The Cangin Languages

Brill's Studies in Historical Linguistics

Series Editor

Jóhanna Barðdal
(Ghent University)

Consulting Editor

Spike Gildea
(University of Oregon)

Editorial Board

Joan Bybee (*University of New Mexico*) – Lyle Campbell (*University of Hawai'i at Mānoa*) – Nicholas Evans (*The Australian National University*) Bjarke Frellesvig (*University of Oxford*) – Mirjam Fried (*Czech Academy of Sciences*) – Russel Gray (*University of Auckland*) – Tom Güldemann (*Humboldt-Universität zu Berlin*) – Alice Harris (*University of Massachusetts*) Brian D. Joseph (*The Ohio State University*) – Ritsuko Kikusawa (*National Museum of Ethnology*) – Silvia Luraghi (*Università di Pavia*) Joseph Salmons (*University of Wisconsin*) – Søren Wichmann (*MPI/EVA*)

VOLUME 21

The titles published in this series are listed at *brill.com/bshl*

The Cangin Languages

Phonological and Morphological Reconstruction and Diachrony

By

John T.M. Merrill

BRILL

LEIDEN | BOSTON

Library of Congress Cataloging-in-Publication Data

Names: Merrill, John T.M. (John Thomas Mayfield), author.
Title: The Cangin languages : phonological and morphological reconstruction and
 diachrony / by John T.M. Merrill.
Other titles: Brill's studies in historical linguistics ; vol. 21 2211-4904
Description: Boston : Brill, 2023. | Series: Brill's studies in historical linguistics,
 2211-4904 ; vol. 21 | Includes bibliographical references and index.
Identifiers: LCCN 2023014377 (print) | LCCN 2023014378 (ebook) |
 ISBN 9789004520028 (hardback) | ISBN 9789004546493 (ebook)
Subjects: LCSH: Cangin languages–Phonology–History. | Cangin
 languages–Morphology–History.
Classification: LCC PL8108 .M47 2023 (print) | LCC PL8108 (ebook) |
 DDC 496.321–dc23
LC record available at https://lccn.loc.gov/2023014377
LC ebook record available at https://lccn.loc.gov/2023014378

Typeface for the Latin, Greek, and Cyrillic scripts: "Brill". See and download: brill.com/brill-typeface.

ISSN 2211-4904
ISBN 978-90-04-52002-8 (hardback)
ISBN 978-90-04-54649-3 (e-book)

Copyright 2023 by John T.M. Merrill. Published by Koninklijke Brill NV, Leiden, The Netherlands.
Koninklijke Brill NV incorporates the imprints Brill, Brill Nijhoff, Brill Hotei, Brill Schöningh, Brill Fink,
Brill mentis, Vandenhoeck & Ruprecht, Böhlau, V&R unipress and Wageningen Academic.
Koninklijke Brill NV reserves the right to protect this publication against unauthorized use. Requests for
re-use and/or translations must be addressed to Koninklijke Brill NV via brill.com or copyright.com.

This book is printed on acid-free paper and produced in a sustainable manner.

Contents

List of Tables   IX
Symbols and Abbreviations   XIII

1 **Introduction**   1
    1.1   The Cangin Languages   3
    1.2   Sources   9
    1.3   Comparison with Drolc (2005)   13

2 **Phonology**   16
    2.1   Consonants   16
        2.1.1   *Voiceless Stops*   17
        2.1.2   *Nasals*   19
        2.1.3   *Implosive Stops*   20
        2.1.4   *Prenasalized Stops*   25
        2.1.5   *Continuants: *f, *s, *h, *H, *x, *ɣ, *w, *y, *l, *r̥, *r*   29
            2.1.5.1   *f and *s   29
            2.1.5.2   Back Fricatives: *h, *H, *x, *ɣ   30
            2.1.5.3   *w and *y   36
            2.1.5.4   Coronal Continuants *l, *r̥, *r   37
        2.1.6   *Consonant Lenition and Loss*   42
        2.1.7   *Consonant Assimilation Processes*   46
    2.2   Vowels   50
        2.2.1   *Basic Vowel Correspondences*   50
            2.2.1.1   High Vowels   50
            2.2.1.2   Non-high Vowels   54
        2.2.2   *ATR Changes and Harmony*   58
        2.2.3   *Vowel Length Changes*   63
        2.2.4   *Vowel Coalescence*   66
        2.2.5   *Medial Vowel Deletion*   70
        2.2.6   *Vowels before *ɣ and *H*   73
        2.2.7   *Irregular Vowel Correspondences*   75
    2.3   Phonotactics and Borrowing   76
        2.3.1   *Word Shape and Proto-phoneme Frequency*   76
        2.3.2   *Borrowing*   79
    2.4   Summary of Sound Changes   88

VI CONTENTS

3 Nominal Morphology 91
  3.1 Noun Class Morphology 91
    3.1.1 *w-* 95
    3.1.2 *n-* 97
    3.1.3 *c-* 101
    3.1.4 *y-, 6-* 103
    3.1.5 *k-* 108
    3.1.6 *f-* 114
    3.1.7 *m-* 118
    3.1.8 *p-* 119
    3.1.9 *nj-* 120
    3.1.10 *t-* 121
    3.1.11 *Saafi Innovations r- and nd-* 124
    3.1.12 *Additional (Fossilized) Nominal Class Prefixes* 125
    3.1.13 *Prefix Resegmentation* 127
    3.1.14 *Additional CV- Agreement Prefixes* 128
    3.1.15 *Non-nominal Class Prefixes: nd-, d-, w-* 129
    3.1.16 *Historical Status of Noun Prefixes* 133
    3.1.17 *Historical Status of Class Agreement* 136
  3.2 Determiners 140
    3.2.1 *Definite and Demonstrative Determiners* 140
    3.2.2 *The Ndut-Paloor Associative Marker -i* 145
  3.3 Numerals 147
  3.4 Derivational Suffixes 151
    3.4.1 *Agent *-oH* 152
    3.4.2 *Attributive *-id* 153
    3.4.3 *Place or Manner *-(oy)aad* 157
    3.4.4 *Nominalizer *-ay* 158
    3.4.5 *Instrument *-oya* 160
  3.5 Summary 160

4 Verbal Morphology 162
  4.1 Pronouns 162
    4.1.1 *Noon-Laalaa* 163
    4.1.2 *Noon-Laalaa-Saafi* 167
    4.1.3 *Ndut-Paloor* 169
    4.1.4 *Proto-Cangin* 170
  4.2 Inflectional Morphology 173
    4.2.1 *Tense and Aspect* 175
      4.2.1.1 Imperfective *-e 176

CONTENTS   VII

4.2.1.2 Past *-í   177
4.2.1.3 Habitual > Future *-an   178
4.2.1.4 Perfective Markers   179
4.2.1.5 Future Auxiliary Construction with 'Come'   180
4.2.1.6 Progressive/Durative Construction with *na   181
4.2.1.7 Presentative Construction Using
           Demonstratives   182
4.2.1.8 Use of the Unmarked Verb   184
4.2.2 *Mood (Imperative, Hortative/Optative)*   185
4.2.3 *Negation*   186
4.2.4 *Plural Subject/Passive *-us*   192
4.2.5 *The Morpheme da*   195
4.3 Derivational Suffixes   198
4.4 Summary   206

5 Cangin in an Areal and Niger-Congo Context   208
5.1 Phonology   212
5.1.1 *Phoneme Inventory*   212
5.1.2 *Lenition of Voiceless Stops in Pre-Cangin*   214
5.1.3 *Development of Pre-Cangin Geminate Consonants*   218
5.1.4 *Phonotactics, Phonological Processes, and Lack of Consonant
        Mutation*   220
5.2 Noun Class   222
5.2.1 *Areal Pressure: Wolof and Sereer*   222
5.2.2 *Etymological Connections*   224
5.3 Verbal Derivational Suffixes   229
5.4 The Place of Cangin within Niger-Congo   232
5.5 Conclusion   234

Appendix 1: Proto-Cangin Lexical Reconstructions   235
Appendix 2: Outside Cognates   269
References   283
Index   287

Tables

1	Selected features of Laalaa and Noon dialects (known innovations in bold)	4
2	Sources of data for each Cangin language	11
3	Reconstructed Proto-Cangin consonant inventory	16
4	Proto-Cangin voiceless stops	17
5	Verb roots with a leniting final voiceless stop in Ndut-Paloor	18
6	Proto-Cangin nasals	19
7	Proto-Cangin initial implosive stops	20
8	Proto-Cangin final implosive stops	21
9	Proto-Cangin intervocalic implosive stops	24
10	Proto-Cangin prenasalized stops	27
11	Early borrowing of prenasalized stops in Cangin languages	28
12	Sporadic reanalysis of nasals as voiced stops and vice versa	29
13	Proto-Cangin *f and *s	30
14	Proto-Cangin *ɣ	31
15	Correspondences for PC *ɣ in other Atlantic languages	31
16	Proto-Cangin *h	32
17	Correspondences for PC *h in Sereer and Wolof	32
18	Proto-Cangin *H	33
19	Borrowing sources of PC roots with *H	33
20	Proto-Cangin *x	34
21	Proto-Cangin initial and final ∅/ʔ	35
22	Proto-Cangin *w and *y	36
23	*w > y before a front vowel in Ndut-Paloor	36
24	Proto-Cangin *l	37
25	Proto-Cangin *ɽ̥	38
26	Correspondences for PC *ɽ̥ in other Atlantic groups	39
27	Proto-Cangin *r	40
28	Deletion of intervocalic consonants in Noon in non-alternating environments	43
29	Lexically-specific deletion of intervocalic consonants in Northern Noon	44
30	Deletion of intervocalic consonants in non-alternating environments	45
31	Isolated deletion of final *ɓ	46
32	Realization of assimilating suffix consonants in Noon and Laalaa	46
33	Noon and Laalaa suffix assimilation with -da 'punctual/narrative'	47
34	Isolated examples of the assimilation of /d/ from *-íd in Noon, Laalaa, and Saafi	48
35	Reconstructed Proto-Cangin vowel inventory	50

36	Proto-Cangin +ATR high vowels	51
37	Proto-Cangin -ATR high vowels	51
38	Raising of unstressed short mid vowels in Northern and Padee Noon	53
39	Proto-Cangin mid and low vowels	54
40	Proto-Cangin *oɣ and *aɣ	56
41	Raising of mid vowels in some Saafi polysyllabic words	56
42	Raising of mid vowels before a palatal coda in Northern Noon	57
43	Backing of front vowels between a labial and palatal consonant in Laalaa	58
44	ATR effect of suffixes with a +ATR vowel	59
45	Historical effect of a +ATR vowel on a preceding vowel	60
46	Reduction to /ë/ in Thiès Noon	61
47	Long +ATR mid vowels in native monosyllabic vocabulary	62
48	Vowel length differences between languages	63
49	Lengthening of final vowels in disyllabic words in Noon and Laalaa	64
50	Words with no final lengthening in Noon	64
51	Laalaa and Saafi vowel lengthening in CVC forms with consonant loss	65
52	Proto-Cangin nouns with a coalesced prefix	66
53	Proto-Cangin nouns with a coalesced prefix resulting in a short vowel	67
54	New instances of coalesced class prefixes	67
55	Stem + suffix vowel coalescence in Northern Noon	69
56	Historical deletion of medial short vowels in Saafi	70
57	Examples of synchronic Saafi medial vowel deletion	71
58	Synchronic medial vowel deletion in Ndut and Noon	71
59	Consonant clusters formed by medial vowel deletion in Proto-Cangin	72
60	Words with Noon /eeh/, Laalaa /eh/	73
61	Lowering of NLS *ih, *eh to NL /ah/	73
62	Lowering of vowels before NLS *h	74
63	Possible vowel changes before PC *ɣ	74
64	Irregular vowel quality correspondences between Ndut-Paloor and NLS	75
65	Other irregular vowel quality correspondences	75
66	Freq. of initial consonants in PC reconstructions (class prefixes in parentheses)	77
67	Frequency of final and medial (subscripted) consonants in PC reconstructions	77
68	Frequency of vowels in reconstructed PC roots	78
69	Potential borrowings into Proto-Cangin	80
70	Some shared borrowings from after the Proto-Cangin period	86
71	Later borrowings from Wolof into Noon and from Sereer into Saafi	87
72	Noun class prefixes of the Cangin languages	92
73	Nouns showing class agreement with a suffixed definite determiner	93
74	Reconstructed Proto-Cangin noun class prefixes	94

75	Some nouns in the default agreement class	96
76	Proto-Cangin reconstructions with a word-initial prenasalized stop	98
77	Proto-Cangin nouns with or without *n- in different languages	100
78	Singular and plural definite nouns in each Cangin language	101
79	Definite singular forms of 'person' in each language	103
80	Definite plural forms of 'person' in each language	104
81	Forms of 'thing' in each Cangin language	106
82	Human nouns with a prefix *bi-	107
83	Nouns in the *k- agreement class	109
84	Additional nouns with a potential *kV- prefix	110
85	Synchronically active kV- prefixes in Noon and Laalaa with examples	110
86	Deverbal nouns with a kV- prefix in Laalaa and Saafi	112
87	f-initial nouns in the *f- agreement class	114
88	Non-f-initial nouns in the *f- agreement class	116
89	Animal nouns reassigned to f- in Ndut-Paloor	116
90	Agreement classes used for PC disyllabic nouns across all modern languages	117
91	Nouns in the *m- agreement class	119
92	Nouns in the *p- agreement class	120
93	Noon and Laalaa nouns in the j- class	121
94	Some Noon and Laalaa plurals in the t- class	122
95	Non-plural nouns with a prefix *tV-	122
96	Sources of some Saafi r- class nouns	124
97	Sources of some Saafi nd- class nouns	125
98	Proto-Cangin *c-initial nouns	126
99	Nouns with other fossilized class prefixes	127
100	The prefix on the definite marker resegmented as part of the root	128
101	Noon demonstratives prefixed with d-	130
102	Non-nominal prefixes in each language	130
103	Words containing a frozen prefix *ndV- or *dV-	131
104	Temporal adverbs containing a prefix *wV-	132
105	Class prefixes with a derivational function in Proto-Cangin	135
106	Number of reconstructed nouns containing each class prefix	135
107	'Goat' with a (proximal) definite determiner and proximal demonstrative	140
108	Suffixed definite determiners	141
109	Demonstrative determiners of each language	141
110	Definite determiners used with each demonstrative in Noon, Laalaa, and Paloor	142
111	Wolof and Sereer determiners (with class markers b- and k-)	143
112	Numerals 1–5 and 10	148
113	Forms of 'two' and 'three' in Noon-Laalaa	148

XII TABLES

114 Nominal derivational suffixes in each language 151
115 The suffix -oh on insect nouns 152
116 Reconstructable agent nouns suffixed with *-oH 152
117 Selected agentive nouns with -oh in each language 152
118 Deverbal nouns formed with -(a)aɗ 157
119 Deverbal nouns with -ah/-aah/-a 159
120 Instrument nouns with Noon -oo, Saafi -oha 160
121 Noon and Laalaa pronouns 163
122 Reconstructed Proto-Noon-Laalaa pronouns 164
123 Saafi pronouns 167
124 Reconstructed Proto-Noon-Laalaa-Saafi pronouns 168
125 Paloor and Ndut pronouns 169
126 Possible Proto-Cangin pronouns 170
127 Verbal inflectional morphemes of each language 173
128 Tense and aspect suffixes of Cangin languages 175
129 Tense/aspect auxiliary constructions in Cangin language 175
130 Proto-Cangin tense/aspect suffixes and auxiliary constructions 176
131 Modal suffixes in each language 185
132 Negative imperative and hortative/optative constructions 188
133 Proto-Cangin verbal derivational suffixes 198
134 Additional verbal derivational suffixes 199
135 Language-specific verbal derivational suffixes 200
136 Noon, Laalaa, and Saafi verbs with the suffix combination *-is-ox 204
137 The rare verbal suffix *-oH 206
138 Evidence for lenition of *t to *s 215
139 Distribution of PC consonants in reconstructed native noun and verb
    roots 216
140 Cangin root-initial *f corresponding to /w/ in other Atlantic groups 217
141 Distribution of vowel length before PC voiceless obstruents in native
    roots 218
142 Development of Pre-Cangin voiceless obstruents into Proto-Cangin 220
143 Noun class prefixes of Proto-Cangin, Wolof, and Sereer 223
144 Etymological connections between class prefixes in Cangin and other
    groups 225
145 'Millet' in various Niger-Congo languages 225
146 Reconstructed class prefixes with /g, j, d, b/ vs. /k, c, t, p/ in N. Atlantic 227
147 Cangin verb extensions with equivalents in Wolof and Sereer 230
148 Anticausative/middle/stative suffixes in Northern Atlantic groups and
    Bantu 232
149 Regular development of singleton consonants in NW Atlantic groups and
    Bantu 271

Symbols and Abbreviations

°, ˘, †, ‡, ◊	used to indicate sources of data for each language—see § 1.2
*	reconstructed forms, mostly Proto-Cangin
**	Pre-Cangin forms, from any stage before Proto-Cangin
NLS	Noon-Laalaa-Saafi
NL	Noon-Laalaa
NdP	Ndut-Paloor
PC	Proto-Cangin
Ser.	Sereer
Wo.	Wolof
BKK	Bainunk-Kobiana-Kasanga
borr.	borrowed
1s, 2s, 3s	1st, 2nd, 3rd person singular
1p, 2p, 3p	1st, 2nd, 3rd person plural
excl, incl	(1st person pl.) exclusive, inclusive
1sS, etc.	1st person singular subject, etc.
1sO, etc.	1st person singular object, etc.
(n), (v)	noun, verb
ACAUS	anticausative
ADJ	adjective-forming
AM	associative marker (NdP)
ASSOC	associative prefix (NL)
APPL	applicative
ATTR	attributive
BEN	benefactive applicative
CAUS	causative
CL-	noun class prefix
COP	copula
DEF	definite
DEM	demonstrative
DET	determiner
DIST	distal
DUR	durative
DV	default vowel (Sereer)
FACT	factitive
FOC	focus
FUT	future

HORT	hortative
IMPER	imperative
IMPF	imperfective
IND.CAUS	indirect causative
INF	infinitive
INST	instrument
MANN	manner
MID	middle distance
NARR	narrative
NEG	negative
OPT	optative
ORD	ordinal number
PASS	passive
PERF	perfective
PL	plural
PROG	progressive
PRST	presentative
PROH	prohibitive
PROX	proximal
PST	past
PUNC	punctual
RED(UP)	reduplicated verb stem
REFL	reflexive
REL	relative clause marker
SUB	subordinator
SUBJ	subject
SUBJ.EXT	subject extraction (Sereer)

CHAPTER 1

Introduction

This study addresses the history of the phonological and morphological systems of the Cangin family of languages spoken in and around the city of Thiès in western Senegal, including a reconstruction of the phoneme inventory, phonological patterns, noun class and other nominal morphology, verbal morphology, and lexicon of Proto-Cangin. Though Senegambia is a region where linguistic relations are often extremely distant, Cangin is a relatively tight-knit language family, and as such the application of traditional methods of comparative linguistics is highly successful in tracing the history of these languages and reconstructing the form of their common ancestor. Cangin is part of the widespread Niger-Congo macro-family, and within it has been assigned to the controversial Atlantic subgroup which includes (among many other members) Cangin's geographically closest neighbors Wolof, Sereer, and Fula. Historical discussion of the Atlantic languages has focused in large part on top-level reconstruction (e.g. Doneux's (1975a) attempt to reconstruct the noun class system of Proto-Atlantic), arguments regarding the internal structure of Atlantic, and comparison with other Niger-Congo languages. However addressing these high-level questions is difficult if not impossible without a solid understanding of the history and reconstruction of the established lower-level families.

The value of historical work on lower-level language families does not only lie in its ability to shed light on more distant linguistic relations. At least equally important is its ability to help our understanding of language change more broadly. Work in historical linguistics cannot be successfully carried out without knowing what sorts of changes are and are not attested, which are more likely, and what the precursors are for each change. This "base of knowledge" within historical linguistics continues to rely largely on a few well-studied families, chief among them Indo-European. The very good reason for this emphasis on Indo-European is that its history is better understood than for any other family of a similar time depth due to the impressive efforts of generations of linguists. Of course many other families have been the focus of diachronic linguistic work, much of which is excellent. However just as most languages of the world remain undescribed or underdescribed, most established or proposed language families have received no careful historical treatment. Just as the continued documentation and analysis of modern understudied languages is of paramount importance to synchronic linguistics, the historical treatment of understudied language families is crucially important

© JOHN T.M. MERRILL, 2023 | DOI:10.1163/9789004546493_002

to diachronic linguistics. This study aims to be a foundation of such an effort for the Cangin family. The goal is not only to determine what can be reconstructed to Proto-Cangin, but also to trace the phonological and morphological changes that have taken place in each language—even those which are rather recent. Up to now, little historical work has been carried out on Cangin. By far the most extensive historical treatment is found in the work of Drolc (2003, 2004, 2005, 2006), but even this is quite preliminary. Drolc's conclusions are briefly compared with those of the present work in § 1.3. Besides Drolc, Pozdniakov and Segerer's (2004) treatment of the Proto-Cangin pronominal system is the only notable contribution to the diachronic study of the Cangin languages.

Part of the reason for the dearth of historical work on Cangin is that the languages themselves have only been relatively recently described. The family was not examined in earnest until the work of Pichl (1966), due in part to the fact that Cangin speakers are members of the larger Sereer ethnicity. As such, they may have been erroneously assumed to speak dialects of the Sereer language. The existence of a "Noon" language as distinct from Sereer was noted by multiple European writers since at least the mid 18th century. These historical references to Cangin populations are collected in Becker (1985). In the mid 19th century, Pinet-Laprade (1865) identified three dialects of a "None" language completely distinct from "Sérère Sine" ("None," "Paror," and "Saafi"), and many other references to a distinct Noon (i.e. Cangin) language emerge in works such as Faidherbe (1865). Tastevin (1936) is the first wordlist for Noon or any Cangin language, postdating more extensive lists for Wolof, Sereer, and Fula by over two centuries. Despite these earlier references, it was not until Pichl brought attention to the family that the first wave of Cangin documentation began in the 1970s and 80s. Recent years have seen the appearance of a number of valuable descriptive works on Cangin languages (Morgan 1996 on Ndut, Soukka 2000 and Wane 2017 on Noon, Dieye 2010 on Laalaa, Pouye 2015 and Botne & Pouille 2016 on Saafi, Thornell et al. 2016, 2016b, 2016c on Paloor and Laalaa). Due to this recent proliferation of descriptive work, we are now in a much better position than ever before to address questions related to the history of the Cangin languages.

This study is organized as follows. Chapter 2 treats Cangin phonology, focusing on the reconstruction of the Proto-Cangin consonant and vowel systems, and identifying the sound changes that took place in each language. This chapter also discusses Proto-Cangin phonotactics and patterns of borrowing from other languages. Chapter 3 treats the nominal morphology, most of which is related to the Cangin noun class system. Chapter 4 treats the verbal morphology, both inflectional and derivational. This chapter also contains a treatment of the Cangin pronoun system. Finally, chapter 5 addresses Proto-Cangin in an areal and genetic context, comparing Cangin phonology and morphology with other Niger-Congo languages, especially those spoken nearby. Appendix 1 contains Proto-Cangin lexical reconstructions presented alongside the modern forms, and Appendix 2 lists potential outside cognates for Proto-Cangin reconstructions.

1.1 The Cangin Languages

The Cangin languages are Noon, Laalaa (aka Lehar), Saafi-Saafi (aka Saafi, Safen), Paloor, and Ndut. They form a very cohesive genetic group with a clear internal organization.

Noon and Laalaa are extremely similar to each other, as are Ndut and Paloor. With better documentation of the dialects of each language, it may turn out that both groups are best seen as dialect continua. Pichl (1977) in fact considers Paloor to be a dialect of Ndut, and Lopis (1980) treats Laalaa as a dialect of Noon. Table 1 presents some features of Laalaa and the three Noon dialect areas, from which it can be seen that they are not easily grouped in a tree-based model, and a subgroup containing all Noon dialects to the exclusion of Laalaa may not be justified. A similar table could likely be produced for Ndut-Paloor dialects pending more extensive documentation. I will use the abbreviations NL for "Noon-Laalaa" and NLS for the "Noon-Laalaa-Saafi" branch. Basic information on the dialects of each language follows, along with the most recent estimate of the number of speakers.

TABLE 1   Selected features of Laalaa and Noon dialects (known innovations in bold)

	Laalaa	Northern	Thiès	Padee
(a) Shared between Laalaa and Northern Noon				
pl. subject marker	**not used**	**-us only w/ NP**	-ës	-us
stem-final ɓ + suffix -ɗ	ɓɓ	ɓp, ɓɓ	ɓp	ɓp
infinitive prefix	ka-	ka-, ki-	kë-	ki-
form of 'know'	únoh	únoh	ínoh	ínoh
'ant sp.' (note 2nd vowel)	kúlbísoh	kúlmbís		kúlmbús
(b) Shared between all Noon dialects				
past tense suffix	-í	**-ee**	**-ee**	**-ee**
NL 1pO *ɗaso(n), 2pO *ɗafín	-ɗason, -ɗëfín	**ɗoo, -ɗïi**	**-ɗuu, -ɗïi**	**-ɗuu, -ɗïi**
nouns w/ y-/ɓ- animate agr.	only 'person'	**all animates**	**all people**	**all animates**
form of 'be many'	yemen	**yewin**	**yëwën**	**yewin**
'dog' lexeme	ɓúu	**baay**	**mbaay**	**baay**
(c) Shared between Northern and Thiès Noon				
possessive marker *nga	ga	ga, **-n**	ngë, **-ŋ**	ga
*f, s, w, y > ∅ / V_V	no	**yes**	**yes**	no
class-agreeing pronouns	-a, -i	-a	-ë	-a, -i
(d) Shared between all but Padee Noon				
/h/ → ∅ / V_V	**yes**	**yes**	**yes**	no
use of def. determiner -um	**no**	rare	**no**	yes
(e) Shared between all but Thiès Noon				
*ND > D in onset	**yes**	**yes**	no	**yes**
final V lengthening	**yes**	**yes**	no	**yes**
(f) Shared between Thiès and Padee				
form of 1s object pronoun	-soo	-yoo	**-ɗoo**	**-ɗoo**
(g) Shared between Northern and Padee Noon				
unstressed NL *e	e	**i**	e/ë	**i**

INTRODUCTION   5

Noon (~25,000 speakers: Soukka 2000: 22)
Noon is spoken in 31 villages in and around the city of Thiès (see Soukka 2000:
27 for a list). The city is called *Cangin* in the Thiès dialect of Noon, which lends
its name to the language family as a whole (an appellation first applied by
Pichl). Thiès is a major city in Senegal, having grown up around the original
Noon settlements during the colonial period. Today the large majority of its
inhabitants speak Wolof as their first language, with Noon speakers confined
for the most part to certain neighborhoods within the city. Soukka (2000) identifies three dialect areas: "Cangin" spoken in the city of Thiès and nearby villages
(here I will use the term "Thiès dialect" to avoid confusion), "Padee" spoken
in the area to the east of the city including the town of *Padee* (Fandène), and
"Saawii" spoken in villages to the north of the city closer to the Laalaa-speaking
area (I will use the term "Northern Noon" for this dialect, since speakers do not
identify themselves by the term *Saawii*, which today refers to a single village
within this region, and furthermore refers to the Saafi language). From the available documentation (which is admittedly lacking for many dialects of other
Cangin languages), Noon exhibits the most dialectal variation of all the Cangin
languages. In some respects the Northern dialect is more similar to Laalaa than
to the Thiès or Padee dialects.

Laalaa (~13,217 speakers: Thornell et al. 2016c: 7)
Laalaa is spoken in 19 villages just to the north of the Noon-speaking area (see
Dieye 2010: 12 for a list), in an area known as *Laa* or *Lehaad* (literally 'end-place,'
whence the language's other common name, Lehar). Neither Dieye (2010) nor
Thornell et al. (2016c) mention any dialectal variation within Laalaa. Laalaa
could itself be taken as a dialect of Noon (as in Lopis 1980), with the designation as a separate language based largely on ethno-cultural grounds. Dieye
(2010: 20) reports that Laalaa speakers understand Noon "perfectly," and while
they generally marry within the Laalaa community, they also often intermarry
with Noon speakers. My Noon consultant Marie Christine Diop (a speaker of
the Northern dialect) finds that Laalaa is mostly but not totally comprehensi-
ble.

Saafi (~200,000 speakers: Botne & Pouille 2016: v, citing Ethnologue)
Saafi (more accurately Saafi-Saafi) is spoken in about 60 villages in an area to
the southwest of Thiès known as *Saafeen* 'Saafi country' (whence the other
common name of the language, Safen). It has by far the most speakers of any
Cangin language, with this number having increased drastically in recent years
(Mbodj cites 30,000 speakers as of 1968). Mbodj (1983: 6) distinguishes three
dialect areas (North, Center, South), and notes that the dialectal differences

6 CHAPTER 1

are minor. Botne & Pouille (2016: v), citing Ethnologue, mention five dialects: Boukhou, Sébikotane, Sindia, Hasab, and Diobass.

Paloor (~22,715 speakers: Thornell et al. 2016: 13)
Paloor is spoken in 26 villages just to the north of Saafeen, and just south of the Ndut-speaking area (see Thornell et al. 2017 for a list). Thornell et al. (2016) identify two dialects, Kajoor in the north and Baol in the south, named for the two kingdoms (aka Cayor and Bawol) whose border the Paloor-speaking area once straddled. Thornell et al. mention that there are very few differences between these dialects. The data in Thornell et al. (2016: 16) is based off of the speech of the southern part of the Paloor-speaking region, though it includes notes on both the Kajoor and Baol dialects. D'Alton's (1983) dissertation is based on the speech of the village of Khodaba, situated within Kajoor. However there are many important differences between the dialect described by D'Alton (henceforth the "Khodaba dialect") and those described by Thornell et al. These latter scholars attribute some of these differences to a stronger influence of Wolof on the northern region, though they do not elaborate on what the specific effects are. D'Alton's lexicon does not contain a higher percentage of Wolof borrowings than Thornell et al.'s (2016b) lexicon. In fact there are many features of the Khodaba dialect that are more conservative based on comparative Cangin evidence. For example if D'Alton's analysis is correct, the dialect of Khodaba has not developed contrastive /é, ó/, which is a conservative feature, and it also exhibits a more conservative determiner system. Of the documented Paloor dialects, the one most similar to Ndut is the Khodaba dialect.

Ndut (~21,200 speakers: Morgan 1996: 1)
Ndut is spoken in 23 villages in an area to the northwest of Thiès. Morgan notes that there are, according to native speakers, six "speech areas" within Ndut. Morgan identifies only two by name, being the "Mt. Rolland" variety which is the basis of Morgan's documentation (though this term generally applies to the entire Ndut-speaking area), and an apparently rather divergent dialect spoken in the village of Palo. Ndut is very similar to Paloor (D'Alton 1983: 11 reports that they are "partially" mutually intelligible), and as with Noon-Laalaa, the designation of Ndut and Paloor as separate languages is based largely on ethnolinguistic self-identification. Notably, the Ndut are Catholic, and the Paloor Muslim (D'Alton 1983: 7). Pichl (1977, 1979) had considered Paloor to be a dialect of Ndut.

The names of the Cangin languages have interesting, though often unclear origins. *Saafi* is likely from PC **sa fi* 'the person,' cf. Paloor *sa f-* 'person.' In Paloor,

INTRODUCTION   7

Saafi refers to the Noon. In Noon, there is a town *Saawii* with no relation to the Saafi people, and until recently Noon speakers referred to themselves as *Saawi* (Lopis 1980: 3). In Saafi, *Saafi* is used to refer to all Cangin speakers (e.g. *Saafi Noon* 'Noon people'). As Pouye (2015: 14) suggests, this was likely the term used by Proto-Cangin speakers to refer to themselves. *Noon* originated as a Wolof exonym (Wolof *noon* 'enemy'), owing to the once inimical relationship between Wolof and Cangin speakers, as detailed in Becker (1985) and D'Alton (1983: 11). It has been applied historically to all Cangin speakers, but currently only to speakers of the language now called Noon. The term *Süli* (an adaptation of *Séeréer*) is used both by Ndut-Paloor speakers and Noon-Laalaa speakers to refer to Ndut-Paloor as a whole—*Ndut* itself is ultimately an exonym of uncertain origin. A folk etymology connects it with the Sereer word *ndut* 'circumcision retreat.' Wolof has *Ndutt* with a final geminate, which if it is a borrowing cannot be recent. *Mont Rolland* is taken from a French place name, the home of one of the priests serving Ndut speakers during their initial conversion to Catholicism (Morgan 1996: 4). *Fefey*, the traditional name for Mont Rolland (Pichl 1977: 41), bears resemblance to Sereer *Feefey* 'people of Saalum' (Sereer *a-Mbey* 'Saalum'), though there is currently no connection between Ndut and the Saalum region far to the south. The origin of *Paloor* and the equivalent Saafi term *Waro* is unclear.

There are two possible etymologies for the place name *Cangin* 'Thiès.' Dieye (2010: 16) reports that according to oral tradition, it is formed from *Caañaak*, the name of the city in at least Northern Noon, with the suffix *-een*. This name is rendered in Wolof as *jànqeen*, supposedly meaning originally 'people from *Caañaak*.' Thus **Caañaak-een* > **Caañk-een* > *Cangin*. This etymology is implausible for a number of reasons. In Saafi, the suffix *-een* (borrowed from Sereer or Wolof) forms a place noun from a proper noun referring to an ethnicity, as in *Saaf-een* 'Saafi country,' so it is unclear why a place name *Caañaak* would take this suffix (the 'group of people' meaning results only when attached to a family name). Phonologically, long vowels are never subject to medial vowel deletion (§2.2.5), long vowels are never shortened (even before clusters), and /ee/ cannot regularly develop to /i/ or /e/. This etymology might be valid if *Cangin* were borrowed directly from Wolof *jànqeen*, but this would leave the form of *Caañaak* unexplained. Paloor does have *Jangin* 'Thiès,' but this is a more recent borrowing from Noon or Wolof. A more likely etymology is that *Cangin* is equivalent to Ndut-Paloor *gin* < **ngin* 'village' with the noun class prefix **ca-* (§3.1.12). Since prefixes are often eroded in Ndut-Paloor, a PC reconstruction **ca-ngin* 'village/town' may be justified—or else **ca-* served as an augmentative prefix in this word. This form was retained in all Noon dialects as †*Cangin* or °*Cagin* (including in Northern Noon *ki-Cagin-*

Cagin 'Thiès Noon dialect'). Note that onset *ng > /g/ occurs in all Noon-Laalaa dialects except Thiès Noon (§ 2.1.4). *Caañaak* might be from a compound of *Cagin* and Noon *yaak* 'big,' i.e. *Cagin yaak > Cagnyaak > Caañaak*. At least in the Northern dialect, Noon speakers refer to Thiès as 'town' in expressions like 'going to town' and 'the way they speak in town,' supporting the idea that *Cagin* was originally simply the word for 'town.'

The Cangin languages are not closely related to any other languages in terms of absolute time depth. Geographically, they are quite conspicuous in being the only indigenous languages of Senegal north of The Gambia besides the much more widely spoken Wolof, Fula, and Sereer. Traditionally Cangin has been grouped within the "(West) Atlantic" subfamily of Niger-Congo. However the status of Atlantic as a family has never been secure, and there is no agreement regarding the subgrouping of languages within this proposed branch of Niger-Congo (see e.g. Güldemann 2018: 180–183). Cangin speakers are all members of the larger Sereer ethnic group, having traditionally shared many of the cultural and religious practices of the Sereer people. However the Cangin languages are entirely distinct from the Sereer language (known as *Sah* or *Seh* in Cangin languages, and often called Sereer-Siin in the literature after the prestige dialect of the historical kingdom of Siin).

All of the Cangin languages except Saafi have been said to be endangered, with the most common reasons cited being migration to urban areas and language shift to Wolof. To be sure, recent history has seen the loss of many traditions among all of the ethnic groups of Senegal. However each of the Cangin languages continues to be transmitted as a first language to children (Morgan 1996: 2, Dieye 2010: 20, Soukka 2000: 23–24, Thornell et al. 2017: 20). It is true that language shift can occur rather quickly within one or two generations, but as of now there is still an appreciable number of villages in which each Cangin language is the primary language of communication within the community. Lüpke and Storch (2013: chapter 5) caution against taking increased multilingualism as a sign of language decline in Africa. Whatever the case, all of the Cangin languages are in serious need of continued documentation, with many dialects being entirely undocumented and both lexical and grammatical documentation being relatively limited. For example the largest lexica for Cangin languages have ~2000–3000 entries, versus the largest dictionaries for Sereer, Fula, and Wolof, each with over 15,000. Efforts to document these languages have increased markedly in recent years, with both the quality and quantity of documentation improving dramatically in the 21st century—but there is still much work left to do.

INTRODUCTION

1.2 Sources

I have drawn from multiple sources for primary data on each Cangin language, privileging those which are more recent and (perhaps as a result) more internally and comparatively consistent. The earliest notable work on Cangin languages was carried out by Pichl (1966, 1977, 1979, 1981), but these sources have a number of deficiencies when compared with more recent work, most notably inaccuracies involving vowel quality, vowel length, and the identification of implosive stops.

For Noon my primary source of data is fieldwork on the Northern dialect carried out by myself and Nico Baier in 2014 and later by myself in 2019 with Marie Christine Diop, a speaker from the town of *Laalaa* (aka Lalane, not to be confused with the Laalaa language) which has produced the largest lexicon of Noon currently available (~1800 entries). The materials from this project including full recordings and transcriptions of elicitation sessions are available online in the California Language Archive. Information on the Padee dialect of Noon comes from Soukka's (2000) grammar—the most extensive for any Cangin language. Some words are also cited from the Padee Noon translation of the New Testament published by Wycliffe Bible Translators. Information and wordforms from the Thiès dialect come from Lopis/Lopis-Sylla (1980, 2010) and Wane (2017). Both researchers frequently disagree regarding ATR values and vowel length both among themselves and when compared to other Noon and Cangin sources, and as such they should be treated with some caution (in all other respects they seem to be accurate). A few words are cited from Tastevin's (1936) and Williams and Williams' (1993) short wordlists (each ~200 words), both of which contain many phonological inaccuracies. Based on the forms given, Tastevin's list represents the Thiès dialect and Williams and Williams' is from a Northern variety.

For Laalaa my primary source is Dieye (2010), a grammar-dissertation with an accompanying lexicon (~1200 entries). Some additional nouns and information on the class system is found in Dieye (2015). A number of forms are also cited from Thornell et al.'s (2016c) lexicon (~1300 entries). The two sources are in almost total agreement with each other, with the only notable differences being the length of some (usually final) vowels and ATR values in a few words. Some words are cited from Pichl (1981), which is the largest lexicon of Laalaa, but is rather inaccurate in transcribing vowels and implosive consonants.

For Saafi my primary source of lexical data is Botne & Pouille's (2016) dictionary (~1600 entries accompanied by a short grammatical description) based on the Sébikotane dialect spoken by the second author. A few forms have also been cited from Stanton (2011), for whom Pouille served as the informant. Much of the grammatical information as well as some wordforms are from Mbodj's (1983) grammar-dissertation on the Boukou dialect and Pouye's (2015) grammar (he does not mention the dialect described, but like Mbodj's grammar it appears to represent a central "ɓoo Saafi" variety). All of these sources are largely in agreement, and the few differences between them are likely true dialectal differences (perhaps with the exception of a number of vowel length discrepancies between sources). A few words are cited from Williams and Williams' (1993) short wordlist.

For Paloor my primary source for lexical data is Thornell et al.'s (2016b) lexicon (~2200 entries). Grammatical information comes from Thornell et al.'s (2016) sketch grammar of the Kajoor and Baol dialects, as well as D'Alton's (1983) grammar-dissertation on the Khodaba variety. Many wordforms are also cited from D'Alton (1983). D'Alton's data has many disagreements with Thornell et al. and (taking comparative evidence into account) other sources on Cangin languages. These discrepancies involve ATR values, vowel length, and implosive vs. egressive consonants. In almost all cases I have privileged Thornell et al.'s data where possible. However D'Alton provides a great deal of valuable information on a dialect that is in some respects crucially different from the dialects described by Thornell et al. (2016). Furthermore D'Alton (1983) is the most extensive description of any Ndut-Paloor variety. A few forms are taken from Soukka and Soukka's (2011) description of Paloor phonology, which is largely in agreement with Thornell et al.

For Ndut my primary source is Morgan's (1996) grammatical overview. Morgan provides no lexicon, but many wordforms are given throughout the text. Secondary sources are Pichl's (1977) lexicon (~3000 entries), and a wordlist (~600 entries) collected by Doneux (unknown year) and made available in the online RefLex database (Segerer and Flavier 2011–2021). Because Pichl treats Paloor as a Ndut dialect, some of the words in his lexicon were collected from Paloor (he identifies three dialects: Mont Rolland, Palo, and Paloor), but I have opted to treat all of these words as Ndut. Doneux's and especially Pichl's wordlists seem to contain many inaccuracies when compared with Morgan and the Paloor sources, mostly involving vowel quality, length, and implosive vs. egressive stops. In particular, Pichl seldom transcribes [-ATR] high vowels, and thus often has [+ATR] high vowels where a [-ATR] vowel is expected. He also often gives a short vowel where a long vowel is expected. A brief description of the Ndut-Paloor noun class system is found in Diagne (2015). Gabriel Guèye produced a number of phonetic studies of Ndut in the 1980s, which I have unfortunately not been able to obtain. Morgan provides some discussion of Guèye's findings.

INTRODUCTION 11

Because the words cited for each language come from different sources (some of which represent different dialects), I have marked forms from different sources using the symbols in Table 2.

TABLE 2   Sources of data for each Cangin language

Noon:	unmarked	Author's fieldwork on the Northern dialect as spoken in Lalane
	°	Soukka (2000) on the Padee dialect
	ˇ	New Testament translation in the Padee dialect
	†	Lopis/Lopis-Sylla (1980, 2010), or Wane (2017) on the Thiès dialect
	‡	Williams and Williams (1993)
	◊	Tastevin (1936)
Laalaa:	unmarked	Dieye (2010, 2015)
	°	Thornell et al. (2016c), a few forms from Soukka and Soukka (2011)
	†	Pichl (1981)
Saafi:	unmarked	Botne & Pouille (2016), a few forms from Pouye (2015)
	°	Mbodj (1983)
	†	Stanton (2011)
	‡	Williams and Williams (1993)
Paloor:	unmarked	Thornell et al.'s (2016, 2016b) lexicon or grammar
	°	D'Alton (1983)
	†	Soukka and Soukka (2011)
Ndut:	unmarked	Morgan (1996)
	°	Doneux's (unknown year) wordlist
	†	Pichl (1977)

With longer examples the following abbreviations are used for citing the original source: Di. = Dieye (2010), So. = Soukka (2000), Wa. = Wane (2017), B.P. = Botne and Pouille (2016), Po. = Pouye (2015), Mb. = Mbodj (1983), Th. = Thornell et al. (2016), d'A. = D'Alton (1983), Mo. = Morgan (1996). Examples cited simply as "Noon" are from my own fieldwork (given with the elicitation session number), as are the few Sereer examples.

I have made some alterations to the spelling conventions used by some authors in order to present a more unified scheme for the Cangin languages and facilitate historical comparison.

For all languages:
– Root-initial glottal stops are not contrastive with zero in any Cangin language, and so these are not written (D'Alton and Mbodj write them while other authors do not, while noting their phonetic presence).

- +ATR marks appear on all +ATR vowels within a word. Dieye as well as Thornell et al. use the convention of only marking one vowel per word.
- In a few cases a word is given inconsistently in multiple locations within the same source, and I have chosen to present the one which is most consistent with other sources and languages—e.g. Dieye (2010) lists Laalaa *tíid* 'walk' and *mey* 'leave' in his wordlist, but *tíd* and *me'* in the body of the dissertation; the first two must be correct, lining up with °*tíin* and °*mey* found in Thornell et al. (2016c) and Noon *tíid* and °*mey*.

For Noon-Laalaa:
- All underlying voiced stops are written as voiced stops, even in coda position where they have nasal allophones (see §2.1.4); e.g. Noon *taab* 'accompany' for /taab/ [taam~taab-].
- Implosive phonemes in intervocalic and coda position are written as implosives, rather than using the symbols for their allophones (see §2.1.3); e.g. Noon *kaɗ* 'go' and *kaɗin* 'go (perfective)' for /kaɗ/ [kaʔ] and /kaɗin/ [karin]. This includes a number of tokens of /ɗ/ in grammatical morphemes that other sources have analyzed as /r/ underlyingly. Noon-Laalaa /r/ is a borrowed phoneme, and with perhaps a few exceptions (e.g. in ideophones), native [r] is always an allophone of /ɗ/.
- Thiès Noon /p, t, c, k/ between vowels/approximants are written as ⟨b, d, j, g⟩ following Lopis-Sylla (2010) in order to draw attention to this unique feature of the Thiès dialect.
- An orthographical hyphen (-) appears between a synchronically active CV-prefix and the root (e.g. Noon *ki-ɓof* 'to cough'), in order to indicate that the prefix is unstressed, and does not trigger the intervocalic allophones of root-initial consonants. For Laalaa the sources are not always clear on which prefixes are active and which are frozen, so in some cases a hyphen may be absent in a Laalaa form where by this scheme it ought to be present.
- Dieye analyzes all tokens of Laalaa final [ʔ] as underlyingly /ɗ/, but for words in which [ʔ] shows no alternation it is not clear that this analysis is correct. As such I have adapted the spelling of Laalaa *ɓo'* 'person,' *pe'* 'goat,' and *sope'* 'ring,' all of which historically (and I suspect synchronically) have a final glottal stop and not /ɗ/.
- Because Dieye's orthography encodes allophony for the implosives (writing intervocalic /ɓ, ɗ, ʏ/ as ⟨w, r, y⟩), he is able to write the intervocalic geminate implosives derived by assimilation (§2.1.7) as simply ⟨ɓ, ɗ, ʏ⟩. I write them here as geminates.

INTRODUCTION 13

For Ndut-Paloor:

- D'Alton's ⟨x⟩ for Paloor is changed to ⟨h⟩ to be consistent with all other sources (D'Alton notes that [h] is the most common realization of this phoneme).
- For the Ndut-Paloor words cited from Pichl (1977), I have followed his suggestion to "replace the [initial] prenasalized sounds with implosives for Mont Rolland and Palo [pronunciation]" since prenasalized stops in this unspecified dialect correspond to implosives in all other Ndut-Paloor dialects and other Cangin languages (see § 2.1.3). Pichl does distinguish the prenasalized stops that correspond to implosives in other dialects from the borrowed prenasalized stops which appear in all dialects—the borrowed prenasalized stops are written with the nasal symbol underlined. Thus there is no risk of overgeneralization when replacing ⟨mb, nd, nj⟩ with ⟨ɓ, ɗ, ʄ⟩ graphically. Pichl also notes that word-final ⟨b, d, j⟩ in his lexicon correspond to implosives in other Ndut dialects. This is indeed the case, but as he does rarely spell words with word-final implosive stops, I have not replaced his ⟨b, d, j⟩ with the corresponding implosive symbols.
- I have removed the space between a noun and a following consonant-initial definite determiner in Ndut and Paloor to be consistent with the convention used in other languages; e.g. *miisma* 'the milk' and not *miis ma* (D'Alton also does not write a space for Paloor).

In some cases I have slightly altered the interlinear glosses of cited examples to unify terminology and analyses across languages. For most examples from D'Alton (1983) and Botne & Pouille (2016), the interlinear glosses are my own, since none are given in the original source. The translations of examples and words from all sources but Morgan (1996), Soukka (2000), Stanton (2011), and Botne & Pouille (2016) are originally in French, and I have adapted these into English as faithfully as possible.

1.3 Comparison with Drolc (2005)

Drolc's (2005) dissertation on historical Cangin phonology and morphology addresses many of the same topics as the present work, and thus a brief comparison is warranted. First, there is a difference in scope—Drolc's study treats only phonological reconstruction and nominal morphology, with no discussion of verbal morphology or nominal derivational morphology. It also does not address contact/areal effects (including the identification of borrowings), or etymological comparisons with other Niger-Congo languages.

There are a number of non-trivial issues on which Drolc (2005) and the present work are in agreement. The most notable are the reconstruction of the pronoun system, treatment of ATR harmony, and treatment of consonant mutation. My own reconstruction of the Proto-Cangin inventory of pronouns (§ 4.1) is extremely similar to Drolc's, and both have a number of significant differences with the system reconstructed in Pozdniakov and Segerer (2004). Drolc reconstructs a very limited ATR harmony system for Proto-Cangin, involving only regressive harmony triggered by a few suffixes, and not affecting high vowels (see also Drolc 2004)—essentially the same as the conclusion that I arrive at here (§ 2.2.2), though I regard the process as entirely allophonic since I do not reconstruct +ATR mid vowels as Drolc does. Regarding initial consonant mutation, which some other sources suggest might have once existed in Cangin (see § 5.1), Drolc finds no evidence for this process in the history of Cangin (see also Drolc 2003)—a conclusion with which I am in complete agreement.

Some notable features of Drolc's analysis with which the present work differs are:

- There is no account of the /l/ vs. /s/ correspondence for which I reconstruct *ɽ (§ 2.1.5.4)
- Nor for the /l/ vs. /t/ correspondence for which I reconstruct *r (§ 2.1.5.4)
- Nor for the /h/ vs. /k/ correspondence for which I reconstruct *x (§ 2.1.5.2)
- The ∅ vs. /h/ correspondence is given the implausible reconstructed value [ɟ], rather than [ɣ] as reconstructed here (§ 2.1.5.2).
- Regular intervocalic deletion of *ɓ, *y in Ndut-Paloor and Laalaa is not identified (§ 2.1.3).
- There is no discussion of the lenition/loss of *f, *s, *w, *y in Noon-Laalaa (§ 2.1.6).
- The development of *w to Ndut-Paloor /y/ before front vowels (§ 2.1.5.3) is not identified. A /w/ vs. /y/ correspondence is mentioned for 'ash,' but reconstructed as *yet (in fact *wet)
- The reconstruction of the vowel system is rather different; Drolc reconstructs the unnecessary +ATR mid vowels *é and *ó, and a number of regular sound changes are not identified (§ 2.2).
- The regular lengthening of word-final vowels in Noon-Laalaa (§ 2.2.3) is not identified. As such the vowel length in determiners (§ 3.2) does not receive a satisfying treatment.
- The noun class *n- (§ 3.1.2) is not reconstructed, and the status of reconstructed initial prenasalized stops as appearing almost exclusively in nouns is not recognized. Instead the exponent *n- is considered a variant marker of the default class.
- Fossilized/rare noun prefixes are not identified (§ 3.1.12).

There are many other minor discrepancies between Drolc's analysis and my own, for which the reader is encouraged to consult the original source. Recall that much of the most extensive and accurate documentation of the Cangin languages was carried out after Drolc's work appeared. One of the consequences of this difference in available data is that Drolc is able to reconstruct significantly fewer lexical items (334 reconstructions) than what I present here (> 600 reconstructions).

CHAPTER 2

Phonology

Proto-Cangin had a simple CVC syllable structure, and avoided consonant clusters and vowel hiatus. Subsequently, various lenition and assimilation changes took place in each language. Notable properties of the PC consonant system include the presence of voiced prenasalized stops without corresponding plain voiced stops, and a somewhat large number of contrastive back fricatives. The development of PC prenasalized stops has given rise to a typologically-notable coda nasalization pattern in most Cangin languages. Proto-Cangin had a seven-vowel system with a distinction between +ATR and -ATR high vowels, which led to the development of ATR harmony systems in all languages but Saafi. §2.1 and §2.2 cover the consonants and vowels of Cangin respectively—both their reconstruction to Proto-Cangin, and their developments in the modern languages. §2.3 examines Proto-Cangin phonotactic patterns, and the ways borrowings were adopted into Cangin languages throughout their history. §2.4 summarizes the sound changes proposed in this chapter.

2.1 Consonants

The set of reconstructed Proto-Cangin consonant phonemes is given in Table 3.

TABLE 3   Reconstructed Proto-Cangin consonant inventory

	Labial	Coronal	Palatal	(Post-)Velar
voiceless stop	p	t	c	k, (')
implosive stop	ɓ	ɗ	y	
prenasalized stop	mb	nd	nj	ng
nasal	m	n	ñ	ŋ
voiceless continuant	f	s, r̥		h, x, H
voiced continuant	w	l, r	y	ɣ

Note these departures from the International Phonetic Alphabet, which also hold for modern forms and forms within phonetic brackets given throughout:

© JOHN T.M. MERRILL, 2023 | DOI:10.1163/9789004546493_003

PHONOLOGY

Cangin letter:	y	(n)j	ñ	y	'
IPA:	ʃ	(ɲ)ɟ	ɲ	j	ʔ

All prenasalized stops are homorganic. The exact realization of the reconstructed phonemes *x and *H is not entirely clear—one of them was uvular [χ]. The phonetic values of *ṛ and especially *r̥ are also far from certain. The following sections will examine each of these consonants, their modern reflexes, and why they are reconstructed as such.

2.1.1 Voiceless Stops
The four voiceless stops *p, *t, *c, and *k can be reconstructed without complication (Table 4). For the most part they are unchanged in the modern languages in all positions.

TABLE 4   Proto-Cangin voiceless stops

PC	Noon	Laalaa	Saafi	Paloor	Ndut	
*pe'	pe' f-	pe' f-	pe' f-	pe' °f-	pe' f-	'goat'
*pon	pon	pon	pon	pon	pon	'fold'
*mi-sip	miip, °mesip m-	mesep m-	misip m-	°misib m-	misip m-	'sauce'
*ɓap	ɓap	ɓap	ɓap	ɓap	°ɓap	'suckle'
*ɓap-íɗ	ɓépíɗ	ɓëpíɗ	ɓapiɗ	ɓëpíɗ		'nurse'
*toɓ	toɓ	toɓ	toɓ	toɓ	°tob	'rain' (n, v)
*teɗ	teɗ	teɗ	teɗ	°teɗ	°tedd	'weave'
*ɓaat	ɓaat	ɓaat	ɓaat	ɓaat	ɓaat	'add/increase'
*hot	ot	ot	ot	hot	°hot	'stink' (v)
*wa/wo-te	wati	wate	woti	wate °f-	wote	'today'
*cangín	cégín	cëgín	cangin	°cigin f-	°cígín, †céegín f-	'worm' (grub)
*ca-oɣ	cooh f-	coh f-	cooh	caa' °f-	°ca', †caa' f-	'elephant'
*hac	ac	ac	ac	hac	hac	'dig'
*hoc	oc	oc	oc	hoc	†hoc	'scratch'
*kaañ	kaañ	kaañ	kaañ	°kaañ	°kaañ	'be sharp, dare'
*kún	kún 'cover'	kún	kun 'cover'	kún	°kún	'close'
*misik	miik, °mesik	mesek	misik	misik	misik	'hurt' (intr.)
*ki-rik	kedik k-	kedek k-	kidik	kilik k-	kilik †k-	'tree'
*pok-ís	pókís	púkís		pokís, °pëkís	°pokís, †pëkís	'untie'

The only regular change to the voiceless stops is that they are allophonically voiced between vowels and approximants in the Thiès dialect of Noon (e.g. †*dúugúl* 'be sick' vs. Northern *díukúl*). In Ndut-Paloor, stem-final voiceless stops are voiced before a following unprefixed definite marker or associative marker (e.g. Paloor *kot* 'foot,' *kod-a* 'the foot'), but voiceless stops in other intervocalic environments are not subject to this voicing (see § 3.1.1 for the likely explanation for this discrepancy). In four common Ndut-Paloor verb roots, a root-final voiceless stop is lenited before a vowel. These are given in Table 5.

TABLE 5   Verb roots with a leniting final voiceless stop in Ndut-Paloor

PC	Noon	Laalaa	Saafi	Paloor	Ndut	
*ɣot	hot	hot	hot	ot~l	ot~l	'see'
*hap	ap	ap	ap	hap~w	hap~w 'beat'	'kill'
*lap	lap	lap	rap	°lap~w	°lap~†β	'mount, climb'
*ɣac~ɣay	hay	hac	hay	ac~y	ac~y	'come'

The root 'come' seems to have shown this alternation already in Proto-Cangin, as the modern languages show reflexes of either *ɣac* or *ɣay*.

There was also likely a glottal stop in Proto-Cangin, but not as a contrastive phoneme. In the modern languages, a glottal stop appears after any CV lexical root and before any vowel-initial root. In other positions (after CVV and polysyllabic vowel-final stems), the status of the glottal stop differs by language. For Paloor, D'Alton always writes a glottal stop after a root-final vowel, as does Mbodj for Saafi. For Ndut, Morgan (1996: 19) notes that the transcription of /ʔ/ in these longer vowel-final roots is inconsistent between sources, and in his own transcriptions most such words do not have a glottal stop. However at least in Ndut CVV roots there is a contrast between /ʔ/ and ∅, e.g. in *ñee* 'take a path' (perfective *ñeete*) vs. *nee'* 'sleep' (perfective *nee'te*), where the tokens of /ʔ/ come from earlier consonants *ɣ or *x. For Laalaa, Dieye (2010: 53–54) does not consider /ʔ/ to be an underlying phoneme, and always analyzes root-final [ʔ] as /ɗ/, as this phoneme has a regular coda allophone [ʔ] (allophones [ɗ] and [r] in other positions). This analysis is probably not warranted, since in words like [ɓoʔ] 'person' no [ɗ] or [r] ever appears (e.g. in the definite forms *ɓiu, ɓoam,* and *ɓea*). In Noon the presence of /ʔ/ is marginally contrastive in polysyllabic vowel-final roots, being always present for verbs, and almost never for nouns. The only example I have encountered of a polysyllabic /ʔ/-final noun is *joku'* 'small pestle.' The presence of [ʔ] is audible, and is also made clear by

PHONOLOGY   19

the addition of a following vowel-initial clitic, which has an epenthetic /n/ after
a vowel (e.g. *fu hot kédí-naa* 'if you see a mortar' vs. *fu hot joku'-aa* 'if you see a
small pestle'). This root is historically *ɗ-final, and the non-diminutive form *koɗ*
'pestle' retains this consonant. All Noon CVV roots have a final glottal stop. The
glottal stop is probably best considered epenthetic in Proto-Cangin, inserted
word-initially before a vowel, and word-finally in a CV(V) lexical word. Crucially, prefixed nouns in Proto-Cangin are never of the shape CV-'VC—instead
the vowel of the prefix coalesces with the root vowel if no root-initial consonant
is present.

2.1.2   *Nasals*
The four nasals *m, *n, *ñ, and *ŋ are unchanged in the modern languages
(Table 6). Note that *ŋ was rare compared to the other nasals.

TABLE 6   Proto-Cangin nasals

PC	Noon	Laalaa	Saafi	Paloor	Ndut	
*mún	mún m-	mún m-	mun	mún m-	mún m-	'flour'
*meex-ir̥	meekis	miikis	meekis	meel	meel	'ask'
*kúum	kúum k-	kúum k-	kuum	kúum k-	°kúum k-	'honey'
*túm	túm	túm	tum	tum, °túm 'put'	tum, †túm 'put'	'do'
*ngumú	gómúu (f-)	°gumuu f-	ngumu °f-	gúmú °f-	°gúmú f-	'hyena'
*naal	naal	naal	naar	naal	°naal †f-	'bull/male animal'
*nuf	nof	nof	nof	nuf	°nuf	'ear'
*hon	on	on	on	hon	hon	'swallow'
*mín	mín	mín	min	mín	mín	'be able'
*kún-ís	kúnís	kúnís	kunis	kúnís	°kúnís	'open'
*ñam	ñam	ñam	ñam	ñam	ñam	'eat'
*ñíf/ñif	ñíf	ñíf	ñif m-	ñif m-	ñif m-	'blood'
*ñiiñ	ñiiñ	ñiiñ	ñiiñoh °f-	°ñíin f-	°ñíiñ f-	'ant'
*ti/pi-wiñ	piiñ, pewiñ p-	píiñ p-	tiwiñ	tiwiñ °k-	tiiñ k-	'metal/iron'
*haañí(nd)	éeñíin	ëëñín, †ëñíd	aañind	héeñí	°héeñí	'coal'
*ŋaɓ	ŋaɓ 'take big bite'	ŋaɓ	ŋaɓ	ŋaɓ	ŋaɓ	'hold betw. teeth'
*ndíiŋ	díiŋ	ndíig	ndiŋ	díiŋ °f-	°díiŋ f-	'owl'

While no regular sound changes affected the nasals, final nasals were rarely
analogically reinterpreted as underlying prenasalized/voiced stops, for which
see §2.1.4.

20   CHAPTER 2

2.1.3   *Implosive Stops*

The three implosive stops *ɓ, *ɗ, and *ɣ have undergone a number of changes in each Cangin language. Word-initially, the implosive stops are unchanged in all languages (Table 7).

TABLE 7   Proto-Cangin initial implosive stops

PC	Noon	Laalaa	Saafi	Paloor	Ndut	
*ɓoo(ɣ)-ox	ɓook	ɓook	ɓook	ɓooh	°ɓooh	'bathe'
*ɓof	ɓof	ɓof	ɓof	°ɓof	°ɓof	'cough/(bark)'
*ɓít	ɓít	ɓít	ɓit	°ɓít	ɓít	'be heavy'
*ɗaaɗ	ɗaaɗ	°ɗaaɗ	ɗaaɗ	ɗaaɗ	†ɗaad	'fermented fish'
*ɗiñ	ɗiñ	°ɗeñ	ɗiñ	ɗiñ °f-	°ɗiñ f-	'louse'
*ɗeɓ	ɗeɓ	ɗeɓ	ɗeɓ	ɗeɓ	ɗeɓ	'be first'
*yaal	yaal	yaal	yaar	yaal	yaal	'man'
*yeek	yeek	yeek	yeek	yeek	yeek	'sing'
*yuH	yoh	yoh	†yoh	yuh	°yuh	'bone'

A rather peculiar change has affected word-initial implosives in an unspecified dialect of Paloor (as recorded in Pichl 1977, 1979), where they have apparently become prenasalized egressive stops. Thus Pichl gives †*mboo* for standard Ndut-Paloor *ɓoo* 'wash/bathe,' †*ndíis* for standard *ɗíis* 'sew,' †*njaal* for standard *yaal* 'man,' etc. Pichl notes no phonetic difference between these stops and borrowed prenasalized stops. Pichl records initial implosives for Laalaa and other Cangin languages, so there is no reason to doubt his transcription of these Paloor sounds.

In other positions, the implosives are subject to various lenitions.

In coda position:

In all Cangin languages coda implosives remain phonemically distinct from other segments, but in some languages they have phonetic realizations which differ significantly from their word-initial allophones. In Saafi, both Mbodj (1983) and Stanton (2011) note that implosives can be allophonically devoiced word-finally, but this does not result in any phonemic neutralization. Botne & Pouille (2016:xiv) describe the Saafi coda allophones as similar to [p, ʔ, tɕ]. More discussion of these Saafi coda allophones is found in Faye and Dijkstra (2004), who approximate them with the symbols [ʔp, ʔt, ʔc]. In Paloor (D'Alton 1983: 24, Thornell et al. 2016: 22), implosives are also devoiced in coda position. D'Alton

PHONOLOGY

writes that this devoicing does not result in neutralization with the voiceless stops, but in practice she very frequently records words with an etymological final implosive as having a voiceless stop or voiced egressive stop (which she also notes as being devoiced in coda position). Both Thornell et al. (2016) and Soukka and Soukka (2011) always list these Paloor words with the historically-expected final implosives (e.g. *lab* 'hit' for D'Alton's *lab*), and Soukka and Soukka note that /b, d, j, g/ are not possible root-finally or in coda position. For Ndut, Morgan writes, "My earlier phonetic transcriptions suggest that the glottalized stops also are unreleased in word final position, leading to an apparent neutralization with voiceless stops in that environment. Articulatory analysis carried out by Gueye (p.c.), however, shows that a laryngeal lowering occurs in such segments" (1996: 13–14). Doneux records final implosives as voiced egressives in Ndut, and Pichl (1977: i) similarly finds that in a dialect of Paloor, final implosives have become voiced egressive stops. In Noon and Laalaa, /ɓ, ɗ, y/ have the allophones [wʔ, ʔ, yʔ] in coda position. For /ɗ/, this allophony results in neutralization with /ʔ/, but its status as /ɗ/ is confirmed by the addition of a suffix; e.g. *dooɗ* [dooʔ] 'stick,' *dooɗ-ii* [doorii] 'the stick.' Tastevin (1936) records coda /ɗ, ɓ/ as voiceless stops in Thiès Noon (◊*pat*, ◊*top*, ◊*bé dəp*, ◊*kop noh* for *paɗ* 'slap,' *toɓ* 'rain,' †*bedëɓ* 'woman,' †*koɓnoh* 'meat'), and /y/ as a semivowel (◊*e loy* 'low,' ◊ *fol m'bul wi* 'marrow' for *looy* 'be short,' † *fumbuluy* 'brain'). Thus it is clear that even at this late date, Noon /ɓ, ɗ/ had not yet fully developed to [wʔ, ʔ] in coda position. Dieye (2010: 72) describes the coda allophones of Laalaa /ɓ, y/ slightly differently: coda /ɓ/ is [ʔ] after a round vowel, and coda /y/ is [ʔ] after a front vowel, though it is quite likely that the glide portion of these phones is simply difficult to perceive in these environments. Examples of word-final implosives are given in Table 8.

TABLE 8   Proto-Cangin final implosive stops

PC	Noon	Laalaa	Saafi	Paloor	Ndut	
*ɗoɓ	ɗoɓ	ɗoɓ	ɗoɓ	ɗoɓ	°ɗob	'bite'
*teeɓ	teeɓ	teeɓ	teeɓ	teeɓ	°teeb	'show'
*ɓaaɓ	ɓaaɓ	ɓaaɓ	ɓaaɓ	°ɓaaɓ	°ɓaab	'travel'
*kuɗ	koɗ k-	koɗ k-	kuɗ	kuɗ °k-	kuɗ k-	'pestle'
*paɗ	paɗ	paɗ	paɗ	paɗ	°padd	'sweep'
*ɗaɗ	ɗaɗ	ɗaɗoh, °ɗaɗ	ɗaɗ	°ɗaɗ	ɗaɗ	'tear/be torn'
*Heey	heey	heey	heey	°heej	heey	'dream' (v)
*may	may	may		may	†may	'suck'
*pay	pay	pay f-	pey	pay 'cricket'	†pay f-	'grasshopper'

22   CHAPTER 2

Due to the neutralization of coda /ɗ/ and /ʔ/ in Noon-Laalaa, a few tokens of each consonant have been reinterpreted as the other, e.g. Noon *joku'* 'little pestle' from **nju-kuɗ*, and *poɗ* 'clap' from **puh*, but this analogical reanalysis is extremely rare.

In intervocalic position:
Saafi implosive stops undergo no change. For Paloor, Thornell et al. report that the implosives are realized with egressive stop allophones [b, d, j] between vowels. Though this allophony is not noted in other Ndut-Paloor sources, transcriptions of individual words seem to confirm the phenomenon throughout the subgroup. In Noon and Laalaa, /ɓ, ɗ, ʝ/ have intervocalic allophones [w, r, y], resulting in neutralization with /w, y/, and depending on analysis the borrowed phoneme /r/. Intervocalic /ɗ/ is a more accurately a tap [ɾ], at least in Noon. In word-initial position, borrowed /r/ is generally a trill. Because the tap can always be analyzed as underlyingly /ɗ/, even in borrowings (e.g. *oɗaas* 'orange'), it can be argued that /r/ appears only word-initially, such that there is not any neutralization with /ɗ/. Crucially, in Northern Noon, the allophones [w] and [y] of /ɓ, ʝ/ do not delete like intervocalic /w, y/ generally do. Examples of these allophonic alternations are given in (1).

(1) Allophonic alternations for Noon implosive consonants
     /ɓeɓ/ 'take'   /kaɗ/ 'go'   /maʝ/ 'suck'
     [ɓewʔ]   [kaʔ]   [mayʔ]

     /ɓeɓ-in/ 'take (perf.)' /kaɗ-in/ 'go (perf.)' /maʝ-in/ 'suck (perf.)'
     [ɓewin]   [karin]   [mayin]

Note that Noon-Laalaa root-final implosives are never actually realized as implosive stops, as the stop allophones occur only in word-initial and postconsonantal position. Synchronically they can be identified as /ɓ, ɗ, ʝ/ because they are in complementary distribution with the sounds [ɓ, ɗ, y]. The only situation which yields an alternation between all three allophones of an implosive involves the derivational suffixes *-iɗ* (benefactive) and *-íɗ* (causative), in which the vowel of the suffix can delete, leaving the implosive in postconsonantal position. For example Northern Noon *jég-íɗ* [jégíʔ] 'teach,' *jég-íɗ-ee* [jégíree] 'taught,' *jég-ɗ-oh* [jéɲɗoh] 'teacher.'

   In fact the change of **ɓ* and **ʝ* to [w, y] in Noon and Laalaa must be rather late, and postdate the diversification of Noon-Laalaa dialects. Laalaa regularly deletes intervocalic **ɓ* and **ʝ*, but crucially does not delete intervocalic /w, y/, and so the implosives cannot have lenited to [w, y] prior to this Laalaa

PHONOLOGY   23

deletion—a change that is not shared with Noon. In Northern (and often Thiès) Noon, intervocalic *w, *y are regularly deleted, as are *f, *s which first voiced to [w, y]. However *ɓ, *ʄ are never deleted in Noon, and thus must not have lenited to [w, y] prior to the deletion of intervocalic /w, y/—a change that is not shared with Laalaa or even Padee Noon. Even rather recent borrowings from European languages have undeleted [w] from intervocalic *ɓ in Noon; e.g. *taawul* 'table' and *céewí* 'key' (earlier *taabul, caabí*) from French *table* and Portuguese Creole *chabi*, cf. Wolof *taabul* and *caabi*. At the time these words were borrowed, Noon intervocalic /ɓ/ must have still been a stop [ɓ].

In non-alternating environments the situation is more complicated. In Ndut-Paloor, when original intervocalic implosives appear in non-alternating environments, they are lenited: *ɓ becomes /h, w, y/, or is deleted, and *ɗ becomes /r/. In Laalaa tautomorphemic intervocalic /ɓ/ is also deleted. In Noon intervocalic /ɓ/ does not delete, but in two words there is somewhat of a metathesis (dependent on dialect) when *ɓ is flanked by round vowels: *ku-ɓú* 'mouth' > Northern *kúuɓ*, Padee *˘kúuw*, but Thiès *◇kuvu* (for /kúwú/); *ku-ɓo* 'child' > Northern *kowu* or metathesized *koow* (Padee *°kowu*, Thiès *†kowo*). Evidence regarding intervocalic *y is scant, but we can be rather sure that *y (like *ɓ) deleted intervocalically in Ndut-Paloor and Laalaa. 'Cloud' and 'sunset' are relevant forms, if the Paloor words contained a suffix historically (/y/ is certainly deleted in Laalaa *múhaad-noh* 'west' from *múuy-oy-aad noy* 'place at which the sun sets'). In *ka-xeyi* 'dirt/sand' there appears to be a metathesis in Noon similar to the examples with *ɓ above. Table 9 shows the development of original intervocalic implosives in each language.

24 CHAPTER 2

TABLE 9 Proto-Cangin intervocalic implosive stops

PC	Noon	Laalaa	Saafi	Paloor	Ndut	
*pe-ɗe(e)m	peɗim p-	píɗím p-	peɗeem	pereem	°pereem	'tongue'
*heɗVf	eɗif, ˇeɗef	aɗaf	eɗef	heref, °heraf	°heref	'be lightweight'
*mi-ɗa	meɗaa m-	meɗa m-	miɗa m-	miraa m-	mira °m-	'salt'
*fúɗíñ	fúɗíñ	fúɗíñ	‡fu'ñuk	°fúrëñë'	†fúríñ	'whistle'
*síkíɗ-ox?	súkúɗúk	súkúɗúk	sikiɗuk	sikiroh	síkírëh	'listen,' L. 'hear'
*(n)ɣaɓit	hawit	hayet f-, °haet	haɓit	geet	°geet	'dung'
*ki-ɓí(s)	kíwíi k-, †kíwís	kiis k-, †kíwís	kiɓi k-	kíi °k-	°kíi k-	'fire'
*haɓaang-ís-ox	éwéegíik		aɓaangsuk	°hëbgísëh	°hëëgísë	'yawn'
*haɓaang-íɗ		ëëgíɗ				'be stupefied'
*ku-ɓo	kowu k-, †kowo	kuu k-	kuɓu k-	kook 'baby'	këë, †kú k-	'child'
*tuɓaaɓ	towaaɓ	†toowᵃ	tuɓaaɓ	tuyaaɓ	†toab	'white person'
*kaaɓaaɓ		kaaɓ	kaaɓaaɓ k-	(°kabaap 'jaw')	†kakaab	'cheek'
*ɓeɓ-íɗ	ɓéɓíɗᵇ	ɓíiɗ			†ɓéyíd	'pick up'
*caɓín			caɓin	céen, °ciin	céhín, °céyín	'moon'
*pi-ɓil	piwil, ɓiwil	píil p-	piɓiir	°pihil		'lower abdomen'
*wu-tuɓa	wutuwaa	wotoa, °watoa	wotɓa			'yesterday'
*ɣooɓ-ox	hooɓukᵇ	°hook	hooɓuk			'pass the day'
*ɣooɓ-íɗ	hóoɓíɗᵇ	°hóyíɗ	hooɓiɗ 'turn night'			'be late at night'
*ɣaaɓi	haawi, †haaɓ(e)	haay				'couscous'
(Wo. dibéer)		°déeɗ			†díhër	'Sunday'
(Wo. tabax)	tawah	†tah	taɓah			'building/build'
(Wo. gobad)	◊goaᶜ	goat			†gaaɗ	'knife'
(Wo. yabóy)	yawóy		yaɓoy	°yawey 'herring'		'sardine'
*Húy-íɗ, -ox	húyíɗ (n)	húuɓ (n)	‡huyi (n)	°huuh (v)	†húuh (v)	'(be) cloud(y)'
*múuy	múuy	°múuy	muuy	múuy		'disappear'
*múuy(-ox)		múu	muuy	muh, °múh		'sun go down'
*ti/ka-xeyi	kakeey, ˇkakay f-	keke, °kekee f-	kekey~ kehey	°tihi' k- 'sand'		'dirt'
*fi-yaang	feyaaŋ f-	feaŋ f-	fiyaang			'bed'

a This is almost certainly *tooɓ*—Pichl usually gives Laalaa final /ɓ/ as ⟨w⟩
b Phonetically [ɓéwíʔ], [hoowuk], [hóowíʔ]; /ɓ/ is identifiable in the unsuffixed roots
c Likely represents *gowad*

PHONOLOGY

However for root-final implosives, intervocalic tokens created by suffixation generally remain stops in Ndut-Paloor, and in Laalaa /ɓ, y/ sometimes persist with the allophones [w, y]. These must have lenited/deleted at one point, but were restored by leveling with the unsuffixed forms. The Laalaa "restoration" of intervocalic /ɓ, y/ as [w, y] was likely based on dialect comparison with Noon, since the regular deletion of intervocalic *ɓ, *y would have left Laalaa with no intervocalic allophones of these sounds. The alternative—deletion of *ɓ, *y, then restoration as [ɓ, y], then lenition to [w, y]—is less likely. Some suffixed forms in each language do exhibit the historically expected deletion/lenition— in fact this process seems to be rather common. Laalaa *tuy* 'room' and *doy* 'inside' with the definite suffix -*aa* become *tua* and *doa*, and Laalaa /mey-íɗ/ 'exit-CAUS' becomes *míiɗ*. There are in fact more examples of the deletion of intervocalic /y/ in Dieye (2010) than of its intervocalic allophone [y], but he does not comment specifically on the deletion phenomenon. Thornell et al. (2016c: 14) give a Laalaa form °*balooh* 'gatherer' from *ɓalaɓ* 'gather' with the agentive suffix -*oh*, hinting at a synchronic intervocalic ɓ-deletion process in Laalaa. Ndut-Paloor *muluɓ* 'water' with the definite suffix -*a* becomes *mulaa*. Ndut *ɓeleɓ* 'woman' with the definite suffix -*a* or associative suffix -*i* becomes *ɓelaa, ɓelii*, and *kakaa* 'the cheek' given by Morgan is the definite form of what is presumably unsuffixed *kakaaɓ* (based on †*kakaab* given by Pichl). Ndut °*teroh* 'weaver' from the verb *teɗ* 'weave' retains the lenited consonant, as does Paloor (Kajoor dialect) *para* 'broom' from *paɗ* 'sweep.' The historically expected alternation is retained in the Paloor verb °*ɗeeɗ~ɗeer*- 'sting,' and Morgan gives a number of examples of root-final /ɗ/ realized as [r] before a vowel in Ndut (e.g. /ɗaɗ-a'-u/ → [ɗaruu] 'tear-APPL-PL'). Pichl (1979: 39–40) reports that in Ndut the regular behavior of ɓ-final verbs is to replace the consonant with /w/ or /y/ before a vowel, giving the example *doy-u-te* from *doɓ* 'bite.' In his vocabulary, he gives two suffixed forms of Ndut †*ɓeɓ* 'take': †*ɓew-il~ɓey-il* 'take again,' and †*ɓe-oh* 'take something.'

2.1.4 *Prenasalized Stops*

The development of the Proto-Cangin prenasalized stops *mb, *nd, *nj, and *ng has given rise to a cross-linguistically remarkable pattern in all Cangin languages but Saafi and the Thiès dialect of Noon. In all but these two varieties, prenasalized stops were denasalized in onset position and deoralized in coda position, yielding alternations between onset voiced stops [b, d, j, g] and coda nasals [m, n, ñ, ŋ]. In Thiès Noon and some dialects of Saafi (those described in Botne & Pouille 2016 and Pouye 2015), they remain prenasalized stops in onsets but become nasals in coda position, yielding alternations of the type [mb~m]. In the dialect of Saafi described by Mbodj (1983: 70), prenasalized stops have pure nasal allophones before a consonant, and /nj, ng/ have pure nasal allophones word-finally, but /mb, nd/ remain prenasalized stops word-finally (however Mbodj also transcribes ⟨m, n⟩ word-finally after a long vowel). The phonemic status of these sounds in the modern languages is not completely straightforward, since the nasal allophones merge completely with the pure nasals /m, n, ñ, ŋ/. In Noon and Laalaa, the alternations are completely regular and phonologically predictable, and as such I believe it is desirable to analyze all tokens of alternating [b~m], etc. as underlying voiced stops /b, d, j, g/. Dieye (2010) adopts this analysis for Laalaa, as does Soukka (2000) for Noon, though the allophones are represented distinctly in her orthography.

(2) Allophonic alternations for Noon egressive voiced stops

/ab/ 'hold'	/mad/ 'resemble'	/paj/ 'get married'	/jag/ 'read'
[am]	[man]	[pañ]	[jaŋ]
/ab-in/ (perf.)	/mad-in/ (perf.)	/paj-in/ (perf.)	/jag-in/ (perf.)
[abin]	[madin]	[pajin]	[jagin]

The same analysis could be applied to Ndut, since Morgan (1996: 14) notes that voiced egressive stops cannot appear in coda position, and verb roots with a historical final prenasalized stop show the expected [b~m]-type alternation. However Morgan chooses to analyze these alternations as phonemic, and as such it is not possible in many cases to determine if a root-final nasal is underlyingly a stop or nasal from his transcriptions (since roots are often not given pre-vocalically). For Paloor, D'Alton and Thornell et al. also analyze these alternations as phonemic, but D'Alton notes all of the alternating roots in her lexicon. Based on the available evidence, the Paloor facts align with the Ndut ones, such that [b~m] etc. could be analyzed as underlying /b, d, j, g/ just as in Noon and Laalaa. Nonetheless, Ndut-Paloor roots will be listed here as they are in the original sources with regards to these final sounds. A selection of Proto-Cangin reconstructions containing prenasalized stops is shown in Table 10.

PHONOLOGY 27

TABLE 10   Proto-Cangin prenasalized stops

PC	Noon	Laalaa	Saafi	Paloor	Ndut	
*mbaang	baag	°baaŋ		baaŋ	baaŋ	'stalk' (n)
*mbíing	bíig, †mbíiŋ			bíiŋ 'hip'	°bíiŋ	'back'
*yamb	yab	yab	yamb	°yab	†yam~b	'accuse'
*so(o)mb	soob	soob		som~°b	som~b	'pound (into flour)'
*pambi	pabi, †pambe f-	pabe f-	pambi °f-	(paan)	(paan †f-)	'chicken'
*ndangal	dagal, †ndangal	dagal	ndangal	dagal °f-	°dagal f-	'scorpion'
*ndíiŋ	díiŋ	ndíig	ndiŋ	díiŋ °f-	°díiŋ f-	'owl'
*mand	mad	man	mand	man~d	man~d	'resemble'
*kínd	kíd	kín	kind	kín~°d	†kín~d	'count'
*yoond	yood	yood	yoond	yoon~d	°yoon~d	'learn' (S. 'move')
*yoond-íɗ	yóodíɗ	yóodíɗ	yoondiɗ	yóodíɗ	°yoodíd	'teach' (S. 'make move')
*njakal	jakal	jakal	njakar	°jakal	†jakal f-	'lizard'
*njol	jol		njol	°jol	†jol f-	'cricket'
*sinja(a)n		sejan		sijaan		'back'
*ngúl	gúl (n, v)		ngul (n, v)	gúl (n, v)	°gúl (v)	'(make) hole'
*ngumú	gómúu (f-), †ngómú	°gumuu f-	ngumu °f-	gúmú °f-	°gúmú f-	'hyena'
*pang	pag		pang-	paŋ~g	paŋ~g	'do' (S. 'work')
*hang	ag	ag	aŋ, °ang-	haŋ~°g	°haŋ	'be wide'
*cangín	cégín, †cëngën	cëgín	cangin	°cigin f-	°cígín, †céegín f-	'worm' (grub)

There were no non-prenasalized voiced egressive stops [b, ɗ, j, g] in Proto-Cangin. In some borrowed vocabulary, there is a spurious sound correspondence between plain voiced egressive stops in all languages except Thiès Noon, e.g. *gaaw* 'be fast' from Wolof (see Table 70 for other examples). These are without a doubt the result of independent borrowing from after the Proto-Cangin period; i.e. there is no evidence for a series of PC plain voiced egressive stops distinct from the prenasalized stops discussed in this section. An alternate analysis might propose that the series under discussion was in fact not nasalized, but acquired nasalization later as a way to reinforce the voicing of these stops. However there are a number of reasons to reject this scenario. For one, this is the series used for borrowings which contain prenasalized stops in other languages, some of which are shown in Table 11 (though more recent borrowings have reintroduced prenasalized stops, see § 2.3.2).

28 CHAPTER 2

TABLE 11   Early borrowing of prenasalized stops in Cangin languages

Cangin	Sereer	Wolof	
*dǐng	dǐng		'fence'
*mbaal	mbaal		'sheep'
*ngiic	ngiic		'jujube tree'
*(H)umb-is	umb	xamb	'rekindle fire'
*sangalí		sànqal	'millet semolina'
Nd. °dut, L. °dút	ndut		'circumcision retreat'
P. °digileñ	ndinglaañ	ndénqleñ	'gums'
N. bap 'underwear'	o-mbap		'pants'
N. tagul, P. tagu		tangor	'mountain'

These are also the sounds that result from prefixing the class marker *n- (see §3.1.2). Furthermore, the spontaneous introduction of nasalization in voiced stops is in fact rather rare, especially in coda position where only a few convincing examples from Austronesian can be found (Blust 2005). For all of these reasons, we can be certain that this series was prenasalized in Proto-Cangin.

Word-initially, almost all instances of Proto-Cangin prenasalized stops are found in nouns, being the result of prefixing the noun class marker *n-. Since a small number of nouns appear both with and without this prefix *n- (across languages and within the same language, see Table 77), it is possible to identify certain consonants that transform into a prenasalized stop when this prefix is added. Coronal *l becomes *nd when prenasalized, and *k, *h, and *ɣ become *ng. It is significant that *h patterns as velar in this regard, just as it does in Fula, Sereer, and Wolof.

In Ndut-Paloor, only historically ND-final verbs exhibit the nasal/oral alternation, with nouns and other parts of speech having only the pure nasal realization. For example, for Noon búig [bíiŋ] 'back' from *mbúing, Ndut and Paloor have non-alternating búiŋ. The Noon form with the distal definite suffix is búig-aa [bíigaa], whereas Ndut has °búiŋ-ë [bíiŋë] with a nasal. The reason for this lack of alternation likely has to do with the timing of when the definite article was grammaticalized as a suffix in Ndut-Paloor. If the coda *ng> [ŋ] etc. changes took place while the definite article was still a free word, nouns with a final *ng would have no possibility of appearing before a vowel within the same word, and so there would naturally be no alternation (*mbúing w-a > *mbúiŋ w-a > búiŋ-ë). In Noon-Laalaa on the other hand, the definite article must have been

PHONOLOGY

grammaticalized as a suffix before the deoralization of coda ND, so that from Proto-NL *[mbíing, mbíingaa], modern [bíiŋ, bíigaa] could develop (*mbíing w-a > *mbíing-aa > bíigaa).

In individual languages, roots which historically ended in a prenasalized stop have sporadically been reinterpreted as nasal-final, and vice versa (Table 12). An example of the first change is *ɓend 'accompany,' in which the alternation has been eliminated in Paloor. Two examples of the second change are *ɓeen 'pick fruit' and *ten 'milk.'

TABLE 12   Sporadic reanalysis of nasals as voiced stops and vice versa

PC	Noon	Laalaa	Saafi	Paloor	Ndut	
*ɓend	ɓed	°ɓen	ɓend-	ɓen	°ɓen~†d	'accompany'
*ɓeen	ɓeed	ɓeen	ɓeen	°been	†ɓeen	'pick/harvest fruit'
*ten	ten	ten		°ten~d	ten	'milk' (v)

For 'pick fruit,' based on the Saafi form (no prenasalized stop even before a vowel) we can be reasonably sure that there was no final prenasalized stop in this root originally, but Noon has ɓeed [ɓeen~ɓeed-]. For 'milk,' we can reconstruct *ten based on the fact that Ndut, Noon, and Laalaa show only [n], with the alternation being analogically introduced in Paloor. Reanalysis has even taken place in some borrowings, like Noon sod 'be tired' from Wolof sonn, and Paloor °múñ~j 'be patient' from Wolof or Sereer muñ. This analogical reinterpretation is possible due to the complete neutralization of the ND and N series in coda position. This reanalysis is not very common, but where it does occur it can sometimes be difficult to determine whether the root was originally ND- or N-final. For example Paloor has °yon~d and Noon yon for 'thresh grain,' and so we cannot know whether to reconstruct *yon or *yond. Even for 'milk,' since there is no Saafi form recorded we cannot be entirely sure that the root was not *tend.

In the Baol dialect of Paloor, intervocalic /d/ (from *nd) has developed to /r/, e.g. saara' 'flee' vs. Kajoor saada' from *saand-oy.

2.1.5   Continuants: *f, *s, *h, *H, *x, *ɣ, *w, *y, *l̥, *r̥, *r
2.1.5.1   *f and *s

The voiceless continuants *f and *s are reconstructed without complication (Table 13), though note that they are subject to lenition or deletion intervocalically in Noon and Laalaa (see § 2.1.6).

TABLE 13   Proto-Cangin *f and *s

PC	Noon	Laalaa	Saafi	Paloor	Ndut	
*faan	faan f-	faan f-	faan	faan	faan	'body'
*fen	fen f-	fen f-	fin f-, °fen f-	fen °f-	°fen f-	'hair'
*ɣaf	haf	haf	haf	af	af	'head'
*nuf	nof	nof	nof	nuf	°nuf	'ear'
*húfir̥/hufir̥	úwis	°úwís	ufis	hufil	°ufil, †hofel	'swell'
*sex	sek	sek	sek	seh	°seh	'wait'
*sís	sís	sís	sis	sís	sís	'tooth'
*soos	soos	soos	soos	°soos	°sos	'be cold'
*fíis	fiis	fíis	fiis	fiis	°fíis	'draw, trace, write'
*misik	miik, °mesik	mesek	misik	misik	misik	'hurt' (intr.)

Paloor and Saafi /s, f/ have voiced allophones [z, v] between voiced sounds.

2.1.5.2   Back Fricatives: *h, *H, *x, *ɣ

Each Cangin language has a single voiceless back fricative /h/, the description of which varies somewhat between languages and sources. Noon-Laalaa /h/ is glottal, though Dièye (2010: 39) notes that in Laalaa it is pronounced as [h~x] in free variation. For Saafi, Pouye (2015: 56) describes /h/ as glottal, voiced to [ɦ] between voiced sounds; Mbodj (1983: 44–45) describes /h/ as pharyngeal, with a free variant [x] before or after pause; Botne and Pouille (2016: xiv) describe /h/ as pharyngeal or uvular before a back vowel (presumably glottal elsewhere). D'Alton (1983: 55) describes the Paloor sound as auditorily most similar to [h], but involving a velar constriction. Pichl (1979: 3) gives Ndut [h~x] in free variation. Other Ndut-Paloor sources describe the sound as glottal.

Reconstruction of the back fricatives is somewhat complicated. There are four regular sound correspondences involving modern /h/. The first represents the development of the voiced velar *ɣ, which is lost in Ndut-Paloor, and develops to /h/ in the other languages (Table 14).

PHONOLOGY

TABLE 14 Proto-Cangin *ɣ

PC	Noon	Laalaa	Saafi	Paloor	Ndut	
*ɣaf	haf	haf	haf	af	af	'head'
*ɣaan	haan	haan	haan	aan	aan	'drum'
*ɣot	hot	hot	hot	ot~l	ot~l	'see'
*ɣac~ɣay	hay	hac	hay	ac~y	ac~y	'come'
*ɣiñ-oɣ	hiñoh	heñoh	hiñoh	iña'	†íñ	'fight'
*yaɣ	yah	yah	yaah, °yah	ya'	ya'	'hand, arm'
*neeɣ	neeh	neh	neeh	ne'	nee'	'sleep'
*waɣ	wah	wah	waah	wa'		'winnowing fan'
*to-ɣo	tooh, °tohoo t-	too t-	toho r-	too k-	too k-	'millet'

The identification of this sound correspondence with a voiced velar is based on comparison with other Atlantic languages (Table 15; see Merrill 2018 for the reconstructed forms).

TABLE 15 Correspondences for PC *ɣ in other Atlantic languages

PC	Sereer	Fula	Wolof	Bainunk-ᴋᴋ	Biaf.-Pajade	Proto-Tenda	
*ɣaɽ/ɣíɽ	a-ngid	gite (pl.)	gët (pl.)	*ci-ggiɽ	*-gəɽä	*-ɣəɽ	'eye'
*ɣam	gom	'am~ngam		Kob. -gom	*gam	*ɣam	'dance'
*i/fa-noɣ	naak	nagge	nag		*-nagä		'cow'
*ɣawúl	gawul (pl.)	gawlo	géwël				'griot'
*noɣ		naange		*bu-nȩg	B. nnagə		'sun'
*ɣaf			gopp (pl.)	*bu-gof	*bu-gafä	*-ɣaf	'head'
*ca-oɣ					*wan-yoogä		'elephant'
*ɣíiñ	giiñ						'roll couscous'
*ɣVnd	gend 'equals/ co-wives'						'be equal'

It will be seen in § 2.2.6 that *ɣ likely had a lowering effect on preceding vowels. As such, while *ɣ originated as a velar consonant, it may have been a voiced uvular fricative by the Proto-Cangin stage.

For the second sound correspondence, Ndut-Paloor has /h/ while the other languages have nothing (or epenthesized /ʔ/). This sound can be reconstructed as *h (Table 16).

32   CHAPTER 2

TABLE 16   Proto-Cangin *h

PC	Noon	Laalaa	Saafi	Paloor	Ndut	
*has	as	as	as	has	has	'(be) new'
*huɓ	oɓ	°oɓ	oɓ	huɓ 'leaf'	huɓ 'leaf/bark'	'bark'
*hund	on, †ond	od	und	°hun	°hun	'skin' (n)
*hút	út 'bake'	út	ut	hút	°hút	'grill'
*hap	ap	ap	ap	hap~w	hap~w 'beat'	'kill'
*neh	ne'	niiy (<*neh-iɗ)	ne'	neh	neh	'draw water'
*níh	ní'	níi	nii, ‡ni'	níh	°níh	'rope'
*yíh~ɗíh	yí'	ɗíi	yii, †yi'	yíh	°ɗíh	'knee'
*ɓuh		ɓúu f-	ɓuu f-, ‡ɓu'	ɓuh f-	ɓuh f-	'dog'
*te/pe-he'	tee' t-, °pee' p-	†peᵃ p-		°tehe' 'palm fiber'	†teh k- 'straw'	'palm midrib'

Unfortunately outside comparisons are not as straightforward for *h (Table 17).
Sereer and Wolof are the only two Northern Atlantic languages which contrast
/h/[1] and uvular /x/ (and only in root-initial position), and they do not show
uniform correspondences with Cangin *h. Sereer has uvular /x/ in 'new,' and
for 'bark/leaf' Wolof and Sereer both have /x/.

TABLE 17   Correspondences for PC *h in Sereer and Wolof

PC	Sereer	Saalum Wolof	
*hon	—	honn	'swallow'
*hoɗ	—	hol	'pound in mortar'
*has	xas	hees	'new'
*huɓ	o-xoɓ 'bark'	xob 'leaf'	'bark/leaf'
*hup	hup	hëpp	'exceed'

Proto-Cangin *hup 'exceed' (Saafi °up, Paloor hup) is especially strong evidence
for reconstructing [h], as it is borrowed from Sereer hup, itself an old borrowing from Wolof hëpp, suggesting that Cangin *h was the phonetically-closest
sound to Sereer and Wolof [h]. Furthermore, [h] is the most likely value simply

---

1   Wolof has lost /h/ in all but the Saalum dialect, for which see Ndiaye (2013: 26) and Dramé
    (2012: 59), who note that wherever other dialects have an initial vowel or optional epenthetic
    /y/ or /w/, Saalum has /h/. Sereer has merged /h/ and /x/ in some dialects, but they remain
    distinct in most of Siin.

PHONOLOGY   33

because it could not be uvular [χ] or voiced [ɣ], as those values are reconstructed for other proto-sounds.

For the third correspondence, all languages have /h/. I take this correspondence as the regular development of a proto-phoneme *H (Table 18).

TABLE 18   Proto-Cangin *H

PC	Noon	Laalaa	Saafi	Paloor	Ndut	
*Heey	heey	heey	heey	°heej	heey	'dream' (v)
*Hul	hol	ol	hor	hul	°hul	'star'
*yuH	yoh	yoh	†yoh	yuh	°yuh	'bone'
*luH(Vy)	looy, °lohoy	looy	rohoy	°luh	°lúh	'(be) short'
*ti/pi-soH	peoh p-, °tesoh t-	pesoh p-	tisoh	°tisoh	tisoh k-	'seeds'
*Hak	hak	hak	hak	hak	†hak	'acacia tree'

The most likely phonetic value for *H is a uvular fricative [χ]. The phonemic
distinction between a glottal [h] and uvular [χ] is found in Sereer as well as
the Saalum dialect of Wolof (and all Wolof at an earlier time), as well as some
nearby Mande languages like Soninke and Susu. As such, it is not at all surprising that Proto-Cangin would have also made this phonemic distinction. This
is the phoneme used for Sereer and Wolof borrowings with uvular /x/ or /q/
(Table 19; *xx > q in both languages).

TABLE 19   Borrowing sources of PC roots with *H

PC	Source	
*misaH	Wo. sàq (< earlier *m-saxx*)	'granary'
*na(a)H	Ser. o-naq 'sorcerer'	'magic healer'
*Húlúɓ	Ser. o-xuluɓ	'river'
*Híl	Ser. xil	'snore'
*Haalís	Wo., Ser. xaalis (from Arabic)	'money/silver'
*Halí	Ser. a-qali, Susu xali	'bow' (weapon)
*taH	Wo., Ser. tax	'cause' (v)
*yaH	Wo. yàq, Ser. yaq	'destroy'
*mbaHane	Wo. mbaxane	'hat'

*H is found in all positions, and appears in native as well as borrowed vocabulary. *H is less common in non-borrowed reconstructions than *h (44 *h vs. 22 *H). It might be tempting to attribute the all-h sound correspondence to dialect mixture, whereby forms with /h/ that arose from *ɣ or *h were borrowed between early Cangin dialects, yielding this relatively less frequent correspondence without the need to reconstruct a separate proto-sound. However the roots in which it appears are extremely basic (e.g. 'star, dream, short'), and it is even found in the nominalizing agentive suffix *-oH. Furthermore there is no independent evidence for dialect mixture of this sort, and so it is necessary to reconstruct *H as a separate phoneme. There is unfortunately only one convincing cognate between Cangin and Sereer involving *H (and none with Wolof), being *Hul 'star,' which in Sereer is o-xoor with a uvular fricative.

For the fourth correspondence, Ndut-Paloor has /h/ (deleted intervocalically and often after a long vowel), and the other languages have /k/. This correspondence is not found word-initially. I reconstruct this phoneme with the symbol *x (Table 20). Note that an all-k correspondence set (from *k) is found in all positions, so this k:h set cannot be traced to *k.

TABLE 20   Proto-Cangin *x

PC	Noon	Laalaa	Saafi	Paloor	Ndut	
*sex	sek	sek	sek	seh	°seh	'wait'
*wax	wak	wak	wak	wah	†wah	'egg'
*la(a)x	laak	laak	raak	lah	lah	'have, happen'
*poox	pook	pook	pok	poo	poo, °pooh	'break'
*loox	look	look	rook	loo y-	loo	'belly'
*ɓoo(ɣ)-ox	ɓook	ɓook	ɓook	ɓooh	°ɓooh	'bathe'
*meex-iṛ	meekis	miikis	meekis	meel	meel	'ask'
*fi-xí	fíkíi f-	fíkíi f-	fiki	fíi °f-	fii, †fíh	'face/before'
*-ox	-uk	-ok	-uk	-oh	-oh	anticausative

The most likely phonetic value for *x is a velar or uvular fricative [x~χ], though it must have been distinct from *H as reconstructed above. Etymological comparisons can be made with the Sereer anticausative suffix -oox (and see Table 148 in chapter 5 for other potential cognates to this suffix), cf. Cangin *-ox, and Sereer naxik 'four,' cf. Cangin *nixiiṛ. Cangin *híix 'breathe' can be compared with Sereer hiiq and Wolof xiix 'rasp, breathe with difficulty,' but these words are sound symbolic, and as such may not represent regular sound correspondences.

PHONOLOGY

The phonetic realization of *H and *x is one of the most puzzling questions in the reconstruction of Proto-Cangin. As argued above, the most plausible value for each consonant is [χ], but they cannot have both been realized as such. There are of course a number of other sounds with which either proto-phoneme might be identified, e.g. a pharyngeal [ħ], a velar [x], a voiced uvular, or a uvular stop [q]. Of these, the only sound found in other languages of northern Senegal is [q] in Soninke, Sereer, and Wolof—though the development of geminate [χχ] to [qq] (later degeminated in Sereer) in all three languages may be a relatively recent development. In §5.1.3 it will be seen that this pair of Proto-Cangin phonemes can be traced to an earlier singleton vs. geminate opposition for a single voiceless uvular obstruent at a Pre-Cangin stage (also seen for other voiceless obstruents). However by the Proto-Cangin stage, consonant duration was likely not the phonetic property which distinguished these two sounds. The question of what exactly this distinguishing property was must be left open for now. The values that I find most likely are uvular [χ] for *H and velar [x] for *x, but these are far from certain. In support of these values, *H seems to have effected the quality of preceding vowels (typical of uvular consonants cross-linguistically), while *x did not (see §2.2.6). Whatever the case, it is clear that Proto-Cangin contained a comparatively large number of back fricatives, a fact which is likely related to its geographic proximity to the originally Berber-speaking area along the western Senegal River (see §5.1.1).

The final relevant sound correspondence is the all-zero (or [ʔ]) set (Table 21).

TABLE 21   Proto-Cangin initial and final ∅/ʔ

PC	Noon	Laalaa	Saafi	Paloor	Ndut	
*on	on	on	on	on	on	'give/offer'
*ú(u)f	úf, ⁺úuf	úf	uuf	°uuf	⁺úf	'pagne'
*iñ	iñ	oñ	iiñ 'snake'	iñ 'things'	iñ	'thing'
*op		op	op	op	°opa	'sweat'
*pe'	pe' f-	pe' f-	pe' f-	pe' °f-	pe' f-	'goat'
*paaní	péeníi f-	pëëní f-	paani f-/n-	póoní °f-	pëëní f-	'monkey'
*saangú	sóogúu f-, ⁺sóongú	°sëëgúu	saangu n-	sóogú °f-	°sëëgú f-	'shadow, shade'
*fi-xí	fíkíi f-	fíkíi f-	fiki	fíi °f-	fii	'face/before'
*mi-ɗa	meɗaa m-	meɗa m-	miɗa, meɗa m-	miraa, °mera m-	mira °m-	'salt'

Due to the existence of this correspondence set both word-initially and -finally, none of the correspondences involving /h/ can be reconstructed as originally ∅ with /h/ inserted in one branch or another.

2.1.5.3 *w and *y

The voiced continuants *w and *y can be reconstructed straightforwardly (Table 22). For the deletion of intervocalic /w, y/ (especially in Noon), see § 2.1.6.

TABLE 22 Proto-Cangin *w and *y

PC	Noon	Laalaa	Saafi	Paloor	Ndut	
*waaɽ	waas	waas	waas	waal	waal	'road'
*woɽ	wos	wos	wos-	wol	°wol	'send'
*waɗ-oɣ	waɗoh	waɗoh	waɗ 'gift'	waɗa'	°woda'	'share'
*saaw	saaw	saaw	saaw	saaw	†saaw	'firstborn'
*ɗeew	ɗeew	(ɗees)	ɗeew	ɗeew	°deu	'lick'
*yaɣ	yah	yah	yaah, °yah	ya'	ya'	'hand, arm'
*yooɓ	yooɓ	yooɓ	yooɓ	yooɓ	yooɓ	'be easy'
*yúun(d)	yúud	yúud	yun	yúun	yúun	'wake up'
*pay	pay	pay	pay 'disperse'	pay	pay	'go'
*looy	looyuk 'mourn'	looy 'flow'	rooy	looy	looy	'cry'
*fa-yúm	‡fëyum	fëyëm f-	fayum	fëyúm °m-	°fëyúm	'fat, grease'

The consonant *y is almost entirely absent before front vowels in PC roots, though the class prefix *y- can appear before front vowels. The one clear exception is *yúíɓ 'limp,' and there is also *(y)eɗ 'give,' with the /y/ present only in Ndut-Paloor, and NLS *(y)úf 'pour,' with /y/ absent in Noon but present in Laalaa and Saafi. Outside cognates for both 'give' and 'pour' contain /y/ (see Appendix 2).

Before a front vowel, *w generally becomes /y/ in Ndut and some dialects of Paloor (Table 23).

TABLE 23 *w > y before a front vowel in Ndut-Paloor

PC	Noon	Laalaa	Saafi	Paloor	Ndut	
*wet	wet	weet	wet	wet, yet	°yet	'ash'
*wíiñ	wíiñ	wíiñ	wiiñ	yíiñ	°yíiñ	'hang dry'
*wees	wees	°wees	wees	yees, †wes	°yees	'throw'
*wic	‡ɥit, (wiiy)	(°wii)	wic	wic, yic	wic	'horn'
*wíiɽ	wíis	°wíis	wiis	yiil, °yíl	°yíil	'dawn (v)'

PHONOLOGY

TABLE 23   *w > y before a front vowel in Ndut-Paloor (*cont.*)

PC	Noon	Laalaa	Saafi	Paloor	Ndut	
*wík	ík	wíik	wik	°yík		'give back'
*wíind	wíid	wíid	wiind	°yíin~d	°yíin	'pour out/decant'
*walínd		wëlíd	wirind	yilin, °yíil	°yéníl	'pay'
*ɣawíɽ			°hawis	óyíl, °owil	°oyíl, †ëyíl	'reduce'
	wes			yíis		'unbraid'

2.1.5.4   Coronal Continuants *l, *ɽ, *r

In addition to *s, three coronal continuants must be reconstructed which have some overlapping reflexes in modern languages: *l, *ɽ, and *r, though the phonetic realization is only secure for the first of these. The most common of the three is Proto-Cangin *l, which is unchanged in all languages except Saafi, where it usually develops to /r/, but sometimes remains /l/ (Table 24).

TABLE 24   Proto-Cangin *l

PC	Noon	Laalaa	Saafi	Paloor	Ndut	
*la(a)x	laak	laak	raak	lah	lah	'have, happen'
*lap	lap	lap	rap	°lap~w	°lap	'mount, climb'
*líif	líif	líif	riif	líif	líif	'be full'
*loox	look	look	rook	loo y-	loo	'belly'
*lox	lok	lok	rok	loh	°loh	'steal'
*luun	luun	luun	ruun	°luun	°luun	'witch, sorcerer'
*naal	naal	naal	naar	naal	°naal †f-	'bull/male animal'
*paal	paal	paal	paar	paal	†paal	'sprout' (v)
*Hul	hol	ol	hor	hul	°hul	'star'
*kel-oH	keloh	kalah	kerah	keloh	keloh 'listen'	'hear'
*liil	liil	liil	liir	liil	°liil	'intestine'
*laal	laal	laal	laar	laal 'be sated'	†laal 'be sated'	'be drunk'
*le(e)lu	leeloo	leloo	leero	lelu	†lelu	'middle/between'
*lam	lam	lam	lam	lam		'inherit'
*loy	luy, †loy	loy	°loy	loy		'knot' (n/v)
*ngúl	gúl (n, v)		ngul (n, v)	gúl (n, v)	°gúl (v)	'(make) hole'
*njol	jol		njol	°jol	†jol f-	'cricket'

The split reflex of *l in Saafi is difficult to explain. Saafi /r/ is the more common reflex, especially in the most basic vocabulary. Saafi /l/ is commonly found in borrowings, even some that can be reconstructed to Proto-Cangin (e.g. *lam 'inherit' from Sereer lam with the same meaning). There are other Sereer borrowings (see § 2.2.6) where the Saafi form matches the Sereer word more closely than in other Cangin languages, and so it appears that for some words, the Sereer word was "reborrowed" into Saafi. However there are enough seemingly non-borrowed tokens of Saafi /l/ to support the idea that some of these are dialect forms borrowed from some other Cangin variety at a time soon after the breakup of Proto-Cangin. The /l/ in 'intestine,' 'middle,' and 'be drunk' can be attributed to a regular dissimilation from the following /r/ (cf. also leere 'dinnertime' from Wolof reer, and hiilir 'be green' vs. Laalaa hiilüil). It is not desirable to reconstruct two separate proto-phonemes based on the two Saafi reflexes, since Saafi /l/ is a rather marginal sound in core non-borrowed vocabulary.

There is a common sound correspondence between /l/ in Ndut-Paloor and /s/ in NLS (Table 25). This correspondence does not appear word-initially. For reasons presented below, I reconstruct it as *ŗ for Proto-Cangin—Pozdniakov and Segerer (2017) suggest [ɬ].

TABLE 25   Proto-Cangin *ŗ

PC	Noon	Laalaa	Saafi	Paloor	Ndut	
*kíiŗ	kíis k-	kíis k-	kiis k-	kíil	kíil †k-	'year'
*waaŗ	waas	waas	waas	waal	waal	'road'
*woŗ	wos	wos	wos-	wol	°wol	'send'
*puuŗ	puus	puus	puus	puul	°puul	'wound' (n)
*haaŗ	aas	aas	aas	haal	haal	'enter'
*tuHuŗ	toos	toos	tuhuus, °tuhus	tuul		'spit' (v)
*ma-ŗúɓ/ŗuɓ	móoɓ, °músú m-	mësú m-	masuɓ m-	muluɓ °m-	muluɓ	'water'
*fV/a-ŗaal	ˇfasaa f-		fisaa r-	alaal	°araal	'chest' (thorax)
*kV-ŗaaɣ	ki-saah	kesah	°kisoh	kalaa	†kal	'last year'

The most convincing outside cognates for Cangin *ŗ are listed in Table 26.

PHONOLOGY   39

TABLE 26   Correspondences for PC *ṛ̥ in other Atlantic groups

PC	Sereer	Fula	Wolof	BKK	Tenda	Biaf.-Paj.	
*ɣír/ɣaṛ̥	a-ngid	gite (pl.)	gët (pl.)	*-giṛ̥	*-ɣəṛ	*-gəṛä	'eye'
*wíiṛ̥	feed	weet-	bët-set			*biiṛ̥	'dawn (v)'
*waaṛ̥				KK *bi-aaṛ̥		*f-aaṛ̥(e)	'road'
*kíiṛ̥ (*kV-híiṛ̥)	o-hiid	hitaande	hat m-				'year'
*tuHuṛ̥	tuxud/duxud	tuut-					'spit'
*taṛ̥			taat w-				'buttock'

Two hypotheses for the realization of PC *ṛ̥ are most plausible, of which I prefer the first.

In all but Sereer, Cangin *ṛ̥ corresponds to a voiceless coronal: /t/ in Wolof and Fula (and Bantu, see Appendix 2), and *ṛ̥ in other groups, which is the lenition of earlier **[t]. Other groups' *ṛ̥ becomes [tt] when geminated. Note that the phonetic value *ṛ̥ is also a reconstruction in other groups, where modern languages have [s, r, l, h] as reflexes. Since other groups' *ṛ̥ can be straightforwardly traced to an earlier **[t], the same is likely true of Cangin *ṛ̥. While a number of Proto-Cangin reconstructions have non-initial *t, it will be seen in §5.1.3 that these come from earlier geminates. Further complicating the situation, there is in fact evidence for the lenition of *t to *s in Proto-Cangin (see Table 138 in chapter 5). I find the following scenario most likely: the lenition of **t to PC *ṛ̥ was a very old change, which affected only tokens of **t which were not word- or stem-initial. The lenition to *s was a later change, which affected post-vocalic tokens of PC *t that were not subject to the earlier lenition—namely those in stem-initial position, and some non-initial tokens in words borrowed after the earlier change. Incidentally, this means that in 'water, chest, last year,' the class prefix must have been frozen at an early date, such that the original root-initial consonant was not treated as root-initial by the time of the **t > *ṛ̥ change.

The second hypothesis relies on the correspondence with Sereer /d/, which might suggest the value of a voiced coronal for the Proto-Cangin sound. The equivalence between Sereer /d/ and Cangin *ṛ̥ is bolstered by the fact that 'year' and perhaps 'spit' appear to be borrowed from Sereer in Proto-Cangin. For 'year,' see the discussion towards the beginning §2.3.2. For 'spit,' many Niger-Congo groups have a form beginning in *tV$_{[back]}$ (cf. Bantu *tʉ́) which is perhaps inherited, and certainly sound-symbolic. However the full form of the root differs substantially between Atlantic groups, making the segment-

for-segment identity between Fula-Sereer *tuxud and Cangin *tuHųr̥ sugges-
tive of borrowing. Assuming that either 'year' or 'spit' is indeed a borrowing
from Sereer, Proto-Cangin *r̥ must have had a sound value similar to the sound
that became Sereer /d/. However, it is far from clear that Sereer root-final /d/
was always voiced. In fact the regular correspondence is /t/ in Fula, and recall
that no other group has a voiced coronal. As such, there seems to have been
a Sereer-specific voicing change. I assume that this change had in fact taken
place in Proto-Fula-Sereer (PFS), with subsequent devoicing in Fula, but even
so it might be that 'year' and/or 'spit' were very old borrowings into Cangin
from before the voicing change. It must be acknowledged that this issue is not
yet resolved, and a better understanding of the history of other Atlantic groups
may force the questions surrounding this Proto-Cangin consonant to be reeval-
uated.

There is evidence for various changes affecting *r̥ when next to a consonant. The two Noon forms *úwis* 'swell' and *úwlis* 'swell even more,' from *húfir̥
and *húfr̥-is* show *r̥ developing to Noon /l/ after a consonant. The second of
these is suffixed with the pluractional/intensive suffix *-is*, causing deletion of
the preceding vowel, and placing *r̥ in post-consonantal position. Ndut and
Paloor each have an irregular suffixed form of *kíil* 'year': Paloor °*kítkí*, Ndut
kirki 'next year.' These forms are seemingly from *kíir̥ k-i* 'the year,' and the
original *r̥ (rather than *l) in this word helps to explain the unexpected consonant changes. Note also Paloor *heltoh*, Ndut *heeltoh* or °*helsoh* 'turn around/look
back' from *Heel-ir̥-ox* (cf. Noon *heeleek*), in which the *r̥ of the suffix becomes
/t/ or /s/ after *l.

Lastly, there is a rare correspondence between Ndut-Paloor /l/ and NLS /t/
that can be reconstructed as *r (Table 27). Another possible value is *[d]. This
sound correspondence is only attested in intervocalic position, and as such *r
is rare in reconstructions.

TABLE 27   Proto-Cangin *r

PC	Noon	Laalaa	Saafi	Paloor	Ndut	
*ɓe-reɓ	ɓeti, †ɓedëɓ	ɓete f-	ɓitiɓ	ɓeleɓ	ɓeleɓ	'woman'
*leɓ	leɓ		riɓ			'female'
*ki-rik	kedik k-	kedek k-	kidik	kilik k-	kilik †k-	'tree'
*(a-)roɣ	atoh (f-)	atoh	atoh °f-	la'	la', †ala	'stone/rock'
*kV-ra	ketaa k-	ketaa k-		°kula		'pot'

PHONOLOGY

The identification of this proto-phoneme with [r] is in part because intervocalic *l, *ɽ, and *t are already reconstructed, but also because of the potential connection between *-reɓ 'woman' and Fula-Sereer *-rew 'woman.' However on the whole, outside comparisons only raise further questions about the history of Cangin *r. All three remaining words have external connections: *kV-ra 'pot' is from the Mande Wanderwort daa (cf. Wolof ndaa, Tenda *-ɗaa); *a-roy 'stone' can be compared with Manjak *pə-laak and Balanta f-làagí; *ki-rik 'tree' appears to be cognate with **t-initial roots like Tenda *-ɽax, Bantu *-tí. Thus Cangin *r corresponds to a number of different sounds in outside groups (*d/r, *l, *t/ɽ), which do not regularly correspond to each other between the groups in question. The reason for the voicing of this consonant as [d] in NLS 'tree' is unclear. This voicing is regular in the Thiès dialect of Noon, but in the other varieties is confined to this root. Word-initially, *r must have merged with *l, as evidenced by the unprefixed root 'female.'

Due to the rarity of *r, a few further comments are warranted to justify its reconstruction. First, this t:l sound correspondence cannot be attributed to the intervocalic lenition of *t, since in NLS 'female' and Ndut-Paloor 'stone' the consonant appears word-initially as /l/ rather than /t/. Second, it is very unlikely that this sound correspondence is the result of the fortition of *l or *ɽ in NLS. Since all of the words with *r are prefixed nouns, it might be proposed that the prefix in each word had the effect of hardening *l or *ɽ to NLS /t/. Indeed, in a number of other Atlantic language groups, certain noun class prefixes induce fortition of root-initial consonants due to the earlier presence of an oral consonant at the end of the prefix (see Merrill 2018). However the specific prefixes on these particular Cangin nouns—namely *ɓi- (§ 3.1.4) and *ki- (§ 3.1.5)—do not induce fortition on any other noun roots, and thus it is very unlikely that the t:l correspondence is the result of fortition-inducing prefixes.

Nonetheless, there is a potential scenario in which the t:l correspondence can be explained by prefix-induced fortition, and while it is unlikely, it must be considered. First, under this prefix-induced fortition scenario it must be assumed that the fortition process had not taken place in Proto-Cangin, since the outcome /t/ is found only in NLS. The prefix *a- on NLS *a-roy 'rock' is not found on any other NLS noun, and as such there is no obstacle to proposing that this particular prefix induced fortition. There is in fact a fortition-inducing noun class prefix a-II in Kobiana-Kasanga within Atlantic, used for small round objects including 'stone' (Kobiana a-bbòong). For *ki-rik 'tree,' the prefix *ki- is reconstructed on a number of other nouns, but it is conceivable that the prefix *ki- on 'tree' was at one time distinct from the prefix *ki- used on other nouns. It could be compared with the Fula fortition-inducing class marker II- -ki used on all tree names (though not leggal 'tree' itself). Noon-Laalaa *ke-taa 'pot' (cf.

Paloor °*kula*) might have the same prefix used for 'tree.' For **ɓe-reɓ* 'woman,' it must be noted that the prefix **ɓi-* is found on only a few nouns in NLS, and the only one that would exhibit fortition is 'woman' (the others being **ɓi-o'* 'person' and Saafi *ɓitif* 'old woman,' which also has /t/ in Ndut-Paloor). Thus there is strictly speaking no obstacle to treating **ɓi-* as a fortition-inducing prefix. Human plural class prefixes of the shape **ɓV-* are found in multiple Atlantic groups, and in general they cannot be reconstructed with a final consonant. However, in the Bak family the marker has the shape *bVk/bVg-* in some contexts. Thus, for each of the three class prefixes that appear on the roots with an initial t:l correspondence, there is a potential connection to be made with a fortition-inducing (or **CVC-*) prefix in another Atlantic group. Nonetheless, the scenario sketched in this paragraph remains implausible. First, since this supposed fortition process took place only in NLS, it cannot have operated in Proto-Cangin, and so CVC- prefixes would have to be reconstructed to Proto-Cangin to allow for the appearance of unfortified /l/ rather than /t/ in Ndut-Paloor. Second, under this scenario all of the roots that show a trace of this fortition process are **l-* or **r̥-initial, which would be quite a coincidence. Next, there is no independent evidence for the idea that the **ki-* prefix in 'tree' and 'pot' was ever distinct from the **ki-* prefix found in other nouns. Finally, the association of the prefix in **a-roy* 'rock' with Kobiana-Kasanga *a-II* (which is a very large class, but found in no other family) is highly speculative.

Since this fortition-based scenario is so unlikely, the reconstruction of a distinct phoneme for the t:l sound correspondence cannot be easily avoided. Nonetheless, it is somewhat unsatisfying to propose a phoneme with such a limited distribution, and other explanations must be considered in the future. It may even be that the t:l correspondence does not have the same origin in all cases. Recall that Ndut-Paloor irregularly lenites /t/ to /l/ in *ot~ol-* 'see,' and this lenition could account for 'tree' and 'pot.'

2.1.6 *Consonant Lenition and Loss*

Various processes of consonant lenition and deletion have operated in each Cangin language. In Saafi and Paloor, /f, s/ are allophonically voiced to [v, z] between voiced sounds. D'Alton and Pouye also note the voicing of /h/ between voiced sounds to [ɣ] in Paloor and [ɦ] in Saafi. The lenition/deletion of implosives in all languages but Saafi is discussed in § 2.1.3.

Noon exhibits a particularly high degree of intervocalic lenition. In the Thiès dialect, /p, t, c, k/ are voiced between vowels and approximants. In the Northern and Thiès dialects, intervocalic /f, s/ as found in the Padee dialect are voiced to /w, y/, and /w, y, h, '/ are subject to deletion (including /w, y/ from **f, *s). In

PHONOLOGY   43

root-internal position or after a historical noun class prefix this deletion is regular in Northern Noon, and occurs with some exceptions in the Thiès dialect (Table 28).

TABLE 28   Deletion of intervocalic consonants in Noon in non-alternating environments

PC	N., T. Noon	Padee Noon	Laalaa	Saafi	Paloor, Ndut	
*caafú	cëw, †cëwuu	°cëwuu	cëëfú f-	caafu	cóofú °f-, °cëëf k-	'fly' (bug)
*ñVfaɗ	ñooɗ, †ñooɗ	°ñafaɗ		ñafaɗ	ñafaɗ, ñofaɗ	'shoe'
*(n-)ku-suun	guun, ‡guyun		guusuud	kusun k-	kusiin, kusuun †k-	'navel'
*misik	miik, †misëk	°mesik	mesek	misik	misik, misik	'hurt' (intr.)
*(pi/ti-)síl	tíil t-, †píil p-	°písíl p-	písíl p-	sir	síl, °síl	'vein'
*mi-sip	miip m-	°mesip m-	mesep m-	misip m-	°misib m-, misip m-	'sauce'
*mi-sook	meek, †meek m-	°misook m-	mesook m-	misook m-	Nd. misook m-	'urine'
*ti/pi-soH	peoh, †peeh p-	°tesoh t-	pesoh p-	°tisoh	tisoh, tisoh k-	'seeds'
*ma-r̥úɓ	móoɓ, †múu m-	°músú m-	mësú m-	masuɓ m-	muluɓ °m-, muluɓ	'water'
*wur̥/úr̥	úwaay, (†)úyaay	°úsaay	wos	us	°wul, wul	'be far'
*ɣawúl	hool, †huul		hëwúl	hawur	(ɓóolu/†ɓëëlú, †ɓol k-)	'griot'
*ka-aɣay	kaay, †kaahay	°kaahay	kaahaay	kahaay	(eye, éeyë)	'three'
*kooɣ wíir̥	kuus, †kuwis	°kuwis	†koh wis	kooh wiis	koope yiil, †ko yíl	'tomorrow'
*ki-yuuŋ	kuuŋ		kiyuuŋ k-, †kúuŋ k-			'shin'
	yooh, †yooh	°yo'oh				'red'

In root-final position, the situation is more complicated, since the consonant is often analogically restored. For example the consonant remains in Northern Noon ñíwís 'bleed' from ñíf 'blood.' Even when the suffixed root shows no possibility of alternation in the modern language, the consonant often remains, as in Northern Noon maayoh 'termite' from the root *maas and úwis 'swell' from *húf-ir̥. In other cases the consonant is deleted as expected, as in tuuk 'stand' from *tof-ox. As with the restoration of Laalaa intervocalic /ɓ, y/ (see §2.1.3), the restoration of Northern Noon /f, s/ as [w, y] must have been influenced by dialectal comparison. Because intervocalic [f, s] first voiced to [w, y] and then were deleted entirely, there would have been no dialect-internal basis for restoring /f, s/ as [w, y], since these phonemes would have had no regular intervocalic allophones after their deletion. It seems that some varieties like that recorded by Williams and Williams (1993) voiced /f, s/ but did not delete them, and the restoration of intervocalic /f, s/ as [w, y] in deleting dialects would have been facilitated by comparison with these varieties. The historical intervocalic deletion sound changes are reflected as a synchronic process of intervocalic deletion in Northern Noon (Table 29). Suffixed nouns and verbs do or do not delete /s, y, h, ʼ/ on a word-by-word basis, with recent borrowings especially liable to resist deletion (/f, w/ never delete synchronically, though /f/ always voices to /w/).

TABLE 29   Lexically-specific deletion of intervocalic consonants in Northern Noon

Noun	-*aa* distal definite	Verb	-*aa* imperative
waas 'road'	**waa**	tes 'remain'	**tee**
kókús 'axe'	**kókóo**	aas 'enter'	**aa**
kooh 'sky'	**koo**	yah 'go'	**yaa**
atoh 'stone'	**atoo**	neeh 'sleep'	**nee**
muus 'cat'	muuyaa	wes 'unbraid'	weyaa
kaas 'cup'	kaayaa	tís 'wash'	tíyaa
ɓoh 'baobab'	ɓohaa	saɗah 'sacrifice'	saɗahaa
maayoh 'termite'	maayohaa	tóh 'smoke'	tóhaa

In Thiès Noon these root-final consonants are always restored except for /h/, e.g. †*edoh* 'use for'+ -*ës* 'passive' → *edoos* (Lopis-Sylla 2010: 83). Wane (2017: 24) notes that root-final /f/ is voiced before a vowel in nouns only (and not verbs), and mentions no synchronic voicing of /s/. No voicing or deletion of these consonants occurs in Padee Noon. The noun class marker *f-* is never voiced or deleted in any dialect (e.g. *fíkíi-f-ii* 'the face'), likely due to analogical reinforcement by agreeing pronouns and determiners in which *f-* is word-initial. On the other hand, *y-* in forms of *ɓo'* 'person' is generally deleted in Northern Noon (e.g. *ɓu-y-ii* ~ *ɓuui* 'the person'), and in Laalaa *ɓ-* is subject to regular intervocalic deletion in plural forms of *ɓo'* (see § 3.1.4).

Deletion of *f, *w, *y, and /h/ from all sources is also witnessed in certain words in Paloor, Ndut, and especially Laalaa (Table 30).

PHONOLOGY

45

TABLE 30   Deletion of intervocalic consonants in non-alternating environments

PC	Noon	Laalaa	Saafi	Paloor	Ndut	
*tuHuɽ	toos	toos	tuhuus, °tuhus	tuul		'spit' (v)
*tof-ox	tuuk	tuuk	tufuk	tofoh		'stand'
*to-ɣo	tooh, °tohoo t-	too t-	toho r-	too k-	too k-	'millet'
*ku-fúc	kúuc k-	kúuc f-	kufic, †kufuc	°kúfúc k-	†kúc k-	'needle'
*mu-ɣon	moon m-	moon m-	muhun	°moon m-	†mun m-	'tear (crying)'
*kaɣand	kaad f-	kaad f-	kahan, °kahand			'house'
*yoɣon	yoon	yoon	yohon			'field'
*ɗafuk	ɗook	ɗook	ɗafuk			'above/over'
(Arabic kāɣ̱iṭ)	kéet, °†këyít	°kéet	kiya	këyít	†kéít	'paper'
*pi-wiñ	piiñ, pewiñ p-	píiñ p-	tiwiñ	tiwiñ °k-	tiiñ k-	'metal/iron'
*luH(Vy)	looy, °†lohoy	looy	rohoy	°luh	°lúh	'(be) short'
*kayoH	kayoh, †keeh f-	kayoh f-	keeh	kaah	°kaah k-	'truth'
*nixiiɽ	nikiis	niikiis	nikis	iniil	iniil	'four'
*meex-iɽ̥	meekis	miikis	meekis	meel	meel	'ask'
*fi-xí	fíkíi f-	fíkíi f-	fiki	fii °f-	fii	'face/before'

In Laalaa (Dieye 2010: 72), /h/ is subject to intervocalic deletion synchronically, e.g. *kalah* 'hear' + -*en* 'perfective' → *kaleen*. The intervocalic deletion of /h/ in Laalaa seems to be regular, with *kaahaay* 'three' as the only clear exception. In Ndut-Paloor /h/ from all sources (*h, *H, *x) is generally deleted intervocalically both within roots and between a prefix and a root, though there are exceptions, e.g. *te-he'* > Paloor °*tehe'* 'palm fiber' and *ti-xeyi* > Paloor *tihi k-* 'sand.' A few examples of Ndut intervocalic /h/ deletion are found throughout Morgan (1996), e.g. /yúh-eh/ → *yéeh* 'know-HAB.NEG,' /yúulëh-inki/ → *yúulínkí* 'perform.libation-do.before.' Otherwise the deletion of intervocalic continuants in languages other than Noon is not a regular change, instead affecting only specific (and generally frequent) lexical items. In Saafi (Mbodj 1983: 214), the root-final consonant of a few common verbs can be deleted before a vowel, e.g. *hay* 'come' + -*iɗ* 'perfective' → *hiɗ* (also in *kaɗ* 'go,' *jom* 'must'). Mbodj also mentions *woy* 'say' as exhibiting this deletion, but historically the /y/ is not part of the root, being extended from forms of the verb with an /i/-initial suffix. As such the modern forms of 'say' without /y/ never had it to begin with. Other than these few verbs and in *keeh* 'truth,' intervocalic consonants were seemingly not subject to deletion historically in Saafi. Recall from § 2.1.1 that in Ndut-Paloor, four common voiceless stop-final verb roots lenite the stop before a vowel.

46   CHAPTER 2

The lenition of intervocalic implosives was discussed in § 2.1.3, but there are also some isolated roots in which word-final *ɓ is deleted in Noon or Laalaa (Table 31).

TABLE 31   Isolated deletion of final *ɓ

PC	Noon	Laalaa	Saafi	Paloor	Ndut	
*ɓe-reɓ	ɓeti, †ɓedëɓ	ɓete f-	ɓitiɓ	ɓeleɓ	ɓeleɓ	'woman'
*ma-ɽúɓ	móoɓ³, °músú m-	mësú m-	masuɓ m-	muluɓ °m-	muluɓ	'water'
*leɓ	le'		reɓ	leɓ 'come close'	†leɓ	'touch'
*tíɓ	tíɓ	tíi	tiɓ	°tíɓ	°tíɓ	'forge'
*pV-huɓ	tóoɓ t-, °puuɓ	póo p-				'leaf'
*kúɓ(-ox)	kúɓ	°kúu		°kúu	†kúuh	'carry (baby) on back'

a   Northern Noon *móoɓ* 'water' loses its final consonant in definite forms (e.g. *móo-m-ii*), cf. Saafi *mas-m-i*. The Thiès Noon form is given as *mu'* or *muu* by Lopis (1980, 2010), and *múu(')* by Wane (2017), which is perhaps /múuɓ/.

It is unlikely that any of these lenition processes operated in Proto-Cangin since none of them take place in all modern languages, with most being confined to one or two languages.

2.1.7   *Consonant Assimilation Processes*

In each language the initial consonant of certain suffixes assimilates to a preceding consonant. The suffixes which undergo this assimilation differ by language, as do the assimilation processes themselves. In Noon-Laalaa the suffixes that undergo assimilation are all those that begin with /ɗ/ (most of which are object pronouns) and the 1st person singular object pronoun (Laalaa *-soo*, Northern Noon *-yoo*, Padee and Thiès Noon *-ɗoo*). Outcomes of Noon-Laalaa consonant assimilation are shown in Table 32, with examples in Table 33.

TABLE 32   Realization of assimilating suffix consonants in Noon and Laalaa

Preceding C	Suffix C becomes Noon	Suffix C becomes Laalaa
/m, n, ñ, ŋ/	/b, d, j, g/ (†/md, nd, nj, ng/)	/b, d, j, g/
/ɓ, ɗ, y/	/p, t, c/	total assimilation
all others	total assimilation	total assimilation

PHONOLOGY   47

TABLE 33   Noon and Laalaa suffix assimilation with *-ɗa* 'punctual/narrative'

	Noon	Laalaa	
ap -ɗa =	appa	appa	'killed'
lom -ɗa =	lomba	lomba	'bought'
ab -ɗa =	abba [amba]	abba [amba]	'held'
ɗoɓ -ɗa =	ɗoɓpa [ɗowʔpa]	ɗoɓɓa [ɗoɓɓa]	'bit'
ɓof -ɗa =	ɓoffa	ɓoffa	'coughed'
naaw -ɗa =	naawwa	naawwa	'laundered'

Note that NL full assimilation to root-final /b, d, j, g/ results in /bb, dd, jj, gg/, in which the first consonant is in coda position, and thus has its nasal allophone. For example Northern Noon *tam-bii* 'isn't hot' and *tab-bii* 'isn't forbidden' are homophonous. In Thiès Noon the sequence of a nasal and prenasalized stop (as in †*kaan-ndii* 'doesn't die') that results from this assimilation process is distinct from a simple prenasalized stop. With a preceding implosive, total assimilation is possible in Northern Noon, though it is less common than the voiceless stop pattern; e.g. *kúɓ-púu* [kúwʔpúu] ~ *kúɓ-búu* [kúwʔbúu] 'carry you (pl.) on one's back.'

In Saafi two suffixes undergo assimilation: the 1st person singular object/possessive pronoun *-so* (Pouye 2015 writes this as a free word) and the narrative marker *-ɗa*. These assimilate to the preceding consonant, becoming /p, t, c/ after /ɓ, ɗ, y/, prenasalized stops after a nasal or underlying prenasalized stop, and assimilating totally to other consonants (Pouye 2015: 129).

(3)   Assimilation of the 1st sg. object pronoun *-so* to a preceding consonant in Saafi

ap po	'kill me'
aaf fo	'repay me'
amb mbo [ammbo]	'hold me'
on ndo	'give me'
reɓ po	'come near me'

In Mbodj's (1983: 168, 215) description, the consonant of the suffix becomes /p, t, c/ after /ɓ, ɗ, y/, and is deleted after other consonants.

48 CHAPTER 2

While /ɗ/ is the NLS consonant that most often exhibits assimilation, /ɗ/ in the verbal suffixes -íɗ 'causative' and -iɗ 'benefactive' (as well as -ɗuk 'pretend to') do not show this assimilation when the suffix vowel is deleted (e.g. Noon jégɗoh 'teacher' from jégíɗ 'teach'). However in two examples with frozen *-íɗ, the consonant does assimilate (Table 34).

TABLE 34   Isolated examples of the assimilation of /ɗ/ from
            *-íɗ in Noon, Laalaa, and Saafi

PC	Noon	Laalaa	Saafi	
*heeñ-íɗ-ox	éeñɗuk	éenjúk		'smell'
*(h)aañ-íɗ-oɣ	éenjoh	ënjóh	aññjoh	'play'

In Ndut-Paloor there are at least three distinct patterns of consonant assimilation. First, in Ndut the plural noun class marker y assimilates completely to a preceding consonant, with the exception of [ʔ] and /h/, after which it remains /y/.

(4)   Assimilation of Ndut plural y (Morgan 1996: 23)

Noun	Def. pl. -y-a	
wic	wicca	'horn'
aan	aanna	'drum'
heey	heeyya	'dream'
les	lessa	'room'
baw	bawwa	'dog's bark'
ɓa'	ɓa'ya	'baobab'
añoh	añohya	'oath'

Plural y does not undergo assimilation in Paloor. The second process affects the perfective suffix -te in both languages. After /p, t, c, k/, /m, n, ñ, ŋ/, and /ɓ, ɗ, y/, the /t/ of this suffix becomes a homorganic voiceless stop. After /f/ and /s/ it assimilates completely. After all other consonants it is unchanged.

PHONOLOGY

(5) Assimilation of Ndut-Paloor perfective -*te* (Morgan 1996: 21)

Ndut verb	Perfective -*te*	
hap	happe	'hit'
lom	lompe	'buy'
súuy	súuycé	'bury'
has	hasse	'be new'
pay	payte	'go'

The third process affects the particle *da*, which serves as the relative clause marker, and is also used in a "presentative" construction (see §4.2.5). This shows the allomorphs *da~ra~na~la* in D'Alton's (1983: 231) description of Paloor, and *da~ra~na~la~nda* in Morgan's description of Ndut. In Khodaba Paloor, the allomorph used is *ra* after a vowel, *na* after a nasal, *la* after /l/, and *da* after all other consonants. Morgan does not specifically comment on the conditioning of the allomorphy, and in his examples *ra* often occurs even after a consonant, with either *da*, *na*, or *nda* after a nasal. Thornell et al. (2016: 90) find that the choice of *ra~na~da* in Paloor is based on dialect. Morgan (1996: 19) finds that any example of the Ndut sequence /l-d/ is realized as [ll]. Lastly, Morgan (1996: 124) notes that when multiple Ndut derivational suffixes appear on a verb, "there tends to be a loss of some of the phonetic material," but provides only one example, which is difficult to analyze: /tas-il-a'-ay/ → [tallilaa] 'remain-again-APPL-FUT.' There are a number of reasons to doubt Morgan's morphological analysis of this word (it may be /tas-il-il-a'-a/), but it is at least clear that the root-final /s/ has assimilated to the consonant of the following suffix.

It is unlikely that any of these assimilation processes operated obligatorily in Proto-Cangin, since none of the particular processes are shared between all modern languages. It may however be that certain consonants in grammatical morphemes, especially *ɗ*, could optionally assimilate to a preceding consonant.

2.2 Vowels

The set of reconstructed Proto-Cangin vowel phonemes is shown in Table 35.

TABLE 35   Reconstructed Proto-Cangin vowel inventory

high +ATR	í, íi		ú, úu
high -ATR	i, ii		u, uu
mid		e, ee	o, oo
low		a, aa	

Notably there were no non-high +ATR vowels, these being subsequent developments of the modern Cangin languages. A brief note is in order on the phonetics of the ATR distinction ("advanced tongue root," though this description may not be articulatorily accurate for the Cangin languages). The high vowel ATR distinction is difficult to hear for non-native speakers, and as such by far the most common type of discrepancy between sources involves the ATR value of high vowels. The phonetic realization of these two series is not IPA [i, u] vs. [ɪ, ʊ] (as for example in English *beat* vs. *bit*), which is a commonly used convention for representing these sets of vowels. From my own experience with Noon, the -ATR vowels are closer to [i, u] as in e.g. Spanish, and the +ATR vowels sound mildly breathy. Detailed phonetic research into the articulation and acoustics of Cangin vowels is unfortunately lacking, but for our purposes it can simply be said that the Proto-Cangin articulation of these high vowels was in all likelihood essentially the same as in the modern languages. The +ATR low vowel /ë/ which develops in most Cangin languages is most similar to [ə]. Modern /ë, é, ó/ are generally described as identical to the Wolof vowels represented with the same symbols, which my own experience with Noon corroborates.

2.2.1 Basic Vowel Correspondences
2.2.1.1 High Vowels
The +ATR high vowels can be reconstructed without complication (Table 36). In Saafi the ATR distinction has collapsed, so that *í and *i are merged as /i/ and *ú and *u as /u/—all other languages maintain this distinction.

PHONOLOGY   51

TABLE 36   Proto-Cangin +ATR high vowels

PC	Noon	Laalaa	Saafi	Paloor	Ndut	
*fiis	fiis	fiis	fiis	fiis	°fiis	'draw/trace/write'
*níil	níil	níil	niir	níil	°níil	'root'
*ɓíiɓ	ɓíiɓ	ɓíiɓ	ɓiiɓ	ɓíiɓ	ɓíiɓ	'breast'
*kíiɽ	kíis k-	kíis k-	kiis k-	kíil	kíil †k-	'year'
*wíiñ	wíiñ	wíiñ	wiiñ	yíiñ	°yíiñ	'hang dry'
*sís	sís	sís	sis	sís	sís	'tooth'
*ɓít	ɓít	ɓít	ɓit	°ɓít	ɓít	'be heavy'
*típ	típ	típ	tip	típ	†típ	'beat (drum)'
*-íɗ	-íɗ	-íɗ	-íɗ	-íɗ	-íɗ	causative
*-ís	-ís	-ís	-is	-ís	ís	reversive
*kúum	kúum k-	kúum k-	kuum	kúum k-	°kúum k-	'honey'
*súuɽ	súus	súusúus	susuus	°súul	°súul	'(be) black'
*ñúus	ñúus (v)	ñúus (n)	ñuus (n)	ñúus (n, v)		'be dark/darkness'
*ɗúuk	ɗúuk	°ɗúuk	ɗuuk			'smoke' (v)
*ɗúuk-ú			ɗuuku r-	ɗúukú	ɗúukë	'smoke' (n)
*múuy	múuy	°múuy	muuy	múuy		'disappear'
*púk	púk	púk	puk	púk	púk	'forehead'
*mún	mún m-	mún m-	mun	mún m-	mún m-	'flour'
*kún	kún 'cover'	kún	kun 'cover'	kún	°kún	'close'
*hút	út 'bake'	út	ut	hút	°hút	'grill'
*púnd	púd		pund	°pún~d	pún~†d	'fly'

For the -ATR high vowels (Table 37), the long vowels are unchanged in all languages. The short vowels *u and *i have regularly developed to /o/ and /e/ in Noon and Laalaa. The change *u > /o/ operated inconsistently in Saafi.

TABLE 37   Proto-Cangin -ATR high vowels

PC	Noon	Laalaa	Saafi	Paloor	Ndut	
*liil	liil	liil	liir	liil	°liil	'intestine'
*miis	miis m-	miis m-	miis m-	miis m-	miis m-	'milk'
*kiih	†kii	kii	kii (nut)	°kiih (nut, oil)	°kii	'palm tree'

TABLE 37 Proto-Cangin -ATR high vowels (cont.)

PC	Noon	Laalaa	Saafi	Paloor	Ndut	
*ɓil	ɓil	°ɓil	ɓiir	ɓil		'young man/boyfriend'
*siili	siili	siili		siili	siili	'Ndut-Paloor/Sereer'
*sing(u)	seg	seŋ, †seg	°singu	sigu	°sugu	'left'
*ɓis	†ɓes	ɓes	ɓis	ɓis		'arrow'
*ki-noH	kenoh k-	kenoh k-	kinoh	°kinoh	†kinoh k-	'waist'
*misik	°mesik	mesek	misik	misik	misik	'hurt' (intr.)
*Humbis		hobes		hubis		'stir'
*sinja(a)n		sejan		sijaan		'back'
*suul	suul	suul	suur	°suul f-	°suul f-	'vulture'
*luun	luun	luun	ruun	°luun	°luun	'witch, sorcerer'
*puuɽ	puus	puus	puus	puul	°puul	'wound' (n)
*nduul	duul	duul	nduur		°duul f-	'monitor lizard'
*luum	luumiin	°luumiin	ruumind	luum	°luum	'be red,' NL 'have light skin'
*Hul	hol	ol	hor	hul	°hul	'star'
*huɓ	oɓ	°oɓ	oɓ	huɓ 'leaf'	huɓ 'leaf/bark'	'bark'
*ɓuk	ɓok	ɓok	ɓok	ɓuk °f-	°ɓuk f-	'mosquito'
*nuf	nof	nof	nof	nuf	°nuf	'ear'
*yuH	yoh	yoh	†yoh	yuh	°yuh	'bone'
*kuɗ	koɗ k-	koɗ k-	kuɗ	kuɗ °k-	kuɗ k-	'pestle'
*hund	on, †ond	od	und	hun	°hun	'skin' (n)
*yut		hotiit	hut	ut	°ut	'be long'
*nu(n)yund	nood	nogon	nuhun	nuun~d	nuŋun, †nugun	'point out'

The Noon-Laalaa lowering change does not occur when a short -ATR high vowel co-occurs with a long vowel of the same quality (/ii/ or /uu/) in the same word. The change does take place when vowel qualities differ, e.g. Laalaa *hotiit* 'be long' < *yut. Examples of this (lack of) change are shown in (6).

(6) Noon-Laalaa [i, u] rather than [e, o] when adjacent to [ii, uu]

Noon		Laalaa	
kipii	'ring'	kuumun	'nose'
nikiis	'four'	miikis	'ask'
fuñuuñ	'millet burrs'	kimiiliic	'lightning'
jutuut	'(be) small'	Ce~Ci-	adj. agr. prefix (/i/ before /ii, uu/)

PHONOLOGY   53

As a result of this lowering change, short [i, u] did not exist in Proto-Noon-Laalaa except as allophones of /e, o/ next to /ii, uu/. Proto-Cangin *e, *o never co-occur with *ii, *uu, and so even though *e, *o did not change from PC to Proto-NL, Proto-NL [e, o] and [i, u] were in complementary distribution. This situation still holds in Laalaa as analyzed by Dieye (2010: 58) (notably, all affixes with /e, o/ have [i, u] when /ii, uu/ is in an adjacent syllable), and possibly in Thiès Noon. The vowels /e/ and /o/ are more than twice as frequent in Noon and Laalaa roots versus /í/ and /ú/, since each mid vowel results from the merger of two Proto-Cangin vowels.

A few notes are necessary regarding the status of /i, u/ in Laalaa and Thiès Noon. For Laalaa, Dieye does list a few words with /u/ and /i/ that cannot be the result of vowel harmony: a series of class agreeing pronouns CL-*i, yin* 'thing,' *ɓu* '2nd pl. pronoun,' *tuy* 'hut,' and the negative suffix -*ɗi*. For these last three Thornell et al. (2016c) have °*ɓú*, °*tuuy*, and °-*ɗii*. For Thiès Noon, Lopis (1980: 77) reports that there is no length contrast for -ATR /ii/ and /uu/, which she notes are longer than the short vowels, but chooses to spell as monographemic ⟨I, U⟩. The analysis is that -ATR short vowel phonemes /i/ and /u/ do not exist in Thiès Noon. However, the Thiès dialect does contain a few words with short /u/ (based on etymological comparison—these are all from PC short vowels), all of which have multiple tokens of the vowel: †*mungul* 'cheek,' †*fumbuluy* 'brain,' and †*kuyu k-* 'girl.' It seems that multiple tokens of Proto-NL *o (whether from PC *u or *o) within the same word sometimes became Thiès Noon [u]. This change is seemingly not regular, cf. †*njogon* 'finger,' †*lohoy* 'be short.' No similar change affected Proto-NL *e, which generally is reduced to Thiès Noon /ë/ in an unstressed syllable.

Subsequent to the Noon-Laalaa *i, *u > /e, o/ change, Northern Noon raised /e, o/ from all sources to /i, u/ in unstressed (i.e. non-stem-initial) syllables, as shown in Table 38. Borrowed words can have non-initial stress, and /e, o/ raise here as well, e.g. in the male given name *Jigaan* with second syllable stress, from Sereer *Jegaan*. This raising took place in Padee Noon for /e/ > /i/, but not consistently for /o/ > /u/. Laalaa preserves the Proto-NL vowels in all of these words, as does Thiès Noon unless the unstressed vowel is reduced to /ë/.

TABLE 38   Raising of unstressed short mid vowels in Northern and Padee Noon

PC	Nor., Pad. Noon	Thiès Noon	Laalaa	Saafi	Paloor, Ndut	
*mi-sip	miip, °mesip m-		mesep m-	misip m-	°misib m-, misip m-	'sauce'
*ki-rik	kedik, °kedik k-	†kedëk	kedek k-	kidik	kilik k-, kilik †k-	'tree'
*(n)ɣaɓit	hawit		hayet, °haet	haɓit	geet, °geet	'dung'
*-iɗ	-iɗ, °-iɗ	†-ëɗ	-eɗ	-iɗ	-iɗ, -iɗ	benefactive

TABLE 38 Raising of unstressed short mid vowels in Northern and Padee Noon (*cont.*)

PC	Nor., Pad. Noon	Thiès Noon	Laalaa	Saafi	Paloor, Ndut	
*pambi	pabi, (°pabu) f-	†pambe f-	pabe f-	pambi f-	(paan, paan †f-)	'chicken'
*ɓe-reɓ	ɓeti, °ɓeti	†ɓedëɓ	ɓete	ɓitiɓ	ɓeleɓ, ɓeleɓ	'woman'
*(nju-)kun	jokun, °jokon j-	†njogon nj-	jokon j-	ndukun	kun, °kun	'finger'
*njaɓul	jawul	†njawol	jawol		P. °jawul	'parakeet'
*nju-kuɗ	joku', °joko' j-		jokoɗ j-			'little pestle'
*ka-no(ɣ)	kanu, °kanu k-	†kanoh k-	kano k-			'calabash'
*ka-mbot	kobut, °kobot °k-		kebot k-		Nd. †kabot	'debt'

However this raising never operated before /h/, such that /oh/ in non-initial syllables is still common in all Noon dialects. As a result of this raising change, while short /i, u/ are very rare in Northern and Padee Noon in stem-initial syllables (as in Laalaa), they are common in unstressed non-initial syllables. The phonotactic effects of these changes involving high vowels are seen even in recent borrowings into Noon like *botuŋ* 'button' from French *bouton*, in which /o/ is preferred in the initial syllable and /u/ in the second, since regular sound changes eliminated /u/ in stressed (stem-initial) syllables and /o/ in unstressed syllables (except before /h/). The existence of a few seemingly non-borrowed Noon roots with /i, u/ like *yug* 'sit' (Pichl gives Laalaa †*yúg* 'crouch') is unexplained.

2.2.1.2 Non-high Vowels

The non-high vowels *e, *o, *a (long and short) can be reconstructed without complication (Table 39).

TABLE 39 Proto-Cangin mid and low vowels

PC	Noon	Laalaa	Saafi	Paloor	Ndut	
*yeek	yeek	yeek	yeek	yeek	yeek	'sing'
*Heey	heey	heey	heey	°heej	heey	'dream' (v)
*keen	keen	keen	keen	keen	keen	'fall'
*wees	wees	°wees	wees	yees, †wes	°yees	'throw'
*seek	seek	seek	seek	°seek	†seega 'dry seas.'	'stop raining'
*sex	sek	sek	sek	seh	°seh	'wait'
*neɓ	neɓ	neɓ	neɓ	neɓ	†neɓ	'be nice'

PHONOLOGY

TABLE 39 Proto-Cangin mid and low vowels (*cont.*)

PC	Noon	Laalaa	Saafi	Paloor	Ndut	
*pe'	pe' f-	pe' f-	pe' f-	pe' °f-	pe' f-	'goat'
*ɗeɓ	ɗeɓ	ɗeɓ	ɗeɓ	ɗeɓ	ɗeɓ	'be first'
*yen	yen	yen	yen	yen	°yen	'laugh'
*loox	look	look	rook	loo y-	loo	'belly'
*yooɓ	yooɓ	yooɓ	yooɓ	yooɓ	yooɓ	'be easy'
*moos	moos	moos	moos	°moos	°moos	'wipe clean'
*ɓoo(ɣ)-ox	ɓook	ɓook	ɓook	ɓooh	°ɓooh	'bathe'
*yoond	yood	yood	yoond	yoon~d	°yoon~d	'learn', S. 'move'
*lom	lom	lom	rom	lom	lom	'buy'
*ɓot	ɓot	ɓot	ɓot	ɓot	°ɓot	'vomit'
*hon	on	on	on	hon	hon	'swallow'
*woṛ	wos	wos	wos-	wol	°wol	'send'
*ɗoɓ	ɗoɓ	ɗoɓ	ɗoɓ	ɗoɓ	°ɗob	'bite'
*waaṛ	waas	waas	waas	waal	waal	'road'
*haaṛ	aas	aas	aas	haal	haal	'enter'
*kaañ	kaañ	kaañ	kaañ	°kaañ	°kaañ	'be sharp, dare'
*yaal	yaal	yaal	yaar	yaal	yaal	'man'
*faan	faan f-	faan f-	faan	faan	faan	'body'
*han	an	an	an	han	han	'drink'
*hac	ac	ac	ac	hac	hac	'dig'
*hang	ag	ag	aŋ, °ang	haŋ~°g	°haŋ	'be wide'
*has	as	as	as	has	has	'(be) new'
*ñam	ñam	ñam	ñam	ñam	ñam	'eat'

Recall that short unstressed *e and *o raise to /i, u/ in Northern and sometimes Padee Noon (§ 2.2.1.1).

The sequence *oɣ develops to /a'/ in Ndut-Paloor. Recall that NLS /h/ and NdP ∅/ʔ are the regular reflexes of *ɣ. The sequence *oɣ contrasts with *aɣ, which must be reconstructed in two lexical roots and a derivational suffix. The development of *oɣ and *aɣ is shown in Table 40.

TABLE 40   Proto-Cangin *oɣ and *aɣ

PC	Noon	Laalaa	Saafi	Paloor	Ndut	
*ɓoɣ	ɓoh	ɓoh	ɓoh	ɓa'	ɓa'	'baobab'
*ca-oɣ	cooh f-	coh f-	cooh	caa' °f-	°ca', †caa' f-	'elephant'
*(a-)roɣ	atoh (f-)	atoh	atoh °f-	la'	la', †ala	'stone/rock'
*noɣ	noh	noh	noh	na'	na'	'sun'
*i/fa-noɣ	enoh f-	enoh f-	inoh	fana' f-	fana f-	'cow'
*-oɣ	-oh	-oh	-oh	-a'	-a'	applicative
*yaɣ	yah	yah	yaah, °yah	ya'	ya'	'hand, arm'
*waɣ	wah	wah	waah	wa'		'winnowing fan'
*-aɣ	-ah	-ah	-aah	-a		nominalizer

Due to the regular change *oɣ > /a'/ in Ndut-Paloor, no correspondence exists between Ndut-Paloor /o(')/ and NLS /oh/. Note that in Saafi, word-final *aɣ becomes /aah/.

Saafi exhibits the raising of *e and *o in some common disyllabic words, as well as in the anticausative/reflexive suffix *-ox (Table 41). This change can be seen as a peripheralization of these mid vowels in post-tonic syllables (similar to the regular Noon change discussed in the previous section), followed by assimilation of the preceding vowel in a few common words.

TABLE 41   Raising of mid vowels in some Saafi polysyllabic words

PC	Noon	Laalaa	Saafi	Paloor	Ndut	
*mu-ɣon	moon m-	moon m-	muhun	°moon m-	†mun m-	'tear (crying)'
*kol-ox	koluk	kolok	kuruk	koloh	koloh	'rise'
*tof-ox	tuuk	tuuk	tufuk	tofoh	†towoh	'stand'
*ku-ɓo	kowu k-, †kowo	kuu k-	kuɓu k-	kook 'baby'	†kú k-	'child' (son/daughter)
*-ox	-uk	-ok	-uk	-oh	-oh	anticausative
*ɓe-reɓ	ɓeti, †ɓedëɓ	ɓete f-	ɓitiɓ	ɓeleɓ	ɓeleɓ	'woman'

The alternative is to reconstruct -ATR high vowels for these correspondences, with vowel lowering in Ndut-Paloor. However there is no phonetic motivation for a lowering change in these specific words, whereas the proposed Saafi

PHONOLOGY

change is phonetically natural. Furthermore *ku-ɓo 'child' (perhaps more accurately *ku-ɓi-o') is the diminutive of *ɓi-o' 'person,' so a reconstruction *ku-ɓu is unlikely.

In Northern Noon, short /e, o/ as found in Padee Noon, Thiès Noon, and Laalaa (whether from *i, *u or *e, *o) has raised to /i, u/ before a palatal coda consonant (and in *bus* 'rear' before /s/, before which the change does not normally occur), as shown in Table 42.

TABLE 42   Raising of mid vowels before a palatal coda in Northern Noon

Proto-NL	N. Noon	Other Noon	Laalaa	Other Cangin	
*mey	miy	°†mey	mey	S. mey	'leave'
*heñ	hiñ	°†heñ	heñ	P. iñ-a'	'fight'
*ɗeñ	ɗiñ	‡ɗeñ	°ɗeñ	S., NdP. ɗiñ	'louse'
*eñ	iñ	°†iñ	oñ	NdP. iñ	'thing'
*weñ	wiñ			P. wañ~j	'make holes for planting'
*weñ	wiñ	†wënj	°woñ		'surpass'
*woy	wuy		woy	S., Nd. woy	'boil'
*woy?	wuy		way, †woy	NdP. woy	'collect firewood'
*loy	luy	†loy		P., S. loy	'knot'
*loy	luy		loy	P., S. luy	'funeral'
*fey	fiy		°foy †f-		'mucus'
*mbos	bus	†mbos			'rear' (n)

Because this change occurs only before a coda consonant, certain suffixed forms retain a mid vowel, e.g. *héñ-ís* 'break up a fight' (vs. *hiñ* 'fight') and *méy-íd* 'make leave' (vs. *miy* 'leave'). There is no evidence for this change before /c/, hence *oc* 'scratch' from *hoc. The sequences /ey/ and /oñ/ are also unaffected, as in *bey* 'call,' *oñ* 'burn food.' As a result of this change, Northern Noon final /ey, oy, eñ, oy/ appear only in borrowings. Finally, in Laalaa there are a few cases where a front vowel becomes a back vowel after a labial consonant and before a palatal consonant, shown in Table 43. No labial consonant is present in *oñ* 'thing,' though see note 80 in Appendix 1 regarding possible cognates to PC *iñ* 'thing' with /o/ in other Atlantic languages.

TABLE 43   Backing of front vowels between a labial and palatal consonant in Laalaa

Proto-Noon-Laalaa	Laalaa	N. Noon	
*fey	°foy †f-	fiy	'mucus'
borr. Wo. féey[a]	°fúy	féey	'swim'
*weñ	woñ	wiñ	'surpass'
*eñ	oñ	iñ	'thing'

a But note Wo. *fóoy* reported for the Lebu dialect

This change is peculiar in that it is at once dissimilatory (from the palatal consonant) and assimilatory (to the labial consonant). Given the very few words in which it occurs, it is difficult to determine the precise environment for this change—note that it does not take place in *bíñ* 'mouse' or *mey* 'leave.'

2.2.2   ATR *Changes and Harmony*

The +ATR vowels *ú and *í trigger changes in preceding vowels in all languages but Saafi, which has totally collapsed the ATR distinction. The modern alternations are as in Figure 1.

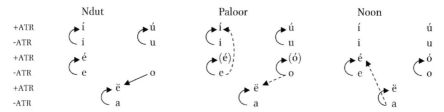

FIGURE 1   Synchronic ATR vowel alternations in Ndut, Paloor, and Noon

The same alternations affect long vowels. For Laalaa the alternations are simply /a(a), e(e), ii, o(o), uu/ → /ë(ë), é(e), íi, ó(o), úu/. The dashed arrows for Paloor represent the alternations described by D'Alton (1983) for the Khodaba variety, which does not contain /é/ or /ó/. The dashed arrow for Noon represents the Northern Noon /a~é/ alternation, equivalent to /a~ë/ in other dialects. The -ATR high vowels do not alternate in Northern or Padee Noon. Their status in Thiès Noon is unclear—Lopis (1980: 105) reports that they do not alternate (but gives no relevant examples), whereas Wane (2017: 36) reports /a, e, i, o, u/ → /ë, é, í, ó, ú/, but for the high vowels his only example is †*kun* 'close,' †*kúnís* 'open,' which is in fact +ATR *kún* in all other Noon and Cangin

PHONOLOGY

sources. The specifics of Thiès Noon vowel harmony are in general unclear. Lopis (1980: 105–107) gives /a, e, o/ → /ë, ë, ú/ as the only alternations, but these are not reflected in Lopis-Sylla (2010). Within roots, Lopis identifies [é, ó] as variants of /e, o/ triggered by a later +ATR vowel, as in †*péengí* 'grass' and †*péení* 'monkey' (in both cases from historical *aa). Recall that short /u, i/ are rare in Thiès Noon, if they exist at all. All of this is complicated by the fact that /ë/ can be either a "true" +ATR vowel (as in causative -*ëɗ* from *-*íɗ*), or a reduced vowel that behaves like a -ATR vowel (as in benefactive -*ëɗ* from *-*íɗ*).

Synchronically, ATR alternations are triggered by suffixes with a +ATR vowel (Table 44). These are causative -*íɗ*, reversive -*ís* (unexpectedly, Thornell et al. (2016: 42) report that -*ís* does not trigger harmony in Paloor), and a few other language-specific suffixes containing /í/.

TABLE 44   ATR effect of suffixes with a +ATR vowel

PC	Noon	Laalaa	Saafi	Paloor	Ndut	
*pon	pon	pon	pon	pon	pon	'fold'
*pon-ís	pónís	pónís	ponis	ponís, °pënís	pënís	'unfold'
*ɓap	ɓap	ɓap	ɓap	ɓap	°ɓap	'suckle'
*ɓap-íɗ	ɓépíɗ, °ɓëpíɗ	ɓëpíɗ	ɓapiɗ	ɓëpíɗ		'nurse'

Leftward-spreading ATR harmony is a feature of all Cangin languages but Saafi. Rightward-spreading harmony exists in Ndut and Laalaa (and Paloor as described by Thornell et al.), where it is reported to trigger the same alternations as leftward-spreading harmony. In fact Laalaa /a/ is not affected by rightward harmony, e.g. *tík-aaɗ* 'kitchen.' In Khodaba Paloor, D'Alton reports that rightward harmony affects fewer vowels (only /i, u, a/ → /í, ú, ë/). No rightward harmony exists in Noon. Rightward harmony must be a more recent development, and was not present in Proto-Cangin. Drolc (2004) reaches exactly this conclusion, and suggests that rightward-spreading harmony developed due to contact with Wolof. It is probable that a purely allophonic ATR harmony system existed in Proto-Cangin, with *a, *e, *o having allophones [ë, é, ó] before *í or *ú in the next syllable. The -ATR high vowels *i and *u were likely not affected. An original high vowel alternation would require a complete leveling in Noon leaving no trace whatsoever, which is unlikely. As in the modern languages, there would have been no situation in which an underlying +ATR *í or *ú could become -ATR.

60   CHAPTER 2

Historically, in addition to the suffix-triggered changes described above, ATR changes triggered by a following *í or *ú are seen within disyllabic roots, on frozen noun class prefixes, and triggered by non-alternating (i.e. lexicalized) suffixes (Table 45). However these historical vowel changes are somewhat different from the synchronic vowel alternations.

TABLE 45   Historical effect of a +ATR vowel on a preceding vowel

PC	Noon	Laalaa	Saafi	Paloor	Ndut	
*paaní	péeníi f-	pëëní f-	paani f-/n-	póoní °f-	pëëní f-	'monkey'
*haañí(nd)	éeñíin	ëëñín, †ëñíd	aañind	héeñí	°héeñí	'coal'
*naand-ís	níidís	níidís	naandis		°nédís	'remind/remember'
*paangí	péegíi (f-)	paagii f-	paangi f-/n-			'grass'
*(h)aañ-íd-oy	éenjoh	ënjóh	aññnjoh			'play'
*paní	péní	pëní f-	pani	póní, °pëní	pëní f-	'sleep' (n)
*panís	pénís f-	pënís f-	panis	pónís	pënís f-	'horse'
*ɓasíl			ɓasil	°ɓësíl	ɓësíil, †ɓësíl	'beget'
*walínd		wëlíd	wirind	yilin, °yíil	°yéníl	'pay'
*walínd-ox	oolduk	°wëldúk	wirnduk			'get revenge on'
*cangín	cégín, †cëngën	cëgín	cangin	°cigin f-	°cígín, †céegín f-	'worm' (grub)
*nang-íd(-oy)	négíd, °nëgídoh, †nëngëdoh	nígídóh		°nígírë	†négér(é)	'gather'
*ka-ndí(d)	kédí k-	këdí k-	kandid	kedi		'mortar/pipe'
*sangalí	ségélíi	†sagalí f-		sëgílí		'millet semolina'
*ɣawír̥			°hawis	óyíl, °owil	°oyíl, †ëyíl	'reduce'
*ɓeer̥-íd	ɓestíd, ˇɓeestíd	ɓéesíd	ɓeesdoh	ɓíilíd	ɓílíd	'tell' (S. 'chat')
*heeñ-íd/ís-ox	éeñduk	éenjúk	(eeñ)	°heeñsoh	°héeñsëh, †hínsë	'smell (good)'
*ñVVk-íd	ñéekíd			ñéekíd	†ñekit	'sew'
*moondíd?	móodíd	móodíd		°moodid	†mëdëh~ moddë	'whisper'
*caafú	cëw, °cëwuu	cëëfú f-	caafu	cóofú °f-	°cëëf k-	'fly' (bug)
*saangú	sóogúu f-, †sóongú	°sëëgúu	saangu n-	sóogú °f-	°sëëgú f-	'shadow, shade'
*kaalú	kóolúu	këëlú			†kúulú f-	'venomous snake'
*ngakúd	gókúd	°gëkúd	ngakud n-	°gëkút	†gokúd f-	'gecko'
*ma-r̥úɓ/r̥uɓ	móoɓ, °músú m-	mësú m-	masuɓ m-	muluɓ °m-	muluɓ	'water'
*fa-yúm	‡fëyum	fëyëm f-	‡fayum	fëyúm °m-	°fëyúm	'fat/grease'
*fa-núf	fónúf f-, ˇfënúf, †fënëf f-	fënúf f- 'eyelash'			°fënúf	'body hair' No. also 'feather'
*ma-púy	mópúy, °mëpúy m-	mëpúy m-		°mëpúy m-		'pus'
*yatús/r̥	yótús, †yúdús	yítús	yatus			'five'

PHONOLOGY   61

First it must be noted that for disyllabic roots with a +ATR vowel in the second syllable, the only vowels possible in the first syllable are *a, *í, or ú (long or short). The only clear examples with a noun class prefix and a +ATR root vowel contain the prefixes *fa- and *ma-. Thus with the exception of 'tell,' 'whisper,' and 'smell' which have frozen suffixes, the only vowel quality which appears before a +ATR vowel in a non-alternating environment is *a. In a few words, *a has assimilated completely to a following *í in one language or another. In Northern Noon, +ATR *[ë] has developed to /é/ before /í/, such that /é/ is the most common +ATR counterpart of /a/ (the only synchronic +ATR triggers contain /í/). Similarly, in Northern Noon [ë] usually develops to /ó/ before /ú/ or in the presence of a labial consonant. In addition to the examples in Table 45: *hóbíɗ* 'repair' from *haɓ* 'be proper/fit'; *tómóoy* 'heat (v)' from *tamoh* 'be hot'; *óbúluk* 'hold on' from *ab* 'hold.' This [ë] > /ó/ change may have also occurred in the Thiès dialect based on *saangú > †sóongú* 'shade.' This same change of *a to /é/ or /ó/—and with essentially the same triggering contexts—can be observed in Paloor and more rarely Ndut. D'Alton, who does not acknowledge the existence of the phonemes /ó/ and /é/ for Khodaba Paloor, transcribes these words with /e/ or /o/, and often writes the historically triggering +ATR vowel as -ATR as well, e.g. *caafú > °coofu* 'fly.' The conclusion to be drawn from all of these changes is that *a before a +ATR vowel was subject to more drastic assimilation when in a non-alternating environment, with the degree of assimilation being somewhat lexically-specific.

In the Thiès dialect of Noon, unstressed vowels often reduce to a central vowel that is transcribed as /ë/, the same as the +ATR low vowel. The main targets of reduction are unstressed Proto-NL *e (from PC *i or *e), and any unstressed vowel in a grammatical morpheme. This reduction is also sometimes seen for stressed /í/ when followed by /ë/. Some examples are given in Table 46.

TABLE 46   Reduction to /ë/ in Thiès Noon

PC	Northern Noon	Thiès Noon	
*ki-rik	kedik k-	†kedek~kedëk k-	'tree'
*ɓe-reɓ	ɓeti	†ɓedëɓ	'woman'
*cangín	cégín (f-)	†cëngën	'worm'
*nang-íɗ	négíɗ	†nëngëɗ-	'gather'
*panís	pénís	†pënís~pënës	'horse'
*líkít	líkít	†lëgët	'cotton'
*ka-, *ki-	ki-	†kë-	infinitive

62   CHAPTER 2

TABLE 46   Reduction to /ë/ in Thiès Noon (*cont.*)

PC	Northern Noon	Thiès Noon	
*ku-	ku-	†kë~ko-	diminutive
*-ox	-uk	†-ëk	anticausative
*-us	-us	†-ës	plural subject/passive
*ɗa	-ɗa~Ca	†-ɗë~Cë	punctual/narrative

The non-high +ATR vowels /ë, é, ó/ were not present in Proto-Cangin as contrastive phonemes. In the modern languages they are generally found only in
borrowed roots when not the result of ATR harmony or (in Thiès Noon) reduction to /ë/. However there is a small number of native roots that have long /ée/
or /óo/, especially in Northern Noon (Table 47).

TABLE 47   Long +ATR mid vowels in native monosyllabic vocabulary

PC	N. Noon	Other Noon	Laalaa	Saafi	Paloor	Ndut	
*ma-ɼúɓ/ɼuɓ	móoɓ m-	°músú, †múu	mësú m-	masuɓ m-	muluɓ °m-	muluɓ	'water'
*(pV/tV-)huɓ	tóoɓ t-	°puuɓ p-	póo p-		huɓ	huɓ	'leaf'
*ɓi-Vɓ	ɓéeɓ	°ɓéeɓ	ɓeeɓ		°ɓéeɓ, ɓeeɓ	ɓéeɓ	'all'
*tV-úH	tóoh	°tóoh, †túuh			túh	†tú	'all'
*ti-ix	téek	°†teek	teek	tiik (n), teek (v)	tii k-	°tii, †téey	'name' (n)
*neex (ne-ox?)	néek	˘niik	neek, °nëëkéy	neek	neek	neeh	'fear' (v)
*fool	fool 'run'		fool 'run'			fóol	fool, †fël	'jump'
*ca(h/ɣ)úc?			cóoc f-		°cooc		'breakfast'
NdP *i-aayV?	(kaay	°†kaahay	kaahaay	kahaay)	eye	éeyë	'three'
*ɗa-(h)uy?	ɗóoy	°ɗuuy	ɗoy	ɗooy			'inside'
*nda/ɗa-(h)um	dóom	°ɗuum	ɗom		doom	†dom	'not yet'
					yéem	yéem	'well' (n)

In 'water' and 'leaf,' Northern Noon /óo/ is clearly the result of vowel coalescence, and interestingly these long +ATR mid vowels can result from the coalescence of two -ATR vowels, as in 'leaf.' Thus it is likely that all of these other
forms with /ée, óo/ were originally disyllabic. The word ɓéeɓ 'all' is certainly historically polymorphemic, containing the plural class prefix *ɓi-, and it is likely
that tóoh 'all' contains the plural/mass class prefix *tV-. Laalaa cóoc 'breakfast'
probably contains the class prefix ca-, cf. Laalaa cëënín 'evening meal' from *nún
'evening.'

PHONOLOGY   63

2.2.3   *Vowel Length Changes*

There are some lexical roots for which languages differ in the length of the
vowel. The most notable examples are given in Table 48.

TABLE 48   Vowel length differences between languages

PC	Noon	Laalaa	Saafi	Paloor	Ndut	
*ca-oy	cooh f-	coh f-	cooh	caa' °f-	°ca', †caa' f-	'elephant'
*ne(e)ɣ <ní-oɣ	neeh	neh	neeh	ne'	nee'	'sleep'
*le(e)ɣ <lV-oɣ	leeh	leh	reeh			'be finished'
*fe(e)y <fV-ey	◊fey			fey, °feey f-	feey, †fey f-	'soil, dirt'
*pe-ɗe(e)m	peɗim p-	píɗim p-	peɗeem, °peɗem	pereem	°pereem, †perem	'tongue'
*la(a)x	laak	laak	raak	lah	lah	'have, happen'
*yú(u)k	yúuk	yúuk	yuuk	yuk	yúk	'shoulder'
*ha(a)y	aay	ay	aay	haay, °hay	hay, †haay	'be spicy/bitter'
*na(a)H	nah, †naah	nah	naah	naah	°naah, †nah	'magic healer'
*su(u)ng	suuŋ/suug	†sug	suung	°suŋ	°suŋ	'elbow'
*le(e)lu	leeloo	leloo	leero	lelu	†lelu	'middle/between'
*so(o)mb	soob	soob		som~b	som~b	'pound (to flour)'
*yu(u)y			yuuy	yuy	†yuc	'embers'

In some cases these discrepancies may be due to errors of documentation, but
this certainly cannot account for the majority of them. The most common sort
of discrepancy is between a short vowel in Ndut-Paloor (often also Laalaa) and a
long vowel in the other languages. Some of these discrepancies unfortunately
receive no explanation. However some of these words contained an original
vowel-vowel sequence across a morpheme boundary: *ca-oy* 'elephant' contains a class prefix *ca-* like a number of other animals (see § 3.1.12), and *ne(e)ɣ*
'sleep' was very likely *ní-oɣ*, cf. the noun *paní* 'sleep' containing a class prefix
pa-. Some of the remaining length discrepancies might be due to unrecover-
able vowel-vowel sequences.

Beyond these cases which may involve an original vowel sequence, there are
two environments in which a difference in vowel length can be explained by
regular sound change. First, Noon (though not the Thiès dialect) and Laalaa
lengthen the final vowel of disyllabic words with no final consonant. Dieye
(2010) does give a few polysyllabic Laalaa words with a final short vowel, but
these are almost all given with a long vowel in Thornell et al. (2016c). Table 49
shows some of the words affected by this final lengthening change.

64 CHAPTER 2

TABLE 49 Lengthening of final vowels in disyllabic words in Noon and Laalaa

PC	Noon	Laalaa	Saafi	Paloor	Ndut	
*paaní	péeníi f-	pëëní f-	paani f-/n-	póoní °f-	pëëní f-	'monkey'
*-íno	-íinoo	-íinó, °-íinóo	yino	yíno	yíněh	'one'
*caafú	°cëwuu	cëëfú f-	caafu	cóofú °f-	°cëëf k-	'fly' (bug)
*su/ki-pi	kipii k-	sope'	kipi 'earring'	°kipi k-	supi	'ring'
*ki-ɓí(s)	kíwíi k-	kiis k-, †kíwís	kiɓi k-	kíi °k-	°kíi k-	'fire'
*mi-ɗa	meɗaa m-	meɗa m-	miɗa, meɗa m-	miraa, °mera m-	mira °m-	'salt'
*saangú	sóogúu f-	°sëëgúu	saangu n-	sóogú °f-	°sëëgú f-	'shadow, shade'
*to-ɣo	°tohoo t-	too t-	toho r-	too k-	too k-	'millet'
*ngumú	gómúu (f-)	°gumuu f-	ngumu °f-	gúmú °f-	°gúmú f-	'hyena'
*fi-xí	fíkíi f-	fíkíi f-	fiki	fíi °f-	fii	'face/before'
*(n-)hila	elaa	elaa	ngila r-	hila	†hílë	'scuffle hoe'
*le(e)lu	leeloo	leloo	leero	lelu	†lelu	'middle/between'
*ndúulú	dúulúu	dúulúu		°dúlú	†dúul	'insect' (L. 'wasp')
*siili	siilii	siilii		siili	siili	'Ndut-Paloor/Sereer'
*kV-ra	ketaa k-	ketaa k-		°kula		'pot'
*sVVmi	siimii		siim, siini	siimi, suumi	suum-	'bead'
*kaalú	kóolúu	këëlú			†kúulú f-	'venomous snake'
*ki-lo		keloo k-	kiro	(°koloj k-)		'pot'
*kí(i)sí		°kíisíi †f-		kísí °f-	†kísí f-	'ocean'

Some of the apparent exceptions to this final lengthening rule in Noon have a final consonant in other languages, though at least 'sleep' and 'chicken' are unexplained (Table 50).

TABLE 50 Words with no final lengthening in Noon

PC	Noon	Laalaa	Saafi	Paloor	Ndut	
*ka-ndí(ɗ)	kédí k-	këdí k-	kandiɗ	kedi	†kédí	'mortar/pipe'
*ka-no(ɣ)	kanu, †kanoh k-	kano k-	kanoh			'calabash'
*nja-no(ɣ)	janu j-	jano j-	njenoh, °njanoh			'small calabash'
*ka-ñík	kéñí k-		kiñi	keñik	†kéñík k-	'bracelet'
*paní	péní	pëní f-	pani	póní, °pëní	pëní f-	'sleep' (n)
*pambi	pabi, †pambe f-	pabe f-	pambi °f-	(paan)	(paan †f-)	'chicken'

PHONOLOGY 65

It is notable that all of the words without the expected lengthening are nouns which are historically composed of a prefix and a monosyllabic root (see § 3.1.12 for the fossilized class prefix *pa-). However as seen in Table 49, many such words do undergo final lengthening. It is possible that the discrepancy can be explained by the chronology of when each noun underwent a stress shift from the historical root to the historical prefix, with only unstressed vowels being affected when the change occurred. This final lengthening can also be seen in a number of grammatical suffixes in Noon-Laalaa, including most object pronouns (e.g. 1st sg. -soo/-yoo from PC *so), but not tense/aspect/mood suffixes.

Second, in Laalaa *CVh roots (and one *CVɓ root) become CVV (Table 51). Note that 'goat' and 'person' with an original epenthetic glottal stop do not undergo this change. This CV>CVV lengthening has occurred also in Saafi as recorded by Botne & Pouille (2016), though these words have short vowels in Williams and Williams (1993), Mbodj (1983), and (depending on the word) Pouye (2015), and thus the change is likely dialectal. Some Saafi words with original final *h now have /y/, originally a hiatus filler before i-initial suffixes that was extended to unsuffixed forms.

TABLE 51   Laalaa and Saafi vowel lengthening in CVC forms with consonant loss

PC	Noon	Laalaa	Saafi	Paloor	Ndut	
*yíh~ɗíh	yí'	ɗíi	yii	yíh	°ɗíh	'knee'
*níh	ní'	níi	nii	níh	°níh	'rope'
*woh (an)	wo'	woo	woo, woy	(won, wan)	(won)	'say'
*ɓuh		ɓúu f-	ɓuu f-	ɓuh f-	ɓuh f-	'dog'
*tíɓ	tíɓ	tíi	tiɓ	°tíɓ	°tíɓ	'forge'
*súh	sú'	†súu	suy	súh	†súh	'be dry'
*leh~lah	le'	lee	ree, raa		†lah, †leh-	'arrive'
*puh	poɗ	puu	poy			'clap'
*sih	se'	sii				'peel fruit'
*pe'	pe' f-	pe' f-	pe' f-	pe' °f-	pe' f-	'goat'
*ɓi-o'	ɓo' y-	ɓo' y-	ɓo' y-	ow, °o' (ɓo-y-a)	ow (ɓëë)	'person'

Though it is tempting to see this change as compensatory lengthening, this characterization would not be accurate. The proto-phoneme *h is lost in all of NLS, and so this loss had probably already taken place in proto-NLS. Thus the lengthening of these vowels in Laalaa and some dialects of Saafi must have

66 CHAPTER 2

postdated the loss of *h in these words, since it is not shared by Noon. The change can be seen as fulfilling a root minimality requirement, where the minimal root is CVV or CVC. Noon instead inserted a glottal stop in these same roots.

2.2.4 Vowel Coalescence

When two vowels come into contact in Cangin languages, the resulting hiatus is generally resolved by assimilation or deletion. A common source of vowel contact involves vowel-initial noun roots prefixed with a CV- class marker. The Proto-Cangin nouns shown in Table 52 are likely of this type.

TABLE 52   Proto-Cangin nouns with a coalesced prefix

PC	Noon	Laalaa	Saafi	Paloor	Ndut	
*ti-ix	téek, ˇ†teek	teek	tiik	tii k-	°tii, †téey	'name' (n)
*kíir̥	kíis k-	kíis k-	kiis k-	kíil	kíil †k-	'year'
*kiil	kiil k-	kiil k-		kiil °k-	kiil k-	'braiding needle'
*kúum	kúum k-	kúum k-	kuum	kúum k-	°kúum k-	'honey'
*miis	miis m-	miis m-	miis m-	miis m-	miis m-	'milk'
*faan	faan f-	faan f-	faan	faan	faan	'body'

In most of these nouns the root contained a long vowel, based on outside cognates and the uniform vowel correspondences between languages. In others the long vowel may result from the coalescence of the prefix with a short root vowel. Most notably, in 'name' the hiatus is resolved differently in each language, as the prefix vowel and short root vowel were still separate entities in Proto-Cangin. These nouns may have had a root-initial *h, as this regularly deletes in NLS and usually deletes between vowels in Ndut-Paloor. Compare *kíir̥ k- 'year' (likely **kV-híir̥) with Sereer (g)o-hiid. In fact only four *h-initial native noun roots are reconstructed (vs. 28 verb roots, see Table 139), suggesting that *h was normally lost after a prefix, preserving the consonant of a prefix which might have otherwise eroded.

The two PC nouns in Table 53 probably contain a prefix, but have a short vowel.

PHONOLOGY

TABLE 53   Proto-Cangin nouns with a coalesced prefix resulting in a short vowel

PC	Noon	Laalaa	Saafi	Paloor	Ndut	
*kuɗ	koɗk-	koɗk-	kuɗ	kuɗ°k-	kuɗk-	'pestle'
*mún	mún m-	mún m-	mun	mún m-	mún m-	'flour'

'Pestle' was likely earlier **ku-hoɗ*, containing the root *hoɗ* 'pound in mortar,' and 'flour' might contain a root cognate with Fula-Sereer *'un* 'pound in mortar.' Based on these forms, it seems that in **CV-VC nouns a vowel was in some cases deleted. There are numerous possible explanations for the different interactions between a prefix and root (the quality of the prefix vowel, the presence vs. absence of a root-initial consonant /h/, the original length of the root vowel, the date at which the prefix and root vowel coalesced), but most are speculative.

Especially in Noon, newer cases of vowel coalescence have arisen when a root-initial consonant still present in Proto-Cangin was deleted intervocalically (Table 54).

TABLE 54   New instances of coalesced class prefixes

PC	Noon	Laalaa	Saafi	Paloor	Ndut	
*ku-fúc	kúuc k-	kúuc f-	kufic, †kufuc	°kúfúc k-	†kúc k-	'needle'
*(pV)-huɓ	tóoɓ t-, °puuɓ	póo p-	oɓ 'bark'	huɓ	huɓ	'leaf'
*(pi-)síl	tíil t-, †píil p-	písíl p-	sir	síl 'tendon'	°síl	'vein'
*ma-ɾúɓ/ɾuɓ	móoɓ, †múu m-	mësú m-	masuɓ m-	muluɓ °m-	muluɓ	'water'
*mu-ɣon	moon c-	moon m-	muhun	°moon m-	†mun m-	'tear (crying)'

In these cases dialects differ in how the hiatus is resolved, though in Noon-Laalaa the result is always a long vowel. There are not enough examples to be able to determine the regular outcomes of each prefix+root vowel combination in each language/dialect.

A number of cases of tautomorphemic vowel coalescence due to the loss of an intervocalic consonant were presented in § 2.1.6 (see Table 28 and Table 30, which also contain additional cases of coalescence between a class prefix and root). However the most common sort of vowel coalescence involves a root-final vowel or deleted consonant followed by a vowel-initial suffix. Coalescence of this sort is a synchronically active process in each language except Saafi, and follows suffix-specific rules of hiatus resolution.

In Paloor, vowel contact arises when definite markers, demonstratives, or the associative marker -*i* are suffixed to a vowel-final noun. The result is a monophthongal long vowel, though D'Alton (1983: 90–91) does not fully describe the outcomes with all possible suffixes, and Thornell et al. (2016: 43–44) discuss only the definite suffix -*a* (and not the associative marker -*i* or the demonstratives -*in* and -*ee*, see §3.2). The outcomes in these two varieties of Paloor differ in some respects.

(7)   Vowel assimilation in Paloor nominal suffixes

Khodaba Paloor (D'Alton)			Paloor (Thornell et al.)		
/mango-a/	→ mangaa	'the mango'	/bíró-a/	→ bíróo	'the office'
/mango-i/	→ mangii	'mango of ...'	/maalu-a/	→ maalaa	'the rice'
/múmë-i/	→ múmíi	'lion of ...'	/héeñí-a/	→ héeñëë	'the coal'
/caabi-a/	→ caabaa	'the key'	/altine-a/	→ altinaa	'the Monday'

In Ndut (Morgan 1996: 18–19) a preceding vowel always assimilates completely to the definite suffix -*a*. With other Ndut-Paloor vowel-initial suffixes (e.g. verbal suffixes), a glide is generally inserted after a preceding vowel. There are a few other cases of coalescence from a deleted final /h/ in Ndut (e.g. /yúh-eh/ → *yéeh* 'know + HAB.NEG'), but Morgan does not comment on this phenomenon explicitly.

In Saafi vowel coalescence occurs in a few common verbs when a root-final consonant is deleted (Mbodj 1983: 214–215). In these cases the resulting vowel is short: /hay-idʼ/ → *hidʼ*, etc. Otherwise vowels do not come in contact within a word in Saafi—notably no vowel-final nouns are assigned to the singular noun class with ∅-marked agreement.

In Laalaa, the deletion of intervocalic /h/ and less often /y/ and /ɓ/ results in vowel contact, and there are a number of vowel-final roots. Dieye (2010: 79–80) gives the following examples:

(8)   Vowel coalescence in Laalaa
      /woo-os/   → woos   'say (passive)'
      /kalah-en/   → kaleen   'hear (perfective)'
      /mey-ídʼ/   → míidʼ   'exit-CAUS'
      /an-í-e/   → anee   'drink-IMPF-PST'

PHONOLOGY 69

In all of his examples, the first vowel assimilates in quality to the following one. Note however the behavior of the distal definite suffix *-aa* in /tuy-aa/ → *tua* 'the hut,' /doy-aa/ → *doa* 'the inside,' and /ɓo'-ɓ-aa/ → *ɓoa* 'the people.'

In Padee Noon a short vowel deletes before a suffixed determiner, e.g. /otu-ii/ → *otii* 'the car' (Soukka 2000: 54). In Thiès Noon the behavior of vowels in contact is not clear, but Wane (2017: 34) notes that the suffix *-oh* drops out before perfective *-ën*, e.g. /keloh-ën/ → *kelën* 'heard.' Vowel coalescence is much more complicated in Northern Noon, where root-final /y, s, h, '/ are usually deleted before a vowel. Depending on the stem vowel and the identity of the suffix, vowel coalescence may result in total assimilation, no assimilation, or a long diphthong. These outcomes are presented in Table 55 (I found no examples with /ii/ or /uu/ in the stem, and there are some other gaps in the data).

TABLE 55   Stem + suffix vowel coalescence in Northern Noon

	í	i	e	a	o	u	ú	íi	ee	aa	oo	úu
-i, -ee, -ii	íi	ii	eei/ei	aai/ai	ooi/oi	uui/ui	úi	—	eei	aai	ooi	—
-in	íiñ	iiñ	eeñ	aañ/aiñ	ooñ/oiñ	uuñ	úuñ	íiñ	eeñ	aañ	ooñ	úuñ
-u(s), -oo	íu	iu	eeu	aau	oou	oou	úu	—	eeu	aau	oou	—
a-initial[a]	ée	ee	ee	aa	oo	oo	óo	—	ee	aa	oo	—

a   These suffixes are: imperative *-a(a)*, hortative *-at*, future *-an*, and the distal definite marker *-aa* (if not preceded by a class marker). The other suffixes are imperfective *-i*, past *-ee*, proximal definite marker *-ii*, perfective *-in*, passive/plural subject *-u(s)*, and negative imperfective *-oo*.

The benefactive applicative suffix *-id́* has the same effect as *-in*, but with /y/ in place of /ñ/. The causative suffix *-íd́* is not very productive, but when it follows a vowel it behaves like benefactive *-id́*, but results in a +ATR vowel. The consonants /ñ/ and /y/ resulting from this coalescence are not only phonetically but also phonologically palatal, as they trigger palatal consonants in a following assimilating suffix, e.g. /ɓey-in-d́i/ → *ɓeeñji* 'called him,' /leeh-íd́-d́ii/ → *léeycii* 'didn't finish.' This change can also be seen in Laalaa /yoloh-íd́/ → *yólóoy* 'straighten.' Some examples of coalescence in Northern Noon:

(9)   Northern Noon vowel coalescence

/tes-ee/	→ tee	'remain' + PST
/ɓay-an/	→ ɓaan	'own' + FUT
/ngalah-ii/	→ ngalai	'ngalakh' + DEF.PROX
/mos-oo/	→ moou	'do ever' + HAB.NEG
/yeeh+a/	→ yee	'be slow' + IMPER

/ɓey-in/	→ ɓeeñ	'call' + PERF
/gañi'-id̪/	→ gañiiy	'win' + BEN
/leeh-íd̪/	→ léey	'be finished' + CAUS

Most of the various vowel coalescence processes of each Cangin language arose after the breakup of Proto-Cangin, as none of the synchronically active processes are shared by the family as a whole. However with some prefixed nouns, coalescence appears to have taken place already in Proto-Cangin (see Table 52, Table 53). Determiners were probably all consonant-initial in Proto-Cangin (with *w-* present on the default class determiners), so no hiatus would have existed at that stage between vowel-final nouns and a following determiner. There is no evidence for vowel-final verb stems in Proto-Cangin, and so no vowels would have been in contact within verbs. There has clearly been a strong pressure throughout the history of the Cangin languages to eliminate diphthongs whenever they arise. Only in Northern Noon are diphthongs commonly encountered, these being seemingly rather recent creations, as they are not shared by other dialects. The specific outcomes of the monophthongization of vowel sequences differ between languages and dialects, and even within the same dialect depending on the morphemes involved. As such, cases of vowel contact must have been resolved differently depending on when they arose in the history of each language.

2.2.5 *Medial Vowel Deletion*

In three-syllable words, an original short vowel in the second syllable is sometimes deleted in each language. This process is by far most common in Saafi. Because most roots are a single syllable, three-syllable roots or two-syllable roots with a frozen prefix are rare, but when they are found, the medial vowel is always deleted in Saafi, and sometimes in Noon (Table 56).

TABLE 56   Historical deletion of medial short vowels in Saafi

PC	Noon	Laalaa	Saafi	
*ku-ɓo i-noɣ	kowinoh k-, †koɓnoh	kuunoh k-	kuɓno	'meat'
*mbaHane	baani	°baane	mbahne r-	'hat'
*wu-tuɓa	wutuwaa	wotoa, °watoa	wotɓa	'yesterday'
*ca(n)kunaɣ	coog(i)naah (f-)	cogona f-	cekna(a)~cakna r-	'nail/claw'
*caCíndo(ɣ)	°cígídóo	cëgídóh f-	°ciɓndo'	'panther'
*fi-nVɣo?	fenoo f-	fenoo	finho r-	'behind' ('rear')

PHONOLOGY   71

Medial vowel deletion arises much more often in the case of suffixation. In a
two-syllable base, vowel deletion before a suffix is once again most common
in Saafi, seen for example when a definite suffix is added to a noun. Two syllable verb roots are much rarer in Saafi, but those that occur can exhibit deletion
(Table 57).

TABLE 57   Examples of synchronic Saafi medial vowel deletion

Unsuffixed noun	Suffixed noun	Unsuffixed verb	Suffixed verb
pambi 'chicken'	pam-f-i	misik 'hurt'	misk-oh
paangi 'grass'	paang-f-i	meekis 'ask'	meeks-oh
kiɓi 'fire'	kiɓ-k-i	haawis 'lessen'	haaws-id-k-oh
kuɓu 'child'	kuɓ-k-i	marak 'look'	mark-is
saangu 'shadow'	saang(u)-n-i	supit 'sew'	supt-aah
saafi 'Saafi person'	saaf-nd-i	hirip 'help'	hirp-oh
maalu 'rice'	maal-nd-i	inah 'know'	inh-is
waro 'Paloor person'	war-nd-i	iling 'thunder'	ilng-is
toho 'millet'	toh-r-i	parah 'pick up'	parh-uud
mango 'mango'	mang-r-i	ɓasil 'beget'	ɓasl-oh
japil 'knife'	japl-i	kerah 'hear'	kerh-idoh
panis 'horse'	pan(i)s-i	suusus 'be black'	suuss-id
pedeem/°pedem 'tongue'	pedm-i	yanaw 'be white'	yanw-id
ɓitif 'old woman'	ɓit(i)f-i	yurah 'go towards'	yurh-id
kahan 'house'	kahn-i	yakak 'big' (adj.)	yakk-i

This deletion is sometimes optional, and is lexically-specific. Examples of Saafi
words that apparently never show deletion are *mida-m-i* 'the salt,' *komak-i* 'the
child,' and *sikiduk* 'listen.' High vowels are seemingly more likely to delete. Synchronic deletion of a medial root vowel is rarer in other languages, but Morgan
(1996: 20) finds that it "may occur" in Ndut when adding a suffix, and a few
examples are found in Noon (Table 58).

TABLE 58   Synchronic medial vowel deletion in Ndut and Noon

Ndut unsuffixed	Ndut suffixed	Noon unaffixed	Noon affixed
kilik 'tree'	kilk-a	malak 'look'	mélk-ís 'taste'
gawa 'grass'	gaw-f-a		malk-iikoh 'notice'
búumíd 'blind person'	búumd-ë	awal 'lend'	awl-uk 'borrow'

TABLE 58   Synchronic medial vowel deletion in Ndut and Noon (*cont.*)

Ndut unsuffixed	Ndut suffixed	Noon unaffixed	Noon affixed
yëkúl 'puppy'	yëkl-ë~yëkk-ë	ɗiik < *ɗesik 'place'	ɗesk-ii
húlúɓ 'ravine'	húlɓ-ë	líkët 'cotton'	pílkët p- 'thread'

The most common environment for medial vowel deletion arises from multiple suffixation, where the vowel of a non-final suffix is often deleted before a vowel-initial suffix (e.g. Noon /ham-iɗ-in/ → *hamɗin* 'danced for'). Most -VC suffixes with a high vowel can be targeted in each language, but applicative *-oy* never is, nor anticausative *-ox* in Ndut-Paloor. The suffixes *-iɗ, *-íɗ, *-ir̥, *-is*, and *-us* are the most common targets (see § 4.3). Noon seems to resist deletion the most, and Noon anticausative *-uk* and reversive *-ís* can only rarely lose their vowel. Deletion is always optional in Noon outside of a few lexicalized examples.

Medial vowel deletion was found in some words in Proto-Cangin, though it was likely less common than in any modern language. Deletion with multiple suffixation is seen for example in 'help' (Noon *abɗoh*, Saafi *ambɗoh*, Paloor °*habda*'), from *hamb-(i)ɗ-ox* or *haɓ-(i)ɗ-ox*, lacking the vowel of benefactive *-iɗ* in all modern forms. See also Table 34 for NLS *(h)aañ-(í)ɗ-ox* 'play' and *heeñ-(í)ɗ-ox* 'smell.' There are other reconstructed words with consonant clusters involving either a single suffix or a frozen prefix, in which an earlier vowel had likely been deleted by the Proto-Cangin stage (Table 59). It cannot be a coincidence that these clusters all contain *l (also true for many of the synchronic examples above), all but one of which are of the form *lND.

TABLE 59   Consonant clusters formed by medial vowel deletion in Proto-Cangin

PC	Noon	Laalaa	Saafi	Paloor	Ndut	
*mílnd-oy			mirndoh	mílë'	míllë'	'be last'
*hayl-ox	ayluk		ayruk	hayloh		'be angry'
*walínd		wëlíd	wirind	yilin, °yíil	°yéníl	'pay'
*wal(í)nd-ox	oolduk	°wëldúk	wirnduk			'get revenge on'
*kúlmbVs	kúlmbís f-	kúlbísóh	kurmburus	°kúlbús f-	†kúlbús f-	'ant sp.'
*kúlndV	kúldí	kúldí k-		kúlë	†kúllë k-	'couscous steamer'
*fi-lndo~lond?	fíldóo		†filndo	filoon, °fulon f-	filoon †f-	'behind/under'
*ca/sa-lngis	celngis c-				†selgis f-	'millet granules'

PHONOLOGY 73

The number of Proto-Cangin words with an obligatorily-deleted vowel must have been low, and given that in modern Noon the process is rather limited (and almost always optional), it was probably not particularly prevalent in Proto-Cangin.

2.2.6 Vowels before *ɣ and *H

In Noon-Laalaa and to a lesser extent Saafi, some vowels develop differently before the back fricatives *ɣ and *H, which merge as Proto-NLS *h. Furthermore, the distribution of Proto-Cangin vowels before these two consonants is notably skewed in favor of lower vowels.

In Noon-Laalaa, only /a(a), o(o)/ commonly appear before /h/. Outside of a few borrowings and Noon *tóoh/túuh* 'all' (see below), the only other vowel attested in this environment is /ee/ in Noon and /e/ in Laalaa, as shown in Table 60.

TABLE 60   Words with Noon /eeh/, Laalaa /eh/

Proto-Cangin	Noon	Laalaa	Saafi	
*ní-oɣ	neeh	neh	neeh	'sleep (v)'
*lV-oɣ	leeh	leh	reeh 'be used up'	'be finished'
*nda-anax yaɣ	daaŋkeeh, °daaŋkah	dankeh, °daaŋkeah	ndaŋkiyaah	'ten'

In all three words, the vowel results from monophthongization. For *ní-oɣ* 'sleep (v),' cf. *pa-ní* 'sleep (n),' and for *lV-oɣ* 'be finished,' cf. Fula *re'-* with the same meaning. The vowel sequence was resolved as long in Noon, and short in Laalaa. In Saafi, all vowels are found before /h/. Proto-Noon-Laalaa had no *u or *i, but the lack of /íh, úh, eh/ has other explanations. Three Saafi words with /ih, eh/ have cognates in Noon-Laalaa (Table 61).

TABLE 61   Lowering of NLS *ih, *eh to NL /ah/

PC	Noon	Laalaa	Saafi	Paloor	Ndut	
*niɣ-ís?	naas	naas	nihis	nís	nís	'remove'
*seH	sah	°sah	seh	°seeh		'Sereer (Siin)'
*leɣ	lah	lah	reh			'rainy season'

From these words it seems that Proto-NLS *e and *i were lowered to /a/ before /h/ in Noon-Laalaa. While Saafi did not undergo these changes, it is possible that certain words in Proto-NLS had already undergone vowel lowering before *ɣ or *H, as shown in Table 62.

TABLE 62   Lowering of vowels before NLS *h

PC	Noon	Laalaa	Saafi	Paloor	Ndut	
*tiɣVr̥?	taas	taas	tahas	°tíil	°tiil	'answer'
*leHet		laat	lahit	°lehed 'nape'	°lehet, †leet	'neck'
*yuH	yoh	yoh	†yoh	yuh	°yuh	'bone'
*luH(Vy)	looy, °†lohoy	looy	rohoy	°luh	°lúh	'(be) short'

Recall that PC *u develops unpredictably to Saafi /u/ or /o/, but it is no accident that /o/ is the outcome before Proto-NLS *h. 'Answer' is difficult to reconstruct —it may have been *tiɣar̥ or even *tiyir̥ if the *ɣ affected both vowels, but either way a high front vowel was lowered to *a in Proto-NLS. Recall also that in Northern and Padee Noon, Proto-NLS *o raises to /u/ in unstressed syllables, but not before /h/ (from Proto-Cangin *ɣ and *H).

In Proto-Cangin, it is conspicuous that few roots can be reconstructed with high vowels before *ɣ and *H (just seven, vs. 27 non-high). There is only one reconstructable root with a +ATR vowel before *ɣ or *H, namely 'all': tóoh in Northern and Padee Noon, †túuh in Thiès Noon, and túh in Paloor. It may have been *tV-úH, containing the plural class prefix *tV- (see § 3.1.10). A few outside comparisons hint at vowel changes before PC *ɣ (Table 63).

TABLE 63   Possible vowel changes before PC *ɣ

Cangin	Fula-Sereer	Wolof	Bainunk-KK	Biaf.-Pajade	Tenda	Manjak	
Saafi seeh		jasig j-	*ja-sẹeg	B. jaasugu		*u-tʋk	'crocodile'
NLS *leɣ	S. ndiig		Ko. bóolug	B. bwa-logu	*-ruu		'rainy season'
				P. pa-tio			
*ɓoɣ	S. ɓaak		Bai. *-ǫog,		*-ɓakk,	*bə-bak	'baobab'
	F. ɓok-ki		*-bokk		*-ɓoɣ?		
*noɣ	F. naa-nge		*bi-nẹg	B. nnagə		pə-nak 'noon'	'sun'
*fa/i-noɣ	*ge-nag	nag w-		*-nagä			'cow'

PHONOLOGY

Most outside cognates have high vowels in 'rainy season' and 'crocodile,' where Cangin (perhaps just NLS) has mid vowels. On the other hand, PC *oɣ corresponds to outside /ag/ in 'sun,' 'cow' and 'baobab' (though both /o/ and /a/ are common for 'baobab,' which may involve borrowing in some groups). Without drawing any specific conclusions, it seems that PC *ɣ influenced preceding vowels, which likely accounts for the skewed distribution of vowels before *ɣ. The same is likely true of *H, though here there are no relevant outside cognates. No other consonants (including *h and *x) involve any similar patterns.

2.2.7 Irregular Vowel Correspondences

The large majority of vowel quality correspondences between cognate roots are regular. However there are a few words in which the consonant correspondences are regular, but the vowel qualities in each language show unexpected discrepancies. Some of these involve an entirely different quality between Ndut-Paloor and NLS (Table 64).

TABLE 64   Irregular vowel quality correspondences between Ndut-Paloor and NLS

PC	Noon	Laalaa	Saafi	Paloor	Ndut	
*ɣaɽ/ɣíɽ	has	koas k-	has	°íl	íl	'eye'
*yúx/yox	yúk	yúukís	yuk	yoh	°yoh	'dry season'
*híd/hed	ís	ísúk, °ís	is	hel	hel	'leave/let (go)'
*ma-ɽúɓ/ɽuɓ	móoɓ, °músú m-	mësú m-	masuɓ m-	muluɓ °m-	muluɓ	'water'
*kím/kaam	kím	kím	kim	°kaam f-	†kaam m-	'morning/tomorrow'
*yúm/yím	yúm	yúm		°yím	†yím	'extinguish'
*ndVVɗ	dooɗ	dooɗ	ndooɗ	dúuɗ	duuɗ, †dood	'stick'

For others, one language has an unexpected vowel quality, or two forms with different vowels are found distributed between different languages (Table 65).

TABLE 65   Other irregular vowel quality correspondences

PC	Noon	Laalaa	Saafi	Paloor	Ndut	
*caac~cec	caac, cic	caaca	caac	caac, cec	caac, cic f-	'grandparent'
*wa/wo-te	wati	wate	woti	wate °f-	wote	'today'
*tas	tes	tas	tas	tas	tas	'stay'
*tís	tes	tís	tis	°tís	°tís	'sneeze'
*kílook	kílóok	cílóok	kilook	kílóok, °kúlok	†kílëk	'marry'
*ku-fúc	kúuc k-	kúuc f-	kufic, †kufuc	°kúfúc k-	†kúc k-	'needle'

TABLE 65   Other irregular vowel quality correspondences (*cont.*)

PC	Noon	Laalaa	Saafi	Paloor	Ndut	
*woy	wuy	woy	woy 'heat'	°waj	†woy	'boil'
*síkíɗ-ox?	súkúɗúk	súkúɗúk 'hear'	sikiɗuk	sikiroh	síkírëh	'listen'
*yún-oH?	únoh, °ínoh	únóh	inah	(yúh)	(yúh)	'know'
	ɓaas 'suck venom'		ɓuus		°ɓaas	'suck'

For a few individual roots the influence of Sereer is a possible explanation: Sereer *o-fiic* 'needle,' *way* 'boil,' *ɓuus* 'suck,' and *o-kilook* 'bride' may have influenced the pronunciation of the synonymous words in individual Cangin languages. In 'listen' it is possible that original *í was rounded in Noon-Laalaa due to the influence of the round vowel in the suffix, and in 'know' an original sequence *yú might have coalesced to /í/. For the others no explanation presents itself, and these may be due to unexplained dialectal variation in Proto-Cangin. Again, it should be stressed that vowel correspondences between Cangin languages are in general entirely regular—the exceptions are relatively few.

2.3   Phonotactics and Borrowing

2.3.1   *Word Shape and Proto-phoneme Frequency*

In all modern Cangin languages syllables are maximally CVC, and this would have been true in Proto-Cangin as well. Furthermore, there is hardly any evidence for tautomorphemic consonant clusters in Proto-Cangin. In the modern languages, tautomorphemic clusters are almost always the result of either vowel deletion or borrowing. The few Proto-Cangin roots with clusters are discussed in § 2.2.5. Almost all are of the form *lND, likely the result of vowel deletion. These few apparent exceptions aside, Proto-Cangin would have had consonant clusters only across morpheme boundaries, and here perhaps only optionally. All reconstructed prefixes are of the shape CV- (except *n-* which results in monophonemic prenasalized stops), and all suffixes are vowel-initial. The modern consonant-initial suffixes (object/possessive pronouns, NLS negative *-dii* and punctual/narrative *-da*) were not grammaticalized as suffixes at the Proto-Cangin stage, and each of these morphemes remains a free word in one or more of the modern languages (the only other candidate is Ndut-Paloor perfective -*te*, which does not appear in NLS). The only significant source of clusters within a word would have been the medial vowel deletion process discussed in § 2.2.5, which was likely always optional.

PHONOLOGY

Recall that *x and *r̥ cannot appear word-initially, and *r appears only intervocalically. Otherwise there are no restrictions on where consonants can appear in a word. The majority of reconstructable lexical roots are monosyllabic (473), but an appreciable number of disyllabic roots are reconstructed (67, of which 27 are borrowed; only 21 are verbs, of which five likely contain a frozen suffix *-Vr̥). The frequency of each proto-phoneme initially, medially (intervocalically), and finally in roots is given in Table 66 and Table 67 (these counts include only roots found in both primary branches of the family). In Table 66, reconstructions in which the initial consonant is part of a noun class prefix are counted separately, with these counts given in parentheses; e.g. 28 reconstructed unprefixed roots are *k-initial, and furthermore 31 reconstructed nouns contain a *k-initial class prefix, for a total of 59 *k-initial reconstructions. I have been rather liberal in deciding which reconstructed nouns contain class prefixes—e.g. *kúlmbVs 'ant sp.' is assumed to contain the diminutive class prefix *ku-, even though it is possible that the initial *k is part of the root. As such, these numbers in parentheses should be taken as maximum counts. Root-initial consonants in prefixed nouns like the *ɗ in *mi-ɗa 'salt' are treated as medial (and not initial) in Table 67.

TABLE 66 Freq. of initial consonants in PC reconstructions (class prefixes in parentheses)

p	27 (11)	t	34 (4)	c	2 (16)	k	28 (31)	ʔ/Ø	12
f	11 (14)	s	40 (2)			h	35	H	14
w	23	l	43	y	19	ɣ	18		
mb	11	nd	8	nj	5	ng	10		
ɓ	33 (5)	ɗ	17	y	16				
m	25 (8)	n	33	ñ	15	ŋ	2		

TABLE 67 Frequency of final and medial (subscripted) consonants in PC reconstructions

p	12_2	t	20_3			c	10	k	42_7	ʔ/Ø	30	
f	21_6	s	33_{11}	r̥	21_3			h	12_1	x	19_2	H 14_3
w	3_3	l	53_{23}	r	0_4	y	9_2	ɣ	11_6			
mb	7_2	nd	24_3			nj	0_1	ng	17_{11}			
ɓ	42_9	ɗ	34_8			y	17_1					
m	22_5	n	44_{10}			ñ	26_2	ŋ	5			

The palatal consonants are on the whole less frequent than those at other places of articulation, though final *ñ is quite common. The palatal stop *c is extremely rare in root-initial position. Of the 18 lexemes reconstructed as *c-initial, all but one are nouns, and all but one of these nouns contains the fossilized class prefix *ca- (see § 3.1.12). The phoneme *ŋ is very rare in comparison with the other nasals. See § 5.1 for further discussion of the distribution of Proto-Cangin consonants and their status in the Pre-Cangin period.

The frequency of vowels in reconstructed roots is given in Table 68. Note that this table includes nouns with a C- prefix like *kiil 'braiding needle' (but not the vowel of CV- prefixes), and thus includes vowels that arose due to the coalescence of a root vowel and prefix vowel. Irregular vowel correspondences are not represented in the table.

TABLE 68   Frequency of vowels in reconstructed PC roots

	a	e	o	i	u	í	ú	aa	ee	oo	ii	uu	íi	úu
1 syll. root	70	38	61	14	25	31	30	57	28	35	7	9	26	14
V1 in 2 syll. root	19	4	3	9	6	8	5	5	1	0	1	0	0	1
V2 in 2 syll. root	12	0	2	9	5	16	8	4	0	1	1	0	0	0

Overall short vowels are more common than long vowels, though not by any great margin. Following the cross-linguistic trend, the vowel quality /a/ is most common, followed by the mid vowels, and then the high vowels. As expected of a 7-vowel "2iie" system, the -ATR high vowels are less common than the +ATR high vowels (see Casali 2008).

There are a number of notable restrictions on vowels in disyllabic roots. With few exceptions, the only long vowel that can appear in either syllable is *aa (two of the five exceptions are borrowings: *siili 'Sereer' and *kílook 'marry'). The mid vowels *e and *o are rare, especially in the second syllable, while all four short high vowels are found in both syllables. Thus, the large majority of reconstructable disyllabic roots (55/67) contain only the six vowels *a, *aa, *i, *u, *í, and *ú out of the 14 Proto-Cangin vowels. Nonetheless, the exceptions include some rather basic vocabulary (e.g. *nixiir̥ 'four,' *hedVf 'be lightweight'), and so the restriction on vowels in disyllabic roots must be viewed only as a tendency. There is only one reconstructed root in which +ATR and -ATR high vowels co-occur: *ngumú 'hyena.'[2] The vowel *a(a) co-occurs with all vowel qualities.

---

2   Noon gómúu, Laalaa guumuu/gúmú/ᵒgumuu, Saafi ngumu, Ndut-Paloor gúmú. *ngamú is

PHONOLOGY

2.3.2 *Borrowing*

Borrowing from surrounding languages, especially Sereer and Wolof, is an important phenomenon in the history of all Cangin languages. Table 69 gives a list of potential borrowings into Proto-Cangin, most of which come from Sereer. Sereer words from my own fieldwork on the Saalum dialect are unmarked, and those found only in Crétois' (1971) multidialectal dictionary are marked with (°)—the source dialect is often not specified for these words. The Sereer /h/ vs. /x/ distinction is guided by the forms in Crétois, as this distinction is not made in the Saalum dialect. Wolof words are from Diouf's (2003) dictionary, with the exception of the apparently archaic forms *buum* 'be blind,' *and* 'stove,' and *xom* 'tortoise' from Kobès' (c. 1869) dictionary. It is likely that some of these are independent borrowings from a time after the breakup of Proto-Cangin, and others like 'heal' are quite possibly cognates rather than borrowings. A list of potential cognates between Proto-Cangin and other Atlantic languages is given in Appendix 2—some of these may in fact be borrowings. The words in Table 69 are reconstructed to Proto-Cangin based on purely linguistic criteria. For example 'white person' is included as it shows completely regular developments in each language from a hypothetical Proto-Cangin form *tuɓaaɓ*, even though the word was probably borrowed into each Cangin language well after the Proto-Cangin period.

---

plausible, but the development of *a to Saafi /u/ and NdP /ú/ would be irregular. The Laalaa form is given inconsistently, and all forms are irregular regardless of the reconstruction. The PC word may be borrowed from Sereer (*g*)*o-moon*.

TABLE 69   Potential borrowings into Proto-Cangin

Source	PC	Noon	Laalaa	Saafi	Paloor	Ndut	
Ser. ꝑiis, °ꝼiis	*ꝼiis	ꝼiis	ꝼiis	ꝼiis	ꝼiis	°ꝼiis	'draw/trace/write'
Ser. o-hiid	*kV-híir̯	kíis k-	kíis k-	kiis k-	kíil	kíil †k-	'year'
Ser. o-kulook 'bride'	*kílook	kílóok	cílóok	kilook	kílóok, °kúlok	†kílëk	'marry'
Ser. ɓaat	*ɓaat	ɓaat	ɓaat	ɓaat	ɓaat	ɓaat	'add/increase'
Ser. yooɓ	*yooɓ	yooɓ	yooɓ	yooɓ	yooɓ	yooɓ	'be easy'
Ser. o-naq 'sorcerer'	*na(a)H	nah, †naah	nah	naah	naah	°naah, †nah	'magic healer'
Ser. a-cakar (root *-jakar)	*njakal	jakal	jakal	njakar	°jakal	†jakal f-	'lizard'
Ser. °a-tangaranga	*ndangal	dagal, †ndangal	dagal	ndangal	dagal °f-	°dagal f-	'scorpion'
Ser. °(g)a-kukuɗaaɗam	*ngakúɗ	gókúɗ	°gëkúɗ	ngakuɗ n-	°gëkút	†gokúɗ f-	'gecko'
Ser. o-ꝼiic	*ku-fúc	kúuc k-	kúuc f-	kufic, †kufuc	°kúfúc k-	†kúc k-	'needle'
Ser. °o-xuluɓ	*Húlúɓ	húlúɓ	°hëlúɓ	huluɓ	huluɓ	húlúɓ	'river/ravine'
Ser. o-roon	*loon	ˇloon-haf	lood	roon	loon	†loon	'calabash bowl,' N. 'skull'
Ser. mer	*meeɗ	meeɗ	†meɗ	meeɗ	°meeɗ	°meed	'be used to'
Ser. °moos	*moos	moos	moos	moos	°moos	°moos	'wipe clean'
Ser. ɗoof 'uproot weeds'	*ɗof	ɗof	ɗof	ɗof	ɗof	†ɗof	'uproot'
Ser. fay, Wo. faj	*pay	pay	pay	pay	pay	†paj	'heal'
Ser. way	*woy	wuy	woy	woy 'heat'	°waj	†woy	'boil'
Ser. jamb	*yamb	yab	yab	yamb	°yab	†yam~b	'accuse'
Ser. o-siid	*síis	síis	síis	siis	síis	°síis	'twin'
Ser. seek 'dry season'	*seek	seek	seek	seek	°seek (v)	†seega (n)	'stop raining, dry season'
Ser. a-ndeer (*-reer, Fu. reed-u)	*le(e)lu	leeloo	leloo	leero	lelu	†lelu	'middle/between'
Ser. gawul (pl.), Wo. géwël	*(ɓi-)ɣawúl	hool, †huul	hëwúl	hawur	ɓóolú	†ɓëëlú, †ɓol k-	'griot'

PHONOLOGY 81

TABLE 69 Potential borrowings into Proto-Cangin (*cont.*)

Source	PC	Noon	Laalaa	Saafi	Paloor	Ndut	
Ser. o-ñafaɗ	*ñVfaɗ	ñood, °ñafaɗ		ñafad	ñafad	ñofad	'shoe'
Ser. meeɓ, Wo. meeb	*meeɓ	°meeɓ		meeɓ	meeɓ	†meb	'lift'
Ser. sooy	*sooy	sooy		sooy	sooy	(†soyñ)	'be lost/disappear'
Ser. joot	*coot	†cot		coot 'go'	coot	†cot	'pass by, cross'
Ser. liir	*liil	liil	liil		liil	liil	'piece of cloth'
Ser. fool	*fool	fool 'run'	fool 'run'		fóol	fool	'jump'
Ser. a-siik, Wo. séq	*siik	siik	siik		°siik	siik	'rooster; NL 'male animal'
Ser. xil	*Hil	hil	hil		°hír	†hilí	'snore'
Ser. ligit	*likit	likët	likët		°likit	†lékit	'cotton,' P. 'thread'
Ser. °soom	*so(o)mb	soob	soob		som–b	som–b	'pound (into flour)'
Ser. giiñ	°yiiñ	hiiñ	hiiñ		°iiñ	†iñ	'roll flour'
Ser. °gurfaan, Wo. xurfaan	*ngulfa(n)	gúwlan (n, v), °gúlfaa (v)	gúlfaad (n)		gulfoo, °gulfa'	†gúlfan f-	'mucus,' 'have a cold'
Ser. liin	*iin	íin	fimúk	iin		†iin	'groan'
Ser. ɗing (v), a-fiing (n)	*ɗing	díg	díŋ	ding	°díŋ~g		'fence' (v/n)
Ser. lam	*lam	lam	lam	lam	lam		'inherit'
Ser. fad	*pad	pad	pad	pad	°pad'kick'		'slap'
Ser. ñed	*ñad	ñad	ñaad	ñad	ñada'		'scold/argue,' L. °be angry'
Ser. °ngud (likely root *hud)	*húd	úd	úd	uf	°húd		'*Guiera senegalensis*'
Ser. tag (pl.; sg. ndag)	*tak	tak	tak	tak	tak		'kinkeliba'
Ser. mal	*mal	mal	mal	mal	mal		'bring luck'
Ser. a-keɓ (n)	*keɓ		keɓ	keɓ	keɓ	†keɓ	'fence' (v/n)
Ser. °op	*op		op	op	op	°opa	'sweat'

TABLE 69 Potential borrowings into Proto-Cangin (*cont.*)

Source	PC	Noon	Laalaa	Saafi	Paloor	Ndut	
Ser. ɓoor	*ɓool	ɓool		ɓoor	ɓool 'uproot'		'strip from branch/stalk'
Ser. o-luuβ	*ku-lúɓ	ˇkúlúɓ		kuluɓ k-	°kúlúb		'horn (instrument)'
Ser. ɓak	*ɓak	ɓak		ɓak 'beside'	°ɓëkíɗ		'set aside,' P. 'move'
Ser. mbaal	*mbaal	baal		mbaal	(°mbal)		'sheep'
Ser. ngiic	*ngiic	giic		ngiic	giic		'jujube tree'
Ser. °kaal 'hunt in group'	*kaal	kaal		kaal	kokaal		'hunt'
Ser. o-raaɓ 'fire to clear field'	*-laaɓ	†kolaɓ		koraaɓ	°palaab		'brush fire'
Ser. a-'eel	*eel?	ˇyaayeel		eel	eel		'cloud'
Ser. saak	*saak	saak		saak		†saak	'scratch about in ground'
Ser. a-feem	*ɗeem	†ɗeem		ɗeemb		°deem	'bat (animal)'
Ser. ɓuus	*ɓVVs?	ɓaas		ɓuus		°ɓaas	'suck,' No. 'suck venom'
Ser. °digiñoox	*tí(n)ɣíñ-ox		tíiñúk	°tingiñ	°tígíñëh		'rub (eyes)'
Ser. síɗ	*síɗ	síɗ	síɗ		síɗ		'strain/sift'
Ser. siiβ	*síɓ(-íɗ)	síɓ	síɓ 'knead'		síiɗ		'pour hot water on cousc.'
Ser. foɗ	*puɗ	poɗ 'crack joints'	†poɗoh 'bone fract. healer'		°puɗsoh		'set broken/dislocated bone,' P. 'stretch joints'
Ser. maad, Fula maat-	*maas	maas 'witness'	maas			maas	'be present'
Ser. forol	*fulVl	folul			°fulil	†fúlíl	'spin thread,' Nd. 'spindle'
Ser. o-leeñ, Wo. salleñ	*ko-leñ	koliñ f-, ‡koleñ			koloñ	†koleñ f-	'sand'
Ser. ɓek	*ɓek	(ek)	(ek)	ɓek	ɓek	†ɓek	'put in'
Ser. laβ	*ka-laɓ	kalaɓ	koloɓ f-	kalaɓ k-			'sword'
Ser. °laɓ 'hit with sword'	*laɓ			laɓ	laɓ	laɓ	'beat, hit'
Ser. ɓasil	*ɓasíl			ɓasil	°ɓësíl	ɓësíil, †ɓësíl	'beget'

TABLE 69   Potential borrowings into Proto-Cangin (*cont.*)

Source	PC	Noon	Laalaa	Saafi	Paloor	Ndut	
Ser. °bet (pl. mbet)	*mbet			mbet	bet	°bet	'throw'
Ser. liiɓ 'think/measure'	*liiɓ?			liiɓ	líɓ, líiɓ	(°níb)	'think'
Ser. ɗel 'peel fruit'	*ɗel?	ɗel 'cut fruit'			ɗeel		'cut outer layer'
Ser. ngoloy, Fula ngolc- (pl.)	*ngolVc	golic			°golac		'vomit milk'
Ser. a-salma	*salma?			salma n-/°r-	salma		'(ritual) spear'
Ser. wey	*wey			wey	°wec		'swim'
Ser. °njootoot, °njutut	*njotot			njotoot	°jotoɗ		'lip'
Ser. ɗaar	*ɗaal	ɗaal	ɗaal	ɗaar			'stoop,' Sa. 'be nonchalant'
Ser. a-koɗu (*gal-goɗu)	*ɣoɗ	hoɗ	hoɗ	hooɗ			'pigeon'
Ser. hul	*(h)úul	úul	úul	ul			'cover'
Ser. °ndap	*ndap	dap	dap	ndap			'granary'
Ser. gend (pl.) 'equals/co-wives'	*ɣVnd	híd	híd	hend			'be equal'
Ser. °dung	*ɗúung	dúug 'squint'	ɗúug	ɗuung			'close eyes'
Ser. faal (pl.; PFS *b>Ser. f)	*waal	waal	waal	waar			'Wolof person'
Ser. ɗang	*ɗaang	ɗaag	ɗëëgísúk 'fall'	ɗaangiɗ			'be stuck up high,' Sa. 'keep sth. off the ground'
Ser. xomb, Wo. xom	*Ho(o)m?		hoom	hom			'tortoise'
Ser. xof (intr.), xuf (tr.) 'startle'	*Hof/Huf		hof	hofiɗ			'be fearful,' Sa. 'frighten'
Ser. yeeɓ	*yeeɓ	yéeɓ		yeeɓ			'rock baby'
Ser. ñakt-oox (v), a-ñakit (n)	*ñakít-ox	°ñëkítuk		ñaktuk, ñakit			'eat breakfast,' Sa. '(eat) lunch'
Ser. °saɓ 'touch'	*saɓ-ís-oɣ	séwíyoh		saɓsoh			'separate,' No. 'break up fight'
Ser., Wo., Mandinka muus	*muus	muus	muus	muus °m-	°múus	°múus m-, †f-	'cat'
Ser. disoox, Wo. tísooli, M. tisoo	*tís	tes	tís	tis	°tís	°tís	'sneeze'

TABLE 69   Potential borrowings into Proto-Cangin (*cont.*)

Source	PC	Noon	Laalaa	Saafi	Paloor	Ndut	
Ser. a-qali, Wo. xala, Susu xali	*Halí	ˇhëlí, ‡hélí	hëlí	°hal	hël~hél, °hil	°hél	'bow' (weapon)
Ser. helaar, Wo. (h)illeer	*(n-)hila	elaa	elaa	ngila r-	hila	†hílë, (°hílëër)	'scuffle hoe' ('hilaire')
Ser. fec (noun o-mbec), Wo. fecc	*mbec	†mbec		mbec	bec	°bec	'dance' (v)
Ser. umb, Wo. xamb	*(H)umb-is	obis	hobes		hubis	†húbís	'rekindle'
Ser. hup, Wo. (h)ëpp	*hup			uup, °up	hup		'exceed'
Ser. mooñ, Wo. moxoñ 'crush'	*mooñ	mooñ				°mooñ	'twist'
Ser. ɓoof 'sit w/ knees together,' Wo. bóof 'brood'	*ɓoof	ɓoof		ɓoof 'sit'		†ɓof	'sit w/ knees together,' Nd. 'lay down (of camels)'
Ser. wiril, Wo. wër	*wíl?	wílal	wíil 'search'	wil	wil, °yiil	†yíd	'turn/spin around'
Ser. sal, Wo. sél 'to branch'	*sal?	sal	sal			†sellik	'intersection'
Ser. ciiɓ-noox, Wo. ciip-atu	*cíiɓ-is-ox	cíiwiik		ciiɓsuk			'tsk' (in disapproval)
Wo., Ser. tax	*taH	tah	tah	tah	tah	tah	'cause' (v)
Wo., Ser. xeeñ	*heeñ	eeñ	éeñ	eeñ	heeñ	†heñ	'smell (good)'
Wo., Ser. yoor	*yool	yool	†yol		°yool		'hang down,' P. 'slide dn.'
Wo. tiit, Ser. diid	*tíit	tíit		tiit		tíit	'fear (v)'
Wo., Ser. muñ (Ar. munya?)	*múñ	múñ	múñ		°múñ~j	†múñ	'be patient'
Wo., Ser. joof	*yof	yof				†yof	'cut dog's ear'
Wo. weñ	*ti/pi-wiñ	piiñ, pewiñ p-	píiñ p-	tiwiñ	tiwiñ °k-	tiiñ k-	'metal/iron'
Wo. dëññ 'nit'	*ɗiñ	ɗiñ	°ɗeñ	ɗiñ	ɗiñ °f-	°ɗiñ f-	'louse'
Wo. loŋ-loŋ	*loŋ-loŋ	log-log	loŋ-loŋ	loŋ-loŋ	°loŋ-loŋ	°loŋ-loŋ	'earring'
Wo. mbaxane	*mbaHane	baani	°baane	mbahne r-	baanu	°baane	'hat'
Wo. taaw	*saaw	saaw	saaw	saaw	saaw	†saaw	'firstborn'
Wo. taal 'hearth'	*taal	taal 'nest'	taal 'hut/nest'	taar 'nest'	taal	†taal	'hut,' Pa. also 'hearth'
Wo. mbaam	*mbaam	(m)baam	(m)baam	mbaam		(m)baam	'pig/donkey'

TABLE 69   Potential borrowings into Proto-Cangin (*cont.*)

Source	PC	Noon	Laalaa	Saafi	Paloor	Ndut	
Wo. jeñ	*yeñ(j)	ye'	†yeñ	yenj	°yeej, °yeen	°yeñ	'push'
Wo. sikket	*súkút?	súgút f-		suket	°súkút f-	†síkét	'billy goat'
Wo. kaabaab 'temple'	*kaaɓaaɓ		kaaɓ	kaaɓaaɓ k-	°kabaap	†kakaab	'cheek,' P. 'jaw'
Wo. yàq, Ser. yaq	*yaH	yah	°yah	yah	yah		'destroy'
Wo. séeréer	*siili	siilii	siilii		siili	siili	'Ndut-Paloor/Sereer'
Wo. sàq (earlier *m-saxx)	*misaH		mesah		misah	†misah	'granary'
Wo. buum (archaic)	*mbúum	búum, †mbúum-	búum		búum	búum	'be blind'
Wo. bor (earlier *bod?)	*ka-mbot	kobut, °kobot k-	kebot k-			†kabot	'debt'
Wo. kaani < Bam. káanì	*kaaní	kééní	këëní			°kéení	'hot pepper' (see appx)
Wo. taab	*taaw	taaw	taaw		°taaw		'swelling/abscess'
Wo. sonn	*son	sod	son		son		'be tired'
Wo. sànqal	*sangalí	ségélíi	†sagalí f-		sëgílí		'millet semolina'
Wo. baroom	*paloom		paloom f-		°palom f-		'antelope sp.'
Wo. and 'stove' (earlier *hand)	*han		an 'hearth'			†han	'hearthstone'
Wo. sew, Fula sew-	*sew-	sewiñ		seew			'be skinny/thin'
Wo. nëb	*nop	nop	†nop	nop	(°nëp)	(†nob)	'rot'
Fula taan (Ser. o-taan 'grand-parent')	*taan	taan(um)	taantaan	taanum	taan	†taan	'uncle'
Semitic *paras (Wanderwort)	*panís	pénís f-	pënís f-	panis	pónís	pënís f-	'horse'
Ar. ṭabīb 'doctor' → Wo., Ser.	*tuɓaaɓ	towaaɓ	†toow	tuɓaaɓ	tuyaaɓ	†toab	'white person'
Ar. xāliṣ → Wo., Ser. xaalis	*Haalís	héelís	hëëlís		heelís	°hélíis, †hílís	'money/silver'
Ar. ṣābūn → Ser. saafu	*saafu	saawu		saafu	°suufu		'soap'
Mandinka háañi, Joola -kaañen	*kaañ	kaañ	kaañ	kaañ	°kaañ	°kaañ	'be brave, dare'
Mande, cf. Bambara dàa	*kV-ra	ketaa k-	ketaa k-		°kula		'pot'

86   CHAPTER 2

These early borrowings exhibit a number of phonological adaptations from the
source words. Because Proto-Cangin had no [b, d, j, g], these are borrowed as
other sounds ({*ɓ, *p, *w}, {*ɗ, *t, *r}, {*y, *c, *y}, {*k, *ɣ}). Other languages'
/r/ is usually borrowed as *l. Sereer and Wolof lack an ATR distinction in the
high vowels, and their /i, u/ are usually borrowed as +ATR *í, *ú. The Sereer
noun class prefix *o-* (earlier *go-*, as preserved in the Ñominka dialect) is borrowed as Cangin *ku-* in a number of words, also in Saafi *koɓang* 'wooden spoon'
from Sereer (*g*)*o-ɓang*. The word 'year' has a particularly interesting history,
as it appears that the singular/plural root alternation in Sereer (*g*)*o-hiid* 'year',
xa-kiid 'years' was incorporated into the Cangin borrowing as **kV-húir̥*, **ti-kúir̥*
(Noon *kúis, tíkúis*).

Borrowing from Wolof and Sereer has continued up to the present day in
all of the Cangin languages. After the diversification of the Cangin languages,
Sereer continued to be the main source of borrowings in Saafi, whereas Wolof
has been the source of most borrowings in the other languages. Some Thiès
Noon words are borrowed into other Noon-Laalaa dialects, which are clearly
identifiable when they contain prenasalized stops. Borrowings from French
are also widespread in all Cangin languages. These later borrowings often
exist across multiple Cangin languages, which can make them difficult to distinguish from borrowings into Proto-Cangin. However these later borrowings
often exhibit sound correspondences that cannot be the result of descent from
a single Proto-Cangin form. For example the shared borrowings in Table 70 have
a plain voiced stop in Saafi, which cannot be descended from a Proto-Cangin
sound. Needless to say, no non-borrowed words show this type of sound correspondence.

TABLE 70   Some shared borrowings from after the Proto-Cangin period

Source	Noon	Laalaa	Saafi	Paloor	Ndut	
Wo. gaaw	gaaw	°gaaw	gaaw	gaaw	†gaw	'be fast'
Wo. daas	daas	daas	daas	daas	†das	'sharpen'
Wo. jér, Ser. jir	†njíil	jëɗ	jir	jér	°jér	'be sick'
Ser. jom	jom, †njom	com, °jom	jom	jom		'must/should'
Wo. jasig	jësík	jësík	jasik		°jísík f-	'crocodile'
Ser. bind, Wo. bind	bíd	°bíin	bind		°bíní	'write'
Ser. jang, Wo. jàng	jag, †njang	°jaaŋ	†jang		°jaŋe	'read, learn'
Wo. dof	dof	†dof	dof		†dof	'be crazy'
Wo. bàjjen/bàjjan	bajën, †ɓajeen		bajjen	bajen	†bajan/bajen	'paternal aunt'
Ser. japil	jépíl, †njëbël		japil	°jëpíl		'knife'

PHONOLOGY

87

TABLE 70 Some shared borrowings from after the Proto-Cangin period (*cont.*)

Source	Noon	Laalaa	Saafi	Paloor	Ndut	
Wo. ban	ban	†ban	ban			'clay'
Wo. bés	bís, †mbes	bées	°bes			'day'
Wo. giñ			giñ	giñ		'swear'
Ser. jof 'be fair/straight'	jof, †njof		jof			'be good'

Note that Thiès Noon does not have plain egressive voiced stop phonemes, so these are adapted as prenasalized stops, or less often implosives, even in very recent borrowings. Many more of these recent borrowings could be listed for each language, and I will not attempt to present a systematic catalog of them here. In my own lexicon of Northern Noon, 39 % of the 1240 unique lexical roots collected can be identified as borrowings (from any time period), and the number seems to be similar for other Cangin languages. This situation is not unusual for the area, cf. 36 % borrowed roots in my Sereer Saalum lexicon.

Unlike the borrowings into Proto-Cangin, later borrowings were often not fully adapted to the native phonological system. As such, borrowing has introduced phonemes in each language that do not exist in native vocabulary. These are tautomorphemic prenasalized stops /mb, nd, nj, ng/ in all but Saafi and Thiès Noon (which retain these sounds from Proto-Cangin), plain voiced stops /b, d, j, g/ in Saafi, word-initial /r/ in Noon and Laalaa (and more rarely in Paloor and Ndut), and in all languages but Saafi the +ATR vowels /é, ó, ë/ (only /ë/ in Khodaba Paloor, /é, ë/ in Ndut) when not conditioned by a +ATR high vowel. Some examples of these more recent borrowings into Noon and Saafi containing novel phonemes are given in Table 71.

TABLE 71 Later borrowings from Wolof into Noon and from Sereer into Saafi

Wolof	Noon		Sereer	Saafi	
dër	dëɗ	'stutter'	dox	doh	'burn'
jën	jën	'fish'	jimb	jim	'plant'
tóx	tóh	'smoke' (v)	xaad	haad	'go home'
géej	géey	'sea'	mag	mag	'smoke' (v)
mboq	mboh	'maize'	gij	gij	'go a long time without'
nguur	nguuɗ	'government'	gen	gen	'live (somewhere)'
ràpp	rap	'fray'	daxit	dahit	'remove couscous steamer'

88   CHAPTER 2

In Noon and Laalaa, foreign /r/ is borrowed as /ɗ/ in non-initial position, due to its intervocalic allophone [r]. Initial /r/ exists in borrowings, but even in borrowings Noon and Laalaa do not generally allow [r] in coda position.

2.4   Summary of Sound Changes

The following sound changes have been identified between Proto-Cangin and the modern Cangin languages:

Proto-Cangin vowel allophony
*a(a), *e(e), *o(o) → *[ë(ë), é(e), ó(o)] / __CV$_{[+ATR]}$

PC > Ndut-Paloor
*ɓ, *ɣ > h~∅ / V__V (usually restored in alternating environments)
*ɗ > r / V__V (usually restored to /ɗ/ in alternating environments)
*ND > D / __V
*ND > N / __{C, #}
*o > a / __ɣ
*ɣ > ∅
*x, *H > h
/h/ (from *h, *H, *x) > ∅ / V__V (usually restored in alternating environments)
*w > y / __V[front] (most dialects)
*ɽ̥, *r > l
*[ó(o)] > ë(ë) (in Ndut and Khodaba Paloor)
*i(i), *u(u) > í(i), ú(u) / __CV$_{[+ATR]}$
changes affecting *[ë(ë)] in a non-alternating environment (see Table 45)

Ndut-Paloor > Paloor
/f, s, h/ > [v, z, ɣ] / between voiced sounds
*[é(e)] > í(i) (Khodaba Paloor)

PC > Noon-Laalaa-Saafi (NLS)
*h > ∅
*ɣ > h
*H > h
*x > k
*ɽ̥ > s
*r > t
*u > o (some exceptions in Saafi)

PHONOLOGY

NLS > **Saafi**
*ND > N / __{C, #} (only for *nj, *ng in some dialects)
/f, s, h/ > [v, z, ɦ] / between voiced sounds
*l > r (remains /l/ in a minority of words, esp. Sereer borrowings; *lVl > lVr)
*ah# > aah (always for PC *aɣ, unclear for non-borrowed *aH)
[+ATR] and [-ATR] vowels merge, including allophones of the non-high vowels

NLS > **Noon-Laalaa (NL)**
/ɓ, ɗ, y/ > [w, r, y] / V__V (innovated and spread after dialect diversification)
/ɓ, ɗ, y/ > [wʔ, ʔ, yʔ] / __{C, #} (also likely after dialect diversification)
*ND > N / __{C, #}
*i, u > e, o / except next to *ii, *uu (if not already in NLS)
*eh, *ih > *ah
V# > VV# / in a polysyllabic word (reverted or never occurred in Thiès Noon)

NL > **Laalaa**
*ɓ, *y > ∅ / V__V (sometimes restored as [w, y] in alternating environments)
/h/ (from *ɣ, *H) > ∅ / V__V
*ND > D / __V
#CV# > CVV (in lexical roots)
e > o / C$_{[labial]}$__C$_{[palatal]}$ (see Table 43; few examples, unclear conditioning)

NL > **Thiès Noon**
/p, t, c, k/ > [b, d, j, g] / between vowels/approximants (not nasals/implosives)
short unstressed vowels often reduced to /ë/, esp. grammatical morphemes

NL > **Northern + Padee Noon**
*ND > D / __V
unstressed e, o > i, u, except before /h/ (generally only e > i in Padee)

NL > **Northern + Thiès Noon**
*f, *s > w, y / V__V
w, y, h, ʔ > ∅ / V__V (often restored in alternating environments, especially in
  Thiès Noon)

NL > **Northern Noon**
*[ë] > é / __Cí
*[ë] > ó / next to a labial consonant or before /ú/ (with exceptions)
e, o > i, u / __C$_{[palatal]}$# (/ey, oñ, oc/ unaffected)

The Ndut-Paloor, Noon-Laalaa-Saafi, and to a lesser extent Noon-Laalaa branches are well-supported by shared sound changes. However there are also certain sound changes which were diffused areally, namely the denasalization of onset *ND in Ndut-Paloor, Laalaa, and Northern + Padee Noon, the allophonic voicing of /f, s, h/ in Saafi and Paloor, and the deletion of intervocalic *ɓ and *y in Ndut-Paloor and Laalaa. It is noteworthy that there are no sound changes which are shared between all dialects of Noon to the exclusion of Laalaa.

CHAPTER 3

Nominal Morphology

The most notable component of the nominal morphology of the Cangin languages is their system of noun class marking, discussed in § 3.1. § 3.2 treats determiners (including the modern definite suffixes), § 3.3 numerals, and § 3.4 the few nominal derivational suffixes.

3.1 Noun Class Morphology

In Niger-Congo terminology, "noun class" refers to a system of marking nouns and/or agreement targets with a set of affixes that distinguish between multiple possible morphological classes. The class of a noun is often more or less arbitrary, but in general classes have at least a partial semantic motivation, and changes in the number value of a noun are usually marked by a change in class. Here "noun class" is taken to encompass both the morphological marking of nouns themselves (here "noun prefixes"), and the agreement patterns that they trigger. These two interrelated systems manifest in different ways across Niger-Congo languages. In some the set of noun markers and agreement markers are a near one to one match, while in others there are major differences between the two. In all cases it is important to clearly distinguish between the system of class markers on nouns and the agreement system.

All Cangin languages have a noun class system. The system of Noon-Laalaa is the most conservative, with Saafi's being somewhat reduced, and that of Ndut-Paloor being even further reduced. In Proto-Cangin, noun class was marked by C- agreement prefixes on determiners and some other vowel-initial targets, and CV- (for one class N-) prefixes on nouns and adjectives, though many nouns were unprefixed, including those in the largest singular class and largest plural class. In the modern languages, many of the original prefixes on nouns must be considered frozen, but some number- and diminutive-based prefix alternations still exist in Noon-Laalaa, where a few class prefixes with a productive derivational function are also found. Table 72 presents the class prefixes of each Cangin language. The C- prefixes are the agreement prefixes found on determiners, and the CV- prefixes are the noun prefixes (or particles from an original prefix) which have a derivational or grammatical function in the modern language. The CV- prefixes in parentheses are not productive.

© JOHN T.M. MERRILL, 2023 | DOI:10.1163/9789004546493_004

TABLE 72   Noun class prefixes of the Cangin languages

Noon	Laalaa	Saafi	Paloor	Ndut	Membership
∅/w-	∅/w-	∅	∅	∅	default sg. class
y-	y-	y-	y-		'person,' 'thing'
n-	n-	n-		†n-	mostly V-final nouns
f-	f-	f-	f-	f-	many animals, misc.
	(fe-VERB)				'rain' nominalization
m-	m-	m-	m-	m-	liquids
(°mi-VERB)	(me-VERB)	(mi-VERB)			liquid nominalizations
k-	k-	k-	k-	k-	miscellaneous
ku-NOUN	ke-NOUN				diminutives
ki-NOUN	ke-NOUN				languages
ki-VERB	ka-VERB	ki VERB			infinitives
ki-VERB	(ka/ke-VERB)	(ka/ki-VERB)			nominalizations
p-	p-				long and flexible
	(pe-VERB)				a few nominalizations
j-, †nj-	j-				diminutives
ji-NOUN	je-NOUN				diminutives
c-	c-	c-	y-	y~C-	default pl. class
ci-VERB/ADJ	(ca-VERB)	(ca-VERB)			nominalizations
ɓ-	ɓ-	ɓ-	(°y-)	w-	'person' pl.
ɓi-NOUN	ɓe NOUN	ɓi NOUN	ɓi NOUN		"indefinite pl."
t-	t-				pl. of k-, p-, (n)j-
tu-NOUN					diminutive pl.
ti-NOUN	te-NOUN				diminutive pl.
ti-VERB/ADJ	(te-VERB)	(ti-VERB)			nominalizations
		r-			(Saafi innovation)
		nd-			borrowings (Saafi)
d-, †nd-	d-	nd-	d-	d-	locative, (manner, time)
di-VERB-aaɗ					locative nominalizations
			ɗ-	ɗ-	manner
w-		w-			temporal

The class agreement patterns differ considerably between the modern languages. All Cangin languages exhibit class agreement on determiners which are suffixed to the noun (including the Ndut-Paloor associative marker -*i*). This is the only form of class agreement in Ndut-Paloor. These agreement markers are best seen as prefixes on the suffixed determiners—note that they never appear after the noun in the absence of a definite suffix, e.g. Ndut *faam* '(a) house,' *faam-f-a* 'the house.' Unsuffixed nouns are common, and so it is not possible to treat the C- agreement markers as nominal suffixes, nor to avoid proposing a class agreement system in any Cangin language. Examples of two

NOMINAL MORPHOLOGY

nouns in the *f-* and *m-* agreement classes with a definite determiner are given in Table 73.

TABLE 73 Nouns showing class agreement with a suffixed definite determiner

Noon	Laalaa	Saafi	Paloor	Ndut	
pe'-f-aa	pe'-f-aa	pe'-f-a	pe'-f-a	pe'-f-a	'the goat'
miis-m-aa	miis-m-aa	miis-m-a	miis-m-a	miis-m-a	'the milk'

Noon-Laalaa and Saafi exhibit a pattern of definite agreement between nouns and agreeing adjective phrases and numerals, whereby the suffixed determiner on the noun is repeated after the adjective or numeral phrase. An example of definite agreement from Noon is given in (10).

(10) tedik**tii** tenak-**tii**   (Noon: 014)
     t-edik-t-ii   *t-enak=t-ii*
     CL.PL-tree-CL.PL-DEF.PROX CL.PL-two=CL.PL-DEF.PROX
     'the two trees'

See § 3.1.17 for more discussion of this definite agreement pattern. Noon-Laalaa has considerably more agreement targets. The *C-* agreement markers appear on non-suffixed (demonstrative) determiners, pronouns, numerals 1–3, some question words ('which, where, how many'), and a few other grammatical morphemes like the focus marker (Noon *-édíi*), all of which are vowel-initial. Noon-Laalaa adjectives and numerals higher than three agree with the head noun using a prefix of the form *Ce-* (Laalaa) or *Ci-* (Noon), as in example (11).

(11) kaad fi-yaak   (Noon: 004)
     kaad   fi-yaak
     house   CL-big
     'a big house'

In Noon-Laalaa (especially Noon) it is necessary to make a distinction between the class agreement pattern seen on definite determiners which are suffixed to nouns, and the pattern seen on all other agreement targets. I will refer to these two patterns as "suffixed determiner agreement" and "general agreement." The ∅ marker and the marker *n-* used in Noon-Laalaa suffixed determiner agreement correspond to *w-* in the general agreement pattern. Furthermore, in the Noon general agreement pattern the semantic factors of animacy and diminutiveness can trigger a different class from that seen on the suffixed definite determiner. Animate nouns (humans and animals in Padee and Northern Noon, and only humans in Thiès Noon) use the agreement markers *y-* (sg.) and *ɓ-* (pl.) in the general agreement pattern, and diminutive singular nouns use *j-*. However only a few nouns take these same agreement markers in suffixed determiner agreement (see § 3.1.4 and § 3.1.9). Examples of these animacy- and diminutive-based agreement marker mismatches are shown in (12) and (13).

(12) baaycaa ɓi-yaak-ɓaa   (Noon: 041)
    baay-c-aa   *ɓi-yaak=ɓ-aa*
    dog-CL.PL-DEF.DIST CL.PL-big=CL.PL-DEF.DIST
    'the big dogs'

(13) ku-baaykii ji-súus-jii   (Noon: 043)
    ku-baay-k-ii   *ji-súus=j-ii*
    DIM-dog-CL-DEF.PROX CL-black=CL-DEF.PROX
    'the black puppy'

To summarize the synchronic agreement patterns: all Cangin languages exhibit agreement on suffixed determiners using a *C-* class marker before the determiner, and in NLS these suffixed determiners are furthermore repeated after modifying adjective and numeral phrases. In Noon-Laalaa, the *C-* class agreement markers appear on a number of other targets, and adjectives and higher numerals exhibit agreement using a *CV-* prefix. The Noon class markers used on suffixed definite determiners and those used on other targets can sometimes differ due to considerations of animacy and diminutiveness.

The reconstructed Proto-Cangin class markers are presented in Table 74.

TABLE 74   Reconstructed Proto-Cangin noun class prefixes

Noun prefix	Det. prefix	Membership
∅	w-	default class
y-, ∅	y-	'person,' 'thing,' perhaps family members
N-	n-	animals, trees?, misc.
mV-	m-	liquids/powders
fa-, fi-, ∅	f-	animals (*fa-*), mass nouns (*fa-*), spatial nouns (*fi-*), misc.

NOMINAL MORPHOLOGY

TABLE 74 Reconstructed Proto-Cangin noun class prefixes (*cont.*)

Noun prefix	Det. prefix	Membership
ki-	k-	infinitives/deverbal, languages, misc.
ka-	k-	infinitives/deverbal, misc.
ku-	k-	diminutives, misc.
pi-	p-	long and flexible
nji-	nj-	diminutive (possible NLS innovation)
ca-, ∅	c-	plural, collective/mass, deverbal/abstract
ti~tu-	t-	plural, collective/mass, deverbal/abstract
ɓi-	ɓ-	'people,' perhaps 'women, men' (*ɓi-* on some sg. human nouns)
(ca-, pa-, sa-, su-, a-, i-)	mostly f-	fossilized prefixes: *ca-* and *pa-* on a number of animal and other nouns, the others on only one or two nouns each
nda-	nd-	locative
wu-	w-	temporal
ɗa-	ɗ-	manner

§ 3.1.1–3.1.11 examine in detail each agreement prefix, along with the cognate prefixes which appear on nouns. § 3.1.12 identifies fossilized nominal class prefixes that do not correspond to any agreement prefix (**ca-*, **pa-*, **sa-*, **su-*, **a-*, **i-*, and Saafi *ndu-*). § 3.1.13 discusses words in which a consonantal affix was reinterpreted as part of the root, or the root-initial consonant was interpreted as a prefix. § 3.1.14 covers two additional types of agreement prefix in Noon-Laalaa. § 3.1.15 addresses the locative, temporal, and manner class prefixes. § 3.1.16 discusses the phonological status of nominal class prefixes in Proto-Cangin, and § 3.1.17 discusses class agreement in Proto-Cangin.

3.1.1 *w-*

By far the largest singular class in each Cangin language is the "default" unmarked class. Nouns themselves are unprefixed, and the post-nominal definite determiner is not preceded by any class-marking consonant. In Noon-Laalaa, the general agreement prefix is *w-*. Nouns in this class do not change their form in the plural, though they take a different agreement pattern (see § 3.1.3). Some of the many nouns reconstructed in the default class are given in Table 75.

TABLE 75   Some nouns in the default agreement class

PC	Noon	Laalaa	Saafi	Paloor	Ndut	
*ɓoɣ	ɓoh	ɓoh	ɓoh	ɓa'	ɓa'	'baobab'
*naal	naal	naal	naar	naal	°naal †f-	'bull/male animal'
*yaɣ	yah	yah	yaah, °yah	ya'	ya'	'hand, arm'
*wet	wet	weet	wet	wet, yet	°yet	'ash'
*waaɽ	waas	waas	waas	waal	waal	'road'
*níh	ní'	níi	nii	níh	°níh	'rope'
*sís	sís	sís	sis	sís	sís	'tooth'
*yú(u)k	yúuk	yúuk	yuuk	yuk	yúk	'shoulder'
*Hul	hol	ol	hor	hul	°hul	'star'
*yíh~ɗíh	yí'	ɗii	yii, †yi'	yíh	°ɗíh	'knee'
*yaal	yaal	yaal	yaar	yaal	yaal	'man'
*nuf	nof	nof	nof	nuf	°nuf	'ear'
*yuH	yoh	yoh	†yoh	yuh	°yuh	'bone'
*hund	on, †ond	od	und	°hun	°hun	'skin' (n)
*puuɽ	puus	puus	puus	puul	°puul	'wound' (n)
*níil	níil	níil	niir	níil	°níil	'root'
*ɓíiɓ	ɓíiɓ	ɓíiɓ	ɓiiɓ	ɓíiɓ	ɓíiɓ	'breast'
*noɣ	noh	noh	noh	na'	na'	'sun'
*ɣaan	haan	haan	haan	aan	aan	'drum'
*ɣaf	haf	haf	haf	af	af	'head'
*nung	noŋ	nog	nung	°nuŋ	nuŋ	'hole (in ground)'
*loox	look	look	rook	loo y-	loo	'belly'

The consonant *w-* is a true marker of this class, as /w/ is never epenthetic else-where. In Saafi, *w-* appears as an inanimate singular marker on some pronom-inal forms, most notably *w-a* 'it.' There is limited evidence that **w-* is frozen on a few nouns, namely **waaɽ* 'road' (cf. Biafada-Pajade **f-aaɽ(e)*, Kobiana-Kasanga **bi-aaɽ*) and NLS **wek* 'night' (cf. NdP **elek*). However the number of w-initial class members is not conspicuously high, and nouns in this class must be considered unprefixed in Proto-Cangin. Whether **w-* appeared on the post-nominal definite determiner is not entirely clear. While it is absent in all of the modern languages, it is likely that the original prefix **w-* was eroded when the definite determiner was grammaticalized as a suffix in each language. Some evidence that **w-* did originally appear on definite determiners is found in Noon-Laalaa, where the definite marker on agreeing adjective phrases is pre-fixed with *w-*, as in example (14) (see § 3.1.17 for more discussion).

NOMINAL MORPHOLOGY

(14) gogaa wi-hood-waa   (Noon: 009)
      gog-∅-aa   *wi-hood=w-aa*
      snake-∅-DEF.DIST CL-long=CL-DEF.DIST
      'the long snake'

The voicing of Ndut-Paloor root-final stops before a suffixed determiner in this class might also be explained by the earlier presence of **w-*; thus **kot w-a* > *kod-a* 'the foot' through fusion of the voiced sound /w/ with the voiceless stop (otherwise Ndut-Paloor stops do not voice intervocalically). Synchronically, it would be possible to identify a floating feature [voice] as the marker of this Ndut-Paloor class, being the reflex of the original prefix **w-*.

3.1.2   *n-*

A class *n-* has been proposed for Saafi (Mbodj 1983: 152–156, Pouye 2015: 115–118, Botne & Pouille 2016: 96–97), Noon (Lopis 1980: 174), and Ndut (Pichl 1979: 9), though in all three languages its status is debatable. Regardless, it is almost certain that Proto-Cangin did contain a class marked by a prefix **n-* on both nouns and agreeing elements. In Noon and Laalaa, /n/ appears in the same position as a class marker with certain nouns.

(15) Some Noon nouns with *n-* before the definite marker
      gómúu-n-ii   'the hyena'
      boogaa-n-ii   'the bee'
      dúulúu-n-ii   'the insect'
      oomaa-n-ii   'the child'

However, on most nouns this /n/ need not be analyzed as a class marker in Noon-Laalaa. It is predictably inserted after any noun in the default class that ends in a long vowel, and these nouns trigger the general agreement marker *w-*. As such, Noon-Laalaa /n/ is analyzed as an epenthetic consonant rather than a class marker by Soukka (2000: 52) for Padee Noon, Wane (2017: 32) for Thiès Noon, and Soukka and Soukka (2011: 50–51) for Laalaa. Epenthetic /n/ is also used before vowel-initial clitics like the subordinator *=aa* 'if/when/once,' and the polar question particle *=e(e)* to avoid hiatus with a preceding vowel. Stanton (2011) also adopts the analysis of /n/ as an epenthetic consonant for Saafi, where *n-* appears only between nouns and a following definite marker. The vast majority of these Saafi nouns are vowel final, and the majority of vowel-final nouns take the marker *n-*.

(16) Some Saafi nouns in the *n-* class
muuma-n-i 'the lion'
nguɓu-n-i 'the mouth'
caafu-n-i 'the fly'
sople-n-i 'the onion'

However in Noon (at least in the Northern dialect), Laalaa, and Saafi, there is a very small number of nouns that take *n-* but do not meet the phonological requirement for n-epenthesis.

(17) Noon, Laalaa, and Saafi nouns with unpredictable *n-* before the definite marker

Noon		Laalaa		Saafi	
yaal-n-ii	'the *yaal* tree'	°ŋaak-n-ii	'the crow'	cafay-n-i	'the girl'
haawi-n-ii	'the couscous'	°haay-n-ii	'the couscous'	ngakuɗ-n-i	'the gecko'
mbúɗú-n-ii	'the bread'			pulohaaɗ-n-i	'the exit'
kílo-n-ii	'the kilogram'				

Thus from a synchronic standpoint, it is necessary to acknowledge at least a "subclass" *n-* of the default class in Noon-Laalaa and Saafi, if not an entirely separate agreement class. Pichl (1979: 9) lists an active class *n-* in Ndut, used for 0.5% of collected nouns. His (1977) lexicon lists 19 nouns in *n-*, 16 of which are borrowings (mostly from Wolof, both vowel- and consonant-final). The three native nouns are †*sosat* 'evening,' †*seega* 'dry season,' and †*ow* 'person.' It is unclear why Pichl lists *ow* as being in the *n-* class, since the definite form is *ɓëë*, with no /n/. Morgan does not mention this class.

The argument for reconstructing *n- to Proto-Cangin relies on a quite different set of facts, but explains the appearance of "epenthetic" /n/ in Noon-Laalaa and Saafi. In word-initial position, the overwhelming majority of Proto-Cangin prenasalized stops appear in nouns and not verbs, as shown in Table 76.

TABLE 76 Proto-Cangin reconstructions with a word-initial prenasalized stop

PC nouns	Noon	Laalaa	Saafi	Paloor	Ndut	
*mbaal	baal		mbaal	°mbal		'sheep'
*mbaang	baag	°baaŋ		baaŋ	baaŋ	'stalk' (n)
*mbaangV	baagii	baagii		°baag	baage	'palm oil'

NOMINAL MORPHOLOGY

99

TABLE 76   Proto-Cangin reconstructions with a word-initial prenasalized stop (*cont.*)

PC nouns	Noon	Laalaa	Saafi	Paloor	Ndut	
*mbaHane	baani	°baane	mbahne r-	baanu	°baane	'hat'
*mbaŋ		°baŋ	mban	°baŋ f-	†bang f-	'weaverbird sp.'
*mbíing	bíig			bíiŋ 'hip'	°bíiŋ	'back'
*mbílím	mbílím	°bílím			†bílím	'dance type'
*mboong-	boogaa, booginoh			bóogúl	†bëgúl f-	'wasp,' No. 'bee'
*mboos	boos	boos			°boos	'well bucket'
*ndangal	dagal, †ndangal	dagal	ndangal	dagal °f-	°dagal f-	'scorpion'
*ndap	dap	dap	ndap			'granary'
*ndíiŋ	díiŋ	ndíig	ndiŋ	díiŋ °f-	°díiŋ f-	'owl'
*ndil			ndel	°dil	†díl	'sitting mat'
*ndook		°dook			†dook f-	'egret/heron sp.'
*ndúulú	dúulúu	dúulúu		°dúlú	†dúul	'insect,' La. 'wasp'
*ndúut	dúut	°dúut		°duud f-	†dúut f-	'Abyssinian ground hornbill'
*nduul	duul	duul	nduur		°duul f-	'monitor lizard'
*ndVVɗ	dooɗ	dooɗ	ndooɗ	dúuɗ	duuɗ, †dooɗ	'stick'
*njakal	jakal	jakal	njakar	°jakal	†jakal f-	'lizard'
*njang		°jaaŋ	njang	jaŋ		'Palmyra palm'
*njaɓul	jawul, †njawol	jawol		°jawul		'parakeet'
*njol	jol		njol	°jol	†jol f-	'cricket'
*njotot			njotoot	°jotoɗ		'lip'
*ngaal		gaal			°gaal	'calabash sp.'
*ngakúɗ	gókúɗ	°gëkúɗ	ngakuɗ n-	°gëkút	†gokúɗ f-	'gecko'
*ngiic	giic		ngiic	giic		'jujube tree'
*ngol-ngol	golgol			°golgol	†golgol	'throat'
*ngong	gog, goŋ	gog	ngoŋ 'viper'	°goŋ f-		'snake'
*ngum			ngum	gum	†gum	'gourd,' Sa. 'heart'
*ngumú	gómúu (f-), †ngómú	°gumuu f-	ngumu °f-	gúmú °f-	°gúmú f-	'hyena'

PC verbs

*ngúl	gúl (n, v)		ngul (n, v)	gúl (n, v)	°gúl (v)	'(make) hole'
*mbec	†mbec		mbec	bec	°bec	'dance' (borr.)
*mbet			mbet	bet	°bet	'throw' (borr.)
*ngúɗ	gúɗ	gúɗ	nguɗ			'cut'
*(n)helis	elis	geles		°gílís	†gelis	'burp'

No such imbalance is seen for other consonant series—even consonants like *k which are part of a class prefix are found in an appreciable number of verbs. This imbalance can be explained if these prenasalized stops are the result of a noun class prefix *n- (or more cautiously a homorganic nasal *N-). Like in neighboring Sereer and Fula (see Merrill 2018: ch. 2, §4), Proto-Cangin root-initial prenasalized stops would have appeared only in morphologically derived contexts, with just a few exceptions. This class *n- has some degree of semantic coherence, as most of the nouns with initial prenasalized stops are animals. There is also potentially a connection with trees, a few of which are reconstructed with a prenasalized consonant. The only collected consonant-final noun that takes n- agreement in Noon is *yaal*, a tree species. Lopis (1980: 174) notes a connection between n- agreement and trees in Thiès Noon, but the two examples she provides are vowel-final. There are furthermore a few nouns which are reconstructed with a prenasalized stop based on one or more languages, but a homorganic non-nasalized consonant based on others (Table 77).

TABLE 77   Proto-Cangin nouns with or without *n- in different languages

PC	Noon	Laalaa	Saafi	Paloor	Ndut	
*(n-)ɣaɓit	hawit c-	hayet f-, °haet	haɓit	geet	°geet	'dung'
*(n-)ku-suun	guun	guusuud	kusun k-	kusiin	kusuun †k-	'navel'
*(n-)ku-ɓú	kúuɓ	kúu k-	nguɓu n-	ɓúk	ɓúk	'mouth'
*(n-)lVVn	leen	†len	reen		°diin, †déen, †len	'kapok tree'
*(n-)hila	elaa	elaa	ngila r-	hila	†hílë, (°hílëër)	'scuffle hoe'
*(n-)luuf	luf, °†luuf	lúuf	nduuf	luuf	°luuf	'forest'
				duuf	†dúf	'thick bush'
*ku-lúŋ	kúlúŋ k-	kúlúŋ k-		kuluŋ °k-	†kúlúŋ	'jug/pot'
*n-ku-lúŋ	gúlúŋ 'jug'			guluŋ	guluŋ	'gourd (spoon)'

These forms can be explained as the same lexical root appearing with either the class prefix *n- or the ∅ marking of the default class. In three words *n- was stacked on the class prefix *ku- in some languages, likely because it was reinterpreted as part of the root.

Unlike nouns in most other classes, nouns in the *n- class did not begin with an "alliterative" prefix in the sense that *mb, *nd, *nj, and *ng are not the same phoneme as the agreement-marking consonant *n. Furthermore, some nouns in the Proto-Cangin *n- agreement class must have begun with other conso-

NOMINAL MORPHOLOGY   101

nants entirely, assuming the nominal marker *n- was lost before consonants
like *s, *y, and nasals. Perhaps due to this lack of alliteration (especially in the
languages with onset denasalization), *n- broke down as an active noun class,
with its members being reinterpreted as part of the default class. However the
original agreement marker *n- persisted before the definite marker, leading to
unpredictability as to whether a noun in the default class took this seemingly
arbitrary element n-. The solution in Noon-Laalaa and Saafi was to drop n- after
a consonant, and retain it after a vowel as a means of avoiding hiatus. At this
time all noun-final vowels were long in Noon-Laalaa due to regular lengthening (see § 2.2.3), explaining why n- is only used after long and not short vowels,
most of which are found in recent borrowings. In Thiès Noon, which did not
undergo final lengthening, short vowel-final nouns take n-. Subsequently, n-
was extended to vowel-final nouns that were not originally in the *n- class, and
in Noon-Laalaa this reanalyzed hiatus-filler n- was further extended to other
morpheme boundaries. In Paloor, *n- was eliminated altogether.

3.1.3   c-

The most widely-used plural class is marked by c- agreement in Noon-Laalaa-
Saafi, and y- in Ndut-Paloor. In Ndut this y- assimilates completely to most
preceding consonants, but remains y- after a vowel or glottal consonant. In
Noon-Laalaa, c- is the plural class used for nouns in the singular classes ∅/w/n-,
f-, and m-, and in Saafi (c-) and Ndut-Paloor (y-) it is the plural class for all nouns
except 'person.' Ndut-Paloor y- is almost certainly lenited from original *c-, a
change which can also be seen in the verb root hac~y 'come.' Doneux (1975a)
suggests that NdP y- be connected with plural class markers of the shape y-
or i- in other Atlantic languages (notably Wolof y-, Bainunk i-, and Manjak i-),
which would require NLS c- and Ndut-Paloor y- to be unrelated class markers.
This scenario is extremely unlikely, as it would require a very large noun class
to be lost without a trace in each branch of the family—especially improbable
in Noon-Laalaa with its highly conservative class system.

   Examples of sg./pl. definite nouns from each language are given in Table 78.

TABLE 78   Singular and plural definite nouns in each Cangin language

PC	Noon	Laalaa	Saafi	Paloor	Ndut	
*níil w-a	níil-aa	níil-aa	niir-a	níil-a	°níil-a	'the root'
*níil c-a	níil-c-aa	níil-c-aa	niir-c-a	níil-y-a	°níil-l-a	'the roots'
*mi-sip m-a	miip-m-aa	mesep-m-aa	misip-m-a	°misib-m-a	°misip-m-a	'the sauce'
*mi-sip c-a	miip-c-aa	mesep-c-aa	misip-c-a	°misib-y-a	°misip-p-a	'the sauces'

102   CHAPTER 3

As in the modern languages, plural nouns in the *c- agreement class were not marked by a prefix or any other change from the singular form in Proto-Cangin. Even for singular nouns with a prefix (like *mi-sip 'sauce'), there is no evidence that the plural nouns would have lost or changed the prefix on the noun itself.

While no prefix appears on plural nouns, there is strong evidence that a noun prefix *ca- did exist in Proto-Cangin which can be identified with the plural agreement marker etymologically. In modern Noon, ci- can be used as a semi-productive nominalizing class prefix, with the resulting nouns in the c-agreement class.

(18) Noon nouns with the prefix ci-

Noon verb/adj.		Noon noun	
pok	'tie/marry'	ci-pok c-	'wedding'
wo'	'speak/say'	ci-wo' c-	'speech/talking'
fool	'run'	ci-fool c-	'running'
súus	'black' (adj)	ci-súus c-	'black' (n)
keen	'fall'	ci-keen-keen c-	'epilepsy'

As with the Noon infinitive prefix ki- from both *ka- and *ki- (see §3.1.5), ci- could derive from *ca- by vowel reduction. There are at least two deverbal nouns prefixed with ca- in Saafi: °cakiim 'dowry' from kiim 'ask,' and capoon 'thatch' from the verb poon 'thatch.' In Paloor there is cesiŋ 'palm wine' (Ndut †císíŋ), a borrowing from Wolof sëng with a prefix ce-, °capoon 'thatch,' and °cikaañ 'work/effort' (Ndut †cakañ) likely from °kaañ 'be brave.' In Laalaa there are a few deverbal nouns with a prefix caa-: °caapay 'diseases cured by traditional medicine' from pay 'cure,' cëënín f- 'evening meal' from *níin 'evening,' and probably caalal c- 'type of food' from lal 'burn.' Noon cuu-kím f- 'breakfast' and cuu-noh f- 'lunch,' derived from kím 'morning' and noh 'sun/noon' with the associative prefix CL-uu- (see §3.1.12), contain a c- class prefix synchronically, though they take f- agreement like many other disyllabic nouns. The Noon-Laalaa mass noun 'trash' (Noon calus c-, Laalaa cales c-, †calos c-) certainly contains this prefix. Developments from a mass/abstract noun class to a plural class are amply attested in Niger-Congo systems, as with Bantu class 14 *bu-, and more relevantly Bainunk-Kobiana-Kasanga *ja-, which may be cognate with the Cangin class.

There is an etymologically-distinct fossilized prefix *ca- that appears on some animal nouns, discussed in §3.1.12. These nouns are count nouns, and do

NOMINAL MORPHOLOGY   103

not take *c*- agreement. Nonetheless, it is possible that some of the mass/abstract nouns mentioned in the previous paragraph in fact contain this distinct **ca*-prefix.

3.1.4   *y-, ɓ-*

Agreement prefixes **y*- and **ɓ*- can be reconstructed for certain singular and plural nouns referring to people, most notably 'person.' Furthermore, the noun 'thing' took **y*- agreement in the singular. Corresponding noun prefixes **y*- on 'thing' and **ɓi*- on a few personal nouns can be identified. This section will first examine the use of the agreement markers **y*- and **ɓ*-, and then the prefixes **y*- and **ɓi*- on nouns.

The noun 'person' is in the singular agreement class *y*- in each modern language except Ndut. The definite forms of 'person' are given in Table 79.

TABLE 79   Definite singular forms of 'person' in each language

	Noon	Laalaa	Saafi	Kh. Paloor	Ndut
proximal	ɓuui~ɓu-y-ii, †ɓu-y-ii	ɓiu	ɓoo-y-i	ɓo-y-a	ɓëë
middle	ɓuum~ɓo-y-um			ɓo-y-e	
distal	ɓoo~ɓo-y-aa, †ɓu-y-aa	ɓe-a/ɓo-a	ɓoo-y-a	ɓo-y-in	
non-spatial		ɓo-am			

The Noon-Laalaa general agreement marker (used for demonstratives, pronouns, etc.) is *y*- for *ɓo'* 'person.' In Laalaa *y*- does not survive before the definite suffix, but is the source of the vowel change in the distal definite form (**ɓoyaa > ɓea*) and the first vowel in the proximal definite form (**ɓoyuu > ɓiu*). The use of *y*- on the definite suffix is confined to the word 'person' in Saafi as well as Thiès Noon. In Northern Noon, nouns referring to family members (*eew* 'mother,' *kéméñkí* 'younger sibling,' etc.) and optionally *ɓeti* 'woman/wife' also take *y*- on the suffixed definite determiner. Singular *y*- does not survive in Ndut or Paloor as described by Thornell et al., where 'the person' has no class marker on the definite suffix (Nd. *ɓëë*, Pa. *ɓóo*, from Proto-Ndut-Paloor **ɓó-y-a*).

In Noon-Laalaa the noun 'thing' (Noon *iñ*, Laalaa *oñ*) takes *y*- agreement. While *y*- appears only as the general agreement marker for 'thing' and not on the definite suffix (e.g. Noon *iñ-ii y-ii*, Laalaa *oñ-uu y-uu* 'this thing'), the Laalaa proximal definite form is *oñ-uu* rather than *×oñ-ii*, cf. the irregular proximal demonstrative *y-uu* (rather than the expected *×y-ii*) for this class. Relatedly, Noon-Laalaa *ya* 'what' is simply a pronoun of the shape CL-*a* (see §4.1) with *iñ/oñ* 'thing' as the referent. In fact, Noon subject questions with *ya* 'what' contain an overt noun *iñ* 'thing,' as in example (19).

(19) iñii weel (da) ya? (Noon: 005)
    iñ-ii   *weel* *(da)* ∅ *ya*
    thing-DEF.PROX break (REL) COP what
    'what broke?' (literally 'the thing that broke is what?')

Saafi *ye* 'what' and Ndut-Paloor *yi(h)* 'what' probably contain the prefix *y-* (agreeing with an original noun 'thing'), but note that the default class prefix *w-* would have become /y/ before the front vowel in Ndut-Paloor (see § 2.1.5.3). Thornell et al. report that Paloor *iñ* 'thing' is used only in the plural, which in effect means that it is always used with the class agreement marker *y-*. While synchronically *y-* can be seen as the Paloor plural marker *y-* (from **c-*), it is likely historically descended from **y-* when used with 'thing.' The same situation holds in Morgan and Pichl's Ndut examples, and in all Ndut-Paloor sources, *y-* is used on demonstrative pronoun bases to mean 'this/that thing.' It is noteworthy that in Wolof, the *k-* agreement class is used with only two nouns, *nit* 'person' and *këf* 'thing,' just like Proto-Cangin **y-*.

The plural of 'person' (and in Thiès Noon optionally †*bedëb* 'woman') uses the marker *b-* on definite determiners in Noon and Saafi. Definite forms of 'people' are shown in Table 80.

TABLE 80   Definite plural forms of 'person' in each language

	Noon	Laalaa	Saafi	Kh. Paloor	Ndut
proximal	ɓo-ɓ-ii, †ɓu-ɓ-ii	ɓe'	ɓoo-ɓ-i	ɓo-y-a	ɓëë-w-ë
middle	ɓo-ɓ-um			ɓo-y-e	
distal	ɓo-ɓ-aa, †ɓu-ɓ-aa	ɓo-a	ɓoo-ɓ-a	ɓo-y-in	

NOMINAL MORPHOLOGY

Recall that *ɓ is regularly deleted intervocalically in Laalaa and Ndut-Paloor, which accounts for the absence of the class marker before the definite marker in these languages. Note the vowel coalescence in Proto-NL *ɓo-ɓ-ii > Laalaa ɓe'. The /w/ in Ndut ɓëëwë is probably from *ɓ, cf. the 3rd plural pronoun wa from *ɓa. The long vowel in the root is likely carried over from the definite singular form ɓëë, where the long vowel is the result of coalescence with the definite suffix -a. In Khodaba Paloor, the plural marker y-[1] from the demonstrative paradigm has been co-opted to replace the lost *ɓ (see § 3.2 for discussion of the Paloor demonstrative forms). This element y- cannot be original in these forms, since like *ɓ, *y was regularly deleted intervocalically in Paloor. Thornell et al. (2016) do not find y- in the plural definite form of 'person,' which in these dialects is ɓó-y-a using the regular Paloor plural class marker y-. The Noon-Laalaa general agreement marker is ɓ- for the plural of ɓo' 'person.'

In Noon, Laalaa, and Saafi, y- and ɓ- are also used on pronominal demonstratives referring to humans, e.g. Noon, Saafi yii/ɓii, Laalaa yuu/ɓii 'this person/these people.' In Noon, the use of y- and ɓ- has expanded, being used as the general agreement marker (but not the suffixed determiner agreement marker) for all human nouns and even animals; e.g. yaalii yi-yaak yii 'this big man,' yaalcii ɓi-yaak ɓii 'these big men.' In Saafi there is a form yaaɓ 'men' (listed as pejorative by Mbodj; Botne & Pouille give yaaɓi 'the guys') in which the historical class marker ɓ- is preserved. This suggests that at least *yaal 'man' in addition to *ɓi-o' 'person' and probably *ɓe-reɓ 'woman' originally took ɓ-agreement in the plural. In Morgan's (1996: 164) Ndut data, w- is also used with the plural of këë 'child' (këë-w-ë), which is historically the diminutive of *ɓi-o' 'person.'

The forms of the noun 'thing' in Cangin languages show some historical peculiarities which can be accounted for by the presence of the class prefix *y-. The forms of words meaning 'thing' or 'something' in the modern languages are shown in Table 81.

---

1 D'Alton in fact gives this prefix as j- for both the demonstratives and in 'people,' but it is y- for demonstratives in Thornell et al. (2016) and in Pichl (1977) and Morgan (1996) for Ndut. D'Alton often misidentifies implosives as egressives, though in this case it must be noted that Paloor implosives have regular egressive allophones in intervocalic position, so the pronunciation of /y/ in the definite forms of 'people' is in fact as an egressive stop. Diagne (2015) gives the Paloor definite plural form as ɓëjjë.

106   CHAPTER 3

TABLE 81   Forms of 'thing' in each Cangin language

Noon	Laalaa	Saafi	Paloor	Ndut	
yen 'something'	yin	in	yin	yin	'thing'
enaama (y-)	°yinaama		inam		'thing'[a]
iñ (y-)	oñ y-	iiñ 'snake'	iñ y-	iñ	'thing'

a   Originally 'the thing in question,' cf. modern Noon *gog-aa-ma* 'the snake in
    question.'

Recall that **i* develops to Noon-Laalaa /e/. For the development of /e/ to Noon
/i/ and Laalaa /o/ in *iñ* and *oñ*, see the end of § 2.2.1.2. It would be possible to
identify two unrelated roots **iñ* and **(y)in* for these modern forms, but it is
more likely that they represent the same root etymologically. First, the discrepancy between /ñ/ and /n/ can be attributed to the earlier presence of the agreement prefix **y-* in definite forms. Thus, modern Noon *iñ-ii* 'the thing' might
be traced to **in y-i*. It is likely that this coalescence had already taken place
in Proto-Cangin, such that the definite forms were **iñ-i* and **iñ-a* with irregular fusion of the noun and definite article.[2] Under this account, the resulting
coalesced consonant /ñ/ was extended to forms without the definite marker.
Furthermore, new regularized definite forms of **(y)in* arose in each language
(perhaps already in Proto-Cangin), leading to the etymological doublet **iñ* and
*(y)in. Second, the unpredictable presence of word-initial /y/ in forms which
are otherwise regular cognates can be attributed to a noun prefix **y-* which
appeared before the noun root itself. A similar discrepancy in the presence of
a noun prefix will be seen shortly for 'person.'

    The few nouns listed in Table 82, most notably 'person' and 'woman,' appear
to be prefixed with *ɓ(V)-*. Recall that for 'woman' the unprefixed form exists as
Noon *leɓ* and Saafi *riɓ* 'female.'

2   A structural parallel exists in Sereer, in which the definite forms of *tig* 'thing' are irregu-
    larly fused as *tig-e*, *tig-aa*, whereas for all other nouns the definite article is a post-nominal
    word/clitic with a class prefix.

NOMINAL MORPHOLOGY

TABLE 82   Human nouns with a prefix *ɓi-

PC	Noon	Laalaa	Saafi	Paloor	Ndut	
*ɓi-o'	ɓo' y-	ɓo' y-	ɓo' y-	ow, ɓó, °o'	ow	'person'
NdP *ɓó-y-a				ɓóo, °ɓo-y-a	ɓëë	'the person'
*ɓe-reɓ	ɓeti, †ɓedëɓ	ɓete f-	ɓitiɓ	ɓeleɓ	ɓeleɓ	'woman'
*(ɓi-)ɣawúl	hool	hëwúl	hawur	ɓóolú	†ɓëëlú, †ɓol k-	'griot'
*ɓi-tif?			ɓitif	ɓitif	°ɓitif	'old woman'
*ɓi-sí?				ɓisi, °ɓísí	†ɓisi	'fisherman/Lebu
(cf. *kísí 'ocean')						Wolof person'

The prefix present on these nouns is the personal plural prefix *ɓi-. Apparently the plural form was extended to the singular in these words, which is somewhat unexpected. Noon-Laalaa ɓa 'who' (being the pronominal base -a with a class prefix) can be added to this list, as it has both singular and plural reference. The vowel of the prefix is *i (note that *e in 'woman' is a phonologically conditioned variant of *i before a mid vowel). The prefix form *ɓi- can also be found in the Noon-Laalaa numeral ɓenak 'two' with personal/animate plural agreement, which would result from *ɓi-anax, but not any other prefix vowel. However the presence of *i here may be insignificant, since the Noon-Laalaa adjective agreement prefixes always contain Proto-NL *e (earlier *i), and these are in fact used on higher numerals, e.g. Noon ɓi-nikiis 'four' with the same class agreement. Ndut-Paloor has a +ATR vowel in the prefixed form of 'person' (recall that in Ndut the +ATR counterpart of /o/ is /ë/). The +ATR vowel can be explained as resulting from the coalescence of the original prefix and root vowels (see Table 47 for other +ATR vowels resulting from coalescence), and as such the noun is reconstructed as *ɓi-o', developing to NLS *ɓo' and NdP *ɓó. The Ndut-Paloor unprefixed form of 'person' o'/ow was probably the original singular form. However synchronically, this unprefixed form is used in the singular and plural as long as no definite marker is present, and the prefixed form is used with a definite marker (though in Thornell et al. indefinite ɓó is also found).

A pre-nominal particle/prefix ɓi (Laalaa ɓe) is used in Saafi, Paloor, and Noon-Laalaa with an indefinite plural function (Dieye 2010 but not Pichl 1981 identifies the Laalaa morpheme as a quantifier meaning 'multiple/many'). The Noon prefix is used only with animate nouns (and only human proper names in the Padee dialect; Soukka 2000: 74).

(20) ɓi yaar   (Saafi: Mb. 161)
     'some men'

(21) ɓi peendal   (Paloor: Th. 29)
     'some chameleons'

(22) ɓa ɓi-baay   (Noon: 050)
     ɓ-a   ɓi-baay
     they CL.PL-dog
     'they're dogs' (i.e. wicked people)

(23) bóo apen ɓe enoh   (Laalaa: Di. 130)
     bóo ap-en   ɓe   enoh
     father kill-PERF multiple cow
     'father has killed multiple cows.'

The same marker is probably found in Laalaa *ɓíjëd* 'sickness' from the verb *jëd*
'be sick' (borrowed from Wolof *jér*). This marker is historically the noun class
prefix *ɓi-*. In all languages but Noon it can be used with both animate and inanimate nouns, though in the dialect of Saafi described by Pouye (2015: 114) it is
only used with humans (the Wolof borrowing *ay* is used for non-humans). At
some previous time *ɓi-* would have been used only with humans as in Padee
Noon, but it is possible that already in Proto-Cangin it had been extended to
other nouns to mean 'some NOUNs.'

3.1.5   *k-*

The *k-* agreement class in Noon, Laalaa, and Saafi contains exclusively k-initial
nouns, and this is true with some exceptions (mainly earlier **p-* or **t-* class
nouns) in Ndut-Paloor. All reconstructable Proto-Cangin **k-* class nouns
(Table 83) are prefixed with **kV-* or begin in **k.

There are a number of other k-initial nouns in the *k-* agreement class in each
modern language. A few nouns (Table 84) are not synchronically in the *k-* agreement class in the modern languages, but might have contained a prefix **kV-*
historically.

NOMINAL MORPHOLOGY

TABLE 83   Nouns in the *k- agreement class

PC	Noon	Laalaa	Saafi	Paloor	Ndut	
*kíir̪ (kV-híir̪)	kíis k-	kíis k-	kiis k-	kíil	kíil †k-	'year'
*kúum	kúum k-	kúum k-	kuum	kúum k-	°kúum k-	'honey'
*kiil	kiil k-	kiil k-		kiil °k-	kiil k-	'braiding needle'
*kúlndV	kúldí	kúldí k-		kúlë	†kúllë k-	'couscous steamer'
*kuɗ	koɗ k-	koɗ k-	kuɗ	kuɗ °k-	kuɗ k-	'pestle'
*ki-rik	kedik k-	kedek k-	kidik	kilik k-	kilik †k-	'tree'
*ki-ɓí(s)	kíwíi k-, †kíwís	kiis k-, †kíwís	kiɓi k-	kíi °k-	°kíi k-	'fire'
*ki-noH	kenoh k-	kenoh k-	kinoh	°kinoh	†kinoh k-	'waist'
*su/ki-pi	kipii k-	sope'	kipi	°kipi k-	supi	'ring,' Sa. 'earring'
*ki-hon-aɣ	koonaah k-	keonah k-				'throat'
*ki-yuuŋ	kuuŋ	kiyuuŋ k-, †kúuŋ k-				'shin'
*ki-lo		keloo k-	kiro	(°koloj k-)		'pot'
*(n-)ku-ɓú	kúuɓ k-, °kuvu	kúu k-	nguɓu n-	ɓúk	ɓúk	'mouth'
*(n-)ku-suun	guun	guusuud	kusun k-	kusiin	kusuun †k-	'navel'
*ku-ɓo	kowu k-, †kowo	kuu k-	kuɓu k-	kook	këë, †kú k-	'child,' Pa. 'baby'
*ko-yo	kui, †kuyu k-	koyo k-	kooy	koy k-	koy k-	'child' (NL 'girl')
*ku-fúc	kúuc k-	kúuc f-	kofooc k-, †kufuc	°kúfúc k-	†kúc k-	'needle'
*ku-lúɓ	ˇkúlúɓ		kuluɓ k-	°kúlúb		'horn (instrument)'
*ku-lúŋ	kúlúŋ k-	kúlúŋ k-		kuluŋ °k-	†kúlúŋ	'pot/jug'
*ko-se/r̪e	‡koye	kose f-	kose k-			'tail'
*ku-mun?	kumun k-	kuumun k-, °kumun, †komoon				'nose'
*ka-mbot	kobut, ˇkobot k-	kebot k-			†kabot	'debt'
*ka-ndí(ɗ)	kédí k-	këdí k-	kandiɗ	kedi	†kédí	'mortar' (NLS), 'pipe' (NNdP)
*ka-ñík	kéñí k-		kiñi	keñik	†kéñík k-	'bracelet'
*ka-no(ɣ)	kanu, †kanoh k-	kano k-	kanoh			'calabash'
*ka-kaan	ˇkikaan k-	kakaan k-	kakaan			'death'
*ka-laɓ	kalaɓ	koloɓ f-	kalaɓ k-			'sword, machete'
*kV-pes	ˇkipes k-	kapes k-	kipes	pes k-	pes	'life'
*kV-r̪aaɣ	ki-saah	kesah	°kisoh	kalaa	†kal	'last year'
*kV-ra	ketaa k-	ketaa k-		°kula		'pot'
*(kV-)ñíin			kiñin k-	ñíin	ñíin	'nose'
	(kókús k-)	kew	kiiw k-			'axe'

The form of the historical prefix on these k- class nouns can be reconstructed as *ki-, *ku-, or *ka- depending on the word. Besides the productive uses explored below, there are no clear semantic generalizations to be made for any of these three prefixes.

110   CHAPTER 3

TABLE 84   Additional nouns with a potential *kV- prefix

PC	Noon	Laalaa	Saafi	Paloor, Ndut	
*kayoH	kayoh f-	kayoh f-	keeh	kaah, °kaah k-	'truth'
*kúlmbVs	kúlmbís f-, °kúlmbús	kúlbísóh	kurmburus	°kúlbús f-, †kúlbús f-	'ant sp.'
*kaɗVɗ	kaɗeeɗ	(kaañiid)		kariɗ, °karaɗ †k-	'tamarind tree'
*kayand	kaad f-	kaad f-	kahan, °kahand		'house'
*kilif	kelif f-/†k- 'butter'			P. °kílíf m-	'oil'
*koleň	koliň f-, ‡koleň			koloň, †koleň f-	'sand' (Ser. o-leeň)

There are three synchronically active *kV-* noun prefixes in Noon-Laalaa
(Table 85), all of which form nouns taking *k-* agreement.

TABLE 85   Synchronically active *kV-* prefixes in Noon and Laalaa with examples

PC	Noon	Laalaa	
*ka-, *ki-	ki- (‡ka-)	ka-	infinitive/deverbal
*ku-	ku-	ke~ki- (but *koas* 'eye')	diminutive
*ki-	ki-[a]	ke~ki-	language

Examples:

*kV-ɗoɓ	ki-ɗoɓ	ka-ɗoɓ	'to bite'
*ku-yaan	ku-haan	ke-haan	'little drum'
*ki-waal	ki-waal	ke-waal	'Wolof'

a   Also used with a reduplicated family name to mean 'the area of the X family
home' (Soukka 2000: 73)

The prefix for languages can be reconstructed as *ki-*, but the other two prefixes
exhibit an irregular vowel correspondence between Noon and Laalaa.

As in many Niger-Congo languages, the Noon-Laalaa infinitive prefix is in
fact a noun class prefix. Noon uses *ki-* (Thiès *kë-*) and Laalaa *ka-*. The Laalaa
infinitive prefix must be reconstructed to Proto-Cangin as *ka-*, since an original prefix *ki-* guided by Noon should have merged with the language prefix
in Laalaa. The vowel in the Noon infinitive prefix *ki-* may be the result of the
reduction of unstressed *ka-*. In Williams and Williams' (1993) Noon wordlist,
the infinitive prefix is *ka-* or (before a +ATR vowel) *kə-*, which all but confirms
the reconstruction *ka-*. However, it is likely that both *ka-* and *ki-* were used

NOMINAL MORPHOLOGY

as infinitive prefixes in Proto-Cangin, either in free variation, or depending on the lexical identity of the verb (see the prefixed nouns in Table 86). The infinitive prefix is found in Saafi as *ki*, though it appears in fewer environments than in Noon-Laalaa. Botne & Pouille do not term it an infinitive prefix (and neither Mbodj nor Pouye mention it at all), but it serves some of the same functions as Noon-Laalaa *ki-/ka-*. Some examples of Saafi *ki* from Botne & Pouille (2016) and Pouye (2015) compared with Noon equivalents using *ki-* are given in (24–33).

Saafi

(24) a yi ris ki jiriɗ (B.P. 36)
    a yi ris ki jiriɗ
    s/he PROG still INF be.sick
    's/he is still sick'

(26) e Cheikh uup ki hut Ibu
    (B.P. 42)
    e C. uup ki hut I.
    it's C. surpass INF be.tall I.
    'it is Cheikh who is taller than Ibu'

(28) 6a hay ki guuree (B.P. 20)
    6a hay ki guur-ee
    they FUT INF farm-E
    'they will cultivate'

(30) mi min ki nup (B.P. 25)
    mi min ki nup
    I can INF run
    'I know how to run [well]'

(32) 6o' nu waaɗ ki marak ndoom
    saafi ... (Po. 278)
    6o' nu waaɗ ki
    person whichever want INF
    marak ndoom saafi
    look tatooing Saafi
    'whoever wants to see Saafi
    tattooing'

Noon

(25) ya lís ki-ɗúukúl (049)
    ya lís   ki-ɗúukúl
    s/he continue INF-be.sick
    's/he is still sick'

(27) Gelaŋ yéɗii wiñ ki-hooɗ Gënút
    (049)
    G. y-éɗii wiñ ki-hooɗ G.
    G. FOC surpass INF-be.tall G.
    'it's Gelaŋ who is taller than Gënút'

(29) 6a hay ki-lín (049)
    6a hay ki-lín
    they FUT INF-farm
    'they will cultivate'

(31) mi mín ki-fool (049)
    mi mín ki-fool
    I can INF-run
    'I know how to run [well]'

(33) kaadcii cii moɗunuun ki-malak
    (028)
    kaad-c-ii
    house-CL-DEF.PROX
    c-ii
    CL-DEM.PROX
    moɗ-unuun ki-malak
    be.pretty-PERF.PL INF-look
    'these houses are pretty to look at'

112   CHAPTER 3

In addition to the use of *ka-/ki-* in infinitive constructions, the prefixes *ke~ki-* and *ka-* are used in both Laalaa and Saafi on a number of deverbal nouns, listed in Table 86.

TABLE 86   Deverbal nouns with a *kV-* prefix in Laalaa and Saafi

Laalaa verb/noun		Laalaa noun	
kaan	'die'	kakaan k-	'death'
pes	'live'	kapes k-	'life'
lam	'inherit'	kalam k-	'inheritance'
luun	'sorcerer'	kaluun k-	'sorcery'
oomah	'child'	kaoomah k-	'youth'
tog	'be widowed'	katoŋ k-	'widowhood'
kín	'count'	kakín k-	'count'
woo	'speak'	kewoo k-	'speech'
ɓof	'cough'	ke-ɓof k-	'cough'
miiliic	'lightning'	kimiiliic k-	'lightning bolt'
ay	'be bitter'	†kiayla k-	'bile'
(Pa. híndíŋ~g	'thunder')	†kí'índíŋ k-	'thunder'
Saafi verb		**Saafi noun**	
kaan	'die'	kakaan	'death'
ñam	'eat'	kañam	'food'
pes	'live'	kipes	'life'
waad̵	'want/love'	°kiwaad̵	'love'
raak	'have'	°kiraak	'possessions'

In Noon, most (though not all) infinitive forms can be used nominally, taking *k*-agreement, e.g. *ki-lín k-* 'farming,' *ki-kaan k-* 'death,' *ki-tíid k-* 'walking.' In Noon-Laalaa, *ki-/ke-* is also found on a few adverbs, most notably Noon *ki-deɓaa*, Laalaa *ke-deɓaan* 'previously' from the verb *deɓ* 'be first.' The use of the prefixes *ki-* and *ka-* on deverbal nouns is historically equivalent to the use of these prefixes as infinitive markers, which supports the idea that both **ki-* and **ka-* were employed in this role in Proto-Cangin. Ndut-Paloor has lost the infinitive/denominal prefix(es) *kV-*, but it survives in a few Paloor verbs where an unstressed prefix *ki-* optionally precedes the verb root, listed in (34).

NOMINAL MORPHOLOGY

(34) Paloor verbs with an optional initial *ki-* (d'A. 132)

kipaŋ ~ paŋ	'do, cook'
kisañ ~ sañ	'leave'
kilac ~ lac	'cut'
kilaan ~ laan	'carry on head'

D'Alton gives only these four forms as part of a discussion of stress. It is unclear whether *ki-* can appear on other Paloor verbs, and whether the forms with *ki-* are used in the same environments as the unprefixed verbs. Morgan (1996: 49) notes that in Ndut *ke* and *ki* are "found in association with some nominalizations of verbal/adjectival forms" but does not provide examples. Pichl (1977) gives Ndut †*kijal k-* 'virility' from the noun/adjective *yaal* 'man/male.' A k-initial nominalizing prefix is also found in Ndut-Paloor °*kúl k-* 'death' from the verb *húl* 'die.' There are also some unprefixed Ndut-Paloor deverbal nouns in the *k-* agreement class like Ndut †*luun k-* 'sorcery' (cf. Laalaa *kaluun k-*) and Paloor *pes k-* 'life' (cf. Laalaa *kapes k-*) in which the prefix has eroded.

The diminutive prefix can be reconstructed as **ku-* based on the Noon form. Laalaa does in fact show evidence of **ku-* in *koas k-* 'eye' from **ku-ɣar̥*, cf. Noon *has* 'eye' and *ku-has k-* '(little) eye.' Otherwise, the Laalaa diminutive prefix has become *ke-*. The Laalaa diminutive prefix *ke-* must be kept distinct from the use of *kuu* 'child' in compounds with a diminutive meaning, e.g. *kuu-pe'* 'kid (young goat),' *kuu-koas* 'pupil (of eye)' (Dieye 2010: 122–123). Drolc (2005: 126) mistakenly takes Laalaa *kuu* (cited as *ku*) as being the grammaticalization source for the diminutive prefix **ku-*. The word *kuu* is in fact from **ku-ɓo* 'child,' which itself contains the diminutive prefix **ku-* that must be reconstructed to Proto-Cangin. This diminutive prefix is not productive in the other Cangin languages, but a few examples of it can perhaps be found in each. Paloor has *kuluñ k-* 'little pestle,' °*kofal k-* 'little calabash,' °*koloj k-* 'small pot.' The most notable Paloor noun containing **ku-* is *kúkóy* or °*kukoy* 'child' (Ndut *kúkëy~këkëy*) existing alongside *koy* 'child' (Ndut *koy*) which itself historically contains the diminutive prefix **ku-* (**ko-yo*, with the vowel seemingly influenced by **ku-ɓi-o'* > NdP **kóo* 'child' in some dialects). For Ndut, Pichl gives †*kofel k-* 'net for a calabash bottle' and †*kiif k-* 'calabash (not too large) for measuring millet' (cf. *if* 'calabash'), as well as a few unprefixed nouns for which *k-* agreement can perhaps be explained by their diminutive meaning: †*cofej k-* 'girl,' °*cëëf k-* 'fly,' and †*nísë k-* 'millet seed.' He lists a Mont Rolland dialect form †*kul* 'star,' a variant of *hul* with the diminutive prefix. Saafi has *komaak* 'child' (cf. Noon *oomaah*) with the historical diminutive prefix. The nouns **ku-ɓo* 'child' (the diminutive of **ɓi-o'* 'person'), **ko-yo* 'child,' and **ku-lúŋ* 'small pot/jug' (but 'large metal pot' in Ndut) can be reconstructed to Proto-Cangin with the diminutive prefix (see Table 83).

114   CHAPTER 3

In Northern Noon, the prefix *ku-* is used frequently, but not usually with a diminutive meaning. Rather, it serves to emphasize the singular number of the noun, as in example (35).

(35) mi hoteeɗa ku-baay ga toonaaɗaa   (Noon: 050)
     mi hot-ee-ɗa   ku-baay ga   toon-aaɗ-aa
     I   see-PST-PUNC CL-dog   PREP sell-NOM-DEF.DIST
     'I saw a dog (of any size) at the market'

In fact in some contexts (including example (35)), the absence of *ku-* on an indefinite noun is ungrammatical. This prefix is also used as a singulative marker on mass nouns, e.g. *ku-maalu k-* 'a grain of rice' from *maalu* 'rice,' *ku-peoh k-* 'a seed' from *peoh p-* 'seeds' (Noon: 014, 021). In the same way, the corresponding plural prefix *tu-* can mark the plurality of a noun, without implying anything about its physical size; e.g. *tu-cooh* 'elephants (regardless of size)' (Noon: 033). This non-diminutive use of *ku-* and *tu-* must be a recent development of Northern Noon, as it is not reported for other dialects or Laalaa. It is noteworthy for being an emerging strategy for marking number on the noun itself, in a reversal of the tendency seen throughout the history of all Cangin languages to level number-based alternations.

3.1.6   *f-*

The *f-* class contains a good number of f-initial nouns in each language, but also many nouns which do not begin with this consonant, many of which are animals. Especially in Ndut-Paloor, there is a very strong tendency for animals to appear in the *f-* class regardless of their phonological form. There are also many nouns with a frozen CV- class prefix which take *f-* agreement in each language, which may ultimately be due to an association between two syllable nouns and *f-* agreement.

A number of **f-* class nouns containing a prefix **fV-* or beginning with *f can be reconstructed to Proto-Cangin (Table 87).

TABLE 87   f-initial nouns in the **f-* agreement class

PC	Noon	Laalaa	Saafi	Paloor	Ndut	
*fen	fen f-	fen f-	fin f-, °fen f-	fen °f-	°fen f-	'hair'
*faan	faan f-	faan f-	faan	faan	faan	'body'
*fe(e)y	◊fey			fey, °feey f-	feey, †fey f-	'soil, dirt'
*fa-yúm	‡fëyum	fëyëm f-	fayum	fëyúm °m-	°fëyúm	'fat, grease'

NOMINAL MORPHOLOGY   115

TABLE 87   f-initial nouns in the *f- agreement class (*cont.*)

PC	Noon	Laalaa	Saafi	Paloor	Ndut	
*fa-núf	fónúf f-, ˇfënúf	fënúf f- 'eye-lash'			°fënúf	'body hair' No. also 'feather'
*fe-keɗ	fekiɗ f-	°fekeɗ			†feked	'millet chaff type'
*i/fa-noɣ	enoh f-	enoh f-	inoh	fana' f-	fana f-	'cow'
*fi-xí	fíkíi f-	fíkíi f-	fiki	fii °f-	fii, †fíh	'face/before'
*fi-lond(o)?	fíldóo		†filndo	filoon, °fulon f-	filoon †f-	'behind/under'
*fi-nVɣo?	fenoo f-	fenoo	fino, finho r-			'behind' ('rear')
*(fi-)ɣal	hal 'door'	hal 'door'	har		°fëël, †fël f-	'outdoors'
*(fi-)níin	níin		niin	fíníin f-	finiin f-	'evening'
*fi-ɗaas	feɗaaf, ˇ†faɗaaf f-	feɗaaf f-	fiɗaaf	firaas f-		'corpse'
*fi-yaang	feyaaŋ f-	feaŋ f-	fiyaang			'bed'
*fi-yon	fiyon f-			°fiyonoh (v)	†fion (v)	'cold'
*fV/a-ɣaal	ˇfasaa f-		fisaa r-	(alaal)	(°araal)	'chest' (thorax)
	fabuy f-	fëbúy f-, †fúy f-			°fuj f-	'brain'
				faam f-	faam f-	'village'
				filíɓ f-	†filíɓ	'inside/interior'
				°fikit f-	†fikít	'millet chaff type'
				°fanay f-	°fanaay, †fanay f-	'antelope'

There is evidence for prefixes of the shape *fi- and *fa-. The prefix *fa- is found on mass nouns ('fat, body hair' and perhaps 'soil/dirt, brain, chaff' at an earlier stage), and in Ndut-Paloor two words for large animals ('cow, antelope'). Other mass nouns which likely contain an original f-initial prefix include: Noon *foñu* 'chaff,' *fuñuuñ* 'millet burrs'; Laalaa *fetoɓ f-* 'rain' from the verb *toɓ* 'rain'; Paloor °*fúkúm* 'sheaf of millet' (cf. Sereer and Wolof *xumb*), *filik f-* 'grass' (cf. *kilik k-* 'tree'); Ndut †*feh f-* 'strips of dried meat,' †*fúrfë* 'eyelashes.' In these words as well as in 'millet chaff' the prefix vowel is not /a/, but in some cases the prefix vowel may have assimilated to the root vowel. The prefix *fi- is found on the spatial words 'before,' 'behind,' and 'inside,' though this spatial meaning does not characterize all *fi-prefixed nouns. The unprefixed noun *ɣal 'door' seems to become 'outdoors' (also 'backyard' in Pichl 1979) with the addition of *fi-, but evidence is only extant in Ndut. Noon *foh*, ˇ*fooh* 'outside' and Ndut °*fëgrë* 'under' and †*fëën* 'nowhere' may also contain this spatial prefix. The two noun prefixes *fa- and *fi- likely once corresponded to two unrelated agreement classes, but these had already become conflated by the Proto-Cangin period. The merger of two (or perhaps more) classes as Cangin *f-* may explain the class's rather eclectic semantics.

116 CHAPTER 3

Not all nouns in the *f- agreement class began with *f. The nouns in Table 88 (most of which refer to animals) do not contain an f-initial prefix, but appear in the f- class in (almost) all modern Cangin languages, and thus were likely in the Proto-Cangin *f- agreement class.

TABLE 88   Non-f-initial nouns in the *f- agreement class

PC	Noon	Laalaa	Saafi	Paloor	Ndut	
*cangín	cégín (f-)	cëgín f-	cangin	°cigin f-	°cígín, †céegín f-	'worm' (grub)
*ca-oɣ	cooh f-	coh f-	cooh	caa' °f-	°ca', †caa' f-	'elephant'
*paaní	péeníi f-	pëëní f-	paani f-/n-	póoní °f-	pëëní f-	'monkey'
*pe'	pe' f-	pe' f-	pe' f-	pe' °f-	pe' f-	'goat'
*panís	pénís f-	pënís f-	panis	pónís	pënís f-	'horse'
*pambi	pabi, †pambe f-	pabe f-	pambi f-	(paan)	(paan †f-)	'chicken'
*ɓuh	(baay f-)	ɓúu f-	ɓuu f-, ‡ɓu'	ɓuh f-	ɓuh f-	'dog'
*caal		caal f-	caar		caal f-	'antelope'
*paloom		paloom f-		°palom f-		'antelope sp.'
*saangú	sóogúu f-	°sëëgúu	saangu n-	sóogú °f-	°sëëgú f-	'shadow, shade'
*paní	péní	pëní f-	pani	póní, °pëní	pëní f-	'sleep' (n)
*kí(i)sí		°kíisíi †f-		kísí °f-	†kísí f-	'ocean'

Examples of animal nouns which are in f- in Ndut-Paloor but not NLS are listed in Table 89.

TABLE 89   Animal nouns reassigned to f- in Ndut-Paloor

PC	Noon	Laalaa	Saafi	Paloor[a]	Ndut	
*nand	nad	nad	nand	nan, nen °f-	°nen f-	'spider'
*suul	suul	suul	suur	°suul f-	°suul f-	'vulture'
*diñ	diñ	°deñ	diñ	diñ °f-	°diñ f-	'louse'
*cangín	cégín	cëgín	cangin	°cigin f-	°cígín, †céegín f-	'worm' (grub)

a   In Thornell et al. (2016a), animal nouns are generally given in the default class, and not f-. Thus this large-scale reassignment of animals to f- appears to be confined to Ndut and the northern Paloor-speaking area.

NOMINAL MORPHOLOGY

It is clear that there was a tendency for animals to take *f- agreement even when they did not contain the corresponding noun class prefix. This reassignment apparently began before the breakup of Proto-Cangin for certain nouns, and continued in Ndut-Paloor afterwards. The basis for this reassignment would have been in part the animals originally prefixed with *fa-. However it is notable that only two animal nouns are prefixed with fa- synchronically: 'cow' and 'antelope' in Ndut-Paloor, and none in NLS. While these are two somewhat prominent nouns (especially 'cow'), the particularly strong association between *f- and animals is somewhat unexpected if based only on them.

In each language there are a number of non-f-initial nouns that do not refer to animals, but take f- agreement. Noon examples include *cenon* 'nape,' *kaad* 'house,' and the borrowed nouns *coh* 'millet husk' and *kéet* 'paper.' Most of these contain a fossilized class prefix like *ca- or *pa-, for which see § 3.1.12 (note that most nouns in Table 88 contain one of these prefixes). In fact most nouns which can be reconstructed with a fossilized prefix are assigned to the f- agreement class in at least one modern language. Monosyllabic f- class nouns like the Noon ones mentioned above can generally be traced to disyllabic forms in Proto-Cangin (e.g. *kayand > kaad* 'house'). It is likely that the association between nouns with a frozen prefix and f- agreement is an incidental consequence of their being disyllabic. Table 90 considers all non-borrowed disyllabic nouns reconstructed to Proto-Cangin, whether prefixed like *mi-da* 'salt' or unprefixed like *ndangal* 'scorpion,' and counts the agreement classes used for these nouns across all five modern languages. For the purposes of this table Noon-Laalaa *n-* is considered a regular allomorph of the ∅/w- class agreement marker, and a few nouns taking *c-* or (in Saafi) *r-* or *n-* agreement are not represented.

TABLE 90   Agreement classes used for PC disyllabic nouns across all modern languages

Initial C	∅/w-	k-	m-	t-	p-	f-
*k	32	54	1	—	—	15
*f	15	—	1	—	—	19
*c	30	2	—	—	—	27
*t/p	23	7	—	4	9	18
*m	6	—	30	—	—	—
other	82	—	—	—	—	20
total	188	63	32	4	9	99

The status of *f-* is very different than for the other "alliterative" agreement classes. While the nouns taking *k-*, *m-*, *t-*, and *p-* agreement are overwhelmingly ones which begin with the alliterative consonant, the nouns taking *f-* agreement can begin in any consonant other than *m. When the alliterative cases are set aside (including f-initial nouns taking *f-* agreement), *f-* stands out as being the only class other than the default class commonly used for disyllabic nouns. For monosyllabic nouns this pattern does not hold. There are far fewer PC monosyllabic nouns which take *f-* agreement, and the few that do are almost all animals like **pe'* 'goat.'

The reason why disyllabic nouns were often assigned to the *f-* agreement class is not entirely clear, but the explanation likely involves the status of the **fV-* noun prefixes themselves. The large majority of Proto-Cangin singular nouns with a CV- prefix contained **kV-*, **fV-*, **mV-*, or **ca-*. The fossilized prefix **ca-* no longer corresponded with an active singular agreement class, but the others did (**k-*, **f-*, and **m-* respectively). The **kV-* and **mV-* prefixes on Proto-Cangin nouns were in general easily identifiable as prefixes, in the former case due to alternation with **tV-* in the plural, and in the later case due to the extremely strong semantic association with mass nouns (mostly liquids). However the **fV-* prefixes would have been less identifiable. They did not alternate in the plural, and taken as a whole nouns with these prefixes did not share any particular semantic property. As such, it may be that f-initial nouns taking **f-* agreement were thought of as unprefixed disyllabic roots, while k-initial and m-initial nouns taking **k-* and **m-* agreement were considered monosyllabic roots with a prefix. Because the large majority of historical roots are monosyllabic, **f-* would have been the only class outside of the default class to contain a significant number of roots that were considered disyllabic. The **f-* class then attracted other disyllabic nouns on a phonological basis, both in the case of other prefixed nouns when the prefix became frozen, and in the case of nouns which truly contained an unprefixed disyllabic root. Because so many animal nouns contained the frozen prefixes **ca-* or (less often) **pa-* or **fa-*, the **f-* class came to be associated with animals, and attracted some monosyllabic animals nouns.

3.1.7 *m-*

The *m-* class contains nouns referring to liquids and a few powders in the modern languages, and almost all of them are m-initial. All of the reconstructable **m-* class nouns (Table 91) are prefixed with **mV-* or begin with **m.

NOMINAL MORPHOLOGY   119

TABLE 91   Nouns in the *m- agreement class

PC	Noon	Laalaa	Saafi	Paloor	Ndut	
*ma-ɹúɓ	móoɓ, °músú m-	mësú m-	masuɓ m-	muluɓ °m-	muluɓ	'water'
*mi-sip	miip, °mesip m-	mesep m-	misip m-	°misib m-	misip m-	'sauce'
*miis	miis m-	miis m-	miis m-	miis m-	miis m-	'milk'
*mún	mún m-	mún m-	mun	mún m-	mún m-	'flour'
*mi-ɗa	meɗaa m-	meɗa m-	miɗa, meɗa m-	miraa, °mera m-	mira °m-	'salt'
*mi-sook	meek, °misook m-	mesook m-	misook m-		misook m-	'urine'
*mu-ɣon	moon c-	moon m-	muhun	°moon m-	†mun m-	'tear (crying)'
*mi-tuHuɽ̥	ˇmitoos m-	metoos m-	mituhuus m-			'saliva'
				muluc °m-	°muluc m-	'saliva'
*ma-púy	mópúy m-	mëpúy m-		°mëpúy m-		'pus'
*mV-leɣi?	maleey m-	melaay~melae m-	merey~mereh m-			'sand'
	°muluy m-	muluul m-				'sap'
(*maal)			maar	maal 'fog'	°maal	'dew'

In Laalaa there are some deverbal *m-* nouns in addition to 'saliva,' 'urine,' and
'sauce' (from the verbs *toos* 'spit,' *sook* 'urinate,' *sep* 'put sauce on dish') formed
by the prefixation of *mV-*: *mokop m-* 'palm wine' from *kop* 'tap palm tree,'
menaaw m- 'laundry' from *naaw* 'launder,' *mítík m-* 'dish/plate of food' from
tík 'cook,' and †*mi'an m-* 'beverage' from *an* 'drink.' The noun prefix can be
reconstructed as *ma-*, *mi-*, or *mu-* depending on the word. A few other liq-
uids/powders have been assigned to *m-* in the modern languages, notably *ñif m-*
'blood' in Saafi and Ndut-Paloor (Noon-Laalaa *ñif* is in the default class), and
Paloor *fëyúm °m-* 'fat/grease' (given in the default class by Thornell et al.) found
in *f-* or the default class in other languages. In addition, Saafi has *ndapalay m-*
'mud,' *paɗ m-* 'dirt,' and *puɗ m-* 'dust.' These were almost certainly not in *m-*
originally, being reassigned by semantic pressure. Saafi *muus* (as recorded in
Mbodj 1983 but not other sources) and Ndut *múus* 'cat' (as recorded by Doneux
but not Pichl) has been reassigned to *m-* due to its initial consonant, and likely
influenced by Wolof *muus m-* 'cat.'

3.1.8   *p-*

The *p-* agreement class is only active in Noon-Laalaa, but must be reconstructed to Proto-Cangin. All reconstructable nouns in the *p-* agreement class
(Table 92) have a prefix *pi-*.

120 CHAPTER 3

TABLE 92   Nouns in the *p- agreement class

PC	Noon	Laalaa	Saafi	Paloor	Ndut	
*pe-ɗe(e)m	peɗim p-	píɗim p-	peɗeem, °peɗem	pereem	°pereem	'tongue'
*ti/pi-soH	peoh p-, °tesoh t-	pesoh p-	tisoh	°tisoh	tisoh k-	'seeds'
*ti/pi-wiñ	piiñ, pewiñ p-	píiñ p-	tiwiñ	tiwiñ °k-	tiiñ k-	'metal, iron'
*pi-ɓil	piwil, ɓiwil	píil p-	piɓiir	°pihil		'lower abdomen'
*(pi-)síl	tíil t-, †píil p-	písíl p-	sir	síl 'tendon'	°síl	'vein'
*píim	píim f-	píim p/f-		°pím		'sorghum'
*pV-huɓ	tóoɓ t-, °puuɓ p-	póo p-		(huɓ)	(huɓ)	'leaf'
*pi-líkít	pílkët p-	pílkët p-		(°likit)		'thread'
*te/pe-he'	tee' t-, °pee' p-	†peª p-		°tehe' 'p. fiber'	†teh k- 'straw'	'palm midrib'
				°pi'in		'palm midrib'
*pV-ɣo	pooh p-	poo p-				'millet plant'

The other attested nouns in this agreement class are Noon *pëw*/°*pëwúu p-* 'palm pinna,' †*piik p-* 'clover,' and Laalaa †*píl p-* 'penis,' †*pínii p-* 'twine' (cf. *níh 'rope'). In Laalaa *pe-* forms a few deverbal nouns: *peheey p-* 'dream' (verb *heey*), *peyen p-* 'laugh' (verb *yen*), and *píhíy p-* 'hiccup' (verb *híy*). The noun prefix can be reconstructed as *pi-* (*pe-* before root *e). Unlike with *kV-* and *mV-*, there is no evidence for other prefix vowels. The *p-* class is used for long flexible objects, though 'metal' and the mass nouns 'seeds, sorghum' are also notable. For 'metal,' Soukka (2000: 64) notes that the Noon noun is mainly used for 'iron wire.' 'Seeds' and 'sorghum' are likely singulative backformations from original *t-* class collective nouns (cf. Padee Noon °*pohoo p-* 'millet seed' alongside °*tohoo t-* 'millet' from *to-ɣo*). The semantic association of *p-* with long, flexible objects is especially clear in the pairs *líkít* 'cotton,' *pi-líkít* 'thread,' and *huɓ* 'bark,' *pV-huɓ* 'leaf.' In a number of *p-* class nouns, the *t-* class plural form has been generalized to both numbers in one or more languages. Proto-Cangin *p-* was evidently a rather small class, which contributed to its loss in Saafi and Ndut-Paloor. When *p-* and *t-* were lost in Ndut-Paloor, some nouns originally in this class pair were assigned to the *k-* agreement class while retaining their original plural prefix.

3.1.9   *nj-*

The *j-* agreement class (Thiès Noon *nj-*) is a rare diminutive class in Noon-Laalaa, used for some *k-* class nouns in which *j-* replaces *k-* on the noun itself, and for 'finger' (Table 93).

NOMINAL MORPHOLOGY   121

TABLE 93   Noon and Laalaa nouns in the *j-* class

Noon j- noun	Diminutive of	Laalaa j- noun	Diminutive of	
janu	kanu k-	jano	kano k-	'calabash'
jetaa	ketaa k-	jeloo	keloo k-	'pot'
joku'	koɗ k-	jokoɗ	koɗ k-	'pestle'
		jëdí	këdí k-	'mortar'
jowu 'girl'	kowu k-			'child'
júlúŋ	kúlúŋ k-			'small pot/jug'
jokun	—	jokon	—	'finger'

Furthermore, there is a Noon prefix *ji-* (Thiès Noon *një-*; Lopis 1980: 142, Wane 2017: 45) that attaches to the full noun and forms diminutive nouns with *j-* agreement, though it is much rarer than diminutive *ku-/kë-*. Wane gives the examples *një-oomaa* 'small child,' *një-kot* 'small foot,' and *një-pënís* 'small horse.' Dieye (2015) notes that the Laalaa cognate prefix *je-* is used only for k-initial nouns, e.g. *je-kaan* 'little house.' Pichl (1981: 11) gives the Laalaa examples †*ji-kedek* 'little tree,' †*ji-kíiní* 'little ram,' and †*ji-ke* 'little branch.' The **nj-* class does not survive in Saafi, but the prefix is found in *njenoh~°njanoh* 'small calabash,' the diminutive of *kanoh* 'calabash.' This class does not exist in Ndut-Paloor. The class prefix is perhaps related to the adjective/verb meaning '(be) small' in all modern Cangin languages (Noon *jutuut*, Laalaa *jítúut*, Saafi *yisuut*, Paloor *jísúut*, Ndut °*yútúut*). Similar forms for 'small' appear in other Atlantic groups, but without the initial CV sequence, e.g. Wolof *tuut*. Based on the form of the Noon-Laalaa CV- prefix (*ji-/je-*) and the vowel change in Saafi *njenoh*, the vowel of the prefix can be tentatively identified as **i*. However recall that Laalaa has altered original diminutive **ku-* to *ke-*, so the evidence for reconstructing **i* in this prefix is somewhat weak. In Proto-Noon-Laalaa **njo-koɗ* 'little pestle' and **njo-kon* 'finger,' the vowel of the prefix was likely influenced by the root vowel. Palatal consonants as well as high vowels are cross-linguistically associated with diminutives, and diminutive morphology is subject to rapid renewal. As such, the prefix **nji-* (or **nju-*) could have easily been innovated at any point in the history of Cangin—it may be a Proto-Cangin innovation, or even a Proto-NLS innovation.

3.1.10   *t-*

In Noon-Laalaa, *t-* is the corresponding plural agreement class for singular nouns in the *k-*, *p-*, and *(n)j-* agreement classes, without exception in most dialects. Furthermore, singular nouns in these classes change their initial /k, p, (n)j/ to /t/ in the plural. Examples are shown in Table 94.

TABLE 94   Some Noon and Laalaa plurals in the *t*- class

Noon sg.	Noon pl.	Laalaa sg.	Laalaa pl.	
kanu k-	tanu t-	kano k-	tano t-	'calabash'
kedik k-	tedik t-	kedek k-	tedek t-	'tree'
kowu k-	towu t-	kuu k-	tuu t-	'child'
kumun k-	tumun t-	kuumun k-	tuumun t-	'nose'
jokun j-	tokun t-	jokon j-	tokon t-	'finger'
°puuɓ p-	°tuuɓ t-	póo p-	tóo t-	'leaf'

No alternations of this type have survived in Saafi or Ndut-Paloor. The regular singular/plural noun prefix alternations *kV~tV-, *pi~ti-, and perhaps *nji~ti- can be reconstructed to Proto-Cangin. Within Noon-Laalaa, there are some exceptional nouns that do not follow this pattern, especially in Northern Noon. Some Northern Noon *p*- class nouns are unchanged and take *c*- agreement in the plural, e.g. *piiñ p*- 'metal,' pl. *piiñ c*- (a plural *tiiñ t*- is possible but rarely used). For *pedim* 'tongue' the plural can be *tedim t*- or *pedim c*-. Pichl (1981: 13) notes two Laalaa *p*- class nouns that undergo no change in the plural: *pídĩm p*-/*c*- 'tongue(s)' and †*píl p*-/*c*- 'penis(es).' As seen in Table 92, a number of *p*-nouns in other dialects have had the *t*- plural generalized to both numbers in Northern Noon, and recall from § 3.1.8 that this same change has occurred for certain nouns in other languages, including Saafi and Ndut-Paloor in which the corresponding agreement class is no longer active. A few Northern Noon *k*-class nouns also have unchanged *c*- plurals, most notably *kúum k*-/*c*- 'honey(s),' but in general *k*- class nouns exhibit *t*- plurals, as do all *j*- class nouns except *joow~jowu* 'girl,' for which the plural is unchanged *joow~jowu* (with *t*- or *c*-agreement), perhaps to remain distinct from *toow~towu* 'children.'

A few non-plural nouns can be reconstructed with a prefix *tV-, listed in Table 95.

TABLE 95   Non-plural nouns with a prefix *tV-

PC	Noon	Laalaa	Saafi	Paloor	Ndut	
*to-ɣo	tooh, °tohoo t-	too t-	toho r-	too k-	too k-	'millet'
*ti-ix	téek, ˇ†teek	teek	tiik	tii k-	°tii, †téey	'name'

NOMINAL MORPHOLOGY

TABLE 95   Non-plural nouns with a prefix *tV- (cont.)

PC	Noon	Laalaa	Saafi	Paloor	Ndut	
*tV-úH	tóoh, °tóoh, †túuh			túh	†tú	'all'
*tu-(h)uy	túuy, °túuy, †túy	tuy, °tuuy	tuy, °tuuy			'hut, room'
*ɗa-(h)uy	ɗóoy, °ɗuuy	ɗoy 'among'	ɗooy			'inside'
				°tútab	†tútaab	'maize'

The noun *to-yo 'millet' is not simply the plural of *pV-yo 'millet plant,' as it is a collective noun referring to millet grain, and not multiple plants. It is likely that *t- originally had a collective as well as plural meaning, such that certain nouns (especially referring to grains/seeds) were in the class by default. Some additional collective nouns which contain this prefix are found in Paloor: tihi' k- 'sand' (from the root *-xeyi, cf. Noon kakeey f-, Saafi kekey 'dirt'), and tí'ín k- 'souna millet.' There are two reasons to believe that 'name' contained a class prefix *ti-. First, it is in the k- class in Paloor, which is reserved for nouns that were once prefixed with *kV-, *pV-, or *tV-. Second is the vowel correspondence, which could result from two short vowels in sequence, but not an original long vowel. The vowel correspondence also points to a prefix in NLS 'hut,' which likely has the same root as 'inside.' It will be seen in § 5.1.2 that Proto-Cangin *t was at best extremely rare at the beginning of native noun roots, as it had generally lenited to *s after an (often eroded) class prefix. As such, it is likely that any non-derived t-initial native noun contains the prefix *tV- historically.

In Noon, ti- is used as a semi-productive nominalizer in much the same way as ci- (see § 3.1.3).

(36) Noon nouns with the prefix ti-

Noon verb/adj.		Noon noun	
wo'	'speak/say/talk'	ti-wo' t-	'speech/talking'
kod	'cry'	ti-kod t-	'crying'
yeek	'sing'	ti-yeek t-	'singing'
yenaah	'funny'	ti-yenaah t-	'something funny'

In Saafi this prefix is not productive, but there is tibooñ 'grilled millet' from the verb booñ 'grill,' and tekeb 'stick' from keb 'fence w/ posts.' In Laalaa a few nouns

124   CHAPTER 3

are given with a prefix *te-*: †*te-wo t-* 'rumor' from *woo* 'say,' and *te-jëdoh-jëdoh*
'pretending to be sick' from *jëd* 'be sick.' The plural of the Noon-Laalaa diminutive prefix *ku-* (Noon)/*ke-* (Laalaa) is *tu-/te-*, and the plural of the less common
diminutive prefix *ji-* (Noon)/*je-* (Laalaa) is *ti-/te-*.

There is evidence for both **i and **u, but not **a, as the vowel of **tV-* in
Proto-Cangin. It is probable that the plural diminutive prefix forms **tu-* and **ti-*
existed in Proto-Cangin alongside singular **ku-* and **nji-* (and perhaps **nju-*),
matching the vowel of the singular prefix. The use of the nominalizer *ti-* in Noon
and the few nominalizations with *ti/te-* in Saafi and Laalaa suggest that **ti-* may
be original, often harmonizing to **tu-* before a round vowel.

3.1.11   *Saafi Innovations r- and nd-*

There are two agreement classes in Saafi that have no equivalent in other Cangin languages: *r-* and *nd-*. The origin of the first of these is the resegmentation of
a root-final /r/ due to the sporadic loss of word-final /r/ in polysyllabic forms.
Thus for *fisaa* 'chest' with a definite form *fisaa-r-i* 'the chest,' the unsuffixed
form would have been at an earlier time **fisaar*, confirmed by comparison with
Paloor *alaal* (from the root **-ɽaal*)—note that the Saafi word is given as †*fisar*
in Stanton (2011). Of the nine *r-* nouns given in Botne & Pouille (2016), four can
be explained by this resegmentation (Table 96).

TABLE 96   Sources of some Saafi *r-* class nouns

Saafi *r-* noun		Source
ngila'-r-i	'the scuffle hoe'	Ser. helaar, Wo. illeer
tangoo-r-i	'the hill'	Wo. tangor
yaɓkoo-r-i	'the old man'	yaɓ + Ser. o-koor 'man' (cf. Noon *ya'ɓu* 'old woman')
fisaa-r-i	'the chest'	PC **-ɽaal*, cf. Paloor *alaal*

Pouye (2015: 117) further gives *mango r-* 'mango' from Wolof *màngoro*, and
hoso r- 'voice' which in Botne & Pouille is *hosor* in the default class. With the
other nouns (*toho r-* 'millet,' *cekna(a) r-* 'fingernail/claw,' *finho r-* 'back,' *ɗuuku
r-* 'smoke,' and *soye r-* 'pot,' as well as *yino r-* 'one' and *mbahne r-* 'hat' in Pouye),
/r/ was extended as a hiatus filler. In *toho* 'millet,' *r-* may be an irregular development of the original class marker **t-*, but there is no evidence for a **t* > /r/
change elsewhere in Saafi.

The Saafi *nd-* class is small, and used almost exclusively for borrowings, all
of which either are or were vowel-final (Table 97).

NOMINAL MORPHOLOGY 125

TABLE 97   Sources of some Saafi *nd-* class nouns

Saafi *nd-* noun		Source
ɓasi nd-	'sorghum'	Ser. ɓasi, Wo. basi < Mandinka bási
jin nd-	'djinn'	Ser. jini, Wo. jinne < Ar. jinn
maalo nd-	'rice'	Ser. maalo < Bambara malo
tal nd-	'paved road'	Wo. tali
sak nd-	'bag'	Portuguese saco (perhaps French sac)
°dole nd-	'strength'	Wo. doole < Ar. dawla

However *nd-* is also used for a few other words like *Saafi* 'Saafi person' and in Mbodj (1983) °*ndamu* 'mother.' The origin of this class marker is quite mysterious, and no hint of it is found in other languages. There is a locative prefix **nd-*, but it is unlikely that this is the source of the Saafi class marker. The Saafi word *ndukun* 'finger' from the root **kun* has a prefix *ndu-*, which might be connected with the agreement class *nd-*. But it is unlikely that a prefix used on only the noun 'finger' would have been extended as an agreement marker for borrowings, while being lost as the agreement marker for 'finger' itself.

3.1.12   *Additional (Fossilized) Nominal Class Prefixes*
Some modern or reconstructable nouns appear to be prefixed with a class marker that does not correspond to one of the reconstructed agreement classes. Most of these nouns appear in the **f-* agreement class, which as discussed in § 3.1.6 attracted many nouns with a frozen prefix, likely due to a phonological association with disyllabic nouns. This section first discusses the most common of these prefixes, **ca-*, and then the rarer **pa-*, **a-*, **i-*, **su-*, **sa-*, and Saafi *ndu-*. The Proto-Cangin inventory of class prefixes was already rather reduced in comparison with more conservative Niger-Congo languages, and so it is likely that the prefixes identified in this section are the last remnants of earlier classes that had died out already in Proto-Cangin.

Remarkably, of all **c-initial nouns that can be reconstructed to Proto-Cangin, most are disyllabic or longer with **ca* in the first syllable. Recall that disyllabic roots are much rarer than monosyllabic roots in Proto-Cangin. With the likely exception of **caac~cec* 'grandparent,' these nouns, shown in Table 98, all contain a fossilized class prefix **ca-*.

TABLE 98   Proto-Cangin *c-initial nouns

PC	Noon	Laalaa	Saafi	Paloor	Ndut	
*ca-oɣ	cooh f-	coh f-	cooh	caa' °f-	°ca', †caa' f-	'elephant'
*caafú	cëw, °cëwuu	cëëfú f-	caafu	cóofú °f-	°cëëf k-	'fly' (bug)
*cangín	cégín (f-)	cëgín f-	cangin	°cigin f-	°cígín, †céegín f-	'worm' (grub)
*caangínV	céengënii	cëgëní f-	caangin	°cegina f-	°cagín, †cégín f-	'large bird sp.'
*ca ...	cooginaah (f-)	cogona f-	cekna~cakna r-	cigilaan	°cigilaan	'nail/claw'
*ca ...	ˇcadam f-	†cadúm f-	candoom	°cëdúm	†caróm f-	'price'
*ca(h/ɣ)VnV	cóoní	°coonee		coona	†coona f-	'soul'
*case?		caase f-	case 'squirrel'	cafe'	†casé f-	'porcupine'
*caal		caal f-	caar		caal f-	'antelope'
*cangayo?		°caagayuu		°cagayo f-	†cagoy f-	'large bird sp.'
*caɓín			caɓin	céen, °ciin	céhín, °céyín	'moon'
*cafay			cafay n-	cafay	†cofej k-	'young girl'
*ca(h/ɣ)úc?		cóoc f-		°cooc		'breakfast'
*caɓol		°cawol			†caal f-	'pelican'
*cangíndo(ɣ)	°cígídóo	cëgídóh f-	°ciɓndo'			'panther'
*cambVnaɣ	cobinaah	cobona f-	caɓnaah			'armpit'
*ca ...				caluɓ °f-	caloɓ f-	'hare'
*caac~cec	caac, cic	caaca	caac	caac, cec	caac, cic f-	'grandparent'

Cognates from other Niger-Congo languages confirm that *ca- is not part of the root for 'elephant' or 'fly' (see Appendix 2). It is notable that so many of the nouns reconstructed with *ca- refer to animals—note also Laalaa *caden f-* 'ant sp.,' *caabaa f-* 'rabbit,' *caan f-* 'monkey,' *cëlbíñ f-* 'hedgehog,' °*calaf* 'red-billed quelea bird,' °*cëdúud* 'fishing owl,' and Saafi *cahuy* 'hippopotamus.' This animal class prefix *ca- is almost certainly etymologically distinct from the plural/mass/abstract class marker *ca- (see §5.2.2 for potential etymological connections in other Atlantic groups). The possibility cannot be excluded that some of the nouns in Table 98 were originally plural forms that were extended to both numbers (cf. *ɓi-o' 'person' and *ɓe-reɓ 'woman,' originally plural forms as discussed in §3.1.4). However the relative semantic coherence of the *ca- prefix on count nouns makes this plural-origin explanation unlikely, and recall that there is no evidence for plural nouns being prefixed with *ca- at the Proto-Cangin stage. Further evidence that these nouns all contain a prefix is the fact that native verb roots are never *c-initial. It seems that originally, *c was not a possible root-initial consonant, and the only native source for word-initial /c/ in Cangin languages is an original *c-initial class prefix. As will be discussed in §5.1.2, earlier **c became Cangin *s, and the *c-initial prefixes likely come from earlier **j-initial prefixes based on outside cognates.

Nouns with the fossilized class prefixes *pa-, *i-, *a-, *su-, *sa-, and Saadi *ndu-* are shown in Table 99. For most of these, the prefix can be identified by its

NOMINAL MORPHOLOGY

alternation with a different prefix in another language. There is evidence for segmenting the prefix in *pa-ní 'sleep' based on *neey 'sleep (v),' likely from earlier *ní-oy containing the applicative suffix, which sometimes forms a verb from a noun root (e.g. Noon *lah-oh* 'spend the rainy season somewhere' from *lah* 'rainy season'). For other nouns, segmenting a prefix is more speculative.

TABLE 99   Nouns with other fossilized class prefixes

PC	Noon	Laalaa	Saafi	Paloor	Ndut	
*i/fa-noɣ	enoh f-	enoh f-	inoh	fana' f-	fana f-	'cow'
*(a-)roɣ	atoh (f-)	atoh	atoh °f-	la'	la', †ala	'stone, rock'
*fV/a-ṛaal	ˇfasaa f-		fisaa r-	alaal	°araal	'chest' (thorax)
*ki/su-pi	kipii k-	sope'	kipi 'earring'	°kipi k-	supi	'ring'
*kun	jokun j-	jokon j-	ndukun	kun	°kun	'finger'
*(sa/ca-)pusa	sapuus, †sabës	sapos	pos	capus	†capós	'flower'
*ca/sa-lngis	celngis c-				†selgis f-	'steamed millet granules'
		†salaak c-b				'possessions'
*paní	péní	pëní f-	pani	póní, °pëní	pëní f-	'sleep' (n)
*paaní	péeníi f-	pëëní f-	paani f-/n-	póoní °f-	pëëní f-	'monkey'
*paangí	péegíi (f-)	paagii f-	paangi f-/n-			'grass'
*pambi	pabi, †pambe f-	pabe f-	pambi f-	(paan)	(paan †f-)	'chicken'
*payVm	payum	payamun	payuum	(°pacool)	(†pacoli)	'inlaw'
*ku/pa-laaɓc	†kolaɓ		koraaɓ	°palaab f-		'brush fire'
*pa-loomd		paloom f-		°palom f-		'antelope sp.'
				°pakale f-		'rat'
				°pakaaf f-		'wild dog'

a   ca- in Ndut-Paloor *capus* is the distinct class prefix *ca-
b   Derived from *laak* 'have'; Pichl (1981: 13) identifies *sa-* as a class prefix synchronically based on this word
c   This root is borrowed from Sereer *raaɓ*, which further confirms that Paloor *pa-* is a prefix in this word
d   Likely borrowed into Proto-Cangin from Wolof *baroom*; even so the initial CV- seems to have been treated as a prefix, given that the Paloor word has non-initial stress.

The prefix *pa- is the most widely distributed of these, being found in a number of words for animals. Two of the Paloor *pa*-initial nouns (°*pakale* and °*palom*) belong to the small set of nouns with second-syllable stress, and historically most such nouns contain a CV- prefix.

3.1.13   Prefix Resegmentation
In a few words the class prefix of the post-nominal definite marker has been reinterpreted as part of the preceding root (Table 100). Most examples involve the *k-* class.

128   CHAPTER 3

TABLE 100   The prefix on the definite marker resegmented as part of the root

PC	Noon	Laalaa	Saafi	Paloor	Ndut	
*(ku-)(h)oomaaɣ	oomaa(h)	oomah	komaak			'child'
*(n-)ku-ɓú	kúuɓ k-, °kuvu	kúu k-	nguɓu n-	ɓúk	ɓúk	'mouth'
*ku-ɓo	kowu k-, †kowo	kuu k-	kuɓu k-	kook 'baby'	këë, †kú k-	'child' (son/daughter)
*fi-ɗaas	feɗaaf, ⁻†faɗaaf f-	feɗaaf f-	fiɗaaf	firaas f-		'corpse'

The reanalysis simply involves reinterpreting a morpheme boundary—e.g.
*koo-k-a > kook-a for Paloor 'baby.' In Ndut-Paloor ɓúk 'mouth,' the original pre-
fix has furthermore been eroded, such that the final /k/ is the only remaining
indication of the noun's original class. There is also Saafi yaaɓ 'men' (from
*yaal ɓ-) mentioned in § 3.1.4, and in Thiès Noon Lopis (1980: 23) notes that
†pënëf is a variant of †pënës f- 'horse.' In both †pënëf 'horse' and NLS 'corpse,' a
sequence /s-f/ has been reduced to /f/.

For a few borrowed nouns in certain languages, the agreement class is influenced by the initial consonant of the noun, e.g. Noon kúdú 'spoon' optionally in
the k- agreement class (also Laalaa †kúdú k- given by Pichl) from Wolof kuddu,
Laalaa †pun p- 'ground tobacco' from Wolof póon, and Ndut °múus m- 'cat,'
found in Wolof, Sereer, and various Mande languages of the area. It could be
said that the root-initial consonant has been reinterpreted as a class prefix in
these few words, though none of them alternate. It is possible that a similar process had taken place for some native unprefixed nouns already in Proto-Cangin,
most notably *fen f- 'hair,' in which *f is likely the root-initial consonant based
on outside cognates. This process is likely responsible for keeñ 'liver' being in
the k- class in Laalaa and (as reported by Pouye) Saafi, since based on comparative data the word-initial /k/ is part of the root (cf. Sereer unprefixed xeeñ,
Bainunk *bu-kiiñ). However, because among borrowings this sort of class reassignment is seen for only a few nouns, it seems that non-etymological class
reassignment based on the root-initial consonant was in fact extremely rare,
and there is no reason to assume that it played any large role in the history of
Cangin.

3.1.14   *Additional CV- Agreement Prefixes*

While all Cangin languages use C- agreement markers, only Noon-Laalaa uses
CV- agreement prefixes, the most common being *Ci-* (Noon) or *Ce-* (Laalaa)
used in adjective/numeral agreement. Noon-Laalaa has two additional CV-
agreement prefixes. The first is the "associative" prefix *Cuu-* meaning 'belonging
to or having to do with NOUN.' An example from Noon is given in (37).

NOMINAL MORPHOLOGY

(37) baayfii fii fuuyoo, faa fuu-Jigaan   (Noon: 028)
      baay-f-ii   *f-ii*   *f-uu-yoo*   *f-aa*
      dog-CL-DEF.PROX CL-DEM.PROX CL-ASSOC-1S CL-DEF.DIST
      f-uu-J.
      CL-ASSOC-J.
      'this dog is mine, that one is Jegaan's'

The associative prefix is often used without an overt head noun, as in Noon
ɓuu-fu 'your people/your family.' Some of these constructions with the associative prefix have become lexicalized, e.g. Noon-Laalaa *ɓuu-kaad* 'family' (*kaad*
'house'), Laalaa *ɓuu-hëët* 'ancestors' (*hëët* 'long ago'), and Noon *cuu-kím* 'breakfast,' *cuu-noh* 'lunch,' and ˇ*cuu-níin* 'supper' (*kím* 'morning,' *noh* 'sun,' *níin*
'evening'). Pouye (2015: 92) notes a Saafi prefix *cu-* meaning 'pertaining to'
which is cognate with Noon-Laalaa *cuu-*. In Wolof, Kobès (1869: 84) records an
equivalent construction with pre-nominal *Cu-*, e.g. *bu-Peer* 'something belonging to Pierre.' This construction is apparently no longer used in standard Wolof.
The Cangin construction may have been influenced by the Wolof one, but it is
possible that it was present in Proto-Cangin.

  The second prefix *Cu-* is used on ordinal numbers, as in the Noon example
(38).

(38) bíyaa wu-kanak-waa   (Noon: 016)
      bís-aa   *w-u-kanak=w-aa*
      day-DEF.DIST CL-ORD-two=CL-DEF.DIST
      'the second day'

Ordinal numbers in Ndut-Paloor and Saafi are unprefixed. There is no apparent source for grammaticalizing this prefix *Cu-*, and nothing similar is found in
surrounding languages. As such there is no reason to preclude its presence in
Proto-Cangin, especially as Ndut-Paloor and Saafi are prone to losing original
agreement prefixes.

3.1.15 *Non-nominal Class Prefixes: nd-, d-, w-*
In each Cangin language, certain prefixes appear on determiner/pronominal
bases to indicate a place, time, or manner. With the exception of a set of *di-*
prefixed locative nouns in Noon (see below), no nouns trigger agreement with
these prefixes, but because they appear in the same position as the nominal
class agreement prefixes, they can be regarded as part of the noun class system. Examples of demonstrative bases with the Noon prefix *d-* are shown in
Table 101.

130   CHAPTER 3

TABLE 101   Noon demonstratives prefixed with *d-*

Noun with demonstrative		Locative/manner/temporal demonstrative	
iñii yii	'this thing'	dii	'here' or 'like this'
iñii yiima	'this thing right here'	diima	'now'
iñaa yaa	'that thing'	daa	'there' or 'like that'
iñaa yaama	'that thing right there'	daama	'(right) there'
iñum yum,	'that thing by you'	duma	'(right) there (by you)'
iñum(m)a	'the thing right by you'		
iñaa yúu	'that thing over there'	dúu	'over there'
iñaa yúune	'that thing way over there'	dúune	'way over there'

The non-nominal prefixes of each language are given in Table 102.

TABLE 102   Non-nominal prefixes in each language

	Prefix	Meaning	Demonstrative/pronominal forms
Noon:	d- (†nd-)	place	all demonstratives, °*da/di* 'there'
	d- (†nd-)	manner	*dii* 'like this,' *daa* 'like that'
	d- (†nd-)	time	*diima* 'now'
	w-	time	*waa, wii* 'when (subordinator)'
	*ɗ-	manner	°*da* 'thus'
Laalaa:	d-	place	all demonstratives, *da/di* 'there'
	d-	manner	*da* 'thus'
	d-	time	*daa* 'when (subordinator),' *déen* 'now'
	*ɗ-	manner	°*da* 'thus'
Saafi:	nd-	place	all demonstratives
	nd-	manner	*ndaa* 'thus'
	w-	time	*wa, wi* 'when (subordinator)'
	ɗ-	manner	*ɗaa* 'that way'
Paloor[a]:	d-	place	all demonstratives
	d-	manner	*di* 'how (subordinator)' *dii* 'how (adverb)'
	ɗ-	manner	all demonstratives
Ndut:	d-	place	all demonstratives
	ɗ-	manner	all demonstratives

a   In D'Alton the meaning of these two prefixes *d-* and *ɗ-* is reversed. This may be a dialectal
    difference, but D'Alton often transcribes implosives as egressives and vice versa.

NOMINAL MORPHOLOGY   131

For Proto-Cangin, the prefixes *nd- 'locative (and perhaps manner),' *d- 'manner,' and *w- 'temporal' can be reconstructed.

All languages use *nd- as the locative prefix, and this can be securely reconstructed to Proto-Cangin. In Noon-Laalaa, the prefix di-/de- can be used on adjectives to form adverbs as part of its function as a manner prefix.

(39) Noon and Laalaa adverbs prefixed with di-/de-

Noon		Laalaa	
di-jówí'	'well'	de-hëɓí'	'well'
di-yóoɓí'	'easily'	de-mëëñí'	'for a long time'
di-gaawí'	'quickly'	de-íiní'	'hard/strongly'

In Noon there is also di-liis 'elsewhere' from the adjective liis 'other' with the locative prefix. It is even possible to use the Noon prefix di- on locative nouns like di-ñamaah 'eating place' from ñam 'eat,' equivalent to unprefixed ñamaah. At least in the Padee dialect (Soukka 2000: 71), these nouns show d- class agreement, as in °di-neehaaddaa 'the place to sleep' from neeh 'sleep.' From this Noon use of di- as a noun prefix, a CV- noun prefix *ndV- can be tentatively reconstructed to Proto-Cangin.

The manner prefix d- is productive in Ndut-Paloor, and survives in Saafi daa 'that way' and Noon-Laalaa °da 'thus,' and as such can be reconstructed to Proto-Cangin. The locative prefix *nd- has expanded in usage considerably in Noon-Laalaa, taking over the function of the manner prefix *d- (also in Saafi ndaa 'thus') and also acquiring a temporal meaning. It is possible that the original function of *nd- included some non-locative meanings, but since it is only completely productive on determiner bases with a locative interpretation in each language, this must be its basic meaning.

The few words listed in Table 103 appear to contain a frozen prefix *ndV- or *dV-. In most cases, the vowel of the prefix was *a. Oddly, *dV- appears to have a locative meaning in these words.

TABLE 103   Words containing a frozen prefix *ndV- or *dV-

PC	Noon	Laalaa	Saafi	Paloor	Ndut	
*nda-anax yaɣ	daaŋkeeh, °daaŋkah	dankeh, °daaŋkeah	ndaŋkiyaah			'ten' (*'at two hands')

132   CHAPTER 3

TABLE 103   Words containing a frozen prefix *ndV- or *dV- (cont.)

PC	Noon	Laalaa	Saafi	Paloor	Ndut	
*nda/ɗa-(h)um	ɗóom, °ɗuum	ɗom		doom	†dom	'not yet'
*ɗa-fuk/x	ɗook	ɗook	ɗafuk			'above/over'
*ɗa-(h)uy	ɗóoy, °ɗuuy	ɗoy 'among'	ɗooy			'inside'
*ɗi-sik	ɗiik ~ ɗesk- °ɗekat		ɗisik	(ɗíkë, °tíke)	(tígë)	'place' (n) 'place' (n)

The temporal prefix *w- can be reconstructed at least for Noon-Laalaa-Saafi, though it does not appear in Ndut-Paloor. Since it is homophonous with the default class marker w-, this temporal prefix may have originally been part of a noun phrase headed by a noun in the default class with temporal reference (i.e. 'that time')—however the resemblance may be coincidental. A corresponding noun prefix *wV- is found on three temporal adverbs, shown in Table 104.

TABLE 104   Temporal adverbs containing a prefix *wV-

PC	Noon	Laalaa	Saafi	Paloor	Ndut	
*kíiɽ (kV-híiɽ)	kíis k-	kíis k-	kiis k-	kíil	kíil †k-	'year'
*wu-(h)íiɽ	wíis	†wís	woyis			'this year'
*wa/wo-te	wati	wate	woti	wate, °watey f-	wote	'today'
*wu-tuɓa	wutuwaa	wotoa, °watoa	wotɓa			'yesterday'

In 'this year' the prefix *wu- can be segmented from the root, but in the other two the segmentation of a class prefix is speculative (though a connection between *wV-te and Wolof tey 'today' is likely, especially given Khodaba Paloor °watey). The use of a unique class prefix for temporal adverbs is also found in the Bainunk-Kobiana-Kasanga family (*jiN-).

Two other non-nominal prefixes can potentially be identified in NLS, though it is doubtful that they originated as class prefixes in Proto-Cangin. The first is *ng-, as seen in the general-purpose preposition *nga (Saafi nga, Thiès Noon ngë, other Noon-Laalaa ga). There are at least two structures that justify the segmentation of ng- as a non-nominal class prefix. First, in Laalaa both ga and gi exist as prepositions, sensitive to distance from the speaker. These are seemingly built on the pronominal bases CL-a and CL-i. The fact that this distinction

NOMINAL MORPHOLOGY

is not made in Noon or Saafi suggests that *gi* is a Laalaa innovation, made either in analogy with the pronouns CL-*a* and CL-*i*, or under the influence of the equivalent Wolof prepositions *ca* and *ci*. Second, in Noon the interrogative word CL-*ada* 'where' agrees with the subject in class, but can also appear as *gada* without class agreement.

(40) fa en gada?   (Noon: 010)
     f-a   *en gada*
     CL-PRO be where
     'where is it?'

(41) fada fa?   (Noon: 010)
     f-ada   *f-a*
     CL-where CL-PRO
     'where is it?'

Thus, *g-* is in alternation with the class prefixes in 'where.' However historically, *gada* is simply the preposition *ga* followed by a pronoun *d-a* containing the locative prefix. Noon class agreement in CL-*ada* 'where' is from the juxtaposition of a CL-*a* pronoun with the locative pronoun *d-a*. This pattern is not employed in other languages for 'where' (Laalaa uses *de*, Saafi *nde*, and Ndut-Paloor *di*(*h*) without class agreement). There is thus no reason to suspect that the preposition **nga* contains a morpheme boundary of any sort historically. However, it seems that *g-* has been analogically segmented and extended in Padee Noon, where *ˇgi-liis* 'of/about another thing' (taking *g-* agreement) is used.

The other potential non-nominal class prefix is *n-*, based on the interrogative word *na*(*h*) 'how' (Noon-Laalaa *na*, Saafi *nah*). Recall that the Noon-Laalaa question words *ya* 'what' and *ɓa* 'who' are simply CL-*a* pronouns containing a class prefix. If *na* 'how' is analyzed in this way, *n-* can be taken as a manner class prefix. This can be compared with the manner class prefix *n-* used in both Wolof and Sereer. However the segmentation of *na* 'how' is extremely speculative—there is no reason to believe that it is truly based on the pronoun CL-*a*, and furthermore the manner class prefix **d-* (as used in Ndut-Paloor *di*(*h*) 'how') must already be reconstructed to Proto-Cangin.

3.1.16 *Historical Status of Noun Prefixes*
In Proto-Cangin, all nouns in the **k-*, **p-*, **nj-*, **t-*, and **m-* agreement classes were marked with an alliterative prefix, as were many if not most nouns in the **f-* agreement class, and some nouns in **c-*, including all deverbal nouns in this

134   CHAPTER 3

agreement class. The status of the noun prefix *n- in Proto-Cangin is not totally clear, since it had likely already fused with the root-initial consonant, resulting in prenasalized stops before some consonants and deleting before others. The greatest question regarding the CV- prefixes on nouns is the identity of the vowel in each prefix. There is certainly evidence for contrastive vowel qualities in class prefixes, as in modern Laalaa *ka-* used for infinitives versus *ke-* used for languages. Within the *f-*, *m-*, and *k-* classes, different vowels can be reconstructed for the CV- prefix depending on the noun. In some cases the vowel appears to be influenced by the quality of the root vowel. However especially in the *k-* class, the root vowel is independent of the prefix vowel for most nouns, e.g. *ka-no(ɣ)* 'calabash,' *ko-yo* 'child,' and *ki-noH* 'waist,' all with the same root vowel. For *k-* there is evidence from the modern languages for reconstructing separate prefixes *ka-*, *ku-*, and *ki-*, but for *m-* and *f-* as well as diminutive *nj-* and plural *t-* it is difficult to know whether the different vowel qualities that can be reconstructed for the CV- prefix on nouns are indicative of multiple originally contrastive class prefixes, or simply the variable assimilation of the vowel of a single prefix to the following lexical root. For *f-*, the existence of contrastive *fa-* and *fi-* on nouns is likely, but for *m-*, *t-* and *nj-* there is no compelling evidence for multiple contrastive noun prefixes. For *p-*, *ɓ-*, and *c-* there is only good evidence for reconstructing *pi-*, *ɓi-*, and *ca-* on nouns. There is a strong tendency for *u and *i in prefixes to become *o and *e before a following mid vowel, but exceptions exist. It is also possible that prefix *u, *i had become +ATR *ú, *í before a +ATR root vowel already in Proto-Cangin. Taking this allomorphy into account, only a three-way vowel contrast between *a, *i~e~í, and *u~o~ú exists in reconstructed class prefixes.

   In modern Noon, there is a distinction between active prefixes like diminutive *ku-* and deverbal *ci-* and "frozen" prefixes like in *meɗaa m-* 'salt' and *feyaaŋ f-* 'bed'. The active prefixes are not part of the stress domain of the noun, are not subject to ATR harmony, and do not trigger intervocalic allophones of root-initial consonants, whereas the frozen prefixes are given stem-initial stress, are subject to ATR harmony, and trigger intervocalic allophones of following consonants. Compare Noon *ki-ɓít* [ki.ˈɓít] 'to be heavy' containing the active infinitive prefix with *kíwíi* [ˈkí.wíi] 'fire' (from *ki-ɓí*) containing a frozen prefix. The behavior of active CV- prefixes in Padee and Thiès Noon as well as Laalaa is not treated in detail in the existing literature, but they seem to function just as in Northern Noon. Wane (2017: 19) notes that the infinitive prefix does not trigger the voicing of voiceless stops in Thiès Noon, and in Padee Noon and Laalaa the implosives are unlenited after an active prefix, e.g. Laalaa *ke-ɓof k-* 'cough' from the verb *ɓof*. In Paloor, D'Alton (1983: 125–142) reports that while most nouns receive initial stress, others (about 5% of collected nouns) are stressed

NOMINAL MORPHOLOGY

on the second syllable. Most of the Paloor nouns with second-syllable stress contain an original CV- class prefix.[3] Thus there is strong evidence that Cangin class prefixes were historically unstressed, which helps to explain why prefixes had only three contrastive vowels, and these vowels were often subject to influence from the root vowel in individual Cangin languages. It is likely that already by the Proto-Cangin period, some class prefixes had lost their phonological status as prefixes in certain nouns, being reinterpreted as part of the noun stem and receiving stem-initial stress.

In Proto-Cangin, a number of CV- class prefixes had a derivational function, just as in modern Noon-Laalaa. At least the prefixes in Table 105 were used with a derivational function.

TABLE 105   Class prefixes with a derivational function in Proto-Cangin

*ki-	infinitive/deverbal, language
*ka-	infinitive/deverbal
*ku-, *tu-	diminutive sg., pl.
*nji-, *ti-	diminutive sg., pl. (perhaps NLS only)
*ca-	deverbal
*ti-	deverbal
*ɓi-	groups of people, perhaps indefinite plural
*mV-	deverbal liquids (likely unproductive)
*pi-	deverbal (likely unproductive)

For nouns more generally, prefixes were quite common in Proto-Cangin—certainly more so than in any modern Cangin language. The number of reconstructed Proto-Cangin nouns (not counting those only found in NLS) with different prefixes is shown in Table 106. The count for *n- includes all reconstructed nouns with an initial prenasalized stop.

TABLE 106   Number of reconstructed nouns containing each class prefix

Ø	n-	kV-	ca-	fV-	mV-	pi-	ɓi-	tV-	pa-	a-	njV-	su-	sa-	i-	y-
140	33	31	16	14	8	7	5	4	4	2	1	1	1	1	1

---

3   The converse is however not true, which points to a general stress shift to the initial syllable in Paloor (cf. Noon-Laalaa frozen prefixes), such that most original prefixes are now stressed as if they were root-initial.

136   CHAPTER 3

Nine of these prefixed nouns can be reconstructed with two possible prefixes
(e.g. *i-noy or *fa-noy 'cow'), and so the total number of reconstructed prefixed nouns is 120, versus 140 unprefixed nouns. This can be compared with
111/519 Laalaa nouns in Dieye's lexicon which contain any sort of etymological
prefix other than *n- (the ratio is even lower for all other Cangin languages).
The phonological status of these prefixes ("frozen" or not) can often not be
determined with any certainty, but it is significant that close to half of reconstructable Proto-Cangin nouns contain a class prefix.

3.1.17 *Historical Status of Class Agreement*
The modern Cangin languages differ markedly in the degree to which elements
agree with the head noun in class. Noon-Laalaa has the most extensive system,
with definite markers, demonstratives, adjectives, and pronouns (among other
targets) showing full class agreement.

(42) Noon and Laalaa agreement with the head noun

Noon	Laalaa	
enoh-f-ii	enoh-f-ii	'the cow'
enoh fi-yaanaaw	enoh fe-yaanaaw	'a white cow'
enoh-f-ii f-ii	enoh-f-ii f-ii	'this cow'
f-a	f-a	'it' (referring to a cow)

Ndut-Paloor and Saafi show agreement only on the suffixed determiners.

(43) Paloor (lack of) agreement with the head noun
　　 koy-k-a　　　　'the child'
　　 koy yaal　　　 'a male child'　　　　　　　　　　　　　　　(d'A. 159)
　　 koy-k-a bee　 'this child'　　　　　　　　　　　　　　　　(d'A. 186)
　　 bee　　　　　 'this one' (referring to any singular entity)

(44) Saafi (lack of) agreement with the head noun
　　 pam-f-i　　　 'the chicken'　　　　　　　　　　　　　　　(B.P. 83)
　　 pambi yin　　 'a small chicken'　　　　　　　　　　　　　(Mb. 196)
　　 pam-f-ii　　　 'this chicken'
　　 w-a　　　　　 'it' (referring to any non-human singular entity)

Saafi does employ the markers *w-/c-* and *y-/ɓ-* on a number of non-suffixed
agreement targets like demonstrative pronouns, but here agreement is based

NOMINAL MORPHOLOGY

on the human/non-human and singular/plural status of the referent, not the class of the noun that the pronoun stands in for. The adjective agreement prefix *Ci- is lost in Saafi and Ndut-Paloor, but appears to be frozen in *wi-liir̥ 'other'; Noon Ci-liis, Saafi wiriis, Paloor yilil.

Noon-Laalaa as well as Saafi exhibit definite agreement between a noun and modifying adjectives—a phenomenon which is rather rare cross-linguistically. An identical definite marker to that on the noun must appear after the modifying adjective/numeral phrase.

(45) Definite agreement in Noon-Laalaa-Saafi
     Noon: pénís-**c-ii** ci-yaanaaw=**c-ii**   (049)[4]
     Laalaa: pënís-**c-ii** ce-yaanaaw=**c-ii**   (adapt. Di. 134)[5]
     Saafi: pans-**c-i** yaanow-**c-i**   (Mb. 195)
          'the white horses'

In at least Noon, adjective phrases can be larger than just the adjective, as with *néekí' baay* 'afraid of dogs' in example (69) given in §3.4.2. For these larger adjective phrases, the agreeing definite determiner appears after the entire phrase, and thus must be considered a clitic. The status of these agreeing definite determiners (suffix vs. clitic) in Laalaa and Saafi is not made clear in the literature. In Saafi the phenomenon of definite agreement has received hardly any attention, and the status of agreement markers other than plural *c-* is unclear. Mbodj (1983: 195) mentions that there is full class agreement for post-adjectival determiners, but only provides examples for the singular ∅ and plural *c-* agreement classes. The only examples in Pouye (2015: 273) of adjective agreement with a noun in another class involve *kofooc k-* 'needle.' In these examples, the post-adjectival determiner does not show class agreement, e.g. *kofooc-k-i yin-i* 'the little needle.' Definite agreement provides the only environment in which the default class marker *w-* appears before a definite marker in Noon-Laalaa (*w-* is not used in Saafi definite agreement).

(46) Noon-Laalaa definite agreement in the default singular class
     Noon: yoon-aa wi-yaak=**w-aa**   (049)
     Laalaa: yoon-aa we-yaakaak=**w-aa**   (Di. 97)
          'the big field'

---

4 As animals are generally treated as animate in Northern Noon (see the discussion before example (12)), the phrase *péníscii bi-yaanaaw-bii* is preferred; however agreement with *c-* on all targets is also acceptable.

5 This is an adaptation of Dieye's example *pe'fii fe yaanaaw fii* 'the white goat.'

In the Saafi definite agreement pattern, all suffixed determiners (including demonstratives, which also impart definiteness on the noun) are obligatorily repeated after a modifying adjective or numeral, as with the proximal demonstrative -*ii* in example (47).

(47) kurcii kanakcii   (Saafi: Po. 160)
kur-c-ii   *kanak-c-ii*
village-CL.PL-DEM.PROX two-CL.PL-DEM.PROX
'these two villages'

Definite agreement operates in a more limited capacity in Ndut and Paloor. In Khodaba Paloor, there is no definite agreement with the proximal (seemingly most basic) definite marker -*a*, but there is with the middle-distance definite marker -*e* and distal definite marker -*in*. However the class prefix is not repeated on the adjective in definite agreement.

(48) Khodaba Paloor definite agreement   (d'A. 303)
pënís-f-a suul   'the black horse' (proximal)
pënís-f-in suul-in   'the black horse' (distal)
faam-f-e has-e   'the new house' (middle distance)

Thornell et al. (2016: 73) report agreement only with -*ee* (in fact a demonstrative in these dialects), but not with -*a* or -*in*. In Ndut, only one copy of the definite marker appears at the end of the noun phrase (if no demonstrative is present), but the "associative marker" -*i* appears on all non-final nominal elements. The class marker appears only immediately after the suffixed noun.

(49) kudki 6ídë   (Ndut: Mo. 48)
kud-k-i   *6ít-a*
pestle-CL-AM heavy-DEF
'the heavy pestle'

However, with plural nouns the plural marker *y~C* does appear on adjectives as well as the head noun.

(50) kuddi 6íttí éeyëyí yeh   (Ndut: Mo. 61)
kud-y-i   *6ít-y-i*   *éeyë-y-i*   *y-eh*
pestle-PL-AM heavy-PL-AM three-PL-AM PL-DEM.PROX
'these three heavy pestles'

NOMINAL MORPHOLOGY

Synchronically the Ndut phenomenon should probably not be seen as definite agreement, but it may have evolved from an earlier definite agreement pattern.

Proto-Cangin nominal agreement was likely quite similar to the modern Noon-Laalaa pattern, with agreement breaking down in Saafi and Ndut-Paloor. In other Niger-Congo noun class systems, adjectives (if they exist) are one of the most common targets of agreement, including in Sereer and Fula (Wolof has no adjectives). Thus it is almost certain that the adjective agreement prefixes of Noon-Laalaa can be traced back to Proto-Cangin. In the modern languages these are of a shape *Ci-* in Noon and *Ce-* in Laalaa, suggesting a segmentable C- class prefix and V- prefixal base. However, historically these CV- agreement prefixes are likely not segmentable, instead being ultimately the same as the CV- prefixes on nouns. At some Pre-Cangin stage, there was probably a near-complete match between the prefix on the noun and the prefix on the adjective, as is often the case in more conservative Niger-Congo class systems. Thus, for the noun prefixes **ku-* and **ka-*, these same two distinct prefixes would have appeared as agreement markers on the adjective. At the Proto-Cangin stage it is possible that this fuller agreement pattern persisted, but it is likely that the vowel *i had been generalized to all adjective agreement prefixes as in modern Noon-Laalaa. Class-agreeing demonstratives and pronominal forms would have also been present in Proto-Cangin. Definite agreement must be reconstructed for Proto-Noon-Laalaa-Saafi, and as it exists in a reduced form in Ndut-Paloor, Proto-Cangin almost certainly exhibited definite agreement.

The breakdown of agreement in Ndut-Paloor and to a lesser degree Saafi likely contributed to the reduction in the number of classes in these languages. The "alliterative" nature of noun class agreement as seen in the following Noon example is a powerful force in reinforcing the active morphological status of class markers.

(51) tediktaa taay-taa ti-yaak-taa taa   (Noon: 018)
     t-edik-t-aa   *t-aay=t-aa*   *ti-yaak=t-aa*
     CL.PL-tree-CL-DEF.DIST CL-three-CL-DEF.DIST CL-big=CL-DEF.DIST
     t-aa
     CL-DEM.DIST
     'those three big trees'

With agreement reduced to a single non-iterated target in Ndut-Paloor (suffixed determiners on nouns) and a single iterated target in Saafi (suffixed determiners on nouns and modifying adjectives/numerals), the alliterative nature of class agreement was weakened considerably, and as a consequence the less frequent agreement classes were lost.

140   CHAPTER 3

3.2 Determiners

3.2.1 *Definite and Demonstrative Determiners*

Determiners in the Cangin languages are of two types: definite determiners suffixed to the noun, and demonstrative determiners which can follow the noun or stand alone as pronouns. In Noon-Laalaa and Khodaba Paloor, a noun must have a definite suffix when it is modified by a following demonstrative determiner. In Saafi, the demonstrative determiners take the place of definite determiners as suffixes on the noun. The patterns of Ndut and of Paloor as described by Thornell et al. (2016) are more complicated. In Ndut two patterns are possible: either a free demonstrative prefixed with *b-* (sg.) or *y-* (pl.) can follow the noun suffixed with the associative marker *-i*, or the demonstrative can be suffixed directly to the noun. In fact it is not always the noun that hosts the demonstrative, but the final noun or adjective of the NP, e.g. *beli-i wun-ee* 'this beautiful wife' (Mo. 49). Thus these "suffixed" demonstratives are probably better termed clitics, but are presented here as in the original sources. Both of these patterns are used in Paloor as described by Thornell et al., but their use is determined by number: the suffixed demonstratives are used in the singular, and the free demonstratives with *y-* in the plural. Suffixed determiners agree with the head noun in all languages, but free word demonstratives agree only in Noon-Laalaa. The noun 'goat' modified by definite determiners and demonstratives in the singular and plural is shown for each language in Table 107.

TABLE 107   'Goat' with a (proximal) definite determiner and proximal demonstrative

Noon, Laalaa:	pe'-f-ii	pe'-f-ii f-ii		pe'-c-ii c-ii	
	'the goat'	'this goat'		'these goats'	
Saafi:	pe'-f-i		pe'-f-ii	pe'-c-ii	
	'the goat'		'this goat'	'these goats'	
Khodaba Paloor:	pe'-f-a	pe'-f-a bee		pe'-y-a yee	
	'the goat'	'this goat'		'these goats'	
Paloor (Thornell):	pe'-f-a		pe'-f-ee	pe'-y-i yee	
	'the goat'		'this goat'	'these goats'	
Ndut:	pe'-f-a	pe'-f-i beh	pe'-f-ee	pe'-y-i yeh	pe'-y-ee
	'the goat'	'this goat'	'this goat'	'these goats'	'these goats'

NLS and Khodaba Paloor have multiple definite suffixes (Table 108) sensitive to the proximity of the noun to the speaker or addressee. All suffixed determiners are preceded by a class marker, though this is ∅ for the default singular class.

NOMINAL MORPHOLOGY

TABLE 108   Suffixed definite determiners

Noon	Laalaa	Saafi[a]		Khodaba Paloor	
-ii	-ii	-i	near (speaker)	-a	near
-aa	-aa	-a	far (from speaker)	-e	not near, visible
-um			near addressee	-in	far, invisible
	-am		general/'whichever'		

a   Botne & Pouille (2016: 99–101) give a somewhat different account of these two suffixes. The
"proximal" -i is taken as the definite suffix, and "distal" -a as the specific indefinite suffix. They
do note, "These suffixes may also be used to indicate spatial proximity, -i indicating a proximal
object, -a a distal object that one cannot see."

The definite suffixes of Noon, Laalaa, and Saafi are similar, but the Khodaba
Paloor suffixes are quite different. Paloor as described by Thornell et al. as well
as Ndut in Morgan's account use only -a. Pichl (1977: 8) also lists -i~e for Ndut,
a proximal definite determiner. This is distinct from the proximal demonstrative, which Pichl gives as -ii~ee. It is likely that Pichl and Morgan are describing
the same system in different terms, with Pichl finding a difference in meaning
between -e and -ee, and Morgan treating them as variants of the same demonstrative determiner.

For demonstratives there are even more proximity-based distinctions made
in each language. These are listed in Table 109. When these demonstratives are
suffixed to the noun (never the case in Noon-Laalaa), the class agreement patterns are the same as for suffixed definite determiners. When they stand as free
words, the agreement markers w-/y-/c-/ɓ- are used in Saafi (sensitive to number and human/non-human status), and b-/y- in Ndut-Paloor (sensitive only
to number). In Noon-Laalaa, demonstratives show full class agreement, with
w- corresponding to ∅ or n- used with suffixed definite determiners (and some
other differences in Noon, for which see § 3.1).

TABLE 109   Demonstrative determiners of each language

Noon[a]	Laalaa	Saafi		Kh. Paloor	Ndut	
-ii	-ii (y-uu[b])	-ii	near: 'this'	-ee	-e/ee/eh	near: 'this/that'
-aa	-aa	-een	far: 'that'		-a	middle-distance
-um		-um	near addressee	-in	-ín	far: 'yonder'
-úu		-oon	farther: 'yonder'	-inin		farther
-úune	-úuní	-oona	farthest	-iniinis		farthest

142   CHAPTER 3

TABLE 109   Demonstrative determiners of each language (*cont.*)

Noon[a]	Laalaa	Saafi		Kh. Paloor	Ndut	
		-eem	'in question'	-aafa	-aaha	'this in question'
				-ínfë	-ínfë	'that in question'
				-i	-i	general 'which'

a   Some further elements can be added after these Noon determiners: -*ma* 'specific reference,'
    -'*ane* 'exact location' in Northern Noon, and in Padee Noon -*y* on -*aa*, -*ii*, and -*úu* with "purely
    spatial" reference (Thiès Noon -*y*).
b   Laalaa *yuu* with *y*- class agreement has an irregular vowel, perhaps due to dissimilation from
    palatal /y/ to make the presence of the consonant more audible. It may also be related to the
    Laalaa *e > o change seen in Table 43.

In Noon-Laalaa and Khodaba Paloor, a match or near-match is required
between the definite marker and following demonstrative (Table 110). Due to
the different number of distinctions made in definite markers and demonstratives, this is not a one-to-one match.

TABLE 110   Definite determiners used with each demonstrative in Noon,
             Laalaa, and Paloor

Noon		Laalaa		Kh. Paloor	
def.	dem.	def.	dem.	def.	dem.
-ii	-ii	-ii	-ii	-a/-e	-ee, -aafa
-um	-um			-e	-ínfë
-aa	-aa, -úu(ne)	-aa	-aa, -úuní	-in	-in(in), -iniinis

A similar pattern is found in Ndut in which both a suffixed and free demonstrative can be used on a noun. Morgan gives multiple examples of this construction (e.g. (57) below), but does not comment on it. It seems to be used when an
additional modifier is present in the noun phrase.

Reconstructing the Proto-Cangin determiner system is far from straightforward. First it can be noted that the definite suffixes resemble the demonstratives in each language. It is clear that the definite suffixes were grammaticalized
from the demonstratives, though to what degree this had already taken place
in Proto-Cangin is not clear. It is possible that in Proto-Cangin there was no distinction at all between these two groups of determiners, and that like in mod-

NOMINAL MORPHOLOGY   143

ern Saafi only a single determiner would have followed the noun. However it is
more likely that some or all of the demonstratives had been grammaticalized as
definite markers in Proto-Cangin, such that much like in modern Noon-Laalaa
and Khodaba Paloor a single determiner would have a definite interpretation,
and the repetition of the determiner would have a demonstrative interpretation. Recall that Proto-Cangin likely had definite agreement between nouns
and agreeing adjectives/numerals (§ 3.1.15).

Because the definite markers and determiners are cognate, it is only necessary to reconstruct a single series of determiners. It may be that only some
of the original demonstrative determiners were used as definite determiners.
There is only one determiner that exists with roughly the same form in each
language, being -*a(a)* with distal/middle-distance reference. In NLS -*ii* can be
reconstructed for proximal reference, but this is not relatable to Ndut-Paloor
-*e(e)* by regular sound correspondences. Noon and Saafi have -*um* for near-
addressee reference, so this can be reconstructed to Proto-NLS. All languages
use a determiner with /n/ for distant reference, but other than the consonant
nothing is shared between groups. To better understand the development of
the Cangin determiner systems, it is useful to compare the determiner systems
of Wolof and Sereer, given in Table 111.

TABLE 111   Wolof and Sereer determiners (with class markers *b-* and *k-*)

Wolof (partial list)		Sereer	
bi	proximal definite	ke	proximal definite
ba	distal definite	kaa	distal definite
bile~bii	proximal dem.	keek(e)	proximal visible dem.
boobu	near addressee dem.	keen(e)	proximal invisible dem.
bale~bee	distal dem.	kaana	proximal visible dem.
boobale	far, but closer to addressee dem.	kaaga	proximal invisible dem.
buu	distal dem. (Lebu dialect)		

The proximal determiners in Wolof (-*i*) and Sereer (-*e*) might explain the /i/ vs.
/e/ discrepancy in Cangin if one or both Cangin subgroups were influenced by
the Wolof or Sereer determiner systems. In Lebu Wolof there is a distal determiner -*uu* (archaic -*u* is noted in the standard dialect with far distal meaning)
which may be the source of Noon -*úu*. What is especially notable in comparing the Cangin systems with those of Wolof and Sereer is that there is really
nothing specific to the Cangin group as a whole regarding determiners. The

only marker common to all of Cangin is distal -*a(a)*, but this is found in Wolof and Sereer as well. Furthermore there is a cross-linguistic tendency to have lower vowels in more distant demonstratives and higher, more front vowels in proximal demonstratives (Woodworth 1991). Thus there is little that can be conclusively said regarding the inventory of determiners in Proto-Cangin. It likely had -*a(a)* for distal reference, a front vowel for proximal reference, and some other determiners for very distant and perhaps near-addressee reference. However even these vague reconstructions are not secure, since aspects of the modern demonstrative systems can be explained by areal and universal tendencies.

The origin of the Ndut-Paloor elements *b*- (sg.) and *y*- (pl.) used on free word demonstratives is unclear. These prefixes *b*- and *y*- are not noun class markers, and have no cognates in NLS. Unfortunately I can find no clue to their origin in any other Cangin language. It is unlikely that *b*- was borrowed from the Wolof class prefix *b*-. It is conceivable that it was made up of a nasal followed by the default class marker *w*- (*N-w- > *mb- > *b*-), but this is entirely speculative and cannot explain plural *y*-. Ndut-Paloor also uses *y*- on demonstratives to refer to an "abstract" notion, as in example (52) from Ndut.

(52) **yee** na húmú paŋ fu ra   (Ndut: Mo. 63)
     y-ee   *na* *húmú* *paŋ* *fu* *da*
     CL-DEM.PROX DUR be.PST do   you REL
     'what you were doing'

This use of *y*- can be attributed to historical agreement with *(*y*)*in~iñ* 'thing,' one of the two nouns in the original *y- agreement class (see § 3.1.4). The Sereer class *k*- and Wolof class *l*- are used in the same way, being the agreement classes of Sereer *tig* 'thing' and Wolof *lëf* 'thing' (archaic).

A final question for Cangin as a whole regards the length of the vowel in -*a(a)* and -*i(i)*/-*e(e)*. In Saafi and Paloor, the definite determiners are short, while the vowel-final demonstratives are long. In Noon-Laalaa they are all long. There are two pressures at work that could explain this discrepancy. First is the universal tendency for more grammaticalized morphemes to exhibit more phonological reduction. This reduction likely accounts for the fact that the definite determiners have short vowels whereas the demonstratives from which they were grammaticalized have long vowels. Second is the lengthening of unstressed final vowels in Noon-Laalaa (see § 2.2.3). It is likely that already in Proto-Cangin the vowels of these determiners were shortened when used as definite determiners, since they are short in both Ndut-Paloor and Saafi. The Noon-Laalaa definite determiners -*ii* and -*aa* are then the result of the regular lengthening

NOMINAL MORPHOLOGY   145

of final vowels in polysyllabic words, which incidentally had the effect of re-merging the form of the definite and demonstrative determiners.

3.2.2   *The Ndut-Paloor Associative Marker -i*

The Ndut-Paloor "associative marker" *-i* is not described as a determiner, but generally appears in the same position as the definite marker *-a*. This suffix *-i* is used on a noun or adjective when it is followed by a modifier within the noun phrase: either an adjective, numeral (in Ndut), free demonstrative, or another noun acting as an inalienable[6] possessor or "relational" noun (e.g. *'stone* house').

(53) faamfi naa'a   (Paloor: Th. 72)
      faam-f-i   naa'-a
      house-CL-AM white-DEF
      'the white house'

(54) ya'i bín   (Ndut: Mo. 47)
      ya'-i   b-ín
      hand-AM SG-DEM.DIST
      'that branch (over there)'

(55) laami huroy   (Paloor: d'A. 296)
      laam-i   huroy
      feather-AM blackbird
      'the blackbird's feather'

If the head noun is modified by a determiner suffix other than *-a* (which is simply replaced by *-i*), an independent word *ki* (Paloor) or *ke* (Ndut) is used.

(56) miismin ki pe'fa   (Paloor: d'A. 297)
      miis-m-in   ki   pe'-f-a
      milk-CL-DEF.DIST AM goat-CL-DEF.PROX
      'the milk of the goat'

---

6 Each Cangin language has two possessive constructions, which are usually described as "alienable" and "inalienable." However as Morgan (1996: 53) notes, this terminology is not particularly accurate, as either construction can in various situations be used for both alienable and inalienable possession. The precise semantics of each construction is outside the scope of this study, and differs somewhat between languages.

146   CHAPTER 3

(57) ginee ke yen beh   (Ndut: Mo. 49)
     gin-ee   ke yen   b-eh
     village-DEM.PROX AM 1p.incl SG-DEM.PROX
     'this village of ours'

On the surface, the Ndut-Paloor associative marker *-i ~ ki/ke* appears to simply
be the 3rd person singular possessive pronoun (see § 4.1), which has the same
two forms in Paloor (Ndut has only *-i*). However this is not entirely accurate
from a historical perspective. Morgan (1996: 49–50) notes the functional similarity of *-i* to the "associative marker" of Bantu (class-agreeing CL-*a*), but in
fact there is a crucial difference between the use of these two elements. The
Ndut-Paloor associative marker is used with adjectives and (in Ndut) numerals, whereas in Bantu these modifiers are directly marked with agreeing class
prefixes, rather than using the particle CL-*a*. Recall that in Noon-Laalaa, all
adjective agreement is marked by a class prefix **Ci-* on the adjective. Compare
the Noon and Paloor equivalent noun phrases in (58–61).

(58) kaad fi-agí'   (Noon: 049)
     kaad   fi-ag-i'
     house CL-be.wide-ADJ
     'a wide house'

(59) ɓeti yi-hóodí'   (Noon: 049)
     ɓeti   yi-hood-i'
     woman CL-be.tall-ADJ
     'a tall woman'

(60) faamfi haŋ   (Paloor: Th. 70)
     faam-f-i   haŋ
     house-CL-AM wide
     'a wide house'

(61) ɓeleɓi út   (Paloor: Th. 70)
     ɓeleɓ-i   út
     woman-AM tall
     'a tall woman'

While the synchronic analysis of the construction in each language is quite
different, they are formally identical: NOUN+CL-i+ADJ. Thus it is likely that
in Ndut-Paloor noun+adjective constructions, the associative marker *-CL-i* is

NOMINAL MORPHOLOGY

directly descended from the agreeing class prefix *Ci- used on adjectives. As for the use of the associative marker in possessive/relational noun+noun constructions, there are multiple possibilities. The first is that the marker -i in the noun+adjective construction was reinterpreted as the homophonous 3rd singular possessive pronoun (explaining the use of ki/ke) and then extended to noun+noun constructions. The second is that the 3rd singular possessive pronoun was independently employed in noun+noun constructions (this being a common source of genitive markers cross-linguistically) without having spread from the noun+adjective construction. Either scenario is plausible, but the fact that the class prefix is used on the associative marker even in noun+noun constructions is evidence for the first. There is however another possible explanation for the appearance of the class prefix in noun+noun constructions. D'Alton (1983: 296–297) writes that the Paloor associative marker is used only when the head noun is definite, e.g. *miis pe'* 'goat's milk' but *miismi pe'* 'the goat's milk' (in which 'milk' but not 'goat' is definite).[7] Morgan (1996: 51–54) also suggests a connection between the use of -i and definiteness in Ndut, though he does not commit to this analysis. Thus it may be that in these noun+noun constructions the form -i is in fact a determiner, perhaps equivalent to the "general" free demonstrative form -i that D'Alton (1983: 192) gives as meaning 'ce, ces de ...', and Morgan (1996: 60) notes "seems to have an anaphoric function that is much like that of the medial term [-a]." In fact in Khodaba Paloor the associative marker is never used in noun+adjective constructions (D'Alton 1983: 302–304), so the class prefix on adjectives probably cannot be the origin of the associative marker in this dialect. In summary, it is likely that the Ndut-Paloor associative marker has multiple origins, being at least two of: an agreeing class prefix *Ci- on adjectives, the 3rd singular possessive pronoun -i ~ ki/ke, and the "general" determiner -i.

3.3 Numerals

Some Cangin numerals exhibit class-based morphological alternations, some of which are irregular. The numerals 1–5 and 10 are shown in Table 112.

---

7 However Thornell et al. (2016: 71–72) find a completely different pattern, in which definiteness of the head noun is marked by placing -a at the end of the entire NP, as in example (53). They do find that the associative marker can sometimes be omitted, but do not note any change in meaning associated with this omission.

148   CHAPTER 3

TABLE 112   Numerals 1–5 and 10

PC	Noon	Laalaa	Saafi	Paloor	Ndut	
*CL-íno(h)	w-íinoo	w-íinó	yiino	yíno	yíněh	'one'
*CL-anax	kanak	kanak	kanak	ana	anah	'two'
*CL-aɣay(V)?	kaay, °kaahay	kaahaay	kahaay, †kaahai	eye	éeyë	'three'
*nixiir̥	nikiis	niikiis	nikis	iniil	iniil	'four'
*yatús/r̥	yótús	yítús	yatus			'five'
				iip	iip	'five'
*nda-anax yaɣ	daaŋkeeh, °daaŋkah	dankeh, °daaŋkeah	ndaŋkiyaah			'ten'
(Fula sappo)				sabboh	sabbo	'ten'

When used as modifiers, numerals behave like any other adjective in Saafi and Ndut-Paloor, being invariant and unprefixed. In Noon-Laalaa, the numeral modifiers 'four' and above generally behave like all other adjectives, taking a class-agreeing prefix *Ci-* (Noon) or *Ce-* (Laalaa), though unprefixed forms are sometimes encountered. 'One' through 'three' are more complicated in Noon-Laalaa, and require some discussion. 'One' shows full class agreement by means of initial consonant alternation; e.g. Noon *w-íinoo, f-íinoo, p-íinoo*, etc. Note that the invariant Ndut-Paloor form of this numeral may contain the class prefix **w-*, with **w* regularly developing to /y/ before a front vowel in most dialects, but may instead contain the class prefix **y-* used with 'thing' and 'person' (as in Saafi). Curiously, the Noon form of 'one' used in counting is irregular °*wítnoo* (Padee dialect), *winnoo* (Northern dialect). The reason for these irregular forms is unknown. Noon-Laalaa 'two' and 'three' (Table 113) are particularly irregular, both when compared with other numerals and when compared between dialects.

TABLE 113   Forms of 'two' and 'three' in Noon-Laalaa

	Counting	c- agreement	ɓ- agreement	t- agreement
Noon 'two'	kanak	kanak	ɓenak, °ɓanak	tenak, °tanak
Laalaa 'two'	kanak	canak, †kanak	ɓenak	†tenak
Noon 'three'	kaay, °kaahay	kaay, °kaahay	ɓaay, °ɓaahay	taay, °taahay
Laalaa 'three'	kaahaay	kaahaay	†ɓehee	†tehay

NOMINAL MORPHOLOGY   149

There are a number of plausible explanations for these irregularities, the most conspicuous of which is the initial /k/ which alternates with the plural class prefixes *ɓ-*, *t-*, and *c-*.

For 'two,' a Proto-Cangin root **anax* would regularly yield Ndut-Paloor *ana(h)*, and should result in NLS *anak*. The actual NLS form is *kanak*, and the initial /k/ must be explained. A reconstruction **xanax* could be considered, as **x* regularly develops to /k/ in NLS and /h/ or ∅ in Ndut-Paloor. However, this would be the only reconstruction with the consonant **x* in word-initial position (see § 2.1.5.2). Furthermore, the Noon-Laalaa forms *ɓenak* and *tenak* would regularly derive from **ɓi-anax* and **ti-anax*, but reconstructions containing a root-initial **x* would have to irregularly lose the resulting /k/. Taking the root **anax* as vowel-initial, the simplest explanation for the /k/ is that it is a class prefix, since it alternates with the class-marking consonants /ɓ/ and /t/. However it cannot be a plural class prefix like *ɓ-* and *t-*. There is no hint of a k-initial plural class prefix in any Cangin language, and there is no support for the idea that the plural prefix **ca-* (see § 3.1.3) would have once contained a velar stop—note that even the class prefix **ki-* never undergoes palatalization. However *k-* may be the familiar singular class prefix in these two numerals. The treatment of certain lower numerals as essentially singular nouns, while rare, has parallels in other Niger-Congo languages. Most notably, Kobiana has *ku-ná(ŋ)* 'two' and *ku-héh* 'three' used in counting, *ku-* being a singular class prefix used for two nouns meaning 'thing.' As for the discrepancy between Noon *kanak* and Laalaa *canak* when modifying a *c-* class noun, it is likely that 'two' originally did not agree overtly with *c-* class nouns, with *canak* (given by Dieye but not Pichl) being an analogical innovation. However it is possible that *canak* is in fact a conservative form showing *c-* agreement, having been leveled out in other Noon-Laalaa dialects. The vowel discrepancy between dialects for *ɓ-* and *t-* agreement forms of 'two' (e.g. Northern Noon *ɓenak* vs. Padee Noon *°ɓanak*) might be due to different resolutions of the vowel sequence in **ɓi-anax*, **ti-anax*, or else the Padee forms with /a/ might be the result of leveling.

'Three' presents similar difficulties. Like 'two,' it exhibits agreement through initial consonant alternation in Noon and Laalaa, and also like 'two' this consonant is /k/ when used in non-modifying contexts and with *c-* class agreement. For Laalaa, Dieye does not comment on *c-*, *ɓ-*, or *t-* class-agreeing forms, but explicitly notes (2010: 145) that 'one' and 'two' exhibit morphological alternations, omitting any mention of 'three.' This omission might be taken as indicating that Laalaa *kaahaay* is invariant, but Pichl does give alliterative forms with *ɓ-* and *t-* agreement. The original form of the NLS numeral was seemingly **ka-aɣay*, with the same singular class prefix found on 'two,' alternating with the plural class prefixes *ɓi-* and *ti-* in agreement, but probably not with *ca-*.

Comparison with the Ndut-Paloor forms (Ndut *éeyë*, Paloor *eye*) is not straightforward. Assuming that the NLS and NdP forms are related, a possible reconstruction is something like *-VɣVy(V)*. This unsatisfying reconstruction can be helped by assuming that the NdP form acquired an initial /i/, as happened without a doubt in 'four' (see below). A form *i-aɣayV* could have developed into the modern NdP forms if the /ia/ sequence monophthongized as a mid front vowel—recall that *ɣ* is regularly lost in NdP. It is however possible that the forms of 'three' are unrelated between the two branches.

Summing up 'two' and 'three,' the most likely scenario is that both vowel-initial roots were optionally preceded by a singular class prefix *k(a)-* in Proto-Cangin when the numerals were not used as modifiers (as in counting). The k-prefixed forms survived in NLS, and the unprefixed forms in Ndut-Paloor. In NLS, class-agreeing forms prefixed with *ɓi-* and *ti-* were used when modifying nouns in the corresponding plural classes. For 'three' and likely also 'two,' the k-prefixed forms were used when modifying *c-* class plural nouns, effectively showing no agreement. Comparison with outside groups is unfortunately of little help. For 'two,' Bainunk *-nakk* may be cognate, which if valid raises the question of how the initial vowel of *-anax* arose, but would provide support for *k-* being a prefix (a reconstruction *ka-nax* would not explain Ndut-Paloor *anah*). For 'three,' nothing similar is found in other Niger-Congo groups, most of which show reflexes of an original form resembling /tatV/.

'Four' develops regularly from *nixiir̩* in each language, except that the Ndut-Paloor form *iniil* contains an initial /i/. This initial vowel is an innovation, as a similar root is found throughout Niger-Congo without an initial vowel (e.g. Sereer *naxik*, Gurmana *nafi*, Proto-Bantu *nàị*). The /i/ was resegmented from the NdP associative marker *-i* which would have been found on the preceding quantified noun. NLS *yatús* 'five' likely contains the root *yaɣ* 'hand.' Numerals 6–9 are made up of 'five' followed by 'and' (NLS *na*, NdP *a*) and the necessary number one through four. In NLS the formula is *yatús na* NUM, subject to various reductions in each language (e.g. Saafi *yatus-na-kanak* ~ *yas-na-kanak*, Noon *yët-na-kanak* 'seven'). In Ndut-Paloor, the formula is *p-a-*NUM (e.g. Paloor *p-a-ana* 'seven'), reduced from *iip a* NUM. 'Ten' has a particularly interesting etymology in NLS, being *nda-anax yay* 'at/like two hands' with the locative/manner prefix *nda-*. Ndut-Paloor 'ten' appears to be borrowed from Fula *sappo*. Multiples of ten are formed in all languages as 'ten' followed immediately by the multiplying number. Numeral bases 100 and higher are borrowed in all Cangin languages.

NOMINAL MORPHOLOGY

3.4 Derivational Suffixes

In each language there are several nominal suffixes which create nouns or adjectives from verb roots. The nominal derivational suffixes of each language are listed in Table 114.

TABLE 114   Nominal derivational suffixes in each language

Noon	Laalaa	Saafi	Paloor	Ndut	
-oh	-oh	-oh	-oh	-oh	agent
-i'~iɗ	-íɗ	(-iɗ)	-iɗ	-iɗ	attributive
-aah~ɗ, °-aaɗ, †-ooɗ	-aaɗ	-ohaaɗ	-aɗ	-aɗ	place or manner
-ah/-aah	(-ah)	-aah	-a	†-a	nominalizer
-oo	-ah	-oha	-a		instrument
-laat (†-la)	-(e)laat				qualityª
-een	-(en)oen, °-ohen				manner
(-oh)		-ohi			leftover

a   The meaning of this suffix in Northern Noon is somewhat different; it attaches to adjectives rather than stative verbs, and creates nouns meaning 'something Adj.,' e.g. *hoodlaat* or *hóodî'laat* 'something long/tall' vs. Padee Noon °*hoodlaat* 'length/tallness.' The Thiès Noon suffix is given as *-la* by Lopis (1980) and *-laat* by Wane (2017).

Most of these suffixes can be reconstructed to Proto-Cangin, and are discussed in the following sections. The Noon-Laalaa quality and manner suffixes (e.g. Noon °*hood-laat* 'length' and *ham-een* 'way of dancing') are specific to this group, and Saafi *-ohi* (e.g. *toon-ohi* 'unsold inventory' from *toon* 'sell') is found in no other language, though it can be compared with Noon *teoh* 'leftover(s)' from the verb *tes* 'remain' with a suffix *-oh*. The second element of the Noon-Laalaa manner suffix (Proto-NL **-oh-en* containing the applicative suffix) is likely borrowed from Wolof *-in* with the same meaning.

Aside from these productive suffixes, there are a few isolated nouns referring to insects in Noon, Laalaa, and Saafi that have a frozen suffix *-oh* (Table 115).

This suffix may be individuative, if the unsuffixed insect nouns were construed as essentially mass nouns. Compare also Sereer *ñiiñax* 'ant' which appears to contain a similar unproductive suffix.

152 CHAPTER 3

TABLE 115 The suffix -oh on insect nouns

PC	Noon	Laalaa	Saafi	Paloor	Ndut	
*maas	maayoh, ˇmaasoh			maas 't. infestation'		'termite'
*ñiiñ	ñíiñ	ñíiñ	ñiiñoh °f-	°ñíin f-	°ñíiñ f-	'ant'
*mboong-	boogaa, booginoh 'bee'			bóogúl	⁺bëgúl f-	'wasp'
*kúlmbVs	kúlmbís f-, °kúlmbús	kúlbísóh	kurmburus	°kúlbús f-	⁺kúlbús f-	'ant sp.'

3.4.1 Agent *-oH

The suffix -oh forms agent nouns in all languages, and can be reconstructed as *-oH. Some agentive nouns which can be reconstructed to Proto-Cangin are given in Table 116.

TABLE 116 Reconstructable agent nouns suffixed with *-oH

PC	Noon	Laalaa	Saafi	Paloor	Ndut	
*teɗ	teɗ	teɗ	teɗ	°teɗ	°tedd	'weave'
*teɗ-oH	tedoh	tedoh	tedoh	°tedoh	°teroh	'weaver'
*níiɗ	níiɗ	níiɗ	niiɗ	níiɗ	⁺níid	'herd/keep livestock'
*níiɗ-oH	níiɗoh	níiɗóh	niiɗoh	níiɗoh	⁺níidoh~níirëh	'herdsman'
*pay	pay	pay	pay	pay	⁺paj	'heal'
*pay-oH	payoh	⁺payoh	payoh	payoh	⁺pajoh	'healer'

Other examples of agentive nouns in each language are given in Table 117.

TABLE 117 Selected agentive nouns with -oh in each language

	Verb		Agentive noun	
Noon:	yeek	'sing'	yeekoh	'singer'
	típ	'beat'	típoh	'drummer'
	jag	'learn'	jagoh	'student'
Laalaa:	toon	'sell'	toonoh	'merchant'
	lín	'farm'	línóh	'farmer'
	ɓag	'sew'	ɓagoh	'tailor'
Saafi:	toon	'sell'	toonoh	'merchant'
	lam	'inherit'	lamoh	'heir'
	naaw	'launder'	naawoh	'washer'

NOMINAL MORPHOLOGY 153

TABLE 117   Selected agentive nouns with -oh in each language
             (cont.)

	Verb		Agentive noun	
Paloor:	loh	'steal'	lohoh	'thief'
	ten~d	'milk'	tedoh	'milker'
	fel	'lie'	feloh	'liar'
Ndut:	loh	'steal'	lohoh	'thief'
	fel	'lie'	feloh	'liar'
	lín	'farm'	línëh	'farmer'

In Noon, these agentive nominals can also be used as adjectives.

(62) baay fi-ɗoɓoh   (Noon: 018)
      baay fi-ɗoɓ-oh
      dog   CL-bite-AGENT
      'a biting dog'

3.4.2   *Attributive* *-iɗ

The Noon-Laalaa suffix -*iɗ* creates adjectives from verbs. The Ndut-Paloor suffix -*iɗ* creates nouns/adjectives from verbs, and despite the difference in the ATR value of the vowel, these suffixes are likely cognate. In Saafi, the cognate suffix -*iɗ* has become further grammaticalized as a marker of perfective aspect. This suffix can be reconstructed to Proto-Cangin as *-*iɗ*.

The Noon-Laalaa suffix is very productive, and forms adjectives from mainly stative verbs. The form of the suffix in Noon is in free variation between -*iɗ* and -*i'* (with the latter being more common), which are homophonous except before a vowel.

(63) baay fi-jówí'   (Noon: 017)
      baay fi-jof-i'
      dog   CL-be.good-ADJ
      'a good dog'

(64) móoɓ mi-wuyí'   (Noon: 029)
      móoɓ mi-wuy-i'
      water   CL-boil-ADJ
      'boiling water'

(65) oomaanaa yi-hóoɗí'-yaa yi-ñaañí'-yaa   (Noon: 042)
oomaa(h)-aa   yi-hooɗ-í'=y-aa
child-DEF.DIST CL-be.tall-ADJ=CL-DEF.DIST
yi-ñaañ-í'=y-aa
CL-be.smart-ADJ=CL-DEF.DIST
'the tall, smart child'

(66) kuum ke-néɓíɗ   (Laalaa: Di. 222)
kuum   ke-neɓ-íɗ
manioc CL-be.nice-ADJ
'some good manioc'

(67) oomahaa we-hëɓíɗ-waa   (Laalaa: Di. 97)
oomah-aa   we-haɓ-íɗ=w-aa
child-DEF.DIST CL-be.generous-ADJ=CL-DEF.DIST
'the generous child'

At least in Noon, the suffix can be used even more productively to form an adjective from almost any verb, including active and even transitive ones.

(68) ɓo' yi-tuukí'   (Noon: 029)
ɓo'   yi-tuuk-í'
person CL-stand-ADJ
'a standing person'

(69) oomaanaa yi-néekí' baay-yaa   (Noon: 029)
oomaa(h)-aa   yi-néek-í'   baay=y-aa
child-DEF.DIST CL-fear-ADJ dog=CL-DEF.DIST
'the dog-fearing child'

It is also possible to use adjectives predicatively with the zero copula.

(70) oomaanaa yaa yi-néekí' baay   (Noon: 029)
oomaa(h)-aa   y-aa   ∅   yi-néek-í'   baay
child-DEF.DIST CL-DEM.DIST COP CL-fear-ADJ dog
'that child is afraid of dogs' (literally 'that child is a dog-fearing one')

Phonologically, the adjective-forming suffix *-í'~íɗ* is unusual in Northern Noon in that it does not trigger the raising of /a(a)/ to /é(e)/. It does generally trigger the +ATR versions of mid vowels. In Padee Noon and Laalaa this suffix does trigger +ATR /ë/ from /a/ (Soukka 2000: 91, Dieye 2010: 221).

NOMINAL MORPHOLOGY

In Saafi there is a perfective aspect suffix *-iɗ* (Mbodj 1983: 211) which is cognate with the Noon-Laalaa adjective-forming suffix. It may also carry on the verbal derivational suffix *-iɗ* 'to have already done' present in Ndut-Paloor and Noon, for which see § 4.3. Saafi *-iɗ* can be reduced to *-i* in the Sébikotane dialect (Botne & Pouille 2016: 115).

(71) a ñaamiɗ   (Saafi: Mb. 211)
   a ñaam-iɗ
   3sS eat-PERF
   'he has eaten'

(72) yaɓkori kosaayiɗ   (Saafi: Mb. 223)
   yaɓko-r-i   kosaay-iɗ
   old.man-CL-DEF.PROX be.sick-PERF
   'the old man is sick'

No other Cangin language has a perfective suffix *-iɗ*, with Noon-Laalaa using *-in/-en*, and Ndut-Paloor *-te*. Saafi uses *-n* (cognate with the Noon-Laalaa suffix) only in the past tense. In explaining how attributive *-*iɗ* evolved to become an aspectual suffix in Saafi, it is useful to consider Noon examples like (68), (69) and (70) above. Because Saafi has lost the adjective agreement prefixes and (like all Cangin languages) has a zero copula, an original copular clause consisting of a noun phrase and adjective phrase could be reinterpreted as a subject noun phrase and a verb phrase. This evolution can be seen in the hypothetical example (73).

(73) Development of attributive *-*iɗ* into a perfective marker in Saafi
  Proto-Cangin: *ɓi-o' yi yi-tofoxiɗ
          ɓi-o'   y-i   ∅ yi-tofox-iɗ
          CL-person CL-DET.PROX COP CL-stand-ADJ
          'the person is standing'; literally 'the person is a
          standing one'
  > (earlier?) Saafi: ɓooyi tufukiɗ
          ɓo'-y-i   ∅ tufuk-iɗ
          person-CL-DEF.PROX COP stand-ADJ
          'the person is standing'; literally 'the person is a
          standing one'
  > modern Saafi: ɓooyi tufukiɗ
          ɓo'-y-i   tufuk-iɗ
          person-CL-DEF.PROX stand-PERF
          'the person is standing'

Furthermore, at least in the Sébikotane dialect described by Botne & Pouille (2016), it seems that the suffix -*i(d)* can still be used as an adjective-forming suffix. Consider the following example, in which the subject is *Isa* and the predicate is *ɓo' kaañi* 'a brave person.'

(74) Isa ɓo' kaañi   (Saafi: B.P. 18)
     Isa ∅   *ɓo'*   *kaañ-id*
     Isa COP person be.brave-ADJ
     'Isa is a brave person'

Even more convincing is the following example, in which the adjective with -*id* exhibits definite agreement with the head noun.

(75) waasi angidi   (Saafi: B.P. xvi)
     waas-i   *ang-id-i*
     road-DEF.PROX be.wide-ADJ-DEF.PROX
     'the wide road'

Neither Mbodj, nor Pouye, nor Botne & Pouille choose to describe -*id* as an adjective-forming suffix in addition to a perfective suffix, but such an analysis is possible and in fact desirable given the available data.

In Ndut-Paloor there is a suffix -*id* which forms attributive nouns from verbs; i.e. 'person/thing having X attribute.'

(76) Ndut and Paloor nouns formed with the suffix -*id*

guuñ	'have leprosy'	guuñid	'leper'	(Paloor: Th. 149)
wom~b	'be weaned'	wobid	'weaned child'	
búum	'be blind'	búumíd	'blind person'	
búum	'be blind'	búumíd	'blind person'	(Ndut: Mo. 122)
reew	'be rude'	reewid	'rude person'	
neeh	'fear'	neehid	'coward'	

Neither D'Alton nor Thornell et al. give examples of this suffix in context, but the two that Morgan gives use the -*id*-suffixed nominal in essentially the same way as predicate adjectives in Noon-Laalaa.

(77) cicso yaal búumíd   (Ndut: Mo. 122)
     cic-so   *yaal* ∅   *búum-id*
     grandparent-my male COP be.blind-ATTR
     'my grandfather is a blind man'

NOMINAL MORPHOLOGY 157

(78) tunki yeh neehiɗ (Ndut: Mo. 122)
     tunk-i   y-eh   ∅   neeh-iɗ
     children-AM PL-DEM.PROX COP fear-ATTR
     'these children are cowards'

Note also Paloor *af miskiɗ* 'headache' (*af* 'head,' *misik* 'hurt') in which the original adjectival function is especially clear. Due to the loss of agreement prefixes on adjectives, it is not clear that there is a true class of adjectives in Ndut-Paloor as distinct from nouns, but these nominals formed with *-iɗ* serve many of the same functions as Noon-Laalaa adjectives formed with *-íɗ*.

It is difficult to reconcile the ATR difference in the vowel of the Noon-Laalaa and Ndut-Paloor suffixes. However recall that the Northern Noon suffix does not trigger a change in root /a/. It is thus likely that the original suffix was *-iɗ*, and was altered to *-íɗ* in Noon-Laalaa. This change was perhaps due to conflation with the causative suffix *-íɗ*, which also commonly appears on stative verbs.

3.4.3 *Place or Manner *-(oy)aaɗ*

The Noon-Laalaa suffix *-aaɗ* forms place nouns from verbs. The Saafi suffix *-ohaaɗ* forms abstract or manner nouns. The Ndut-Paloor suffix *-aɗ* forms manner nouns. Examples from each language are given in Table 118.

TABLE 118   Deverbal nouns formed with *-(a)aɗ*

	Verb		Derived noun	
Noon:	neeh	'sleep'	neehaah~ɗ-	'sleeping place'
	fet	'light fire'	fetaah~ɗ-	'fireplace'
	toon	'sell'	toonaah~ɗ-	'market'
Laalaa:	níiɗ	'herd'	níiɗaaɗ	'pasture'
	tík	'cook'	tíkaaɗ	'kitchen'
	fool	'run'	foolaaɗ	'racetrack'
Saafi:	tiind	'walk'	tiindohaaɗ	'walking/gait'
	waaɗ	'love'	waaɗohaaɗ	'love'
	woy	'speak'	woyohaaɗ	'way of speaking/speech'
	ñaañ	'be smart'	ñaañohaaɗ	'intelligence'
Paloor:	wan	'speak'	wanaɗ	'way of speaking'
	tíl	'walk'	tílëɗ	'way of walking'
	ñam	'eat'	ñamaɗ	'way of eating'

TABLE 118   Deverbal nouns formed with -(a)aɗ (cont.)

	Verb		Derived noun	
Ndut:	won	'say'	wonaɗ	'way of saying'
	tíl	'walk'	tílëɗ	'way of walking'

In Saafi this suffix is morphologically complex, containing the applicative suffix -oh from *-oy. The Noon-Laalaa suffix probably also contained *-oy, as *-oy-aaɗ would develop to -aaɗ by regular sound change in both languages. Thiès Noon has -ooɗ for this suffix (Wane 2017: 49), which confirms the earlier presence of the applicative suffix at least in Noon. The Ndut-Paloor suffix likely also contained *-oy, as this regularly develops to -a'. The Ndut-Paloor short vowel is in fact evidence for a complex suffix (*-a'-aaɗ > -aɗ), as two vowels in contact often resolve as a short vowel in this subgroup (see §2.2.3). The difference in meaning between languages (place vs. manner vs. general nominalizer) can be attributed to the fact that applicative *-oy can have either a locative or manner (or instrumental) meaning. As such, it is likely that *-aaɗ was simply a general nominalizer, with the locative and manner meanings of these nouns supplied by applicative *-oy.

The Noon suffix is phonologically irregular. Besides differing between dialects (-aaɗ in Northern and Padee Noon, -ooɗ in Thiès), this suffix becomes -aah word-finally in Northern Noon, merging with the rare nominalizer -aah from *-ay. In Northern Noon the suffix -aah~ɗ can also form instruments in much the same way as -oo (see §3.4.5).

(79) Northern Noon instrument nouns with -aah~ɗ-
    dîl   'grind with roller'   dîlaah~ɗ-   'rolling pin'
    tík   'cook'   tíkaah~ɗ-   'stove' (but also 'kitchen')
    yug   'sit'   yugaah~ɗ-   'seat'

This function may derive from the instrumental use of applicative *-oy. However this use of -aah~ɗ may be historically from the nominalizer *-ay (see next section).

3.4.4   Nominalizer *-ay

A nominalizing suffix -aah (Saafi, Noon) or -ah (Noon, Laalaa) exists in Saafi, Noon, and Laalaa. Paloor has a suffix -a which forms instrument and place nouns. Pichl (1979: 34) lists this suffix as [†]-a or [†]-ah for Ndut, but gives few examples of its use. Example nouns are shown in Table 119.

NOMINAL MORPHOLOGY 159

TABLE 119   Deverbal nouns with *-ah/-aah/-a*

	Verb		Derived noun	
Noon:	an	'drink'	anaah, °anah	'alcohol'
	ñam	'eat'	ñamah	'food'
	sok	'sow'	tooh ti-sokaah	'millet for sowing'
	yen	'laugh'	yenaah	'funny' (adjective)
Laalaa:	tog	'trample'	togah	'shoe'
	lag	'close'	lagah	'door'
	ñam	'eat'	ñamah	'food'
Saafi:	lam	'inherit'	lamaah	'inheritance'
	sok	'sow'	sokaah	'seed'
	an	'drink'	anaah	'beverage'
	rom	'buy'	romaah	'merchandise'
	tip	'beat drum'	tipaah	'song of praise'
Paloor:	fiis	'write'	fiisë	'writing implement'
	booh	'bathe'	booha	'bathing place'
	wan	'speak'	wana	'microphone'

The basic meaning of this nominalizing suffix in Noon and Saafi is 'thing that is VERBed.' However in Laalaa, Dieye (2010: 126) reports that its basic meaning is instrumental, which is certainly true of at least 'shoe.' In addition, Noon-Laalaa uses this suffix in the noun 'throat' (Noon *koonaah k-*, Laalaa *keonah k-*), a nominalization of the verb *on* 'swallow.' In Paloor the suffix is instrumental as well, and can also form place nouns. It seems then that the original suffix had a rather broad range of uses. The suffix can be reconstructed to Proto-NLS as *-aɣ*, with the long vowel in Saafi following from a general lengthening of final /ah/ to /aah/, as in *yaah* 'hand' and *waah* 'winnowing fan' from **yaɣ* and **waɣ*. The inconsistent length of the vowel within Noon is irregular. The Northern dialect has *-aah* (perhaps influenced by **-aaɗ* with which it has merged) in all words except *ñamah* 'food,' while Padee and Thiès Noon have *-ah*, though Soukka and Wane both report only *ñamah* 'food' and *anah* 'drink.'

In Laalaa, instrumental nominals formed with *-ah* can be used as adjectives, similar to the use of agentive *-oh* in Noon.

(80) fetil we-apah paloom   (Laalaa: Di. 285)
      fetil we-ap-ah   paloom
      gun CL-kill-INST antelope
      'an antelope-killing gun'

160   CHAPTER 3

Verbs can also be suffixed with -*ah* in Laalaa, which is not found in any other language, and as such is likely an innovation.

(81) fetilaa apahan paloom   (Laalaa: Di. 217)
fetil-aa   ap-ah-an   paloom
gun-DEM.DIST kill-INST-FUT antelope
'the gun will be used to kill antelopes'

3.4.5   Instrument *-oya*

A suffix -*oha* forms instruments in Saafi, as does -(*uk*)*oo* in Noon. Examples are shown in Table 120.

TABLE 120   Instrument nouns with Noon -*oo*, Saafi -*oha*

	Verb		Derived noun	
Noon:	an	'drink'	anukoo	'cup'
	gúɗ	'cut'	gúɗukoo	'cutting tool'
	nen	'shave'	nenukoo	'razor'
	ac	'dig'	acukoo	'digging tool'
Saafi:	liiɓ	'think'	liiɓoha	'brain'
	ñaam	'eat'	ñaamoha	'eating utensil'
	toon	'sell'	toonoha	'market'
	ɓoof	'sit'	ɓoofoha	'seat'
	paɗ	'sweep'	paɗoha	'broom'

Both suffixes derive from *-oya* containing the applicative suffix *-oy*. In Noon the suffix is preceded by anticausative -*uk*, which is somewhat unexpected given the semantics of this suffix. The Paloor nominalizing suffix -*a* may also be from *-oya* (either in addition to, or instead of *-ay*), as it forms instrument nouns. The regular development of this suffix in Ndut-Paloor would be *-oya* > *-a'a* > -*a*.

3.5   Summary

This chapter has explored the history of Cangin nominal morphology. The most notable component is the Cangin noun class system, which still operates in each language. Noon-Laalaa's system is quite conservative both in terms of

NOMINAL MORPHOLOGY

noun prefixation and agreement, while Saafi and especially Ndut-Paloor have undergone erosion of many noun prefixes, and have reduced both the number of agreement classes and the number of agreement targets. The Proto-Cangin class system was quite similar to modern Noon-Laalaa, but likely with more productive derivational functions for various class prefixes, and overall more prefixed nouns. Furthermore, a number of PC noun prefixes can be identified that are not part of the synchronic class system of any modern language, though they were likely already frozen in Proto-Cangin. Taking into account these "fossilized" prefixes and the fact that a number of agreement classes correspond to multiple reconstructed noun prefixes (e.g. *fa- vs. *fi-), Proto-Cangin possessed a rather large number of contrastive noun prefixes, most with identifiable semantic content. However, as in the modern languages, most PC nouns would have been unprefixed, and shown no alternation between singular and plural forms. Among the large number of agreement targets (at least adjectives, numerals, determiners, and pronouns), perhaps the most notable agreement phenomenon involves the definite determiners. In addition to showing class agreement, definite determiners were involved in a definite agreement pattern whereby the entire post-nominal determiner was repeated after all agreement targets in the noun phrase, resulting in noun phrases containing a large number of alliterative agreement markers. This same pattern persists in Noon-Laalaa, but was reduced to varying degrees in the other languages. The inventory of determiner bases is difficult to establish for Proto-Cangin, as they are seemingly subject to a number of pressures: erosion due to grammaticalization, recycling of demonstrative determiners as definite determiners, areal pressure from Wolof and Sereer, and universal sound symbolic associations. Numerals behave on the whole like other agreement targets, but their reconstruction presents some unique challenges. Notably, only the numerals 1–4 can be reconstructed to Proto-Cangin. Each language has a few noun-forming derivational suffixes, most of which are reconstructed straightforwardly to Proto-Cangin.

CHAPTER 4

Verbal Morphology

The verbal morphology of the Cangin languages is exclusively suffixing, though they also employ preverbal auxiliaries in some constructions. Proto-Cangin subject and object pronouns were not grammaticalized as affixes on the verb. The verb exhibited subject number agreement via a suffix *-us* used with a plural subject, but otherwise Proto-Cangin had no subject or object agreement. Various tense, aspect, and mood categories were marked by inflectional suffixes or auxiliary constructions. Like other languages of the area, Proto-Cangin had a relatively large inventory of derivational verbal suffixes (called "extensions" in the Africanist literature), which marked constructions such as the causative and benefactive. §4.1 examines the pronominal system, §4.2 the inflectional morphology, and §4.3 the derivational suffixes.

4.1   Pronouns

Because the pronouns of Proto-Cangin were not grammaticalized as affixes, they are not properly within the scope of verbal morphology. However because they have become suffixes in Noon-Laalaa and (by some accounts) Saafi, I will address them for the sake of completeness. The Proto-Cangin pronominal system has previously been treated by Pozdniakov and Segerer (2004) as well as Drolc (2005). In many respects my conclusions are in agreement with these researchers, but in other respects I differ from Pozdniakov and Segerer, notably in the reconstruction of the plural pronouns and on the topic of class-agreeing pronouns. For the most part I am in agreement with Drolc, though minor differences do exist between her account and my own.

The pronominal system of the Cangin languages is rather complicated from a historical perspective. It will be useful to first examine each subgroup (Noon-Laalaa, Noon-Laalaa-Saafi, and Ndut-Paloor), and then compare between them. In each language there is a distinction between a subject pronoun series, object pronoun series, and possessive[1] pronoun series. The possessive series shares

---

1   These are the pronouns used for "inalienable" possession (though see the footnote on page 147), and are placed directly after the head noun. The more common possessive construction uses NLS **nga* (*> -ŋ* or *-n*) or NdP associative *-i* between the possessed noun and the possessor (be it a full NP or a pronoun).

© JOHN T.M. MERRILL, 2023 | DOI:10.1163/9789004546493_005

VERBAL MORPHOLOGY

much with the object series. Many object and possessive pronouns exhibit assimilation to the final consonant of the preceding verb or noun in Noon-Laalaa and (for 1st person sg. *so*) Saafi. These assimilation processes are discussed in §2.1.7—the forms listed is this section are the unassimilated forms that appear after a vowel.

4.1.1 Noon-Laalaa

The Noon and Laalaa pronoun systems are given in Table 121. The plural possessive pronouns are the same as the plural object pronouns.

TABLE 121 Noon and Laalaa pronouns

Nor. Noon:	Subject sg.	Subject pl.	Object sg.	Object pl.	Possessive sg.
1st (incl.)	mi	ɗoo	-yoo	ɗoo	-yoo
1st excl.		ɗii		-ɗii	
2nd	fu	ɗúu	-ɗaa	-ɗúu	fu
3rd	CL-a	CL-a	-ɗi, CL-a	CL-a	ci

Padee Noon:	Subject sg.	Subject pl.	Object sg.	Object pl.	Possessive sg.
1st (incl.)	mi	ɗu	-ɗoo	-ɗuu	-ɗoo
1st excl.		ɗí		-ɗii	
2nd	fu	ɗú	-ɗaa	-ɗúu	-fu
3rd	CL-a/i	CL-a/i	-ɗi, CL-a/i	CL-a/i	-ci

Thiès Noon:	Subject sg.	Subject pl.	Object sg.	Object pl.	Possessive sg.
1st (incl.)	më	ɗuu[a]	-ɗoo	-ɗuu	-ɗoo
1st excl.		ɗii		-ɗii	
2nd	fë	ɗúu	-ɗaa	-ɗúu	-fë
3rd	CL-ë	CL-ë	-ɗe, CL-ë	CL-ë	-ce

a Lopis-Sylla (2010) and Wane (2017) give opposite ATR values for *ɗúu* and *ɗuu* (both in subject and object position). The ones presented here are from Lopis-Sylla, which match the vowels of the Padee dialect and are historically expected when compared with Laalaa and Saafi. If Wane is in fact correct, a 1st plural inclusive form *ɗúu* could be derived from the hypothetical form *ɗúso* discussed in the next section; however there would be no clear explanation for a 2nd plural form *ɗuu*, which has a +ATR vowel in all other Noon-Laalaa sources.

164   CHAPTER 4

TABLE 121   Noon and Laalaa pronouns (*cont.*)

Laalaa:	Subject sg.	Subject pl.	Object sg.	Object pl.	Possessive sg.
1st (incl.)	me~mi	se~si (†sú)	-soo	-ɗason/h, °-ɗasoo[b]	-soo
1st excl.		ɓoy		-ɗëfín	
2nd	fo~fu	ɓu (°†ɓú, †ɗú)[c]	-ɗaa	-ɗúu	-fo
3rd	ye, CL-a/i	CL-a/i	-ɗe, CL-a/i	-ɗawa	-ce

b   Dieye (2010: 151) gives -ɗasoh as the possessive pronoun, vs. the object pronoun -ɗason. However Thornell et al. (2016c) give the pronoun as -ɗaso(n) or -ɗasoo in either role, indicating that the presence of the final nasal is simply optional regardless of whether it is used as a possessive or object pronoun.

c   Thornell et al. (2017c) give this form as ɓú with a +ATR vowel. Pichl (1981) also gives ɓú, though he is on the whole very inaccurate with ATR values. Pichl (1981: 31) found a single speaker who used ɗú. The form ɓu given by Dieye is peculiar in having the short vowel /u/ which is generally not found in Laalaa except as an allophone of /o/. However since this pronoun comes from ɓo' 'person,' a +ATR vowel would be unexpected. This issue is perhaps resolved by the 1st plural inclusive form sú given by Pichl, as opposed to se given by Dieye and Thornell et al. (apparently a dialectal difference). The form sú seems to represent se in which the vowel was replaced through the influence of ɗú, and so this is also likely the source of the vowel in the form ɓú.

"CL" stands for a noun class prefix, as in the Northern Noon class-agreeing pronouns *ya, wa, ka, fa, ma, pa, ja, ɓa, ca,* and *ta*. Both Laalaa and Padee Noon have a proximal (*CL-i*) vs. distal (*CL-a*) distinction in class-agreeing pronouns, while Northern and Thiès Noon do not. The 3rd sg. human pronoun is *ye* in Laalaa, as opposed to expected *yi* and *ya* (as in Padee Noon). For 3rd sg. object pronouns, *-ɗi/-ɗe* is used for a human object, and a class-agreeing pronoun for non-human objects. For 3rd pl. pronouns, the form *ɓa* (or *ɓi, ɓë*) is used for people, which is a normal class-agreeing form (agreeing with *ɓo'* 'people').

Outside of the class-agreeing pronouns, the main points of disagreement between dialects are the vowel in the 1st plural inclusive pronoun, and the unique Laalaa plural subject pronouns. The system of Proto-Noon-Laalaa can be reconstructed as in Table 122.

TABLE 122   Reconstructed Proto-Noon-Laalaa pronouns

Proto-NL:	Subject sg.	Subject pl.	Object sg.	Object pl.	Possessive sg.
1st (incl.)	me	se, (ɗaso)	-soo	-ɗaso	-soo
1st excl.		ɓo-ɓ-ii, (ɗafín)		-ɗafín	
2nd	fo	ɓo, ɗú	-ɗaa	-ɗúu	fo
3rd	CL-a	CL-a	ɗe, CL-a	CL-a	ce

VERBAL MORPHOLOGY

The question of which of the object and possessive pronouns had already become suffixes is not entirely straightforward—the distinction between a suffix and an immediately post-verbal (for objects) or post-nominal (for possessors) clitic or independent word is a question of analysis even in the modern languages. However good evidence comes from the vowel length of the pronouns. Those which underwent final lengthening (see § 2.2.3) must have been incorporated as suffixes or clitics, while those that did not were still phonologically independent words. This criterion cannot be used for *-dafín and *-daso (which may have been *-dasoo based on the form with a long final vowel given by Thornell et al. 2017c), but I have considered them to be suffixes at this stage in line with the other 1st and 2nd person object suffixes. It must however be noted that *-dafín and *-dúu do not trigger ATR harmony, pointing to a rather recent grammaticalization.

The singular pronouns are reconstructed mainly without complication. Recall that *i, *u had become /e, o/ in Noon-Laalaa, accounting for the forms *me and *fo, which we will see had high vowels in Proto-Cangin. The 1st person singular object/possessive pronoun *-soo has been changed to -doo in the Padee and Thiès dialects of Noon through contamination with the other d-initial pronoun forms. The Northern dialect retains the expected -yoo with regular voicing of intervocalic /s/. Note that all of these d-initial object pronouns as well as *-soo assimilate to a preceding consonant, such that in most environments there would be no distinction between -soo/-yoo and the innovated -doo.

The 3rd person pronouns (except for the human singular object pronoun *de) are formed by a class prefix followed by -a or -i, seemingly a reduced form of the demonstratives -aa and -ii. However it is likely that the forms with -i are innovations of Laalaa and Padee Noon, since they are not found in the other Noon dialects, Saafi, or Ndut-Paloor, which all have only -a (Thiès Noon -ë). Since *i had already become /e/ in Noon-Laalaa, there can be no Proto-NL form with short *i, as this should be -e in Laalaa and Thiès Noon (note that Thiès Noon does not reduce /e/ to /ë/ in -de and -ce, so there is no evidence of -i ever existing in this dialect). The pronoun -i could be traced to Proto-NL if it was in fact a long vowel *-ii that later shortened in Laalaa and Padee Noon, but note that the Saafi and Ndut-Paloor pronoun -a is short. Thus it is likely that the class-agreeing pronominal base -a was always short, and that no counterpart -i existed until it was innovated in Laalaa and Padee Noon in analogy with the demonstratives -aa and -ii. This issue is quite complicated and probably cannot be answered completely satisfactorily. It is likely that the pronominal base *-a is itself ultimately reduced from the demonstrative *-aa. Thus there is likely a real etymological connection between the class agreeing pronouns, demonstratives, and definite markers that continued to be apparent to speak-

166 CHAPTER 4

ers throughout the history of each language, such that the innovation of a new member of one category on the basis of another would not be at all unexpected. At any given point in time it is difficult to say which of the determiner/pronominal bases would have been employed in which of these three roles, and what the length of the vowel would have been when serving in each role. In Laalaa the 3rd person singular human subject pronoun *y-a has become *ye* due either to the influence of the palatal segment on the following vowel, or else contamination with the object pronoun -*ɗe*.

The plural pronouns are more complicated. First, Laalaa has distinct subject forms of the 1st and 2nd person pronouns, whereas Noon uses identical forms to the object pronouns (with only a vowel length distinction in Padee). For the 1st plural inclusive *se*, it is hard to see how this could have been innovated, and thus it is probably conservative. The Laalaa forms *ɓoy* (1st excl. subject) and *ɓu* (2nd pl. subject) are transparently grammaticalized from NLS *ɓo-ɓ-i* 'the people (proximal)' and *ɓo'* 'people.' It is difficult to know whether these are Laalaa innovations, but since forms of *ɓo'* are also used as plural pronouns in Saafi, these were probably present in Proto-Noon-Laalaa. It may be that the "object" pronouns could also be used as subject pronouns as in Noon, such that there was a subject-exclusive series, and a more general series of pronouns that could be used in either subject or object position. However note that 1st plural inclusive *-ɗaso* contains the 1st and 2nd singular object pronouns. Since *-ɗaa* and *-soo* (earlier *ɗa* and *so*) can never be subject pronouns in any Cangin language, it is quite likely that *ɗaso* was also originally only used in object position, with the generalization to subject position being an innovation of either Noon and Saafi separately, or Proto-NLS which was reverted in Laalaa.

The second issue is the form of the plural pronouns that are shared between Noon and Laalaa. Since Noon often deletes intervocalic *s and *f (see §2.1.6), the /s/ and /f/ of the Laalaa forms -*ɗaso(n)* (1st pl. inclusive) and -*dafín* (1st pl. exclusive) must be original. Note that -*ɗaso(n)* is morphologically segmentable as -*ɗa-so*, containing the object pronouns -*ɗaa* (Proto-Cangin *ɗa*), and -*soo* (Proto-Cangin *so*)—thus 'you-me.' The optional final /n/ in this pronoun is presumably due to contamination with 1st pl. exclusive -*ɗafín*, in which the /n/ can be reconstructed to Proto-Cangin based on comparison with Ndut-Paloor *fun*. These two pronouns can be reconstructed as *ɗaso* and *ɗafín*, essentially the same as the Laalaa forms. In *ɗafín*, after the deletion of the consonants *f and *n in Noon, the vowels of the resulting form *ɗĕí* would naturally coalesce to /ii/. In *ɗaso*, Noon unstressed /o/ becomes /u/ (regularly in Padee and Northern Noon, though in Thiès Noon this is not a regular change, see §2.2.1.1), and the resulting form *ɗau* resolved to *ɗoo* in the Northern dialect, and *ɗuu* in Padee and Thiès. There are at least two parallels to this disparate outcome of

VERBAL MORPHOLOGY 167

monophthongization across Noon dialects: Proto-NL *ma-súɓ 'water' > North-ern *móoɓ*, Thiès †*múu*; Proto-NL *pe/te-oɓ 'leaf' > Northern *tóoɓ*, Padee °*puuɓ*. In all three words, the Northern dialect develops a mid vowel, while the other dialects develop a high vowel. Another dialectal discrepancy is the length of the vowel in the 1st and 2nd person plural subject pronouns, which is short in Padee and long in the other two dialects. The historically expected forms would be *ɗuu/ɗoo* and *ɗii* with long vowels, having descended from *ɗaso* and *ɗafín*, and *ɗú* with a short vowel as attested in Saafi. In Northern and Thiès Noon, the vowel of subject *ɗú* was lengthened, influenced both by *ɗuu/ɗoo* and *ɗii* as well as the object form -*ɗúu*, in which the final vowel regularly lengthened. In Padee Noon, the vowel of *ɗuu* and *ɗii* shortened in subject position, perhaps influenced by *ɗú*, but also likely due to phonological reduction. Lastly, Laalaa has altered the 3rd person plural object pronoun *ɓ-a* to -*ɗawa* from the expected -(w)a, with the insertion of /ɗa/ being a sort of contamination from the 1st plu-ral forms -*ɗaso(n)* and -*ɗafín*.

4.1.2 Noon-Laalaa-Saafi
The Saafi pronouns are given in Table 123.

TABLE 123 Saafi pronouns

Saafi:	Subject sg.	Subject pl.	Object sg.	Object pl.	Poss. sg.
1st (incl.)	mi, ŋ-[a]	ɗus, ɓoo, ɓoci, °ɓoɓem	-so	ɓoo, ɓoci, °ɓoɓem	-so
1st excl.		ɗif[b], ɓoo, ɓoci, °ɓoɓi		ɓoo, ɓoci, °ɓoɓi	
2nd	fu	ɗu	-ɗa	-ɗu	-fu
3rd	a, wa	ɓa, ca	-ɗe[c]	-ɓa, -ca	-ce

a In Mbodj (1983: 78) and Pouye's (2015: 128) descriptions this is a homorganic nasal. Pouye furthermore gives a form *ma* along with *mi*, which is the result of the extension of the proxi-mal/distal distinction from the definite markers to the 1st sg. subject (perhaps also influenced by Wolof *ma*). Pouye also lists a form *ñam* used with subject focus, the origin of which is unclear; perhaps *iñ-a mi* using 'the thing' as a focus marker.

b Also *ɗafi* and *ɗifi* in different dialects. Mbodj (1983: 6) makes a three-way dialectal distinction between *ɗafi Saafi*, *ɗifi Saafi*, and *ɓo Saafi* based on the 1st pl. exclusive pronoun used in each dialect. Pichl (1973) gives *ɗafi*.

c Pouye (2015: 112) also gives a form *ɗa* used with 3rd sg. non-human objects, not found in other descriptions. This is likely a retention of earlier *wa* used in object position, but with contam-ination from human *ɗe*.

Pouye (2015) lists all Saafi pronouns as free words, and there is no clear reason to prefer one analysis over the other. The major difference between the Saafi and reconstructed Noon-Laalaa systems is the use of additional forms of *ɓo'* 'person' in Saafi. The Proto-Noon-Laalaa-Saafi pronoun system is reconstructed in Table 124.

TABLE 124   Reconstructed Proto-Noon-Laalaa-Saafi pronouns

Proto-NLS:	Subject sg.	Object sg.	Subject/object pl.	Poss. sg.
1st (incl.)	mi	so	se/si, ɗaso, ɗúso?, (forms of ɓo')	so
1st excl.			ɗafín, (forms of ɓo')	
2nd	fu	ɗa	dú, (forms of ɓo')	fu
3rd	CL-a	ɗe, CL-a	CL-a	ce

One difference in these reconstructed forms from those of Noon-Laalaa is the vowel length in *so(o)*, *ɗa(a)*, and *dú(u)*. Because Ndut-Paloor as well as Saafi have short vowels for these three forms, it is best to reconstruct short vowels. Noon-Laalaa lengthens final vowels in polysyllabic words (though not regularly in the Thiès dialect, see Table 49), and as these three forms had become grammaticalized as suffixes, they were subject to lengthening. 3rd singular *-ɗe/-ɗi* has retained a short vowel in Noon-Laalaa presumably because it grammaticalized as a suffix at a later time than the 1st and 2nd person pronouns.

The Saafi singular forms are only minimally changed from the Proto-NLS forms. 1st person *mi* can optionally be reduced to *ŋ-*, and 3rd sg. human **y-a* is reduced to *a*. The full range of non-human 3rd person singular pronouns (*fa, ka, ma*, etc.) are reduced to *wa* with default class agreement. Saafi evidence clarifies the original quality of the vowels in **mi*, **so*, **fu*, **ɗe*, and **ce*, since unlike Noon-Laalaa, Saafi never merges Proto-Cangin **i* and **e*, and while **u* does sometimes become Saafi /o/ (see §2.2.1.1), the only source for /u/ in an originally monosyllabic word is **u* or **ú*.

Saafi 1st plural exclusive *ɗafi* is the most conservative of the forms *ɗafi/difi/dif*, and confirms the Noon-Laalaa reconstruction **ɗafín*. Recall that Saafi /i, u/ raises a preceding vowel to match it in a few common words (see Table 41). Thus **ɗafín* [ɗĕfín] would have developed to **difín* in certain Saafi dialects before being reduced to *dif* in Sébikotane Saafi. There is unfortunately less data available on the inclusive form *dus* found only in Botne & Pouille (2016). This could derive from **ɗaso* through the stages **ɗaso > *ɗasu > *ɗusu > dus*. However another possibility is that it derives from a hypothetical form **dú-so*, containing

VERBAL MORPHOLOGY

2nd plural *dú rather than 2nd singular *da. Without additional information (which may exist in other Saafi dialects), both possibilities must be considered. There is no cognate in Saafi to Laalaa 1st plural inclusive *se*, but if it is to be reconstructed to Proto-NLS, it could have had the vowel *i or *e, as these merge in Noon-Laalaa. Otherwise the only difference between Saafi and Noon-Laalaa is which forms of ɓo' 'person/people' are used as plural pronouns. Both Laalaa and Saafi use the proximal definite *ɓo-ɓ-i as a 1st plural exclusive pronoun, so this can be reconstructed to Proto-NLS.

4.1.3 *Ndut-Paloor*
The pronouns of Ndut and Paloor are given in Table 125.

TABLE 125   Paloor and Ndut pronouns

Paloor:	Subject sg.	Subject pl.	Object sg.	Object pl.	Poss. sg.	Poss. pl.
1st (incl.)	mi	yen	so	yen	so, -so	yen
1st excl.		fun		fun		fun
2nd	fu	ɗon	ɗo	ɗon	ko, -u	kon, -un
3rd	ɗi, ɗee	ɓa	ɗi	wa	ki, -i	wa

Ndut:	Subject sg.	Subject pl.	Object sg.	Object pl.	Poss. sg.	Poss. pl.
1st (incl.)	mi	yen	so	yen	-so	yen
1st excl.		fun		fun		fun
2nd	fu	ɗon	ɗo, †ro, †ru	ɗon	-u, (-o)	ɗon, -on
3rd	ɗi, †ri, †re	wa	ɗi, †ri, †re	wa	-i	wa

The Paloor 3rd singular subject pronoun *ɗi* is found in Kajoor (including Khodaba), and *ɗee* in Baol. D'Alton also notes a form *ɓoo* with 1st plural reference: "Dans le parler de Khodaba, on relève l'emploi fréquent de *ɓoo* 'gens' à valeur de 'nous,' 'on'" (1983: 207). Pichl (1977: 21) gives this same pronoun as *ɓë* or *ɓo* for Ndut.

Because they are so similar, there is no need to give a separate Proto-Ndut-Paloor reconstruction. The lenition of *ɓ to /w/ in the 3rd plural pronoun is unsurprising given that this consonant deletes intervocalically in this group (see Table 9). Ndut exhibits this lenition even in subject position, while Paloor retains *ɓa*. Otherwise the only differences between Ndut and Paloor are in the possessive pronouns. The suffixed Paloor forms are used with inalienable possession (e.g. *koy-u* 'your child'), and the free forms with alienable possession following a noun with the associative marker *-i* (e.g. *mey-i ki* 'his field'). The suffixed forms are simply reduced from the free forms, with the exception of 2nd singular *-u*, which likely comes from *fu* (as used in NLS) rather than *ko*. For this 2nd singular possessor in Ndut, Morgan only gives forms with *-u*, but lists *bo~bu* as the form meaning 'yours' (cf. *bi so* 'mine'). However there is no indication that a form *ko* ever existed in Ndut, as this form *bo* is likely from **bi ɗo* (cf. the Ndut 2nd plural suffix *-on* reduced from *ɗon*). The Paloor 2nd plural form *kon* is probably an innovation (based on *ko* in analogy with *ɗo, ɗon*), though it is not impossible that it once existed in Ndut and was replaced by the subject/object form *ɗon*.

4.1.4 *Proto-Cangin*

For the singular and 3rd person pronouns, NLS and Ndut-Paloor are essentially in agreement, and so these can be reconstructed to Proto-Cangin mostly without issue. However the 1st and 2nd plural forms are quite different, and these differences cannot be accounted for by sound changes operating on unified proto-forms. The reconstruction of Proto-Cangin pronouns in Table 126 gives all of the plural pronoun forms that might have existed in Proto-Cangin based on each branch. However it is likely that some of these were innovations of one branch or the other, and were not present in Proto-Cangin.

TABLE 126   Possible Proto-Cangin pronouns

Proto-C:	Subject sg.	Object sg.	Subject and object pl.	Possessive sg.
1st (incl.)	mi	so	se/si, yen, ɗaso, (ɗúso?)	so
1st excl.			fun/fín	
2nd	fu	ɗa/ɗo	dú, (ɗan/ɗon?)	fu, (ko, pl. kon?)
3rd	CL-a, (ɗe?)	ɗe, CL-a	CL-a	ke

In addition, forms of **ɓi-o'* 'person/people' were likely employed as 1st and 2nd person plural pronouns, as in all modern languages but Noon.

For the singular pronouns a few points are unclear. The 3rd person sg. human pronoun **ɗe* was certainly used as the object pronoun, but is only used as a subject pronoun in Ndut-Paloor. The loss or extension of **ɗe* in subject position is a conceivable change in either group. The vowel of **ɗe* as well as (in Paloor only) possessive **ke* has raised to /i/ in Ndut-Paloor (though Pichl reports both *re* and *ri* from **ɗe*), which is not a regular change. Mid **e* must be original in these

VERBAL MORPHOLOGY

forms, since Saafi never lowers original *i, and in Ndut the cognate to Paloor *ki* is *ke* (an allomorph of the associative marker, see § 3.2). The Baol Paloor subject pronoun form *dee* may be partially explained by the original form **de*, though the vowel length is not. The vowel of the 2nd singular object pronoun (NLS *da*, Ndut-Paloor *do*) cannot be resolved, as there is no regular a:o correspondence between NLS and NdP. Original **da* may have been altered to *do* by contamination with 1st person **so* in Ndut-Paloor, but it might also be that original **do* was influenced by the 3rd person pronouns **cl-a* in NLS. For the 3rd person possessive pronoun, given **ce* in NLS and **ke* in Ndut-Paloor, it is likely that the original form was **ke*, with the NLS form undergoing an irregular palatalization triggered by the following front vowel. The Paloor 2nd singular possessive pronoun *ko* is probably an innovation, though it may be original. The Paloor pairs *di : ki* (3rd sg.) and *do : ko* (2nd sg.) appear on the surface to speak to an original morpheme **k-* in the two possessive forms, but it is more likely that second person *ko* was created in analogy with third person **de : ke*, since *ko* is found only in Paloor. Pozdniakov and Segerer (2004) argue for such a morpheme *k* and identify it with the possessive construction using **nga* in NLS. A connection between these two morphemes (if *k* is indeed a morpheme) is unlikely, since *nga* is an independent preposition in NLS with a wide range of meanings, only one of which is 'of.' The primary function of *nga* is thus not as a possessive marker—this is a secondary development, and is exclusive to NLS. Finally, Ndut-Paloor lacks all of the historical class-agreeing pronouns except for plural **ɓa*. These were lost in Ndut-Paloor, in which class agreement more generally has been greatly reduced.

There is little agreement between NLS and Ndut-Paloor in the plural pronouns. First it must be noted that three of these (only one of which is found outside of Ndut-Paloor) end in the segment *n. Intriguingly, in Fula and Sereer the 1st and 2nd plural pronouns also end in /n/ (Ser. *'in* 'we,' *nuun* 'you pl.'; Fula *en* 'we (incl.),' *min* 'we (excl.),' *on* 'you pl.'). Pozdniakov and Segerer (2004) suggest that /n/ in these plural pronouns can be attributed to a plural suffix containing /n/ in Proto-Atlantic. This question is beyond the scope of this study, but it must be noted that there is no independent Cangin evidence (i.e. outside of the pronominal system) for a plural suffix of any sort (Saafi uses *-een* on family names to mean 'people in family X,' but this is borrowed directly from the Sereer and Wolof suffix with the same meaning). Compare this with Wolof, in which the sg./pl. 2nd person pair *nga/ngeen* is formed with the synchronically active suffix *-een*. In Cangin it may be that one or two plural pronouns happened to end in *n, and this was then seized upon as a marker of plural pronouns and extended to other plural pronouns. Whatever the case, there is a tendency among languages of the area to employ a final /n/ in 1st and 2nd plural pronouns, whether due to shared inheritance or areal pressure. It was shown in § 4.1.1 that this final /n/ was optionally extended to *daso in Laalaa. The Ndut-Paloor 2nd person pair *do : don* may be an innovation of this group, with *don* being created from the singular pronoun with the addition of /n/; or else this pair may have already existed in Proto-Cangin. There is no reasonable source for the innovation of NLS 2nd plural *dú, and so this must be reconstructed with the same form to Proto-Cangin. With the existence of PC *dú, it is perhaps more likely that Ndut-Paloor *don* is an innovation, but it is possible that these two forms coexisted in PC.

For the 1st plural exclusive pronouns, recall that *daso (and perhaps *dúso) is a compound pronoun, made up of a 2nd and 1st person pronoun in sequence. This pronoun may be an innovation of Proto-NLS, or may have existed in PC— regardless it would have originally been an object pronoun, only later being extended to subject position. The other two forms, Ndut-Paloor *yen* and the Laalaa subject pronoun *se* cannot be easily explained as innovations, and thus one or both likely existed in Proto-Cangin. It is unlikely that these two forms are related, as Ndut-Paloor never exhibits voicing of *s to /y/ and Laalaa does not lose final *n in pronouns. Nonetheless it is conceivable that *s was irregularly voiced in this single grammatical morpheme in NdP, with /n/ added by contamination from other plural pronouns. An original pronoun *se/si can be compared with coronal-stop-initial 1st plural pronouns found throughout Niger-Congo, noted by Güldemann (2018: 117) as characteristic of the family (a number of previous sources propose a reconstruction *ti/tu, while Güldemann himself gives the more tentative "pseudo-reconstruction" $TV_{[high]}$). While the pronoun is s-initial in some groups, this can derive from earlier *t as in the Mel group. There is in fact evidence for a **t > *s change in Cangin prehistory (see Table 138), so cognacy with outside t-initial forms is plausible. The connection here is highly speculative, but provides at least some hint that the Laalaa pronoun is indeed conservative, and has the best chance of representing the most archaic 1st plural PC pronoun.

Finally, the 1st plural exclusive pronouns are likely related: NLS *dafín and Ndut-Paloor *fun*. The element *da* (originally the 2nd person singular object) in the NLS form was added by contamination from *daso (as with the addition of *da* in the Laalaa 3rd plural object pronoun -*dawa* from earlier *ɓa). The remaining discrepancy is in the quality of the vowel (*í vs. *u), which cannot be resolved. It is unlikely that Ndut-Paloor *fun* has any relation to 2nd singular *fu, since the 1st plural exclusive pronoun specifically excludes a 2nd singular participant.

VERBAL MORPHOLOGY

4.2 Inflectional Morphology

Within each of Noon-Laalaa-Saafi and Ndut-Paloor the verbal inflectional systems are quite similar. However between the two groups there are a great many differences, and as such the state of verbal inflectional morphology in Proto-Cangin is somewhat unclear. However the two groups share a number of affixes and auxiliary constructions, and furthermore there is evidence that some of the constructions specific to one group or the other were grammaticalized after the breakup of Proto-Cangin. The verbal inflectional morphemes found in each language are given in Table 127. In multi-word constructions, "V" stands for the verb stem.

TABLE 127   Verbal inflectional morphemes of each language

Noon	Laalaa	Saafi	
-us	-os	-u(s)	passive, Noon pl. subj.
-ee	-í	-ee	past
-an	-an	-an	future
-in	-en	-iɗ (pres.), -n (past)	perfective
-i	-e	-ang	imperfective/habitual
-ɗa	-ɗa	-Ca, (past -ee-ɗa)	narrative/punctual
-a(a)	-a	-a	imperative sg.
-at	-at	-at	hortative/opt., imper. pl.
-ɗii	-ɗi, °-ɗii	-ɗi	negative
-oo	-oo	-uhu (derivational)	imperfective/hab. negative
kaa V(-at)	kaa/caa V(-at)	°ka V(-at)	prohibitive (pl. with -at)
haat/°hanat ki-V	haɗat/caɗat ka-V	kanat ki V, kina(at) V	neg. optat. (+Saafi prohib.)
hay ki-V	hac ka-V	hay (ki) V-e(e)	future
CL-ii/-aa/-um V	(e) CL-ii/-aa V	yii V	progressive
(en) na ki-V	en na ka-V	na V-e	progressive

Paloor	Ndut		
-u	-u		passive/pl. subj.
-í			past
-te	-te		perfective
	-e		imperfective (?)
-an	-a'		habitual

174   CHAPTER 4

TABLE 127   Verbal inflectional morphemes of each language (*cont.*)

Paloor	Ndut	
-e/-í	-e/-í	imperative (sg./pl.)
-a/-aa	-a/-un	hortative/optative (sg./pl.)
-ay~ii/-uy~ii	-ay/-uy	negative (sg./pl.)
-eh	-eh/-íh	habitual negative (sg./pl.)
V V-o	V V-o	"acquired state"
e/in V ɗa	ee/aa/ín V ɗa	"presentative"
ka V	ka V	prohibitive
na V	na V	durative
ac V-e	ay V-e	future
ɗii/ɗee		negative future auxiliary
neh/nii	†neh	negative copula

For Ndut, Pichl (1979: 34–44) gives a somewhat different set of verbal inflectional suffixes, but with very few examples. In addition to perfective *-te* and imperfective *-e* (which he terms "narrative"), he has *-a* 'aorist' (but also 'in the state of ..., V-ing') and *-en/an* 'durative,' though all of the examples with this suffix are translated using the future tense. This last suffix is probably cognate with NLS future *-an* and Paloor habitual *-an*. The suffix *-a* may be equivalent to the habitual suffix *-a'* given by Morgan (1996: 92–95), who himself notes that the meaning of this suffix is unclear. Pichl also gives a preverbal negative particle *i* (sometimes given as *ii*), which may be equivalent to Paloor future negative *ɗii*, though Pichl's examples are not usually translated with the future tense. The remainder of this section will examine the use and evolution of inflectional verbal morphology in Cangin.

VERBAL MORPHOLOGY

4.2.1 *Tense and Aspect*

The tense and aspect suffixes of each language are given in Table 128.

TABLE 128 Tense and aspect suffixes of Cangin languages

Noon	Laalaa	Saafi	Paloor	Ndut	
-ee	-í	-ee	-í		past
-an	-an	-an			future
-in (†-ën)	-en	-iɗ, -een	-te	-te	perfective
-i (†-ë)	-e	-ang	-an	-a', -e	habitual/imperfective
-ɗa (†-ɗë)	-ɗa	-ɗa			punctual/narrative

Botne & Pouille give Saafi -*ang* as an inflectional morpheme, though it is listed as a derivational suffix by Mbodj (1983: 127) and Pouye (2015: 101–102), who give it as -*aŋ*. Since Mbodj mentions that it cannot co-occur with a perfective suffix, it seems reasonable to treat it as inflectional in this dialect. However Pouye presents rather different facts regarding -*aŋ*. It has habitual rather than more generally imperfective meaning, and is always accompanied by copying of the verb stem, e.g. *kosaayaŋ kosaay* 'fall habitually ill.' Mbodj give -*aŋ* with two meanings, 'être en train de,' and 'avoir l'habitude de,' which matches up with both of the meanings given in the other sources. This is likely an innovative Saafi suffix which was originally derivational, but become further grammaticalized as an inflectional suffix in some dialects. Alternately, it might be related to PC habitual *-*an*, with the unexplained addition of a final [g]. For the NLS suffix -*ɗa*, see § 4.2.5.

In addition to verbal suffixation, the Cangin languages use auxiliary constructions to express certain tense and aspect categories, shown in Table 129.

TABLE 129 Tense/aspect auxiliary constructions in Cangin language

Noon	Laalaa	Saafi	Ndut-Paloor	
hay ki-V	hac ka-V	hay (ki) V-e(e)[a]	ac/ay V(-e)	future
(en) na ki-V	en na ka-V	na V-e	na V	progressive/durative
DEM V	(e) DEM V	Cii V	DEM V ɗa	progressive/presentative

a Long -*ee* in Botne & Pouille (2016), and short -*e* in Pouye (2015)

176   CHAPTER 4

The reconstructable PC tense/aspect suffixes and auxiliary constructions are
given in Table 130.

TABLE 130   Proto-Cangin tense/aspect suffixes and
             auxiliary constructions

*-e	imperfective
*-í	past
*-an	habitual
*SUBJ γac ka-V-e	future
*SUBJ (hen) na ka-V(-e)	progressive/durative
*SUBJ (hen) DEM V ɗa	presentative

In addition, the Ndut-Paloor perfective suffix -te may be traceable to Proto-
Cangin.

4.2.1.1   Imperfective *-e

The suffix *-e can be reconstructed to Proto-Cangin as a marker of imperfective aspect. Noon-Laalaa uses a marker -i/e (Thiès Noon -ë) which has been
described as habitual, but which at least in Northern Noon is more broadly
imperfective. Some examples of Northern Noon -i acting as an imperfective
suffix (rather than more narrowly habitual) are given in (82) and (83). Each i-
suffixed verb in these examples describes an action that takes place over some
period of time, but does not recur habitually.

(82) mi lapi-naa, fu hayyoo ki-yen   (Noon: 018)
      mi lap-i=aa   fu   hay-yoo ki-yen
      1sS drown-IMPF=SUB 2sS FUT-1sO INF-laugh
      'if I'm drowning, you'll laugh at me'

(83) ya ñami-naa, ya kéekídidi, ya weeyidi yohcaa (Noon: tree braiding story)
      y-a ñam-i=aa   y-a kéekíd-i-di   y-a wees-i-di
      he eat-IMPF=SUB he   mock-IMPF-3sO he   throw-IMPF-3sO
      yoh-c-aa
      bone-CL.PL-DEF.DIST
      'as he ate, he mocked him, and he threw the bones to him'

Some examples of the Laalaa "habitual" suffix -e are also better characterized
as imperfective, like example (151) given later on. In fact Dieye (2010: 343–354)

VERBAL MORPHOLOGY 177

glosses this suffix as "INAC" (*inaccompli*) throughout his text, where it always has a more generally imperfective (rather than habitual) meaning. Recall that unstressed *e becomes /i/ in Northern and Padee Noon (§ 2.2.1.1). This vowel is expected to lengthen word-finally in Noon-Laalaa, but did not. The same is true of all three -V inflectional suffixes in Laalaa (also -*í*, -*a*) so it seems that these patterned like CV grammatical words in escaping the lengthening change.

Ndut uses an inflectional suffix -*e* that Pichl identifies as "narrative," and as the affirmative counterpart to -*eh*, which in other Ndut-Paloor sources is the habitual negative. Thus -*e* seems to be a habitual/imperfective suffix. This interpretation is consistent with most but not all of Pichl's examples with -*e*. Morgan does not arrive at a final analysis for -*e*, but speculates that it might be an irrealis marker, and notes that it tends to appear in constructions with the auxiliaries *waď* 'must' and *lah* 'must' (1996:111). With these auxiliaries, he often identifies -*e* as the imperative suffix, but in the two clear examples of -*e* that do not involve these auxiliaries (or the future construction, see below), the interpretation is clearly imperfective/habitual. These examples are reproduced as (84) and (85) below.

(84) ... ɗi húmú homa' faam wohe tuŋka   (Ndut: Mo. 113)
     ɗi húmú hom-a'   faam woh-e   tuŋka
     3s be.PST stay-APPL home watch-E children
     '[when he became old], he was staying at home to watch the children'

(85) fu yúh 6ele66a sobe raa ...   (Ndut: Mo. 113)
     fu yúh   6ele6-y-a   sob-e   ɗa
     2s know woman-PL-DEF pound-E REL
     'you know the women when[ever] they pound ...'

In addition to the use of imperfective *-*e* in Noon-Laalaa and Ndut without auxiliaries, the suffix -*e* is used in the Ndut-Paloor and Saafi future construction with **yac* 'come,' and also in the Saafi progressive construction with *na* 'with,' both of which are aspectually imperfective. Examples of the future construction are shown in § 4.2.1.5, and examples of the Saafi progressive construction are shown in § 4.2.1.6.

4.2.1.2   Past *-*í*
The past tense suffix appears to be cognate between Noon and Saafi -*ee*, and then between Laalaa and Paloor -*í*, but it is not at first clear whether these two suffixes can be connected. Ndut does not use the past tense suffix (Morgan 1996: 87). It is quite likely that Noon and Saafi -*ee* is historically from **-í-e*, being the

past tense and imperfective suffixes in sequence. Dieye (2010: 208) gives exactly this analysis for Laalaa -ee. The -ATR vowel in Laalaa -ee is unexpected given the +ATR vowel in -i, but accepting Dieye's analysis, there is no phonological obstacle to seeing Noon and Saafi -ee as having the same origin as Laalaa -ee. This irregular form -ee can then be traced to Proto-NLS. It is notable that Noon past tense -ee cannot co-occur with imperfective -i, which is further evidence that -ee in fact contains the imperfective suffix historically. Synchronically, neither the Noon nor the Saafi suffix is described as having an imperfective interpretation, but in fact Noon -ee is generally used with aspectually imperfective events, as opposed to -ee-da (with the punctual suffix -da, see § 4.2.5) used for aspectually perfective events. Compare the two Noon verbs in example (86), in which the first event is logically imperfective, and the second perfective.

(86) waa mi enee ga Dakaad, mi hoteeda Kodu   (Noon: 004)
      waa   mi en-ee   ga   D. mi hot-ee-da   K.
      when 1sS be-PST PREP D. 1sS see-PST-PUNC K.
      'when I was in Dakar, I saw Kodu'

Saafi -ee is also used for imperfective events, with perfective events instead employing -een. Saafi -een need not contain the suffix -ee, since -een would naturally result from the coalescence of earlier *i-(h)en, being the combination of the past tense suffix and the perfective particle (h)en discussed below. Thus it is quite likely that Noon and Saafi -ee is indeed cognate with Laalaa -ee, being a phonologically irregular combination of the original past tense suffix *-i and the imperfective suffix *-e.

4.2.1.3   Habitual > Future *-an

The Noon-Laalaa future suffix -an is likely cognate with the Paloor habitual suffix -an. The direction of change would be from habitual to future, owing to the implication that if something is done habitually, it will be done again in the future. This future suffix is found in Saafi, though perhaps not in all dialects. It is mentioned only in Pouye (2015: 170–171), and is used with "circumstantial focus," i.e. to focus on the future time, as opposed to the more basic future construction with the auxiliary *hay*. Soukka (2000: 182) also notes a difference between these two future constructions in Noon, with -an being an "assertive future."[2] This distinction does not seem to exist in Northern Noon, and Wane does not note it for Thiès Noon.

---

2   "The assertive future aspect appears as predictions or as decisions made beforehand about

VERBAL MORPHOLOGY 179

4.2.1.4 Perfective Markers

The Proto-Noon-Laalaa perfective suffix was *-en. Noon -in/-ën is the result of regular vowel changes in unstressed syllables. Based only on Noon-Laalaa evidence, the vowel quality cannot be conclusively determined for Proto-NLS, since *i and *e merged in Noon-Laalaa. In Saafi the cognate suffix is used as part of the past perfective suffix -een, with -idʼ used in the present. As Saafi -een is the result of the coalescence of past -í and perfective -Vn, the vowel in the perfective suffix must be *e, since *-í-in would result in long /ii/ rather than /ee/. Saafi -idʼ is grammaticalized from the attributive suffix *-idʼ (see § 3.4.2). Ndut-Paloor has no cognate to -en, and the Ndut-Paloor perfective suffix -te has no cognate in NLS. In Noon-Laalaa there is a particular form of the perfective suffix in combination with the passive/plural suffix *-us (see § 4.2.4): Laalaa and Padee Noon -uunun, Thiès Noon -uunën, and Northern Noon -unuun. In Thiès Noon and Laalaa the perfective suffix can also co-occur with the past tense suffix (Noon -ee, Laalaa -í) as Thiès Noon -eenën, Laalaa -ínín. In all of these suffix combinations there is one more /n/ than expected, and further-more the vowel of the perfective suffix has been influenced by the preceding suffix. There are two possible sources for this additional /n/, which likely origi-nated in Proto-Noon-Laalaa. The first possibility is that the extra /n/ is due to the perfective suffix being doubled. Under this scenario -en could have been a suffix even in Proto-Cangin. However doubling of inflectional suffixes is not attested anywhere else within Cangin, and it is not clear what the motivation for doubling would be, since one /n/ is sufficient to signal the presence of the perfective suffix. The more likely origin of this extra /n/ is as the epenthetic /n/ used elsewhere in Noon-Laalaa to avoid vowel hiatus. Under this scenario, the perfective suffix was a free word or clitic that was grammaticalized rather late. If -en were already a suffix in Proto-Cangin, any resulting hiatus would have been resolved already before the Proto-NLS stage. The use of epenthetic /n/ outside of the noun is specific to Noon-Laalaa, and so if the /n/ in question is epenthetic, it indicates that -en could not have been a Proto-Cangin suffix. The likely grammaticalization source for this suffix is the particle hen found in Noon. Soukka (2000: 148) identifies hen as an adverb meaning 'just,' and Wane (2017: 275) identifies it as a "particle of restriction." In Northern Noon hen is extremely common, and has the same meaning as -in in many situations; for example mi seguk hen and mi seguk-in 'I'm left-handed' are judged to be equiv-

---

actions in the future that thus are very sure to happen" (Soukka 2000: 182). This meaning fol-lows from the suffix's origin as a habitual marker, since asserting that an action takes place habitually essentially predicts that it will recur in the future.

180 CHAPTER 4

alent in meaning. This particle *hen* might in turn be grammaticalized from the verb *(h)en* 'be' (in which case a reconstruction *(H)en* is warranted), but might be unrelated.

There is no evident grammaticalization source for Ndut-Paloor perfective *-te*. Since an imperfective suffix can be reconstructed to Proto-Cangin, it is possible that the language also made use of a perfective suffix, and *-te* based on Ndut-Paloor is effectively the only candidate. However no PC suffix is consonant-initial, and so if it was present it likely had the form *-Vte*.

4.2.1.5 Future Auxiliary Construction with 'Come'

The use of *ɣac~ɣay* 'come' to express future tense is common to all Cangin languages.

(87) baayfii hay ki-ñam (Noon: 001)
    baay-f-ii   hay   ki-ñam
    dog-CL-DEF.PROX come INF-eat
    'the dog will eat'

(88) koh húɓín, hac ka-toɓ lee ga fíkíi (Laalaa: Di. 172)
    koh húɓ-en   hac   ka-toɓ   lee ga fíkíi
    sky be.cloudy-PERF come INF-rain soon
    'the sky is cloudy, (and) it will rain soon'

(89) ɓa hay ki guuree (Saafi: B.P. 20)
    ɓa   hay   ki   guur-ee
    3pS come INF farm-E
    'they will farm'

(90) mi ay ñame (Paloor: Th. 106)
    mi   ay   ñam-e
    1sS FUT eat-E
    'I will eat'

(91) don ay ri lah (Ndut: Mo. 65)
    don ay   di   lah
    2pS FUT 3sO have
    'you (pl.) will have it'

The original construction can be reconstructed as *ɣac ka-V-e*, using the infinitive form of the verb (likely with *ki-* instead of *ka-* for some verbs, see §3.1.5)

VERBAL MORPHOLOGY   181

followed by the imperfective suffix *-e. The infinitive marker *ka/ki- was lost in
Ndut-Paloor (and is optional in Saafi), and the suffix was lost in Noon-Laalaa
(and is optional in Ndut). Alternately, it may be that the imperfective suffix *-e
was added in Saafi and Ndut-Paloor, since the use of an inflectional suffix on
an infinitive verb is somewhat unexpected. However even in modern Noon,
the plural subject marker -us is used on infinitive verbs, so there is not in fact
a strict prohibition on the presence of inflectional suffixes on infinitive verb
forms.

4.2.1.6   Progressive/Durative Construction with *na

All languages use the preposition *na 'with' before the verb in an aspectual construction. This construction is described as progressive for Noon and Laalaa,
and durative for Ndut-Paloor. For Saafi it is mentioned only by Pouye (2015:199),
who terms it a "presentative progressive." In Saafi the verb is suffixed with -e
(originally the imperfective suffix), just like verbs following the future auxiliary
hay.

(92) mi (en) na ki-ñam wa   (Noon: 005)
      mi (en) na   ki-ñam w-a
      1sS (be) with INF-eat CL-PRO
      'I'm eating it'

(93) Konjool en na ka-wook atoh   (Laalaa: Di. 202)
      K. en na   ka-wook   atoh
      K. be with INF-gather stone
      'Konjool is gathering stones'

(94) a na soke toho ha   (Saafi: Po. 200)
      a   na   sok-e toho   ha
      3sS with sow-E millet NEG
      'he's not sowing millet'

(95) mi na pay   (Paloor: d'A. 226)
      mi na   pay
      1sS DUR go
      'I'm leaving'

(96) yaafa na díis if   (Ndut: Mo. 89)
      yaa-f-a   na   díis if
      mother-CL-DEF DUR sew calabash
      'the mother was sewing a calabash'

182   CHAPTER 4

The use of a preposition ('with,' 'on,' 'at,' etc.) to mark the progressive is common cross-linguistically. The preposition *na* 'with, etc.' still exists in NLS and Ndut-Paloor, though it is used somewhat differently in the two branches. This construction may have once used the overt copula **(h)en* obligatorily as in Laalaa, but since all Cangin languages make use of a zero copula in some constructions, it was likely always optional.

4.2.1.7   Presentative Construction Using Demonstratives

Noon-Laalaa uses particles which are segmentally identical to the class-agreeing demonstratives *CL-ii*, *CL-aa*, and (in Noon) *CL-um* in a verbal construction which has a progressive interpretation. Given that the far distal *CL-úu* is not used as a progressive marker in Noon, it might be more accurate to say that these are grammaticalizations of the definite determiners, rather than demonstratives—but recall that these have the same ultimate origin. Dieye (2010: 197) terms this construction "presentative"[3] in Laalaa. In Laalaa this construction uses an optional particle *e* (*i* before proximal *-ii*) before the progressive particle. This progressive construction also exists in Saafi, but does not show full class agreement. Botne & Pouille (2016) give examples with both *yii* and *wii* as the progressive marker (for human and non-human singular subjects respectively), but also note *kii*, used in two examples with the subject *a* 's/he.' Pouye (2015: 167) gives *yii* for 3rd singular subjects, *ɓii* for 1st plural subjects, and *dii* for all other subjects (probably from **de yii* 's/he who is ...' using the human 3rd person singular pronoun **de*, perhaps in addition to the other ɗ-initial pronouns).

(97) díi ɓii ñam   (Noon: 001)
      díi   *ɓ-ii*   *ñam*
      1p.excl CL-PROG.PROX eat
      'we (excl.) are eating'

(98) baayfaa fúu'ane faa fool   (Noon: 023)
      baay-f-aa   *f-úu-'ane*   *f-aa*   *fool*
      dog-CL-DEF.DIST CL-DEM.FAR.DIST-PRECISE CL-PROG.DIST run
      'that dog right over there is running'

---

3 "Le présentatif ne s'emploie qu'avec des verbes d'action pour indiquer des événements en cours de réalisation, inachevés au moment de l'énonciation. Le présentatif a une valeur de présent inaccompli." (Dieye 2010: 197).

VERBAL MORPHOLOGY   183

(99) enohfii fii ñam paagii   (Laalaa: Di. 198)
      enoh-f-ii   f-ii   ñam paagii
      COW-CL-DEF.PROX CL-PRST.PROX eat   grass
      'the cow is eating grass'

(100) ɓoa e ɓaa pay   (Laalaa: Di. 198)
       ɓo'-ɓ-aa   e ɓ-aa   pay
       person-CL.PL-DEF.DIST E CL-PRST.DIST go
       'the people are leaving'

(101) a yii tik   (Saafi: B.P. 116)
       a   yii   tik
       3sS PROG cook
       'she is cooking'

The element *e* found in Laalaa is presumably original—it may be reduced from
en 'be.'

There is a similar construction in Ndut-Paloor that employs a demonstrative with a relative clause in a "presentative" construction.[4] While none of the
Ndut-Paloor sources treat this presentative construction as involving progressive aspect, Morgan translates the Ndut construction using the progressive.
Structurally, this construction is parallel to the NLS construction just discussed
(subject + demonstrative + verb), except for the presence of the relative clause
marker *da* in Ndut-Paloor (see § 4.2.5 for more on **da*). In Paloor the subject
is followed by a particle *e* (for proximal reference) or *in* (for distal reference).
As D'Alton herself surmises, these must be equivalent to the demonstratives -*e*
and -*in*, but without the prefixes *b*- and *y*- seen in other demonstrative forms
(Pichl 1979: 10–11 notes these unprefixed demonstrative forms in other contexts
in Ndut). D'Alton translates this construction with French 'voici' (with *e*) or
'voilà' (with *in*). In Ndut (Morgan 1996: 104–107), all of *ee*, *aa*, and *ín* (unprefixed
demonstratives with a lengthened final vowel) can be used in this construction,
and the relative marker is not always employed.

(102) ɓuhfa e doɓ da   (Paloor: d'A. 233)
       ɓuh-f-a   e   doɓ da
       dog-CL-DEF.PROX DEM.PROX bite REL
       'here's the dog (that) bites' (orig. 'voici le chien (qui) mord')

---

4 D'Alton (1983: 232) defines this construction as follows: "La modalité "présentatif" est utilisée
   pour situer le sujet de la proposition dans l'espace (fonction spatiale) et en outre le désigne
   (fonction épidéictique)."

(103) Mustafa ee nee' ra   (Ndut: No. 105)
     M. ee   nee' ɗa
     M. DEM.PROX sleep REL
     'Mustafa is sleeping'

(104) Benjamin aa faanohte tigalka ra   (Ndut: Mo. 106)
     B. aa   faan-oh-te   tigal-k-a   ɗa
     B. DEM.MID lay-REFL-PERF bed-CL-DEF REL
     'Benjamin is lying down on the bed there'

The use of a relative clause in this construction is rather straightforward—for (102) the meaning would have originally been roughly 'the dog (here) is the one that bites.' In fact D'Alton translates all of these presentative constructions with both a matrix and relative clause, as in example (102). The NLS and Ndut-Paloor constructions likely have a common origin, with the form of the Ndut-Paloor construction being original. The relative marker *da* was lost in the NLS construction, and as it is optional in Ndut it may not have been required in Proto-Cangin. The change in meaning from presentative 'the SUBJECT (here/there) is the one that VERBs' to progressive 'the SUBJECT is VERBing' follows from the implication that if a situation is "presented" as relevant to the current speech context, it likely involves an ongoing action.

4.2.1.8   Use of the Unmarked Verb

All Cangin languages use the unmarked verb stem in a temporally and aspectually "basic" sort of construction, though the exact meaning seems to differ somewhat between languages.

(105) baayfii ñam tooh   (Noon: 001)
     baay-f-ii   ñam tooh
     dog-CL-DEF.PROX eat millet
     'the dog eats/ate millet' (one time)

(106) Laalaacii an mokop   (Laalaa: Di 192)
     laalaa-c-ii   an   mokop
     laalaa-CL.PL-DEF.PROX drink palm.wine
     'the Laalaa drink palm wine'

(107) ɓa ñaam   (Saafi: Mb. 208)
     ɓa ñaam
     3p eat
     'they eat'

VERBAL MORPHOLOGY   185

(108)   mi ñam   (Paloor: Th. 89)
         mi ñam
         1sS eat
         'I eat'

(109)   ɗi ot yin   (Ndut: Mo. 168)
         ɗi ot yin
         3s see thing
         'he sees something'

Dieye (2010: 191) terms this the "aorist" in Laalaa.[5] D'Alton (1983: 221) uses "zero aspect" for Paloor,[6] and Thornell et al. (2016: 89) the "simple present."[7] In Mbodj (1983) this Saafi construction is common, and translated with the French simple present, but he does not comment on its usage beyond the fact that it is temporally present and aspectually imperfective. Botne & Pouille (2016) do not mention the construction. The use of the unmarked verb with an essentially atemporal meaning can be reconstructed for Proto-Cangin.

4.2.2   Mood (*Imperative, Hortative/Optative*)
The imperative and hortative/optative constructions are marked by verbal suffixes in each language, shown in Table 131.

TABLE 131   Modal suffixes in each language

Noon	Laalaa	Saafi	Paloor	Ndut	
-a/-aa[a]	-a	-a	-e	-e	imperative sg.
-at	-at	-at	-í	-í	imperative pl.
-at	-at	-at	-a	-a	hortative/optative sg.
-at	-at	-at	-un, °-aa	-un	hortative/optative pl.

a   Short utterance-finally and long otherwise

---

5   "Dans les énoncés simples, l'aoriste sert généralement à représenter des faits génériques ou des vérités générales, des faits ponctuels."

6   "L'aspect zero est utilise pour denoter un proces, pur et simple, ou un fait dans sa totalite."

7   "Le présent (simple) en paloor met l'action, le processus ou l'état qui est comporté dans le verbe à la situation actuelle."

186   CHAPTER 4

In each language the imperative is used only with 2nd person subjects, and no pronoun is employed. With the Ndut-Paloor hortative/optative there is no restriction on the subject, and it is always expressed. The NLS hortative/optative differs only in that no 2nd person subject can be used (or more accurately they are unexpressed, and the imperative and hortative/optative can be considered a single mood).

(110)   a. ñama   (Noon: 025)
            'eat!' (sg.)

        b. ñamat
            'eat!' (pl.)

        c. ya ñamat
            'may he eat!'

        d. ɗoo ñamat
            'let's eat!'

From the examples given by Morgan (1996: 119), it appears that the Ndut singular imperative suffix is omitted before an object pronoun; e.g. *lomiɗ-∅ so guro!* 'buy cola nuts for me!' This omission is not described for any other Cangin language, but is found in Wolof, which may have influenced the Ndut construction.

It is likely that the NLS imperative *-a* and Ndut-Paloor optative *-a* are cognate, but otherwise the two branches employ entirely different markers. NLS *-at* would not have originally been associated with plurality, with this optative suffix being used for plural commands because *-a* is reserved for singular addressees. The Ndut-Paloor singular/plural suffix pairs do not resemble subject number marking from elsewhere in the language, where *-u* is used with plural subjects.

4.2.3   *Negation*

The most basic mark of negation is *-ɗi(i)* in NLS, and *-ay* in Ndut-Paloor. All languages use a preverbal particle **ka* in prohibitions. Noon-Laalaa has a habitual/imperfective negative suffix *-oo*, and Ndut-Paloor a habitual negative suffix *-eh*. In Noon-Laalaa there is a negative auxiliary *gaa*, and in Saafi there is a clause-final negative particle *haa* (*ha* in Pouye 2015). Paloor has a preverbal negative future particle *ɗii/ɗee* and a negative copula *neh* (also present in Ndut).

VERBAL MORPHOLOGY

The suffixes -ɗi(i) and -ay are likely unrelated.[8] Besides their phonological differences, NLS -ɗi(i) appears very late in the verb, followed only by the object pronouns, which were only recently grammaticalized as suffixes. Furthermore, in Noon -ɗii patterns with the object suffixes in being able to stand outside of the verb if hosted by a dummy infinitive prefix ki-.

(111)   mi na kiɗii ki-yeek dii   (Noon: 035)
        mi na   ki-ɗii   ki-yeek   d-ii
        1sS with INF-NEG INF-sing here
        'I'm not singing here'

Thus it must be that like the object suffixes, negative -ɗi(i) was grammatical-ized as a suffix rather recently. In fact Pouye (2015: 195) analyzes it as a free word in Saafi, though it appears to always immediately follow the verb. On the other hand, Ndut-Paloor -ay is one of the earliest verbal inflectional suffixes, preceded only by plural/passive -u. Furthermore it can appear on a historically infinitive verb in the durative construction with *na*.

(112)   fu na ñamay yin   (Paloor: d'A. 254)
        fu   na   ñam-ay   yin
        2sS DUR eat-NEG thing
        'you aren't eating anything'

While derivational affixes can appear on infinitive forms, the appearance of an inflectional affix is from a historical perspective less expected. Thus NdP -ay may have originally been a "privative" derivational affix in the same vein as Wolof -adi, Sereer -atar, and Saafi/Laalaa -adi meaning roughly 'to not VERB.' Pichl (1979: 39) analyzes this suffix as simply -y, with -a being his 'aorist' suffix.

The Paloor preverbal negative particle *ɗii* (Kajoor Paloor) or *dee* (Baol Paloor) (Thornell et al. 2016: 127) is almost certainly cognate with the NLS negative suf-fix, and thus can be reconstructed to Proto-Cangin as *ɗii. The Paloor particle is used for future negation.

(113)   yen ɗii neh wate   (Paloor: Th. 127)
        yen   ɗii   neh   wate
        1pS.incl NEG.FUT draw.water today
        'we won't draw water today'

---

8   The resemblance between Ndut-Paloor -ay and Laalaa *hay*, which Dieye (2010: 252) terms a negative (future) auxiliary, is coincidental. As Dieye notes, *hay* is a reduction of *hacci*, the negative of *hac* 'come/future auxiliary.'

188 CHAPTER 4

From a historical perspective it is significant that Paloor *dii* is restricted to future constructions, and that **dii* appears on a different side of the verb in Paloor versus NLS. A possible explanation is that the Paloor particle is a reduction of **ɣac dii*, a negation of **ɣac~ɣay* 'come' (Paloor *ac~y*) which is used as an auxiliary in affirmative future constructions in all Cangin languages. Paloor *dii* would then be cognate with the Laalaa negative future auxiliary *hay* (and Noon *hayyii*), also from **ɣac dii*. This scenario would explain both the position of the Paloor marker before the main verb, as well as its restriction to the future construction. D'Alton lists this particle as *dii* or *jii* (in free variation), which lends support to the idea that it was once preceded by a palatal consonant (recall the tendency for /ɗ/ to assimilate in place to a preceding consonant as discussed in § 2.1.7).

In negative imperatives/prohibitions and negative hortative/optative constructions, all Cangin languages use preverbal particles/auxiliaries, shown in Table 132 (S stands for the subject, and V for the verb stem).

TABLE 132   Negative imperative and hortative/optative constructions

	Neg. imper. sg.	Neg. imper. pl.	Neg. hort./opt. sg.	Neg. hort./opt. pl.
Noon:	kaa V	kaa V-at	S haat/°hanat ki-V	S haat/°hanat ki-V
Laalaa:	kaa/caa V	kaa/caa V-at	S haɗat/caɗat ka-V	S haɗat/caɗat ka-V
Saafi (BP):	kana V	kanat ki V	?	?
Saafi (Pouye):	kin(a) V	kinaat V	?	S kinaat V
Saafi (Mbodj):	ka V	ka V-at	?	?
Paloor:	ka/{ki na} V	ka/{ki na} V-í	S ka/{ki na} V-a	S ka/{ki na} V-aa
Ndut:	ka/†kanka V	ka/†kanka V-í	?	?

The particle/auxiliary *ka* (Noon-Laalaa *kaa*, also Laalaa *caa*) is used in prohibitions in all Cangin languages. The Proto-Cangin form was probably **ka*, which was likely grammaticalized from a verb **kaɗ~ka'* 'refuse,' still used in Ndut-Paloor.

(114)   kaa kaɗ Caañaak   (Noon: 022)
        kaa   kaɗ Caañaak
        PROH go   Thiès
        'don't go to Thiès! (sg.)'

VERBAL MORPHOLOGY

(115) kaa kún tua (Laalaa: Di. 253)
kaa kún tuy-aa
PROH close hut-DEF.DIST
'don't close up the hut! (sg.)'

(116) ka ñaam (Saafi: Mb. 212)
ka ñaam
PROH eat
'don't eat! (sg.)'

(117) ka fel (Paloor: d'A. 257)
ka fel
PROH lie
'don't lie! (sg.)'

(118) ka na yees tunka la' (Ndut: Mo. 102)
ka na yees tunk-a la'
PROH DUR(?) throw children-DEF stone
'don't throw rocks at the children! (sg.)'

The long vowel in Noon-Laalaa *kaa* is not easy to explain, since Noon-Laalaa does not lengthen final vowels in monosyllabic words. The long vowel may be due to the presence of the imperative suffix -*a* on this original auxiliary **ka*. Botne & Pouille (2016: 115) give this particle as *kana* for Saafi, and Pouye (2015: 197) gives it as *kin(a)*. Thornell et al. (2016: 130) note that *ki na* can be used in place of *ka* in Paloor. Note that this form *ki na* does not seem to contain the "durative" particle *na*, as it is semantically equivalent to the use of *ka* (as such I suspect that Morgan's gloss "DUR" in (118) is inaccurate). D'Alton (1983: 259) gives some examples with *kan* in place of *ka*, but she analyzes this as a reduction of *ka na* containing the durative marker *na*. Pichl (1977: 73) mentions a Ndut form †*kanka* which serves as a "stronger" version of *ka*. For 2nd person prohibitions, no subject pronoun is used (though D'Alton 1983: 257 provides one such example from Paloor). For 2nd person plural prohibitions, the imperative plural suffix (NLS -*at*, Ndut-Paloor -*i*) is used after the verb in each language.

(119) kaa wo'at na ɓuɓaa ɓaa (Noon: So. 189)
kaa wo'-at na ɓo'-ɓ-aa ɓ-aa
PROH speak-HORT with person-CL.PL-DEF.DIST CL.PL-DEM.DIST
'don't speak to those people! (pl.)'

(120) kaa ñamat ga ceepii   (Laalaa: Di. 253)
       kaa   ñam-at   ga ceep-ii
       PROH eat-HORT of rice-DEF.PROX
       'don't eat any of the rice! (pl.)'

(121) ka ñaamat   (Saafi: Mb. 212)
       ka   ñaam-at
       PROH eat-HORT
       'don't eat! (pl.)'

(122) ka hëmí   (Paloor: d'A. 257)
       ka   hom-í
       PROH sit-IMPER.PL
       'don't sit! (pl.)'

(123) ka na yéesí tunka la'   (Ndut: Mo. 102)
       ka   na   yees-í   tunk-a   la'
       PROH DUR(?) throw-IMPER.PL children-DEF stone
       'don't throw rocks at the children! (pl.)'

For the negative of the hortative/optative in Noon-Laalaa, a particle/auxiliary
of the form *haat* (Northern Noon), °*hanat* (Padee Noon), *caɗat/haɗat* (Laalaa)
is used, followed by an infinitive verb. This auxiliary contains the hortative suffix -*at*, and may be related to prohibitive *kaa*, though /k/ and /h/ cannot be
regularly derived from each other. The discrepancy between /ɗ/ in the Laalaa
form and /n/ or ∅ in Noon is unexpected.

(124) ɗoo haat ki-miy   (Noon: 048)
       ɗoo   haat   ki-miy
       1pS.incl NEG.OPT INF-leave
       'we mustn't leave!'

(125) wati, ken hanat ki-wo' an nohii tamin   (Noon: So. 189)
       wati ken   hanat   ki-wo'   an   noh-ii   tam-in
       today nobody NEG.OPT INF-say that sun-DEF.PROX be.hot-PERF
       'today, may nobody say that the sun is hot!'

(126) se caɗat ka-ñam ga ceepii   (Laalaa: Di. 255)
       se   caɗat   ka-ñam ga ceep-ii
       1pS.incl NEG.OPT INF-eat of rice-DEF.PROX
       'we mustn't eat any of the rice'

VERBAL MORPHOLOGY 191

For Saafi, Botne & Pouille (2016) give a phonologically similar form *kanat* used for prohibitions with a 2nd person plural addressee, which is followed by a verb with the historical infinitive prefix *ki*.

(127) kanat ki ñam   (Saafi: B.P. 115)
       kan-at   ki   ñam
       PROH-HORT INF eat
       'don't eat! (pl.)'

This use of *kanat* is seemingly equivalent to *ka V-at* as found in Mbodj (who does not mention a form *kanat*). Pouye (2015: 198) gives *kinaat* in place of *kanat*, and in his examples the infinitive prefix is not used. Botne & Pouille do not mention whether *kanat* can be used with non-2nd person subjects in a negative hortative/optative construction, but Pouye gives an example of *kinaat* with this function.

(128) komakci kinaat pul ŋ kahni woti   (Saafi: Po. 198)
       komak-c-i   kina-at   pul   nga   kahand-i
       child-CL.PL-DEF.PROX PROH-HORT leave PREP house-DEF.PROX
       woti
       today
       'may the children not leave the house today!'

Based on its phonological form and its use with infinitive verb forms, Saafi *kanat* is likely cognate with the Noon-Laalaa negative hortative/optative auxiliaries *haat*, °*hanat* and *hadat~cadat*. All of these forms seem to be built on a base *kaC* with the hortative/optative suffix -*at*. Paloor (and perhaps Ndut) simply uses *ka* (or Paloor *ki na*) for the negative optative.

(129) di ka saña Jangin   (Paloor: d'A. 258)
       di ka   sañ-a   Jangin
       3S PROHIB go-OPT.SG Thiès
       'may he not go to Thiès!'

A likely origin for the negative particle *ka* and its various suffixed permutations (Saafi *kana~kina*, *kanat~kinaat*, Noon *haat*, °*hanat*, Laalaa *hadat~cadat*) is the verb *kad~ka'* 'hate/refuse' found in Ndut-Paloor.[9] Verbs meaning 'hate/refuse'

---

9 For Ndut, Pichl gives †*ka'a* 'refuse' with the applicative suffix, †*kad* 'forbid, refuse, interrupt,'

are commonly used as clausal negators in the area; e.g. Wolof (*bañ*), Kobiana (*-geñ*) and modern Noon-Laalaa (*sag*). The phonological reduction of **kaḍ* to **ka* would have likely already taken place in Proto-Cangin, and the h-initial forms *hadat* (Laalaa) and *haat*, °*hanat* (Noon) might also be attributed to phonological weakening of original **kaḍ* following its grammaticalization. The /n/ in Saafi *kanat* and Padee Noon °*hanat* is likely not the epenthetic /n/ seen elsewhere in Noon-Laalaa (see § 3.1.2), since its use outside of nouns is a Noon-Laalaa innovation. Rather, this /n/ appears to be the same as that found in Paloor *ki na*, and thus can be traced to Proto-Cangin. There may have been a variant **kan/kin* of the negative verb **kaḍ~ka'*, though if so the origin of the /n/ is unexplained. Due to the phonological irregularities involved, the association of some or all of these negative auxiliaries/particles with **kaḍ~ka'* 'refuse' is not entirely secure, but I believe it to be the most plausible scenario.

The Noon-Laalaa negative copula *gaa* (Proto-NL **ngaa*) and the Saafi clause-final negator *haa* are almost certainly related. NL **ngaa* likely derives from **en yaa* containing the copular verb *en*—note that under this account, the position of the negative particle **yaa* after **en* is in line with the postverbal position of Saafi *haa < *yaa*.

It is likely that the Ndut-Paloor negative copula *neh* is simply from *en-eh*, the habitual negative of *en* 'be.' D'Alton (1983: 262) lists this negative copula as *nii*, which is likely from *en-ay*, or else **en ḍii*. The problem with these etymologies is that *neh/nii* appears after the predicate, whereas *en* 'be' appears between the subject and predicate. The NdP habitual negative suffix *-eh* itself is confined to this subgroup. The equivalent Noon-Laalaa suffix *-oo* is unrelated. It can appear on infinitive verbs, and as such likely originated as a derivational suffix. In fact Pouye (2015: 102) treats the cognate Saafi suffix *-uhu* as a "privative" derivational suffix, e.g. *hot-uhu* 'to never see.' The suffix can be reconstructed to Proto-NLS, and if it existed in Proto-Cangin could have had the form **-oyo* or **-uyu*.

4.2.4 *Plural Subject/Passive *-us*

The suffix **-us* (Noon, Saafi *-u(s)*,[10] Laalaa *-os*, Ndut-Paloor *-u*) has two functions. First, it serves as the passive marker. Second, it marks agreement with

---

    †*ka'il* 'refuse again' with the repetitive suffix, and a noun †*ka'ë* 'hate.' Morgan gives *kaa'* 'refuse, hate.' For Paloor, Thornell et al. give *kaa'* 'refuse' and *kada'* 'refuse, hate' with the applicative suffix. D'Alton gives °*kad* 'refuse.'

10   The Saafi form *-uḍ* or *-uuḍ* given by Mbodj (1983) and Pouye (2015) respectively is simply the passive suffix followed by the perfective suffix *-iḍ*. Though Botne & Pouille (2015) do not list this suffix with /s/, many of their examples contain it. It is not known whether this /s/ ever surfaces in dialects other than Sébikotane.

VERBAL MORPHOLOGY 193

a plural subject. The passive function is found in all Cangin languages, but the plural agreement function is not present in Saafi or Laalaa, where there is no special marking of verbs with plural subjects. It must be stressed that in Noon and Ndut-Paloor this is a single suffix, and not two homophonous suffixes (D'Alton 1983: 275, Morgan 1996: 95, Soukka 2000: 176). It shows the same idiosyncratic allomorphy regardless of its meaning, and there is no special form of the suffix when it marks both a plural subject and passive voice simultaneously. Examples (130–136) contain *-us* with a passive meaning. In (131) the subject of the passive verb is plural.

(130) mi kañu Jóoɓ   (Noon: 029)
       mi kañ-us   Jóoɓ
       1sS give.last.name-PASS Diop
       'I'm named Diop'

(131) ñoodcaa edseeda Kodu   (Noon: 008)
       ñood-c-aa   ed-us-ee-da   K.
       shoe-CL.PL-DEF.DIST give-PASS.PL.SUBJ-PST-PUNC K.
       'the shoes were given to Kodu'

(132) kuunohkaa ñamussi   (Laalaa: Di. 236)
       kuunoh-k-aa   ñam-os-di
       meat-CL-DEF.DIST eat-PASS-NEG
       'the meat hasn't been eaten'

(133) wa tikuusa   (Saafi: B.P. 116)
       wa tik-us-da
       it   cook-PASS-NARR
       'it was cooked' (narrative form)

(134) wa tikseedi   (Saafi: B.P. 116)
       wa tik-us-ee-di
       it   cook-PASS-PST-NEG
       'it wasn't cooked'

(135) di límú Haay   (Paloor: d'A. 213)
       di lím-u   haay
       3s give.birth-PASS Khaye
       'she was born in Khaye'

194   CHAPTER 4

(136)   ɗi húmú ɓooyu ɗih?   (Ndut: Mo. 127)
        ɗi húmú ɓooy-u   ɗih
        3s be.PST wash-PASS how
        'how was he washed?'

Examples (137)–(139) contain *-us* as a plural subject agreement marker.

(137)   oomaacii hamseeɗa   (Noon: 002)
        oomaah-c-ii   ham-us-ee-ɗa
        child-CL.PL-DEF.PROX dance-PL.SUBJ-PST-PUNC
        'the children danced'

(138)   ɓa nehute   (Paloor: d'A. 281)
        ɓa   neh-u-te
        3pS draw.water-PL.SUBJ-PERF
        'they drew water'

(139)   yakka fúsúu ya'yi so   (Ndut: Mo. 89)
        yak-y-a   fús-a'-u   ya'-y-i   so
        bird-PL-DEF flee-APPL-PL.SUBJ hand-PL-AM 1S
        'the birds escaped from my hands'

In Northern Noon the plural subject marker is used only with full noun phrase
subjects and not pronouns, but in other Noon dialects and Ndut-Paloor it is
used with all plural subjects.

   Both the passive and plural subject marking function must have been present in Proto-Cangin. Of these, the plural subject marking function is original, with the passive meaning developing from it—a development which had
already taken place in Proto-Cangin. A plural subject marker can come to mark
the passive due to the use of an impersonal plural subject "they." This exact construction is found in Wolof (which has no productive morphological passive
construction), as in example (140).

(140)   gis nañu ko   (Wolof)
        gis na-ñu   ko
        see PERF-3pS 3sO
        'they saw him' OR 'he was seen'

In this Wolof example, the interpretation can be the same as for the equivalent
passive construction in other languages—in fact it is not necessary that mul-

VERBAL MORPHOLOGY 195

tiple people saw him, as even if only one person saw him this sentence could be used. In Cangin then, the original (Pre-PC) construction would have been something like in the reconstructed example (141).

(141) **ɓa ɣot-us   de
       3p see-PL.SUBJ 3s
       'they saw him' OR 'he was seen'

Eventually the "dummy" subject *ɓa was dropped, allowing the object to move into the vacant subject position, and resulting in the passive construction. The loss of the plural subject marking function is an innovation of Saafi and Laalaa.

The form of this suffix must have been *-us, with the final consonant being deleted in Ndut-Paloor, and often in Saafi. Even in Noon and Laalaa, the consonant is generally deleted word-finally (with the vowel lengthening to -uu in Laalaa). It may be that the consonant was optionally deleted word-finally even in Proto-Cangin.

4.2.5 The Morpheme ɗa

In the modern languages there are two morphemes of the shape ɗa, one of which is grammaticalized from the other: a relative marker ɗa in Noon and Ndut-Paloor, and an aspectual marker -ɗa in NLS. The relative marker *ɗa may in turn be grammaticalized from the manner-class pronoun *ɗ-a 'thus' (see §3.1.15). The Noon and Ndut-Paloor relative marker ɗa appears at the end of the relative clause. Note that in Paloor (and in Ndut with pronominal subjects) the subject is postverbal in relative clauses. In Noon ɗa is often omitted in relative clauses, and in Saafi and Laalaa it is not used at all.

(142) téeɗée Kodu lom ɗa   (Noon: 006)
       téeɗí-aa   K. lom ɗa
       book-DEF.DIST K. buy REL
       'the book that Kodu bought'

(143) yin wante fu kope ra   (Paloor: d'A. 305)
       yin   wan-te fu kope ɗa
       thing say-PERF 2sS God REL
       'what you have said to God'

(144) miisma húmú filiɓ if ra   (Ndut: Mo. 141)
       miis-m-a   húmú filiɓ if   ɗa
       milk-CL-DEF be.PST inside calabash REL
       'the milk that was in the calabash'

Phonologically, *da* is a free word in Noon, always pronounced as [ɗa], while in Ndut-Paloor it can be analyzed as a clitic, undergoing assimilation to the preceding consonant (see § 2.1.7), intervocalic lenition to *ra* (which has been generalized to other environments in Ndut), and vowel harmony with a preceding +ATR vowel. Relative clauses are used not only with a nominal head, but in temporal relative clauses.[11] In Noon these are headed by *waa* or *wii* 'when,' but in Ndut-Paloor there is no overt head. Saafi uses *dah* in temporal clauses headed by *wa/wi* 'when,' and also in a headless construction which generally has a conditional meaning, but is translated in example (147) as temporal. Saafi *dah* is not used in normal relative clauses.

(145) waa mi ham ɗa ...   (Noon: 025)
       w-aa mi ham   ɗa
       when 1sS dance REL
       'when I danced ...'

(146) wa ɓoya eɗ finho ɗah ...   (Saafi: B.P. 11)
       wa   ɓo'-y-a   eɗ finho ɗah
       when person-CL-DEF give back REL
       'when the man turned his back ...'

(147) wek reeyangee ɗah, a ɓoofang ɓoof ...   (Saafi: B.P. 43)
       wek   ree-ang-ee   ɗah a ɓoof-ang ɓoof
       night arrive-HAB-PST REL 3s sit-HAB   sit
       'whenever night came, s/he sat ...'

(148) yeɗ ɗi miis ɗa, sañce   (Paloor: d'A. 314)
       yeɗ ɗi miis ɗa   sañ-te
       give 3s milk REL leave-PERF
       'when he gave the milk, he left'

(149) yéelúu wa ɓa'a rah ...   (Ndut: Mo. 59)
       yéel-a'-u   wa ɓa'-a   ɗa
       look-APPL-PL.SUBJ 3p baobab-DEF REL
       'when they looked at the baobab ...'

---

11   In Noon also with locative/manner clauses headed by a *d-* prefixed demonstrative; e.g. *daa ya kaan ɗa* 'the way that he died,' *daa Kodu kaɗoh ɗa* 'where Kodu went.' D'Alton does not mention these locative/manner expressions in Paloor.

VERBAL MORPHOLOGY 197

It is probably from this temporal construction that the second function of *da* arose. In Noon, Laalaa, and Saafi, there is a verbal inflectional suffix *-da* that is described as either "punctual" (by Soukka 2000) or "narrative." At least for Noon, the term "punctual" is more apt, as this is a very common suffix that is frequently used outside of purely narrative contexts.[12] The basic meaning of *-da* is difficult to pinpoint, but one common usage is in strings of events which happen in a temporal sequence.

(150) ɓoɓaa yugussa, mi líssa ki-ham   (Noon: 013)
       ɓo'-ɓ-aa   *yug-us-da*   *mi lís-da*
       person-CL.PL-DEF.DIST sit-PL.SUBJ-PUNC 1sS continue-PUNC
       ki-ham
       INF-dance
       'the people sat, and I kept dancing'

The punctual/narrative suffix can follow the past tense suffix in each language,[13] but cannot co-occur with aspectual markers such as the perfective suffix, and as such *-da* is identified as an aspectual suffix in each language. If this suffix was originally employed like the relative marker *da* in Paloor, it must have originally been used only in the first of two temporally sequenced clauses (roughly "when [clause A], [clause B]"), but came to be reinterpreted as an aspectual marker on the verb and was then spread to other clauses. Exactly this original construction is found in Laalaa, where Dieye (2010: 201) comments on it as an unexpected use of *-da* to mean 'when' without the word *bi* 'when.'

(151) me ñameeda jën, me jëd   (Laalaa: Di. 201)
       me ñam-í-e-da   *jën me jëd*
       1sS eat-PST-IMPF-NARR fish 1sS be.sick
       'whenever I ate fish, I fell ill'

This Laalaa construction is historically cognate with the Ndut-Paloor construction seen in example (148). Strong evidence for the cognacy of relative *da* and the aspectual marker *-da* is found in Noon, where relative *da* cannot co-occur

---

12   Botne & Pouille (2016: 115) use the term "narrative" for this suffix, but add in a footnote: "This suffix is found primarily in texts, hence use of the term narrative here. Dijkstra (n.d.) considers it to be a thematic connector, and not simply a narrative form."

13   Botne & Pouille (2016: 115) identify the combination of past *-ee* and narrative *-da* as "inceptive" in Saafi.

198 CHAPTER 4

with -*da* or the perfective aspectual suffix -*in*, as seen in example (152) (recall from § 4.2.1 that perfective -*in* is also grammaticalized from a clause-final particle).

(152) a. baayfaa oomaanaa feek ɗa   (Noon: 017)
         baay-f-aa   oomaa(h)-aa   feek ɗa
         dog-CL-DEF.DIST child-DEF.DIST hit   REL
         'the dog that the child hit' (unmarked tense and aspect)

       b. baayfaa oomaanaa feekee ɗa
          'the dog that the child hit' (past tense -*ee*)

       c. *baayfaa oomaanaa feekin ɗa
          (ungrammatical with perfective -*in*)

       d. *baayfaa oomaanaa feekeeɗa ɗa
          (ungrammatical with punctual -*ɗa*)

This restriction on *ɗa* co-occurring with -*ɗa* or -*in* is confirmed only for Northern Noon. The relative marker *ɗa* also does not co-occur with aspectual suffixes in any of the examples in Soukka (2000) and Wane (2017), but they do not specifically comment on this restriction. In Ndut-Paloor there is no similar restriction on the co-occurrence of *ɗa* and aspectual suffixes, since *ɗa* never grammaticalized as an aspectual suffix in these languages.

4.3   Derivational Suffixes

Verbal derivational suffixes (aka extensions) are much more uniform across the Cangin languages than the verbal inflectional morphology. As such there is relatively less to say about them from a historical perspective. The suffixes in Table 133 can be reconstructed to Proto-Cangin.

TABLE 133   Proto-Cangin verbal derivational suffixes

PC	Noon	Laalaa	Saafi	Paloor	Ndut	
*-oɣ	-oh	-oh	-oh	-a'	-a'	applicative (+recip. in NLS)
*-iɗ	-iɗ	-eɗ	-iɗ	-iɗ	-iɗ	benefactive applicative
*-íɗ	-íɗ	-íɗ	-iɗ	-íɗ	-íɗ	causative

VERBAL MORPHOLOGY

TABLE 133   Proto-Cangin verbal derivational suffixes (*cont.*)

PC	Noon	Laalaa	Saafi	Paloor	Ndut	
*-i̥r	°-is, -iis	-es	-is(oh)	-il	-il	iterative
*-ís	-ís	-ís	-is	-ís	-ís	reversive
*-ox	-uk	-ok	-uk	-oh	-oh	anticausative/reflexive
*-is(-oɣ)	-is(oh)	-esoh	-isoh	-is	-is(a')	intensive/pluractional
*-íɗ-ox	RED-ɗuk	RED-ɗuk	-(i)ɗuk	-ɗóh	-ɗëh	pretend
*-iɗ	-iɗ (?)			-iɗ	-íɗ	'have already done'

Other extensions with the same function are used across languages, but probably cannot be reconstructed to Proto-Cangin (Table 134).

TABLE 134   Additional verbal derivational suffixes

Noon	Laalaa	Saafi	Ndut	
-luk	-elok	-(i)ɗuk		factitive (borr. Wolof -lu?)
REDUP-ɗiɗoh	-it	-(i)toh		co-participation
-(i)née[a]	-a(a)	-a	†-i	itive ('go V') (Nd. borr. Wo. -i)
-aat(is)	-aatis		-aat	iterative (borr. Wolof -aat)
	-aaɗi, †-aɗi[b]	-aɗi		privative ('to not V') (cf. Wo. -adi)

a This suffix was originally something like *-(*e*)*nese*, and has a number of irregularities in Northern Noon. The vowel /i/ only surfaces after a consonant cluster, e.g. *toon-ɗ-inée* 'go sell for someone.' It has an allomorph *-nes* before an assimilating consonant, e.g. *lom-nes-sa* 'went to buy' with punctual *-ɗa*. The vowel deletes before a vowel-initial suffix, e.g. *lomnu* from /lom-née-us/. Padee Noon has *-nee* with the vowel deleted before another vowel (Soukka 2000: 172–173). Thiès Noon has two apparently free variants, *-nee* and *-naas* (Wane 2017: 165–166).

b Neither Dieye nor Pichl list this suffix, but Dieye gives *neɓaaɗi* 'be unwell' (*neɓ* 'be good/well'), and Pichl gives †*ñañaɗi* 'not be smart' (*ñaañ* 'be smart'). The Saafi suffix is given only by Mbodj.

Some (generally less common) suffixes are confined to one language or another. These are listed in Table 135. Most of these are borrowed from Wolof or Sereer, but some are unexplained.

200 CHAPTER 4

TABLE 135   Language-specific verbal derivational suffixes

Laalaa:	-el	causative (borr. Wolof -al?)
	-itan[a]	exitive ('go V elsewhere') (borr. Wolof -aan, -taan?)
	-ah	instrumental (see § 3.4.4)
Saafi:	-e	venitive ('come V')
	-uhu	privative (Pouye); PC *-uɣu/oɣo? see § 4.2.3
	-andoo	simultaneous (borr. Wolof -andoo)
	-tin	"parachievement"
	-oot	'V by one's self' (borr. Sereer -ood)
	-it	separative (borr. Sereer -id)
	-(i)tidoh	emphatic reciprocal
	-ndoh	secondary action (equivalent to Sereer -loox)
Ndut-Paloor:	-ante	reciprocal (borr. Wolof -ante)
	Pa. -al, Nd. -il	causative/transitivizer (unproductive, borr. Wo. -al)
	Nd. -inki	do before
	Pa. -kin	achievement
	Pa. -as	'lightly' (unproductive)

a   The synonymous Wolof suffix is -*aan*, but the rare suffix -*taan* seems to be related. Wolof -*taan*
is found for example in *taa-taan* 'go around collecting rainwater' from the verb *taa* 'stagnate
(of rainwater).'

The function of each of the reconstructable derivational suffixes is mostly the
same between languages, and the synchronic descriptions can be consulted for
a more detailed explanation of their usage. A brief discussion of the function
and form of each suffix follows.

The applicative suffix *-oɣ* adds an additional "applied" object which can be
an instrument, location, or manner.

(153)   mi ñama' ya'   (Paloor: Th. 157)
         mi ñam-a'   ya'
         1sS eat-APPL hand
         'I eat with my hand'

(154)   dii mi hamoh da   (Noon: 025)
         d-ii   mi ham-oh   da
         MANN-DEM.PROX 1sS dance-APPL REL
         'the way that I danced'

VERBAL MORPHOLOGY 201

In addition, the applicative suffix functions as the reciprocal suffix in NLS. This function is likely original (or else PC had no reciprocal suffix), since Ndut-Paloor uses reciprocal -*ante* borrowed from Wolof. The applicative suffix is also used as an antipassive suffix in at least Noon-Laalaa (Wane 2017: 138–141, Dieye 2010: 247–248, see §5.3).

The benefactive applicative suffix *-*iɗ* adds an object with the semantic role of beneficiary.

(155) a tikɗi wa ɓoci   (Saafi: B.P. 104)
  a tik-id-iɗ   wa ɓoci
  3sS cook-BEN-PERF it 1p
  'she did cook it for us'

(156) mii hamiɗti   (Noon: 006)
  mi y-ii   ham-id-ɗi
  1sS CL-PROG.PROX dance-BEN-3sO
  'I'm dancing for him'

Thornell et al. (2016) report that in Paloor *-*iɗ* has merged with the causative suffix as -*íɗ*, but they are distinct in D'Alton's description.

The causative suffix *-*íɗ* increases the valence of the verb by adding a causer as the subject and demoting the original subject to object position.

(157) fu tëëkíɗ ɗi feey   (Ndut: Mo. 128)
  fu took-íɗ ɗi feey
  2sS sit-CAUS 3s ground
  'you sit him on the ground'

(158) Nafi lóosíɗin oomahaa feaŋfii   (Laalaa: Di. 242)
  N. loos-íɗ-en   oomah-aa   feaŋ-f-ii
  N. descend-CAUS-PERF child-DEF.DIST bed-CL-DEF.PROX
  'Nafi lowered the child from the bed'

The causative suffix is most commonly used on intransitive bases, such that Soukka (2000: 162–163) terms it the "transitive" suffix, but it can also be used with transitive bases. Its function is essentially the same as Wolof -*al* and Sereer -*in*, the "direct causative" suffixes, rather than Wolof -*loo*, and Sereer -*noor*, the "indirect causative" suffixes. In Noon, Laalaa, and Saafi there is another extension that has been called "causative," and that Soukka (2000: 164) identifies as "factitive" (Noon -*luk*, Laalaa -*elok*, Saafi -*ɗuk*) which has the same function as

202   CHAPTER 4

Wolof *-lu* and Sereer *-noox*. The meaning is close to "to cause to be Ved," and in Saafi, Wolof, and Sereer this complex suffix is made up of the causative and anticausative extensions in sequence.

(159)   ya oɗluk tohootaa ga mësíidaa   (Noon: So. 164)
         y-a oɗ-luk   tohoo-t-aa   ga mësíid-aa
         3sS grind-FACT millet-CL-DEF.DIST at machine-DEF.DIST
         'she has the millet ground at the machine'

The Saafi suffix may have been calqued from Sereer or Wolof, though its function is essentially compositional from the function of the causative and anticausative suffixes together. Noon *-luk* and Laalaa *-elok* are "semi-borrowed" from Wolof, in that the Wolof suffix *-lu* has been altered so that the native Noon-Laalaa anticausative suffix appears in place of the Wolof anticausative *-u*. In Noon and Laalaa (Dieye 2010: 246), the suffix *-luk/-elok* can be combined with applicative *-oh* to yield an indirect causative suffix. Saafi also has an indirect causative suffix *-idukoh* formed in the same way, though no source comments on it specifically.

(160)   mi foollukoiñ oomaacaa   (Noon: 049)
         mi fool-lukoh-in   oomaah-c-aa
         1sS run-IND.CAUS-PERF child-CL.PL-DEF.DIST
         'I made the children run'

(161)   Clotilde soobelokoen oomahcaa tootaa   (Laalaa: Di. 246)
         C. soob-elokoh-en   oomah-c-aa   too-t-aa
         C. pound-IND.CAUS-PERF child-CL.PL-DEF.DIST millet-CL-DEF.DIST
         'Clotilde made the children pound the millet.'

(162)   ɓa neeɓɗukohi ɗi   (Saafi: B.P. 29)
         ɓ-a neeɓ-idukoh-iɗ   di
         3p be.angry-IND.CAUS-PERF 3sO
         'they have angered him/her'

This complex indirect causative suffix *-l-uk-oh* (Noon), *-el-ok-oh* (Laalaa), *-id-uk-oh* (Saafi) (CAUS-ACAUS-APPL) is a morpheme-by-morpheme equivalent to the Wolof and (historically) Sereer indirect causative suffixes *-loo* (Wolof *-al-u-e*) and *-noor* (Sereer **-in-oox-ir*, with **-ir* being the Proto-Fula-Sereer applicative).

The iterative suffix **-ir* means 'to V (once) again,' e.g. Paloor *yen-il* 'laugh again,' Noon *kaɗ-iis* 'go again.' The long vowel in the Northern Noon form is

VERBAL MORPHOLOGY   203

from a duplication of the suffix as *-is-is*, which Soukka (2000: 171) notes is common in Padee Noon. Because /s/ regularly deletes intervocalically in Northern Noon (see § 2.1.6), *-is-is* as found in Padee Noon has developed to *-iis*. This suffix has a regular allomorph *-iss* before a vowel-initial suffix, which historically triggered the deletion of the vowel of the second copy of the suffix; e.g. *kadiis* 'go again,' *kadissin* 'went again,' from Proto-NL **kad-es-es*, **kad-es-es-en*. Thiès Noon uses both †-*is* and †-*siis*.

The form of the reversive suffix **-is* is straightforward; e.g. **pon* 'fold,' **pon-is* 'unfold.' Thornell et al. (2016) report that this suffix does not trigger ATR harmony in Paloor, which must be an innovation. All other languages, including Khodaba Paloor as described by D'Alton, exhibit ATR harmony with **-is*. The Cangin reversive suffix (like that of Wolof and Sereer) has a somewhat broader range of semantic uses when compared with English *un*-; note e.g. **daang-is* 'take down from up high' from **daang* 'be stuck up high,' **naand-is* 'remember' from **naand* 'forget,' and Noon *héñís* 'break up a fight' from *hiñ* 'fight.'

The anticausative/reflexive suffix **-ox* reduces the valence of the verb by removing the object, with the subject being the notional passive participant. The subject may or may not also be the notional active participant—if so the verb has a reflexive interpretation, and if not the interpretation is anticausative, with no implication of an actor/active participant.

(163) mi yúudindi   (Noon: 007)
       mi yúud-in-di
       1sS wake-PERF-3sO
       'I woke him up'

(164) mi yúudukin   (Noon: 002)
       mi yúud-uk-in
       1sS wake-ACAUS-PERF
       'I woke up' (no agent)

(165) ya tíyindi   (Noon: 023)
       y-a tís-in-di
       3sS wash-PERF-3sO
       'he washed him/her'

(166) ya tísukin   (Noon: 026)
       y-a tís-uk-in
       3sS wash-REFL-PERF
       'he washed himself' (*ya* is both agent and patient)

204   CHAPTER 4

This is probably the most common verb extension in each Cangin language, and is also commonly used as a denominal suffix, e.g. Noon *sagacuk* 'be a guest' from *sagac* 'guest.'

The intensive/pluractional suffix *-is* is unproductive and rather uncommon in all languages, and in NLS it is almost always followed by applicative *-oh*. Its most common use is with verbs of separation, e.g. Saafi *ngud-s-oh* 'cut into pieces,' Paloor *lac-is*, Ndut †*lec-s-a*' 'cut into little pieces.' However it is also found in e.g. Noon *tík-is* 'stack up' from *tík* 'put.' Based on the few verbs in which it is found, it is probably best termed a pluractional suffix (as in Botne & Pouille 2016), rather than "intensive." This suffix also combines with *-ox* in Noon (Padee *-suk*, Northern *-iik*), Laalaa (*-esok*), and Saafi (*-isuk*) to mean roughly 'do multiple times in an unimportant way.' Pouye (2015: 96) terms this suffix combination "deprecative." Examples from each languages are given in Table 136.

TABLE 136   Noon, Laalaa, and Saafi verbs with the suffix combination *-is-ox*

Northern Noon

tíid	'walk'	tíidiik	'take a walk'
wo'	'speak'	wo'iik	'speak to self'
ñam	'eat'	ñamiik	'snack'
pag	'do'	pagiik	'play house'

Laalaa (Dieye 2010: 225)

tíid	'walk'	tíidísúk	'take a walk'
woo	'speak'	woisuk	'speak to self'
ñam	'eat'	ñamesok	'nibble at'
an	'drink'	anesok	'sip'

Saafi

nup	'run'	nupsuk	'jog'
ñam	'eat'	ñamsuk	'eat small portions of food throughout the day'
tiind	'walk'	tiindsuk	'take a walk'
toon	'sell'	toonsuk	*'faire le petit commerce'*

VERBAL MORPHOLOGY

Since it implies doing an activity multiple times or for an extended period of time, this complex suffix must contain the pluractional suffix *-is and not repetitive *-iṛ, which is used for repeating an action only once.

The complex suffix *-id-ox means 'pretend to V.' It is reconstructed with +ATR *í based on the Ndut-Paloor form -dëh/dóh, but the first vowel is always deleted except rarely in Saafi (Mbodj gives mark-iduk 'pretend to look'), and perhaps for this reason it never triggers ATR harmony. As Dieye (2010: 224) suggests, the exceptional high vowel of the Laalaa form -duk (as opposed to -dok) is likely explained by an earlier form *-iduk, though it is unclear why the vowel is -ATR. Wolof and Sereer have a suffix with the same meaning, also composed of the causative and anticausative suffixes (see §5.3). In Noon-Laalaa, the verb stem is reduplicated with this suffix, which also occurs in Wolof and Sereer. It may be that this suffix was not present in Proto-Cangin, but rather was calqued from Wolof and Sereer into the Cangin languages after they split. In Saafi a few verbs use -(i)suk with this "pretendative" meaning instead of -(i)duk, e.g. kaalsuk 'pretend to hunt,' which is not too dissimilar from the meaning of -(i)suk 'do multiple times in an unimportant way' discussed above.

The suffix -id 'to have already Ved' is found in Paloor (listed by D'Alton but not Thornell et al.) and Ndut (where Morgan lists it as -íd). D'Alton (1983: 273) mentions that it is very productive, but provides only a few examples of suffixed verbs out of context. This suffix also exists in Noon, though it is not particularly common, and is not noted by Soukka (2000) or Wane (2017). It can co-occur with the benefactive applicative suffix -id, making its presence particularly clear.

(167)   mi dékkí'dindi   (Noon: 040)
        mi dékkí'-id-in-di
        1sS harvest.peanuts-BEN-PERF-3sO
        'I harvested peanuts for him'

(168)   mi dékkí'iddindi   (Noon: 040)
        mi dékkí'-id-id-in-di
        1sS harvest.peanuts-BEN-ALREADY-PERF-3sO
        'I already harvested peanuts for him'

In two reconstructable verbs, there is what seems to be a frozen suffix *-oH, which unexpectedly appears as -ah in Saafi (Table 137). This same suffix appears in 'know' at least in NLS.

TABLE 137   The rare verbal suffix *-oH

	Noon		Laalaa	Saafi	Paloor	Ndut	
*kel-oH	keloh		kalah	kerah	keloh	keloh 'listen'	'hear'
*yul-oH	ˇyoloh 'stand straight'		yoloh	yurah	°yuloh	yuloh	'go straight/forward'
*yún-oH?	únoh, °ínoh		únóh	inah	yúh	yúh	'know'

Paloor °*kel* and Ndut †*kel* 'hear' (D'Alton gives °*keloh* as 'listen') confirm that **kel-oH* is indeed bimorphemic. In Ndut there is an unsuffixed verb *yul* 'go straight.' Judging by these two verbs, this suffix may have had a durative meaning, but it was almost certainly not productive in Proto-Cangin. There also appears to be an unproductive suffix *-ír* of unclear meaning found in **fúd-ír* 'breath/blow' (cf. **fúd* 'light fire') and perhaps also **yawír* 'reduce' and **pídír* 'itch.'

Two privative suffixes ('to not V') are found in NLS. Laalaa and Saafi use *-adi* on some verbs, borrowed from Wolof *-adi*. It might have been independently borrowed, especially given the vowel /i/ in Laalaa, which should have become /e/ if it was present in Proto-NLS. The second is **-uɟu* or **-oɟo* (Saafi *-uhu*, NL imperfective/habitual negative *-oo*), which was present in Proto-NLS, and perhaps in Proto-Cangin.

Of the other suffixes found in individual languages, itive *-a* 'to go V' might be reconstructable to Proto-Cangin, as it is found in Laalaa and Saafi. Otherwise these suffixes are borrowed or have an unclear origin. There is an especially high number of additional derivational suffixes in Saafi, and most are borrowed from Sereer or Wolof. Most of these are given only by Pouye (2015), and thus may be dialectal.

4.4   Summary

This chapter has explored the history of Cangin verbal morphology. All Cangin languages have a large number of verbal inflectional categories, expressed as suffixes on the verb or with auxiliary constructions. A number of these have been innovated, but most can be reconstructed to Proto-Cangin, including suffixes for past tense and imperfective and habitual aspects, and auxiliary constructions for future tense and progressive aspect. Negation strategies are notably innovative in each branch, involving grammaticalization of various auxiliary verbs, particles, or derivational "privative" suffixes in each branch. Proto-Cangin verbs had no person marking for either subjects or objects, but there was an obligatory suffix agreeing with a plural subject, which was grammaticalized as a passive suffix through an impersonal construction ("they saw him" = "he was seen"). Subject pronouns have remained free words in all modern languages, but some object pronouns have become suffixes (but not agreement markers) in some languages. Like many Niger-Congo languages, Proto-Cangin had a large inventory of verbal derivational suffixes or "extensions" used both in valence changing constructions like causatives and applicatives, and with more adverbial meanings like the reversive and iterative. These derivational suffixes are on the whole more stable than the inflectional morphology, but languages have also borrowed a number of extensions from Wolof or Sereer.

CHAPTER 5

Cangin in an Areal and Niger-Congo Context

The Cangin languages are held to be members of the Niger-Congo family, as they share some basic lexical roots and noun class markers found throughout the family. This chapter discusses the features of Cangin languages and Proto-Cangin which can be fruitfully compared with other Niger-Congo languages, especially the other Atlantic languages, and in particular Wolof and Sereer. While Atlantic was first proposed as a genetic unit, its validity has long been in doubt, and my own view is that neither Atlantic nor any large subset of Atlantic languages form a demonstrable subgroup. As a term of convenience I will use "Northern Atlantic" as proposed in Sapir (1971) to refer to these established Niger-Congo groups: Cangin, Fula-Sereer, Wolof, Bainunk-Kobiana-Kasanga (BKK), Tenda, Biafada-Pajade, and Bak (Joola languages, Manjak-cluster languages, and Balanta). I will not discuss Nalu or Mbulungish both because of their geographic position (south of the groups listed), and the paucity of available data. Segerer (2000) suggests that Bijogo be included within Bak, but the issue is unresolved.

It is entirely unclear what Cangin's closest relative is within Niger-Congo. It is certainly not particularly closely related to the Fula-Sereer group, despite Cangin speakers being ethnically Sereer. Any genetic relation between Cangin and another Niger-Congo group must involve a considerable time depth, and as such there is much about the history and structure of the Cangin languages that cannot be explained by appealing to genetic inheritance. On the other hand, much of the structure of the Cangin languages can be attributed to areal pressure. The Niger-Congo languages of northern Senegal—i.e. Wolof, Sereer, Fula, and the Cangin languages—have come to share many properties that are not the result of shared genetic inheritance. An in-depth study of these areal effects would be very welcome, but is outside the scope of this study. A short list of areal features common to Noon, Sereer, and Wolof is given below to illustrate the point. Note that some of these features have a wider distribution, being found also in languages to the south.

© JOHN T.M. MERRILL, 2023 | DOI:10.1163/9789004546493_006

CANGIN IN AN AREAL AND NIGER-CONGO CONTEXT

i) Lexical items with shared idiosyncratic polysemy

Noon	Sereer	Wolof	
kumun	o-ñis	bakkan	'nose, life'
kot	(o-)jaf		'leg, time (countable)'
waas		yoon	'road, time (countable)'
yooɓ	yooɓ	yomb	'be easy, be cheap'
kowu	o-ɓiy	doom	'child, fruit'
pok	hum	takk	'tie, marry'
sag	fañ	bañ	'hate, refuse'
kaak	xom	duul	'defecate, lie'
laak	jeg	am	'have, happen, be (existential)'
kañ, kéñ-íɗ	sim, sim-in		'have family name (in passive),' 'greet'
aaw	jof		'head towards, be about'

ii) Calqued idioms

Noon	Sereer	Wolof	Idiom meaning	Literal meaning
yégís haf	weer xoox	dëgër bopp	'be stubborn'	'be hard'+'head'
bi léey	boo yut	ba noppi	'afterwards'	'until finish'
laak faan	jeg cer	am yaram	'be fat/obese'	'have body'
waas-soo gaa ga	a-fat es ref-ee teen	sama yoon nekk-u ci	'it's none of my business'	'my road isn't in it'

iii) Post-nominal class-agreeing definite determiners with a distal/proximal distinction

Noon	Sereer	Wolof	
baay	o-ɓox	xaj	'a dog'
baay-f-ii	o-ɓox ol-e	xaj b-i	'the dog' (proximal)
baay-f-aa	o-ɓox ol-aa	xaj b-a	'the dog' (distal)

iv) A rich inventory of derivational verbal affixes, many with shared idiosyncratic functions. For example each language has an applicative suffix that can be used for instrumental, locative, and manner applied objects (but not beneficiaries), and which is also used as an antipassive suffix (Noon *-oh*, Sereer *-it*, Wolof *-e*, see § 5.3 for more).

v) Use of a marked preverbal focus construction

	'I like couscous' (no focus)	'I like *couscous*' (object focus)
Noon:	mi waaɗ haawi	haawi wédii mi waaɗ
	mi waaɗ haawi	haawi w-édii mi waaɗ
	1sS like couscous	couscous CL-FOC 1sS like
Sereer:	bugaam saaɗ	saaɗ bugum
	bug-a-um saaɗ	saaɗ bug-um
	like-DV-1sS couscous	couscous like-1sS.FOC
Wolof:	bëgg naa cere	cere laa bëgg
	bëgg na-ma cere	cere la-ma bëgg
	like PERF-1sS couscous	couscous FOC-1sS like

vi) In Noon and Sereer: use of a productive suffix that can form adjectives from almost any verb, even retaining the argument structure of the verb (Noon *-i*, see § 3.4.2, Sereer *-u*)

vii) Use of only two "pure" prepositions (i.e. not basically nouns, verbs, or subordinators). Noon *ga* and Wolof *ci/ca* can both be used pronominally without a following noun phrase ('in it/from it,' etc.).

Noon	Sereer	Wolof	
ga	no	ci/ca	'in, at, on, by, etc.'
na	fo	ak	'with, and'

CANGIN IN AN AREAL AND NIGER-CONGO CONTEXT   211

viii) Use of a complementizer 'that' as a quotative particle (Noon *an*, Sereer *ee*, Wolof *ne*)

ix) Use of a post-verbal subordinator (a suffix in Sereer and Wolof and an enclitic in Noon) to mean both 'once/when' and 'if' (the Wolof construction also uses a clause-initial marker *bu*).

Noon		Sereer	Wolof		
ɗoo	kaɗ=aa	i=ndet-angaa	bu	nu	dem-ee
1p.incl	go=SUB	1pS=go-SUB	if/when	1pS	go-SUB
'when/if we go'		'when/if we go'	'when/if we go'		

Note that all other subordinators are clause-initial in each language, e.g. Noon *bi*, Sereer *boo*, Wolof *ba/bi* 'until,' and Wolof *ndax* 'whether/in order that,' which has been borrowed into Noon and Sereer.

x) Use of a lexical verb as a clausal negator before non-finite verbs. In Noon (*sag*) and Wolof (*bañ*) this verb means both 'hate' and 'refuse,' and Sereer *ñak* means 'lack.'

(169)   mi waaɗ ki-sag ki-ñam   (Noon: 011)
            mi waaɗ ki-sag   ki-ñam
            1sS want INF-refuse INF-eat
            'I want to not eat'

(170)   a buga waana ñak o njaw   (Sereer)
            a=bug-a   w-aana   a=ñak o=njaw
            3S=want-DV those.people 3S=lack INF=cook.PL
            'he wants those people to not cook'

(171)   mënumaa bañ a dem ca céet ga   (Wolof: Diouf 2003: 61)
            mën-ul-ma   a   bañ   a   dem c-a céet   g-a
            can-NEG-1sS INF refuse INF go   to   wedding CL-DEF.DIST
            'I can't not go to the wedding'

xi) In Noon and Sereer: grammaticalization of definite determiners as preverbal markers of progressive aspect. The Noon progressive markers show full class agreement, while the Sereer progressive markers are sensitive only to number, using the personal singular (*ox-*) and personal plural (*w-*) class agreement prefixes (similar to the Saafi construction, see § 4.2.1.7).

Noon det.	Noon prog.	Sereer det.	Sereer prog.	
CL-ii	CL-ii	ox-e, w-e	a-x-e, a-w-e	proximal determiner/prog. marker
CL-aa	CL-aa	ox-aa, w-aa	a-x-aa, a-w-aa	distal determiner/prog. marker
CL-um	CL-um			near-listener det./prog. marker

What is important is that these languages make use of parallel linguistic structures, even though the lexemes and morphemes used in them are not demonstrably cognate. Moreover this areal influence is not a recent phenomenon, and was certainly a force that affected Proto-Cangin (recall from § 2.3.2 that many borrowings, especially from Sereer, can be identified in Proto-Cangin). Today, multilingualism in Wolof is seemingly universal among Cangin speakers, though for Saafi (where multilingualism in Sereer is common) the picture is less clear. Many Paloor speakers also speak Saafi, but otherwise multilingualism between Cangin languages is not reported. Unfortunately the situation prior to Pinet-Laprade (1865) is unknown, but given the patterns of borrowing and the fact that Cangin speakers had close political and cultural ties with Sereer speakers, it is likely that many if not most Proto-Cangin speakers were multilingual in Sereer, and many also in Wolof. There is no good evidence for past multilingualism in any other language. Many of the phonological and morphological properties of Proto-Cangin as reconstructed in chapters 2–4 can be attributed to areal pressure, no doubt facilitated by this multilingualism. The remainder of this chapter will explore the properties and structures of Proto-Cangin within an areal context, as well as a broader Niger-Congo comparative context.

5.1 Phonology

5.1.1 *Phoneme Inventory*

The Proto-Cangin consonant inventory is most similar to Sereer out of all its neighbors. The existence of three implosive stops /ɓ, ɗ, ʄ/ is shared with Fula and Sereer. As in Sereer, Fula, and (at least historically) Wolof, Proto-Cangin word-initial prenasalized stops are for the most part morphologically derived (see § 3.1.2). As in Sereer and Saalum Wolof, there is a distinction between a glottal fricative /h/ and a uvular fricative /χ/ (either *x or *H in Proto-Cangin). With the addition of the third back fricative (*H or *x) and the voiced fricative *ɣ, Proto-Cangin would have had the richest inventory of back fricatives among the Atlantic languages.

The relatively large number of back fricatives is likely related to the fact that Cangin is spoken near the northern extremity of the Niger-Congo area, in proximity to Zenaga Berber with which it may have been in contact in the past. Prior to the Muslim conquest of North Africa, Berber was much more widely spoken in southern Mauritania and even northern Senegal, where Zenaga Berber is still spoken by a small community (see Taine-Cheikh 2008). In fact Berber was the principal language of the coastal area north of the Senegal River even in the 17th century. Furthermore, oral tradition holds that both Sereer and Cangin speakers once lived farther north, in the Senegal River valley. If correct, there is a good possibility of meaningful areal influence between Proto-Cangin speakers and Berber speakers, though the time depth at which this situation would have held is not clear. A careful investigation into the potential influence between Berber and the Atlantic languages of northern Senegal does not exist, and would be very welcome. It seems that there are hardly any lexical borrowings between the two groups, so the contact cannot have been intense, but there is still the possibility of typological features being areally diffused between them. Zenaga has /x, ɣ, h, ħ, ʕ, q, ʔ/; the pharyngeals are borrowed, though frequent (Taine-Cheikh 2008: lxxi–lxxii).

Perhaps the most notable difference between the PC consonant system and that of the surrounding languages is the lack of plain egressive voiced stops. PC *ɣ and *l can be connected with the voiced stops /g/ and /d/ in other languages (see Table 15 for *ɣ). It is likely that these sounds were once stops, but had lenited in Proto-Cangin. The history of Pre-Cangin **b is more difficult to establish, but it also likely lenited. A **b > *w change is suggested by outside cognates for 'dawn.' PC *pe' 'goat' might appear to be a counterexample, as some other Atlantic groups show *b—however this root is found with both /b/ and /p/ throughout Niger-Congo groups (cf. Idoma òpí), and is furthermore likely imitative of a goat's bleating, so it would be unwise to propose any regular sound correspondence based on this root.

Cangin	Fula-Sereer	Wolof	Bainunk	Biaf.-Paj.	Tenda	
*wíiɍ	*beed	bët-set		*biiɍ		'dawn (v)'
*pe'	*ban-be	béy w-	*fa-bę̧		*ji-fe 'sheep'	'goat'

It is striking that only two *w-final roots can be reconstructed: *saaw 'firstborn' and *deew 'lick.' 'Firstborn' was likely borrowed from Wolof taaw in the Pre-Cangin period, and 'lick' may be an irregular development from the same root as *-deem 'tongue.' A likely explanation for this gap is that *w deleted or fused with the preceding vowel word-finally. The best support for this idea comes from *to-yo 'millet,' which is likely cognate with Fula-Sereer *ri-gaab and Wolof dugub (with du- being a fossilized class prefix). Given the b-final root in these other two groups, the Cangin word might have developed as **dV-gab > **tV-yaw > *to-yo, supporting both the **b > *w change, and the elimination of final *w. Whatever the case, it is very likely that plain voiced egressive stops were present at some Pre-Cangin stage, but had changed their phonetic realization by the time of Proto-Cangin.

The Proto-Cangin vowel inventory (*í, i, e, a, o, u, ú) is crucially different from those of its neighbors, though it is encountered in a number of more distant Niger-Congo languages. The two-way split in the high vowels but not mid or low vowels (a "2i1e" system, see Casali 2008) is characteristic of many Benue-Congo languages, most notably Proto-Bantu, though there the distinction was probably not one of ATR. The Bainunk and Joola languages as well as Balanta all spoken in Guinea Bissau and southern Senegal have a 9/10 vowel system with an ATR distinction for mid and low as well as high vowels (only mid and high in Balanta), but the "2i1e" system found in Proto-Cangin is otherwise found only in some Manjak-cluster languages within Northern Atlantic. Subsequent developments in the vowel systems of each Cangin language were probably influenced by contact with Sereer and Wolof. Saafi (which borrows most heavily from Sereer) has lost the original ATR distinction, yielding a five-vowel system identical to that of Sereer. The other languages, which have borrowed more heavily from Wolof, have developed contrastive +ATR mid vowels as found in Wolof, and in Noon-Laalaa short *i, *u became /e, o/ (see §2.2.1.1) yielding an identical inventory of short vowels in Wolof and Laalaa (later developments reintroduced short /i, u/ in Noon).

5.1.2   *Lenition of Voiceless Stops in Pre-Cangin*

There is evidence in the history of a number of Northern Atlantic groups, including Fula-Sereer and Wolof, for the regular lenition of singleton voiceless stops. In Fula-Sereer this change seems to have affected all voiceless stops when not in a cluster, with the exception of *t. This lenition change had already taken place prior to the Proto-Fula-Sereer stage, such that no tokens of singleton *p, *c, or *k can be reconstructed to PFS outside of clusters, whereas *f, *s, and *x are common. Wolof seems to have undergone essentially the same change (presumably through areal pressure), such that until rather recently singleton

/p/ and /c/ were rare, and found only as the first consonant of certain nouns, being the result of a class-induced fortition process (/k/ was more common in this position, as /k/ in class prefixes did not lenite, see Merrill 2021). The recent (likely late 19th century) word-initial denasalization of /mp, nc, nk/ has yielded many more tokens of these voiceless stops in modern Wolof, but it is still the case that word-final and intervocalic singleton /p, c, k/ are extremely rare. The lenition of voiceless stops was much less general in the history of Cangin. Pre-Cangin velar **k seems not to have lenited at all, but it is very likely that earlier **c lenited to *s, and that **p lenited to *f outside of root-initial position. The history of **t is more complicated, as it seems to have undergone two lenition changes, first to *r̥ when not root-initial, and later to *s for certain post-vocalic tokens not affected by the first change.

Regarding **t, first recall from § 2.1.5.4 that *r̥ likely originated as the lenition of **t (only root-finally or after a frozen prefix), as it does in a number of other Atlantic groups. However, there is also scattered evidence (shown in Table 138) for the lenition of *t to *s when comparing between different Cangin forms, and with other Atlantic groups.

TABLE 138 Evidence for lenition of *t to *s

Cangin *t	Cangin *s	Other Atlantic	
	*saaw	Wolof taaw	'firstborn'
	*saaf	Pajade ka-taaf	'leaf'
	La. se	Bijogo ti- (many t-initial in Niger-Congo)	1st pl. pronoun
	*maas	Joola Fo. maat, Fula maat-, Ser. maad	'be present, witness'
	*síis	Fula siwt-aa-ɗo, Ser. o-siid	'twin'
	*-ís	FS -it, BKK *-uɽ, Tenda *-ətt, etc.	reversive suffix
No. jutuut, La. jítúut, Nd. °yútúut	Sa. yisuut, Pa. jísúut	Wolof tuuti, Joola Fonyi tiiti, etc.	'small'
*tíɓ	*sísíɓ 'smith'		'forge'
NdP *tík	NLS *ɗisik		'place' (n)

The Cangin-internal alternations in 'forge/smith' and 'place' suggest that adding a prefix triggered a change from *t to *s, but the evidence is very limited, and it is not immediately clear what conclusions to draw. Furthermore, there are a number of *t-initial Cangin roots which correspond to *t/r̥-initial roots in other groups (e.g. *toɓ 'rain'). This issue is clarified by examining the distribution of Proto-Cangin consonants in nouns vs. verbs root-initially, and

216

in all roots root-finally, as shown in Table 139. All borrowings are excluded from these counts, and roots which are not obviously basically nominal or verbal (e.g. *loy 'knot,' both a noun and verb) are excluded from the root-initial counts. Recall that *x and *r̥ cannot appear word-initially, and thus can only appear root-initially in prefixed nouns.

TABLE 139 Distribution of PC consonants in reconstructed native noun and verb roots

	p	t	c	k	ɓ	ɗ	y	m	n	ñ	ŋ	ND	f	s	h	H	x	w	r̥	l	y	ɣ
Verb-initial	17	21	0	15	19	9	9	14	19	7	1	0	3	13	28	4	0	17	0	25	7	9
Noun-initial	11	2	1	10	12	6	7	4	14	6	0	25	4	19	4	5	2	6	3	13	9	11
Root-final	11	13	7	33	33	30	15	17	43	20	4	47	19	29	12	10	19	1	19	37	9	11

While the number of reconstructed noun roots is overall lower than the number of verb roots, the asymmetry for *t is particularly striking—it is almost entirely absent at the beginning of nouns. Of the two *t-initial noun roots, *teeng 'ball of food' appears only in Saafi in Paloor (perhaps borrowed in Paloor), while *taṛ 'buttock/trunk' (not found in Noon-Laalaa) has no explanation (but cf. Wolof taat 'buttock'). It is also notable that for *s-initial roots there are more nouns vs. verbs than for any other consonant. The tentative conclusion regarding root-initial **t is that it remained *t in Proto-Cangin in word-initial position (as in verbs), but lenited to *s post-vocalically. This change implies that all nouns were at one time prefixed, such that even the initial consonant of unprefixed Proto-Cangin nouns was at an earlier stage preceded by the vowel of a class prefix. This sound change **t > *s / V__ had already taken place by the Proto-Cangin period, and a few innovative *t-initial roots (including some nouns) entered the language after the change. Perhaps *taṛ 'buttock' was an early borrowing from Wolof, and as such was never prefixed. By the Proto-Cangin stage, new nouns could be derived from *t-initial verb roots without triggering a change, e.g. *mi-tuHuṛ 'saliva' from *tuHuṛ 'spit.' This proposal accounts for the correspondences in Table 138 by regular sound change, and also accounts for the low number of *t-initial noun roots in Proto-Cangin. However it does not account for the 13 *t-final roots in Proto-Cangin, which were subject to neither the earlier lenition to *r̥, nor the later lenition to *s. These were earlier geminates, as argued in §5.1.3. It is likely that *maas 'be present' and *súis 'twin' were borrowed from Fula-Sereer with singleton *t, after the lenition to *r̥, but before the lenition to *s. The reversive suffix would be the only non-borrowed example of a final **t(t) developing to *s. If it is related to the

CANGIN IN AN AREAL AND NIGER-CONGO CONTEXT

suffixes in other groups, it was likely originally a geminate (as in Tenda), escaping the original lenition to *ɽ, but then degeminated as a sort of phonological reduction in a grammatical morpheme, before undergoing the later postvocalic lenition to *s.

Regarding **p, it is notable that while 27 non-borrowed *p-initial roots are reconstructed, only seven non-borrowed *f-initial roots are reconstructed. Proto-Cangin *f is certainly a native sound, appearing in class prefixes and pronouns as well as lexical roots, but it does not appear with the frequency it enjoys in Fula, Sereer, and Wolof, where it is the lenition of an earlier stop. Cangin *p does in fact correspond to /f/ root-initially in other groups (see e.g. *púl 'leave,' *poh/puh 'clap,' and *pus 'flower' in Appendix 2), and so it seems that root-initial *p did not undergo lenition in Cangin. Root-initial *f corresponds to /w/ in other Atlantic groups (Table 140), and earlier **w is the only source for Cangin *f in this position.

TABLE 140 Cangin root-initial *f corresponding to /w/ in other Atlantic groups

Cangin	Fula-Sereer	BKK	Tenda	Joola	Manjak	
*caa-fú	*-wuC	*-wuɽund	*-wu (?)	*-wú	u-wu	'fly'
*fen	S. wil		*-waan	*ka-wal	ka-wɛl	'hair'
*faan-ox	S. wond-oox	*-waan-ah			wɛntɽ-a	'lie down'
*fúɗ	*wuuɗ					'blow/whistle'
*fu	S. wo					'you (sg.)'

Root-final *f is more common, and does correspond to /f/ in other Atlantic groups (most notably in *nuf 'ear' and *ɣaf 'head'). This correspondence points to a regular lenition of **p to *f root-finally in Proto-Cangin, assuming that /f/ in all of these groups can be traced to an earlier stop. As with *t, PC root-final *p comes from an earlier geminate.

Palatal *c is reconstructed at the beginning of only one native Proto-Cangin root (*caac~cec 'grandparent'), though it is found at the end of some roots (from an earlier geminate), and in the two class prefixes of the form *ca-. It is likely that in the prefixes, *c derives from earlier **j by a general devoicing of stops in prefixes (see §5.2.2). Singleton **c (if it was not already a fricative in Proto-Niger-Congo) lenited to PC *s.

For velar *k, outside cognates (see especially *keeñ 'liver') as well as the large number of PC roots beginning and ending with *k strongly suggest that original **k was not affected by lenition (e.g. to *h or *x). While root-final *k can likely be traced to an earlier geminate in some words, a geminate origin cannot explain why root-final *k is almost three times more common than *p, *t, or *c. It must be that **k simply never lenited in any position, and that both *h and *x are entirely etymologically distinct from the voiceless stop.

5.1.3 Development of Pre-Cangin Geminate Consonants

In a number of other Atlantic groups (at least Wolof, Fula-Sereer, Bainunk-Kobiana-Kasanga, Tenda, and Biafada-Pajade), geminate and singleton consonants contrast in stem-final (and medial) position, e.g. Wolof *xët* 'page' vs. *xëtt* 'tension trap,' or Fula *haɓ-* 'fight' vs. *haɓɓ-* 'tie up.' In some modern languages the geminates have degeminated (e.g. the Tenda languages, in which the earlier geminates are now stops, and the singletons are continuants), but can be recovered through historical reconstruction. There was no gemination contrast in Proto-Cangin, but there is strong evidence that such a contrast existed at an earlier, Pre-Cangin stage. Like in other Atlantic groups, geminates would not have been found in word-initial position, and as no Cangin prefixes triggered gemination, they were not found root-initially.

Given the evidence for the lenition of root-final (and root-medial) **p, **t, and **c to Proto-Cangin *f, *r̥, and *s presented in §5.1.2, there must be some other source for Proto-Cangin *p, *t, and *c in this position. The existence of earlier geminates provides a simple explanation for these segments. Crucially, there is independent evidence that these voiceless stops were earlier geminates; namely, they are not preceded by long vowels in native roots. Vowel shortening before geminate consonants is a common phenomenon across a number of languages, including Wolof (though unlike in Wolof, long vowels are common before prenasalized stops in Proto-Cangin). The same prohibition against long vowels is found for root-final *H, which suggests that it is also derived from an earlier geminate in this position. Table 141 shows the number of native roots in which a short vs. long vowel appears before each of the relevant Proto-Cangin voiceless obstruents.

TABLE 141   Distribution of vowel length before PC voiceless obstruents in native roots

	_f#	_r̥#	_s#	_k#	_x#	_p#	_t#	_c#	_H#
short V	13	10	15	18	8	11	12	5	8
long V	6	9	12	13	9	0	1	0	1

CANGIN IN AN AREAL AND NIGER-CONGO CONTEXT 219

Before the consonants which arose from earlier singletons (*f, *r̥, *s, *k, *x), both long and short vowels are found, but before those that come from geminates (*p, *t, *c, *H), only short vowels appear. The two exceptions are *ndúut 'Abyssinian ground hornbill' and *laaH 'river/marsh.' The second may be borrowed from Wolof *dex* 'river,' and is not found in Noon-Laalaa (see § 2.2.6 for other examples of vowel-lowering before *H). Saafi *laah* is conspicuous in having /l/, a consonant most often found in borrowings. The root for 'small' (e.g. Noon *jutuut*, Saafi *yisuut*) is another potential exception, but it is sound-symbolic, and resembles similar sound-symbolic roots in nearby languages. It is unclear if it should be reconstructed to Proto-Cangin, and if so in what form.

The fact that *x and *H pattern as a singleton/geminate pair is important in determining their phonetic realizations. Their distribution is exactly parallel to *f vs. *p and *r̥ vs. *t, where the stop results from either a root-initial singleton or a non-initial geminate, and the continuant from a non-initial singleton. This parallelism would suggest that *H was a voiceless uvular stop, and *x a voiceless uvular continuant. However these phonetic values are unexpected given the modern reflexes (*H > /h/ in all languages, and *x > NLS /k/, NdP /h/), which if anything points to the opposite values. Recall also that *H is used without exception for borrowings from Wolof and Sereer with the uvular fricative /x/. One likely reason for the distinct development of the uvular pair is that the Pre-Cangin singleton sound was a fricative [χ], as opposed to the other voiceless obstruents, which were all stops: [p], [t], [k], and [c] (though the realization of this last consonant as a stop, affricate, or fricative is less clear). As such, the Pre-Cangin uvular pair would have been phonetically [χ, χχ], as opposed to e.g. [p, pp]. By the Proto-Cangin period, the phonetic properties distinguishing these two earlier sounds was no longer duration, but unfortunately there is no obvious indication of what exactly the phonetic distinction was. Given the facts from borrowings, [χ] is more likely as the value for *H, which would mean that it had not changed its Pre-Cangin pronunciation in root-initial position, and earlier geminate **[χχ] had simply degeminated. As for *x, perhaps singleton **[χ] had fronted to velar [x] in non-initial position. A value of [q] would explain the modern reflexes more easily, but it seems very unlikely that in the same position, [χχ] would have developed to [χ], while singleton [χ] became [q].

The outcome of Pre-Cangin singleton and geminate voiceless obstruents (minus *h) is summarized in Table 142.

TABLE 142 Development of Pre-Cangin voiceless obstruents into Proto-Cangin

Pre-Cangin	**p	**t	**c	**k	**x	**pp	**tt	**cc	**kk	**xx
Proto-C root-initial	*p	*t (>s)	*s	*k	*H					
Proto-C non-initial	*f	*r̥	*s	*k	*x	*p	*t	*c	*k	*H

The assumption of earlier geminates, along with the lenition of singleton **c, **t, and non-root-initial **p discussed in §5.1.2, explains two notable phenomena in Proto-Cangin. First, the contrast between *t/*r̥, *c/*s, and *H/*x is found only in non-root-initial position—the same environment where a geminate/singleton contrast is more likely to be found cross-linguistically. Second, in native roots long vowels are not found before the consonants *p, *t, *c, and *H, which derive from earlier geminates in non-root-initial position. Finally, there is no evidence for an earlier gemination contrast in consonants other than the voiceless obstruents. If such a contrast existed, it left no trace in Proto-Cangin.

5.1.4 Phonotactics, Phonological Processes, and Lack of Consonant Mutation

As in most Atlantic languages, Proto-Cangin syllables are maximally CVC, and there are no restrictions on what consonants can appear in a syllable onset or coda (with the exception of *r, found only between vowels). Most Northern Atlantic languages including Cangin differ from a number of other Niger-Congo groups in having a basic monosyllabic root shape for both nouns and verbs, rather than CVCV (as with e.g. Bantu noun roots). The second vowel in these CVCV roots is unpredictable, and thus is likely original in Proto-Niger-Congo noun roots, but there is no hint of the vowel's earlier presence in Cangin (compare Bantu *-jògù 'elephant' with a full vowel, Biafada-Pajade *-yoogä with a reduced vowel, and Cangin *-oy with no vowel). There are only seven non-borrowed CVCV roots reconstructed for Proto-Cangin, vs. over 400 non-borrowed CVC roots and 33 CVCVC roots.

Consonant clusters were avoided in Proto-Cangin. With a few exceptions, they would have been found only across a morpheme boundary when the vowel of a -VC suffix optionally deleted before another suffix (see §2.2.5). Prenasalized stops are amply attested at the end of Proto-Cangin roots, as they are in all Northern Atlantic groups and in many other Niger-Congo subgroups. In word-initial position, they are morphologically derived (see §3.1.2 on the noun prefix *n-), just as in the history of Wolof, Sereer, and other nearby Atlantic languages.

There are few phonological processes which are shared between Cangin and the surrounding languages. In particular, intervocalic voicing or lenition is not a synchronic process in Wolof, Sereer, or Fula. One phenomenon which is notably present in Wolof as well as Cangin languages is the progressive assimilation of suffix consonants to an immediately preceding stem-final consonant (see § 2.1.7), e.g. Noon /leeh-ɗii/ → *leehhii* 'isn't finished.' Cross-linguistically, progressive assimilation is much rarer than regressive assimilation, and thus it is noteworthy that this phenomenon is found in multiple languages in the area. In Wolof this assimilation is seen in the reversive suffix *-Ci* (e.g. *yeb, yebbi* 'load, unload,' *suul, sulli,* 'bury, unbury') and historically in transitive pairs like *jur* 'bear child,' *juddu* 'be born,' which must result from the assimilation of the anticausative suffix *-(k)u* (see Merrill 2018: 275–279). Drolc (2004) attributes the development of progressive ATR harmony in Ndut-Paloor to contact with Wolof, though there is much disagreement in the literature about the precise nature of Wolof vowel harmony. Medial vowel deletion (§ 2.2.5) is common in Sereer for short high vowels, and in Wolof for a few suffixes like *-al.*

One phenomenon that is certainly not shared between Cangin and the other languages of the area is consonant mutation (found in Sereer, Fula, Wolof, Bainunk-Kobiana-Kasanga, Biafada-Pajade, and Tenda). There have been suggestions that Cangin shows traces of consonant mutation, most notably in Storch (1995), who reconstructs a three-grade Proto-Cangin mutation system (based on what are in fact regular phonologically conditioned root-final alternations as well as errors in Pichl's transcriptions of word-initial consonants), but also subsequently in Gottschligg (2000) and Pozdniakov and Segerer (2017: 5). For example Storch cites the Noon forms *ʔi ~ gih ~ nyih* 'knee,' which in fact represents non-alternating *yi'.* Pichl was inaccurate in transcribing implosive stops especially in his initial (1966) work, and in doing so he settled on many often inconsistent approximations. Gottschligg mentions only the alternation arising from **(ɓe-)reɓ*, which simply shows different regular outcomes of **r* in initial and intervocalic environments (see the discussion in § 2.1.5.4). The three examples that Pozdniakov and Segerer cite are: a) Laalaa *gúd* 'cut,' *ngúd* 'stump'—native Laalaa words cannot begin with a prenasalized stop, and so this noun must be a borrowing from Thiès Noon *ngúd*; b) Paloor *wët* 'surpass,' *mbët* 'be numerous'—native Paloor words cannot begin with a prenasalized stop, nor can they have /ë/ as the sole root vowel; *mbët* is borrowed from Wolof *mbët* 'in great quantity,' while *wët* has no cognate or obvious borrowing source (neither word is found in Thornell et al. 2016b); c) Saafi *nuhun* 'point at,' *ndukun* 'finger'—both words have secure, unrelated Cangin etymologies, with 'point out' being from **nuyun*, and 'finger' from the root **kun* with a prefix—there is no evidence for any alternation between **y* and **k*, nor between initial **n* and **nd*.

Consonant mutation arose in Fula, Sereer, and Wolof when the final consonant of CVC- noun class prefixes and (in Fula and Sereer) pronouns fused with the following root-initial consonant (see Merrill 2018). In Proto-Cangin there is no evidence for final consonants in class prefixes with the exception of the *n- class, and subject pronouns never grammaticalized as affixes on the verb. Regarding the *n- class prefix, the main reason why it never led to a system of consonant mutation is that (at least by the Proto-Cangin stage) nouns in this class did not alternate from singular to plural, and it was not used as a deverbal nominalizing class. Thus there were very few roots that could appear both with and without the *n- class prefix. However there are at least two such roots in Paloor, and they show the expected alternations: *kuluŋ* 'pot,' *guluŋ* 'gourd spoon,' and *luuf* 'forest,' *duuf* 'bush' (also Noon *kúlúŋ k-*, *gúlúŋ*, both 'jug'). Mbodj (1983: 133) cites a single noun as showing traces of a mutation system in Saafi, being *sisi6* 'smith,' derived from *ti6* 'forge' (both reconstructable to Proto-Cangin). This alternation is the result of the postvocalic lenition of *t discussed in §5.1.2 (see Table 138), which is not morphologically conditioned in any way. The t~s alternation in this pair is unique, as agentive nouns are generally formed with a suffix *-oH*, and never by prefixation. Finally, it is possible that at least two class prefixes, *ca-* (for animals) and *ka-* originally ended in nasals (see §5.2.2), but by the Proto-Cangin period these would not have been identifiable as part of the prefix.

5.2 Noun Class

5.2.1 *Areal Pressure: Wolof and Sereer*

Noun class systems are often taken as the most distinguishing feature of Niger-Congo languages; see e.g. Güldemann's (2018: 123) comment that "The hallmark of typical Niger-Congo languages is a system of noun classification involving both marking on the noun and nominal agreement." Sereer, Fula, and Wolof as well as the Cangin languages exhibit noun class systems which are assumed to be inherited from Proto-Niger-Congo. However due in part to the incredible time depth since the breakup of Niger-Congo, many of the individual noun class markers of the different Atlantic families are not obviously cognate. Regardless of their degree of cognacy, the development of these systems has trended towards an areally-distinct profile between Cangin and Sereer and especially between Cangin and Wolof. Noun class in all of these languages (and Fula[1]) was once marked by CV(C)- prefixes on the noun and agreeing elements.

---

1 In Fula the original prefixes have become suffixes, and the system as a whole is more conser-

CANGIN IN AN AREAL AND NIGER-CONGO CONTEXT   223

However these have all been subject to erosion such that there is much less prefixal material on the noun itself, and agreeing determiners are marked with a
C- or (for Sereer) VC- prefix. Table 143 gives the class markers of Proto-Cangin,
Wolof, and Sereer (roman numerals represent the consonant mutation grade
enforced on the root-initial consonant).

TABLE 143   Noun class prefixes of Proto-Cangin, Wolof, and Sereer

Proto-C noun	PC determiner	Wolof det.	Sereer noun	Sereer det.	Semantics
y-, ∅	y-	k-	o-II	ox-	personal sg.
∅	w-	b-	(gi-)I	l-/r-	
ka-, ku-, ki-	k-	g-	(gi-)III	n-	
fa-, fi-, ∅	f-	w-	(g)o-I	ol-	
pi-	p-	j-	(g)a-II/III	al-	
N-	n-	l-	fa-III, ∅	f(an)-	
mV-	m-	m-	(f)o-I	ol-	incl. liquid
nji-	nj-	s-	o-III	onq-	incl. dimin.
			(g)a-III, gi-III	al-	augmentative
ɓi-	ɓ-	ñ-	∅-I	w-	personal pl.
ca-, ∅	c-	y-	∅-II	k-	pl.
ti~tu-	t-		a-II	ak-	pl.
			xa-II	ax-	pl.
			fo-/fi-/fu-III	n-	dimin. pl.
nda-	nd-	f-, c-		m-, t-	locative
ɗa-	ɗ-	n-		n-	manner
wu-	w-	(b-)		y-	time

Table 143 is not arranged with any etymological considerations in mind, but
only to show the typological similarities in class marking between the three
languages. The Sereer system is the most conservative, as it preserves morphologically active noun prefixes for most classes. However the prefix has eroded
entirely for some common classes, and remains only as a single vowel for most

---

vative than in the other languages. I will not compare the Fula class system here, but it should
be noted that it has not evolved in the same way.

others. The Ñominka dialect retains g-initial forms of certain prefixes, but in other dialects these are eroded as well. Wolof is not generally analyzed as having class prefixes on nouns synchronically. A system of CV(C)- noun prefixes did once exist in Wolof, but has been almost entirely eroded (see Merrill 2021). Most nouns in Cangin languages are also synchronically unprefixed, though some morphologically active prefixes remain in Noon-Laalaa, which also preserves the singular/plural prefix alternation for nouns in the *t-* plural class. For both Wolof and the Cangin languages, the main mark of class is the C- prefix on agreeing determiners. This is to a large extent true in Sereer as well, where the original CV(C)- prefixes have been reduced to C- or VC- on determiners—compare the determiner prefix *fan-* of the Ñominka dialect with *f-* of the Siin and Saalum dialects.

To summarize, while all of these systems once marked class with CV(C)- prefixes on nouns and agreeing elements, the areal typological profile has trended towards no marking on the noun itself, and a C- marker on agreeing determiners. This profile has been almost totally achieved by Wolof, Ndut-Paloor, and Saafi, mostly achieved by Noon-Laalaa, and partially achieved by Sereer. The changes which resulted in this typological shift were not shared in the genetic sense, but are rather evidence that areal pressure has played an important role in the development of Wolof, Sereer, and the Cangin languages.

5.2.2 *Etymological Connections*

From a wider Niger-Congo perspective, Proto-Cangin class marking is fairly typical in that nouns are marked with CV- prefixes, and trigger agreement on various targets. The PC class system is notable for the large number of unprefixed nouns, which is almost certainly the result of the erosion of one or more common class prefixes in the Pre-Cangin period. Turning to specific etymological comparisons, there are few class prefixes for which clear connections can be made with other Niger-Congo subgroups. The most convincing are listed in Table 144, comparing the Cangin markers with those of other Northern Atlantic groups, Proto-Bantu, and Ditammari, a Gur language of the Oti-Volta subgroup (Sambiéni 2005). Comparisons with other groups are of course possible, but Bantu and Gur are two groups within Volta-Congo (i.e. the unproven subgroup of Niger-Congo containing all of the non-Atlantic languages which are uncontroversially included in the family) in which the class systems are both well-studied and seemingly quite conservative.

CANGIN IN AN AREAL AND NIGER-CONGO CONTEXT 225

TABLE 144   Etymological connections between class prefixes in Cangin and other groups

Cangin	Fula-Sereer	Wolof	BKK	Tenda	Biaf.-Paj.	Joola	Ditammari	Bantu	Semantics
*ɓi-	*ɓe-			*ɓə-	*ɓə-	*bVk-	ba-	*ba-	personal pl.
*mV-	Fula -ɗam	m-	*ma-, *muN-	*maŋ-	*maN-	*mu-	ma-	*ma-	liquids
*ti~tu-	*ri-	*dV-	*di-	*də-	*di~du-		di-	*du-	incl. 'millet'
*pa-			*fa-	*fa-	*fa-		fa-		some animals
*fa-	*ban-?	w-			*waN-				some animals

By far the strongest connections involve personal plural *ɓi- and liquid *mV-, which recur with similar forms throughout Niger-Congo. Another fairly strong connection can be made between Cangin *ti~tu- (as found on *to-yo 'millet' and a few other nouns referring to grains) and prefixes of a shape *di- or *du- in other groups, also used with 'millet' and some other mass nouns, especially grains. This connection relies on the assumption that earlier **d devoiced in this Cangin prefix (see below). Words for 'millet' in other Atlantic groups, Ditammari, and Proto-Bantu are listed in Table 145.

TABLE 145   'Millet' in various Niger-Congo languages

Cangin	Fula-Ser.	Wolof	BKK	Bassari	Pajade	Ditammari	Bantu
*to-yo	*ri-gaab	dugub j-	KK *di-hind, Bai. *di-tiit	dəfàx 'millet,' də̂lí 'sorghum,' dəɓàc 'sprouted millet'	tə-ppa 'millet/grain,' tə-pər 'grilled millet,' tə-pombo 'millet sp.'	dī-yòò	*du-bèdé

Bainunk-Kobiana-Kasanga *di- and Biafada-Pajade *di~du- are small though synchronically active classes that contain a number of other nouns referring to grains and other mass nouns. Proto-Biafada-Pajade voiced egressive stops were devoiced in Pajade, accounting for the form of the prefix tə~ti~tu- (Biafada has li~lu-). In Wolof and Tenda (exemplified by Bassari), the prefix is fossilized in a few mass nouns (cf. also Wolof ditiñ j- 'millet sp.,' deret j- 'blood'), but does not correspond to an active agreement class. A Fula-Sereer class *rin- (Fula III- -ri) containing a number of mass nouns can be reconstructed, but 'millet' specifically appears to have *ri- (based on Fula gaw-ri with no nasal mutation). Bantu class 11 is a large class with semantics centered on long objects, but the existence of 'millet' in this class is significant, and it does house a few other mass nouns like *du-cèngà 'sand' and *du-gὺmbí 'dust.' For the use of Cangin *ti~tu- as a plural class, a comparison with the Bantu plural class 13 *tu- and/or Gur collective/plural *tɪ~tʊ is probably more apt. It is also possible (though much more speculative) that in the few PC singular count nouns with *tV- like *ti-ix 'name,' the prefix is cognate with Bantu class 5 *di- and its cognates in other Niger-Congo groups.

Within the Atlantic area, classes of the approximant shape *fa-* and *wa-* are found in a number of groups, both containing almost exclusively animals. These can likely be connected with Cangin *pa-* and *fa-* respectively. Recall that there is a regular correspondence between Cangin *f with /w/ in other Atlantic groups (Table 140), and Cangin root-initial *p corresponds to /f/ in other Atlantic groups. While only two Ndut-Paloor animal nouns are prefixed with *fa-* ('cow, antelope'), the *f-* agreement class is strongly associated with animal nouns, and most nouns with the fossilized prefix *pa-* refer to animals. Some languages outside of Atlantic have an animal class prefix *fV-*, e.g. tiMap (aka Amo) *fə-* and Kom *fɨ-* within Benue-Congo. Sambiéni (2005) identifies an animal class **fa* in Gur (cf. Ditammari *fā-nàa-fà* 'cow,' tiMap *fə-ná*, Ndut-Paloor *fana'f-*), and Miehe et al. (2012: 33) reconstruct a separate Gur animal class *wa*. The f-initial class markers have speculatively been connected with Proto-Bantu diminutive *pɨ-*, but this association is far from secure, especially for the Gur marker. Cangin *fa-* might also be compared with the Fula-Sereer class *ban-* (F. III- -wa, S. fa-III, fan-) used for a number of large or dangerous animals.

In attempting to draw any further connections with class markers elsewhere in Niger-Congo, it becomes apparent that there are some crucial differences in the inventory of consonants found in Cangin class markers versus other groups. Most conspicuously, prefixes with /g/ are very common elsewhere in Atlantic, and these tend to include some of the largest classes in each group. Cangin has no prefixes with *ɣ, which as seen in Table 15 can be connected with /g/ in other groups. The voiced egressive stops /b/ and /j/ are also common in class prefixes elsewhere in Atlantic, but are naturally absent in Cangin, as Proto-Cangin does not have *b or *j. Furthermore, whereas Cangin has *c in the prefix *ca-* and *p in the prefixes *pi-* and *pa-*, these two consonants are rare or entirely absent in other Atlantic class systems. The nominal class prefixes beginning in each of /g, j, d, b/ and /k, c, t, p/ in different Atlantic protolanguages are shown in Table 146 (note that original voiceless stops have lenited in some groups, especially Tenda and Biafada-Pajade). A raised "X" indicates that the prefix triggers gemination/fortition of the root-initial consonant. There is weaker evidence for the prefixes in parentheses, either because they are not found throughout the entire subgroup, or are only found fossilized in certain nouns without a corresponding agreement class. Bak is not included in the table because original voiced egressive stops were devoiced (except /g/ in Balanta). For the reconstructed prefixes, see Merrill (2018), and Merrill (2021) for the Wolof prefixes.

CANGIN IN AN AREAL AND NIGER-CONGO CONTEXT   227

TABLE 146   Reconstructed class prefixes with /g, j, d, b/ vs. /k, c, t, p/ in N. Atlantic

	Cangin	Fula-Sereer	Wolof	BKK	Tenda	Biaf.-Paj.
g	—	gal-, gol-, gun-, go-, ge-, gan-	gu-, ga(N)-	gu-, guN-, (ga-), (gaN-)	gaŋ-, geŋ-, gəŋ-, goŋ-	gaN-, guN-, (gu-)
j	—	—	ja-	ja-, ji-, ja(N)-, jiN-	jə-	ji-
d	—	ri(n)-, re-, ru-	(dV-)	di-, da-, diN-	er-, (də-)	di~du-
b	—	ban-, (bo-)	bu-, baˣ-	bu-, baˣ-, bi-, ba-	—	bu-, baˣ-, bo-
k	ka-, ku-, ki-	han-, ho-, hiC-	ka-, kV-	kaN-, ka⁽ˣ⁾-, ku-, kuN-, ki-, ki⁽ˣ⁾-	xaC-, xoC-, (xoŋ-), (xo-)	kuˣ-, (ko-), (kaˣ-)
c	ca-	—	saN-, siˣ-	ciN-, ciˣ-, (ca-)	ʃaŋ-, ʃeŋ-	(saa-, saˣ-)
t	ti~tu-	—	—	ta-, taˣ-, tiN-	(ɽaC-)	—
p	pi-, pa-	—	—	fa-, (faN-)	fa-	fa-, faa-

Assuming that the class systems of Cangin and the various other Atlantic groups descend from the same original Niger-Congo system, a reasonable hypothesis is that voiced egressive stops in class prefixes were devoiced in Cangin. Evidence for this process was seen above in connecting Cangin *ti~tu- with *di~du- in other groups. However, unlike in Pajade and most of the Bak group, Cangin did not devoice original voiced egressive stops in other positions, so the hypothesis must restrict this devoicing change to Cangin class prefixes. A plausible explanation for this development is that class prefixes were one of the only environments in which the original egressive voiced stops appeared in word-initial position, where they escaped the lenition that regularly targeted these sounds in other positions. However since the same development did not take place in unprefixed verbs, it is simplest to assume that the devoicing change specifically affected consonants in class prefixes. There are numerous other cases in Niger-Congo languages where sounds in noun class markers develop differently from the same sounds in lexical roots.

For the velar stops, devoicing of **g would explain the lack of Cangin *ɣ-initial markers, but there are no particularly clear connections to be drawn between Cangin k-initial prefixes and g-initial prefixes in other groups. Furthermore, the existence of multiple k-initial prefixes in these other groups suggests that the Cangin k-initial prefixes can be traced to original k-initial prefixes in Niger-Congo, independently of whether they are also the reflexes of original g-initial prefixes. For Cangin *ca-, the devoicing hypothesis is somewhat more explanatory. Recall that in addition to being used as the largest plural agreement class, many animal nouns are prefixed with *ca-. While no comparable c-initial classes are found in other groups, ʙᴋᴋ has a plural/collective class *ja- (used as one of the personal plural classes, and for some other plural nouns including those in the *ta^X- singular class), and a class *ja(N)- containing a number of animals (including 'hippopotamus, crocodile, elephant,' cf. Cangin *ca-oy 'elephant,' Saafi cahuy 'hippopotamus'). Evidence is also found in Wolof for *ja- on some animal nouns, e.g. jasig j- 'crocodile' and janaab j- 'cat.' Wolof j- is used as a collective agreement class for some j-initial personal nouns, and Babou and Loporcaro (2016) treat it as a true plural class. Cangin p-initial class prefixes are also potentially relevant to this hypothesis. While *pa- can be connected with f-initial classes in other groups (see above), *pi- has no obvious outside cognates. By the devoicing hypothesis it might be connected with b-initial prefixes in other groups, but no particularly convincing connections can be made on a semantic basis. Thus there is no direct support for the idea that Cangin prefix *p can come from earlier **b, and it is unclear what happened to original **b-initial prefixes in Cangin.

A number of other Cangin classes are difficult to connect with outside classes. The personal singular class *y- does not resemble personal singular classes from elsewhere in Atlantic and Niger-Congo, where the marker is typically either u-, a-, mu-, or a combination of these. But recall that Proto-Cangin *y- is in truth not a class for singular nouns referring to people, but a class for the two nouns 'person' and 'thing' (much like Wolof k-). The default class marked by *w- agreement and no prefix on the noun is particularly difficult to draw conclusions about, as the marker itself could have a variety of different sources: a prefix u-, a larger prefix Cu-, or some prefix in which the original consonant (perhaps /b/) developed to /w/. Depending on its earlier form, it might be compared with the large Bak class *u- (found in Balanta and the Manjak cluster) or various *bu- classes like the Wolof "default" class b-, but there is really no compelling argument to be made for cognacy with any outside class in particular. The rare fossilized prefixes *sa- and *su- are found on too few nouns to allow for fruitful etymological comparison. The nasal prefix *n- is too phonologically small to be reasonably identified with any outside class, and besides n-initial nominal class markers are exceedingly rare in Northern Atlantic groups. The fossilized prefixes *a- and *i- fall victim to both of the aforementioned problems.

Finally, there is some evidence that two Proto-Cangin CV- prefixes were in fact originally CVN- with a final nasal at some earlier stage. These final nasals may provide evidence for cognacy with specific class prefixes elsewhere in Atlantic. ᴘᴄ root-initial prenasalized stops are for the most part only found in nouns with no CV- prefix, these being originally in the *n- class (see §3.1.2).

CANGIN IN AN AREAL AND NIGER-CONGO CONTEXT 229

However, when the fossilized prefix *ca- is removed from the reconstructed singular nouns that contain it (mostly animals, see § 3.1.12), seven roots begin with prenasalized stops, e.g. *cangín 'worm/grub.' It is thus likely that this prefix earlier contained a final nasal, which before certain consonants was deleted, and before others resulted in a voiced prenasalized stop. This prefix *caN- can likely be identified with the Bainunk-Kobiana-Kasanga prefix *jaN-, mainly found on animal nouns (e.g. Gubëeher *jan-kaŋ 'megabat,' Kobiana *jandattóol 'wasp'). The other relevant prefix is *ka-, though the evidence here is much more limited. There are perhaps only five nouns which can be reconstructed with this prefix (infinitive/deverbal *ka- aside), two of which contain voiced prenasalized stops: *ka-ndí(d) 'mortar' and *ka-mbot 'debt' (likely borrowed from Wolof *bor). Of the other three, *ka-laɓ 'sword' is borrowed, and two have nasal-initial roots. Thus it is likely that *ka- was at an earlier time *kaN-, or else there may have been two earlier prefixes, *ka- and *kaN-. Prefixes of the shape *kaN- and *gaN- are found in other groups, most notably BKK *kaN- which also contains 'mortar.' It must be stressed that these prefix-final nasals would not have had any synchronically-active status in Proto-Cangin, at best leaving traces of their earlier presence.

It is quite reasonable to assume that the Cangin inventory of class prefixes is on the whole descended from a unified Proto-Niger-Congo class system, and that cognates for each Cangin class prefix exist in other Niger-Congo groups. However in practice only about half of the reconstructed Proto-Cangin prefixes have convincing etymological connections in outside groups. A hypothesis which assumes the devoicing of original Niger-Congo voiced egressive stops in Cangin prefixes allows the shape of prefixes as a whole to be reconciled with other groups, but is only moderately helpful in identifying specific cognate class prefixes. The idea that many Cangin class prefixes are entirely unrelated to class prefixes in other Niger-Congo subgroups is difficult to argue against, and in the absence of convincing proposals to the contrary, this alternate viewpoint must be seriously entertained.

5.3 Verbal Derivational Suffixes

The verbal derivational suffixes (or "extensions") of Wolof, Sereer, and the Cangin languages are quite similar in function, especially for the most common ones. All but two of the extensions that can be reconstructed for Proto-Cangin have equivalents in Wolof and Sereer, despite the fact that almost none of them appear to be cognate (Table 147).

TABLE 147 Cangin verb extensions with equivalents in Wolof and Sereer

Proto-Cangin	Wolof	Sereer	
*-íɗ	-al	-in, -and	direct causative
*-ox	-(k)u	-oox	anticausative/reflexive
*-oɣ	-e	-it	applicative, antipassive
*-iɗ	-al	-an	benefactive applicative
*-ís	-Ci	-it	reversive
*-i̥r	-aat	-axin, -atin	iterative
*(RED)-íɗox	RED-lu	RED-loox	pretendative
NLS *-is-ox	-antu	-loox	unimportant/deprecative
NLS *-oɣo/uɣu	-adi	-afar	privative
LS -a, N -née	-i	-ik	itive
NL *-el-ok	-lu (-al-u)	-noox (-in-oox)	factitive
NL *-el-ok-oh	-loo (-al-u-e)	-noor (*-in-oox-ir)	indirect causative
*-is(-oɣ)	—	—	intensive/pluractional
*-iɗ	—	—	'have already done'

First it must be noted that a large inventory of verb extensions is common in Niger-Congo and in Africa more broadly. However there are some specific characteristics of the extensions of these languages of northern Senegal which cannot be attributed to wider areal patterns or inheritance from Niger-Congo. For example see the discussion of the complex causative suffixes in §4.3, which are formed in the same way in Wolof, Sereer, Noon-Laalaa, and Saafi.

Perhaps the most conspicuous similarity between these languages is the function of the applicative suffix. Cross-linguistically, applicatives can add objects with many different semantic roles. In Cangin, Sereer, and Wolof the applicative suffix is used for the same inventory of applied objects: instruments, locations, and manners. In all of these languages there is a separate applicative suffix for beneficiaries. Furthermore, the applicative suffix in all of these languages somewhat paradoxically also functions as an antipassive suffix, which eliminates an underlying object, rather than adding one (see Renaudier 2012 for Sereer and Voisin-Nouguier 2002 for Wolof). This function is found at least in Noon (Wane 2017: 138–141), but is not mentioned for other languages, perhaps because it is not a particularly common construction in any of the languages which exhibit it.

(172) mi eɗoiñ kopaɗ   (Noon: 001)
       mi ed-oh-in   kopaɗ
       1sS give-APPL-PERF money
       'I gave (out) money'

(173) xaj bi du màtte   (Wolof: Voisin-Nouguier 2002: 310)
       xaj b-i   di-ul   màtt-e
       dog CL-DEF.PROX be-NEG bite-APPL
       'the dog won't bite'

(174) oxe naa xaate'aa cooxit   (Sereer)
       ox-e naa   xaate'-aa   coox-it
       who SUBJ.EXT judge-PROG give-APPL
       'the referee gave (the signal)'

Another similarity which certainly cannot be attributed to coincidence is the existence of a suffix meaning 'to pretend to V;' e.g. Noon *dek-dek-duk*, Sereer *ram-ram-loox*, Wolof *tëx-tëx-lu* 'pretend to be deaf.' This is accompanied by reduplication of the verb stem in Sereer, Wolof, and Noon-Laalaa, though not in the other Cangin languages. The suffix is complex in each language, being (historically) composed of the causative and anticausative suffixes (Cangin *-*id-ox*, Wolof *al-u*, Sereer *-il-oox*, though Sereer *-il* is borrowed from Wolof and mainly confined to Wolof borrowings). This morphological construction is essentially calqued between all of these languages, and probably originated in Wolof, since borrowing from Sereer or Cangin languages into Wolof is rare.

As found throughout Niger-Congo, most Cangin extensions contain a coronal consonant. The small shape of extensions along with the rather restricted set of consonants found in them makes etymological comparison between groups extremely difficult, as discussed in Hyman (2014). Among the Cangin extensions with a coronal consonant, none have clear cognates in other languages. Reversive *-*is* can be compared with the many reversive suffixes containing /t/ in other groups, e.g. Fula-Sereer *-*it*, BKK *-*uɽ* (earlier *-*ut*), and Tenda *-*ətt*—but an etymological connection would require the irregular development of **t(t) to PC *s in this position (see the discussion in §5.1.2). Of the two Proto-Cangin extensions without a coronal consonant, anticausative *-*ox* has likely cognates in many Niger-Congo groups, where this suffix (often termed "middle," "stative," or "neuter") tends to contain a back consonant, in contrast with the more common coronal extensions (Table 148).

232   CHAPTER 5

TABLE 148   Anticausative/middle/stative suffixes in Northern Atlantic groups and Bantu

Cangin	Fula-Ser.	Wolof	BKK	Tenda	Biafada-Pajade	Joola	Bijogo	Bantu
*-ox	*-oox	-(k)u	*-ah	*-a	B. -oo, P. -a, -oᵃ	*-o	-ɔk	*-ik

a   Meyer (2001: 99–103) terms -a 'middle' and -o 'passive,' noting that they are often used in combination as -a-o

The Cangin applicative suffix *-oy has, to my knowledge, an entirely unique shape among Niger-Congo groups, in which the equivalent suffix generally contains a coronal consonant.

5.4   The Place of Cangin within Niger-Congo

While Cangin's inclusion in the Niger-Congo family (or "Atlantic-Congo" if controversial groups are excluded) has not to my knowledge been challenged, its place in the Niger-Congo family tree is not agreed upon. While many have expressed skepticism about the validity of Atlantic (see e.g. Güldemann 2018: 180–183), the only proposals that make specific claims about Cangin also accept Atlantic (or a subset of these languages) as a valid subgroup. The most notable claims are found in Sapir (1971), a lexicostatistical study that assigns Cangin to "Northern Atlantic" (see the beginning of this chapter for a list of languages), and in Pozdniakov and Segerer (2017), who also treat Cangin as a primary branch of a North Atlantic subgroup (equivalent to Sapir's Northern Atlantic but without Bak). See Merrill (2018: 373–389) for critiques of both proposals.

Subgrouping at large time depths is extremely difficult to establish, such that for most of the world's macro-families there is little agreement on the highest-level structure of the family tree (cf. Indo-European, Uralic, Sino-Tibetan), even when the set of languages included in the family is not in question. To convincingly establish a subgroup, it is necessary to demonstrate shared innovations from the higher-level protolanguage that characterize that subgroup. These can be sound changes, lexical innovations, morphological developments, or any other type of change. Since there is no agreed-upon reconstruction of Proto-Niger-Congo or any protolanguage ancestral to Cangin, assessing whether shared innovations can or cannot be established between Cangin and any other Niger-Congo language is difficult. However, there are three areas in which I believe this question can be fruitfully assessed, and in all three there is no evidence for subgrouping Cangin with any other language or languages.

The first area is sound change, especially regarding consonants. Appendix 2 (Table 149) presents a tentative reconstruction of the Proto-Niger-Congo consonant system based on regular correspondences between Northern Atlantic groups and Bantu. The major changes to singleton consonants in roots from PNC to Proto-Cangin are:

a) Lenition of all voiced egressive stops
b) Lenition of **p, **t when not in word/root-initial position
c) Merger of **c and **ţ as *s
d) **l > *n
e) **j~y is often lost

Comparing with the protolanguages of other Northern Atlantic groups and with Proto-Bantu, these changes do not suggest any obvious subgrouping. Change (a) is seen only in Tenda, (d) in Bainunk-Kobiana-Kasanga and Tenda, and (e) only in Bijogo. Lenition of voiceless stops similar to change (b) is found in a number of Atlantic groups, but never in the same way as in Cangin. Cangin is notable for preserving **p in word/root-initial position and **k in all positions, while in all other groups that exhibit lenition **p and **k are affected. The development of **t is also unique in Cangin. Change (c) is extremely widespread both in the Atlantic area and elsewhere in Niger-Congo (including Bantu), and for exactly this reason it is not a useful diagnostic for subgrouping. Only Bainunk, Joola, Manjak, and Bijogo exhibit distinct reflexes for **c and **ţ—Bantu has *c which is a fricative in all modern languages but Swahili. Regarding vowels, recall that the PC vowel inventory is more similar to that of Proto-Bantu than to any Atlantic language—but pending a reconstruction of the PNC vowel system nothing concrete can be said for now.

The second area is morphology, especially noun class. As discussed in § 5.2.2, many Cangin noun class markers have no identifiable outside cognates, and most of those with cognates appear in many different Niger-Congo groups including ones outside of the Atlantic area. There are very few verbal morphemes with outside cognates, and the few convincing ones like anticausative *-ox are extremely widespread. Recall also that no system of consonant mutation has developed in Cangin, setting it apart from a number of other Atlantic groups.

The last area is lexicon. Potential cognates between Cangin, other Northern Atlantic groups, and Bantu are presented in Appendix 2. While this list will doubtless grow in the future, the number of cognates identified after extensive comparison is rather low, and does not speak to a period of shared lexical innovation between Cangin and any other language. Within Northern Atlantic, I have been able to identify between 35 and 60 convincing cognates with most groups, ~15 with Bijogo, and with Bantu or Benue-Congo ~30. There is no outside group that shares more than a few exclusive cognates with Cangin (i.e. cognates not found in any other group).

5.5 Conclusion

While many developments in the history of Cangin languages can be attributed to a linguistic area which includes at least Wolof and Sereer, there are no convincing shared phonological or morphological innovations from a putative Proto-Niger-Congo language that can be used to subgroup Cangin with any other Niger-Congo language. In fact very little of Proto-Cangin morphology has clear outside cognates at all. Setting aside the areally-driven typological parallels with Sereer and Wolof, the phonological and morphological systems of Proto-Cangin do not closely resemble those of any other Niger-Congo subgroup in particular. This observation also holds for lexical cognates. The conclusion must be that Cangin experienced an extremely long period of independent development, separate from any other extant Niger-Congo language or subgroup. Based on our current understanding, it is not unreasonable to treat Cangin as a primary branch of Niger-Congo (and I suspect that the same could be said of various other Atlantic subgroups). Given its genetic isolation within Niger-Congo, Cangin is potentially of outsized importance in addressing questions related to the reconstruction and diachronic development of Niger-Congo as a whole. It is hoped that this study will allow for Cangin evidence to be given a more prominent position in discussions of these larger questions.

APPENDIX 1

Proto-Cangin Lexical Reconstructions

Reconstructions preceded by a raised "b" are (likely) borrowings—most into Proto-Cangin, but some are probably shared borrowings from after the diversification of the Cangin languages. See Table 69 for the borrowing sources. Paloor has borrowed some words from Saafi, so words which appear only in these two languages should be viewed with caution. Reconstructions preceded by a raised "c" have possible cognates in other Atlantic languages, listed in Appendix 2. Class prefixes, including frozen/fossilized ones (not separated with a hyphen), are underlined. Even some prefixes separated with a hyphen were likely frozen and treated as part of the root in certain words.

	Noon	Laalaa	Saafi	Paloor	Ndut	
			PC *p			
c*paɓ	†paɓ	†paw	paɓ	paɓ	°pab	'wing'
*paɗ	paɗ	paɗ	paɗ	paɗ	°padd	'sweep'
*paɗ			paɗ m-		†pad/par	'dirt/trash'
b*paɗ	paɗ	paɗ	paɗ	°paɗ 'kick'		'slap'
b*paloom[1]		paloom f-		°palom f-		'antelope sp.'
*paní	péní	pëní f-	pani	póní, °pëní	pëní f-	'sleep' (n)
b*panís[2]	pénís f-	pënís f-	panis	pónís	pënís f-	'horse'
c*pang	pag	†paag/pag 'shake'	panguk 'work'	paŋ~g	paŋ~g	'do'
*pay	pay 'pass by'	pay	pay 'disperse'	pay	pay	'go'
b*pay	pay	pay	pay	pay	†paj	'heal'
*pay-oH	payoh	†payoh	payoh	payoh	†pajoh	'healer'
*pay	pay	pay f-	pey	pay 'cricket'	†pay f-	'grasshopper'
*paal	paal	paal	paar	paal	†paal	'sprout' (v)
*paaní	péeníi f-	pëëní f-	paani f-/n-	póoní °f-	pëëní f-	'monkey'

---

1 As a borrowing from Wolof *baroom*, *pa* is not an etymological prefix here, but was likely treated as one given that it is unstressed in Paloor.

2 Ultimately from an Afro-Asiatic language (likely Semitic *paras*), but cannot be a recent borrowing from Arabic *faras*. Between Atlantic groups, the root shows mostly regular correspondences for **pali(n)c~pala(n)c*, e.g. Manjak *u-mpəlɪnc*, Konyagi *i-péḷàcá*, Balanta *fálás*, and earlier Wolof † *fars*. Thus the borrowing must be extremely old in the area. Cf. Central Chadic *pirisʸ*, e.g. Daba *pilís* (Gravina 2014: 156), also likely borrowed from Semitic.

© JOHN T.M. MERRILL, 2023 | DOI:10.1163/9789004546493_007

APPENDIX 1

(*cont.*)

	Noon	Laalaa	Saafi	Paloor	Ndut	
			PC *p			
c*pe'	pe' f-	pe' f-	pe' f-	pe' °f-	pe' f-	'goat'
*pes	ˉ†pes	pes	pes	pes	pes	'live'
*kV-pes	ˉkipes k-	kapes k-	kipes	pes k-	pes	'life'
*peend-?			peendoha n-	pendal °f-	peedal f-	'chameleon'
*su/ki-pi	kipii k-	sope'	kipi 'earring'	°kipi k-	supi	'ring'
*píɗíɽ	pídĩs		piɗis		†píríl	'itch'
*píim	píim f-	píim p/f-		°pím		'sorghum'
*píix	píik	píik	piik	°píy	†píi	'gather' (NL 'harvest')
*poox	pook	pook	pok	poo	poo, °pooh	'break'
*pooy	pooy	pooy		pooy	†poy	'wring'
*pok	pok	pok	(tok)	pok	pok	'tie, attach'
*pok-ís	pókís	púkís		pokís, °pëkís	°pokís, †pëkís	'untie'
*pon	pon	pon	pon	pon	pon	'fold'
*pon-ís	pónís	pónís	ponis	ponís, °pënís	pënís	'unfold'
*pongVluɓ	pooguluy, †pëngëlëɓ			°pogalub	°pugulub	'heel'
*poond	pood	pood	poon	poon	†pon	'thatch/cover (roof)'
*ca-poond			capoon	°capoon	†pon	'thatch' (n)
b*puɗ	poɗ	†poɗoh		°puɗsoh		No. 'crack joints,' La. 'healer of bone fractures,' Pa. 'stretch joints'
c*(sa/ca-)pus	sapuus, †sabës	sapos	pos	capus	†capós	'flower'
c*puuɽ	puus	puus	puus	puul	°puul	'wound' (n)
*púɗ	púɗ		puɗ	°púd		'powder (type)'
*púk	púk	púk	puk	púk	púk	'forehead'
c*púl			pul	°púl	púlëh 'appear'	'leave'
*púnd	púd		pund	°pún~d	pún~†d	'fly' (v)
*ma-púy	mópúy m-	mëpúy m-		°mëpúy m-		'pus'
c*puh/poh[3]	poɗ	puu	poy	°poos	†póos	'clap'

---

3 The NdP form contains pluractional *-*is*. The Laalaa form is better explained if the root vowel is *u, but NdP seem to indicate *o.

PROTO-CANGIN LEXICAL RECONSTRUCTIONS

(cont.)

	Noon	Laalaa	Saafi	Paloor	Ndut	
			PC *t			
ᵇ*taH	tah	tah	tah	tah	tah	'cause'
ᵇ*tak	tak	tak	tak	tak		'kinkeliba'
*tam	tam	tam	(dam)	tam	°tam	'be hot/burn'
*tap	tap	tap	tap 'hit, sting'	tap 'pierce'	†tap 'sting, ram'	'pound'
ᶜ*taṟ			tas	tal	°tal	'buttock/trunk'
*tas	tes	tas	tas	tas	tas	'stay'
ᵇ*taal⁴	taal 'nest'	taal 'hut/nest'	taar 'nest/kitchen'	taal	†taal	'hut,' Pa. also 'hearth'
ᵇ*taan	taan(um)	taantaan	taanum	taan	†taan	'(maternal) uncle'
*taañ(-íɗ)	taañ				téeñíd	No. 'be pregnant out of wedlock,' Nd. 'impregnate out of wedlock'
*(yin) taaŋ⁵			inaa-taang, taaŋ	yin-taaŋ f-	†yin-taŋ	'animal'
*taas(-ox)	taayuk, ˇtaasuk	taasok	taas	taas	†taas 'doubt'	'deny'
ᵇ*taaw	taaw	taaw		°taaw		'swelling/abscess'
ᶜ*teɗ	teɗ	teɗ	teɗ	°teɗ	°tedd	'weave'
*teɗ-oH	tedoh	tedoh	tedoh	°tedoh	°teroh	'weaver'
*ten	ten	ten		°ten~d	ten	'milk' (v)
*teeɓ	teeɓ	teeɓ	teeɓ	teeɓ	°teeb	'show'
*teemb			teemb 'meet'	°teem~w⁶	°teem	'be equal'
*teeng			teeng	°teŋ		'ball of food'
*tiɣVṟ?	taas	taas	tahas	°tíil	°tiil	'answer'
*ti̱-ix	téek, ˇ†teek	teek	tiik (n), teek (v)	tii k-	°tii, †téey	'name' (n)
*tíɓ	tíɓ	tíi	tíɓ	°tíɓ	°tíb	'forge'

---

4 Likely borrowed from Wolof *taal* 'hearth,' especially since native Cangin *t-initial noun roots are perhaps nonexistent. The sense 'hearth' is only found in Paloor, but a development 'hearth > home/hut > (nest)' is natural (cf. Latin *focus* 'hearth > home'). A connection with Kobiana *baal* 'home' (unrelated to the Wolof word) is possible (assuming a frozen prefix *b-*), but unlikely. If valid, the Cangin word would contain a prefix *t-*, but there is no evidence from agreement to support this idea.

5 D'Alton (1983: 125) gives *yin-taan f-*, taken to mean 'thing of maternal uncle.' However as all other sources have /ŋ/, these terms are likely unrelated.

6 This is the only example of an [m~w] alternation, and D'Alton does not comment on it in the text. It may be a typo for the common *m~b* alternation, but Pichl (1979: 40) does note *ham~hav-ute* for *hamb* 'have' in Ndut.

238 APPENDIX 1

(*cont.*)

	Noon	Laalaa	Saafi	Paloor	Ndut	
			PC *t			
*sísíɓ[7]			sisiɓ	°sisip	†sísíb	'smith'
*tík	tík	tík	tik	tík		'cook'
*tík	tík	†tík			tík	'put, be next,' La. 'be more/again'
*típ	típ	típ	tip	típ	†típ	'beat (drum)'
*tíɽ̥	tís	tís	tis 'brush teeth'	tíil, °tíl		'wash by scrubbing'
ᵇ*tís	tes	tís	tis	°tís	°tís	'sneeze'
ᵇ*tí(n)ɣíñ-ox	(tíiñuk, tígíñuk)[8]	tíiñúk	°tingiñ	°tígíñëh		'rub (eyes)'
*tíind~tíɽ̥[9]	tíid	tíid	tiind	tíl	tíl	'walk'
ᵇ*tíit	tíit		tiit		tíit	'fear (v)'
ᶜ*toɓ	toɓ	toɓ	toɓ	toɓ	°tob	'rain' (n, v)
*fi-toɓ		fetoɓ f-				'rain' (n)
*tof	tof	tof				'set down'
*tof-ox	tuuk	tuuk	tufuk	tofoh	†towoh	'stand'
*tong	tog	tog		toŋ~°g	†toŋ~g	'stomp/trample'
ᵇ*tuɓaaɓ	towaaɓ	†toow	tuɓaaɓ	tuyaaɓ	†toab	'white person'
ᶜ*tuHuɽ̥[10]	toos	toos	tuhuus, °tuhus	tuul		'spit' (v)
*mi-tuHuɽ̥	ˉmitoos m-, †medos m-	metoos m-	mituhuus m-			'saliva'
*túm[11]	túm	túm	tum	tum, °túm 'put'	tum, †túm 'put'	'do'
*teh/tah	te'		te', tey~tay	°tah	†tah	'take back'
*tV-úH	tóoh, †túuh			túh	†tú	'all'

---

7   Formed from *tíɓ by partial reduplication, later subject to the postvocalic *t > *s change, i.e. **V-tí-tíɓ > *sísíɓ. This is the only word to use this derivational strategy, which is perhaps taken from the regular Sereer pattern for forming agentive nouns (e.g. ño' 'sew,' o-ñoo-ño' 'tailor').

8   'Put on a headpad' and 'lay head on cushion' respectively; seems semantically unrelated, but the perfect phonological match is conspicuous.

9   Explained if the root is *tí(h) with a different frozen suffix in each branch. The NdP suffix would be iterative *-iɽ̥, but *-Vnd does not exist independently.

10 From Cangin-internal evidence both *tuHuɽ̥ and *tuyuɽ̥ are equally possible, since intervocalic /h/ from all sources is usually deleted in Paloor, and *ɣ is deleted everywhere in Paloor. The choice of *H is based on Sereer duxud/tuxud 'spit,' which is either a cognate or the borrowing source of the Cangin word.

11 Possibly related to words for 'work' in other Niger-Congo languages, e.g. Benue-Congo *-tomo, but these are derived from a verb 'send,' cf. Bantu *-túm.

PROTO-CANGIN LEXICAL RECONSTRUCTIONS

(cont.)

	Noon	Laalaa	Saafi	Paloor	Ndut	
PC *c						
ᶜ*ca-oɣ[12]	cooh f-	coh f-	cooh	caa' °f-	°ca', †caa' f-	'elephant'
*caɓín		caɓin		céen, °ciin	céhín, °céyín	'moon'
*caɓol?		°cawol			†caal f-	'pelican'
*cafay			cafay n-	cafay	†cofej k-	'young girl'
*cangayo?		°caagayuu		°cagayo f-	†cagoy f-	'large bird sp.'[13]
*cangín	cégín (f-), †cëngën	cëgín f-	cangin	°cigin f-	°cígín, †céegín f-	'worm' (grub)
*case?		caase f-	case 'squirrel'	cafe'	†casé f-	'porcupine'
*ca(h/ɣ)úc?		cóoc f-		°cooc		'breakfast'
*ca(h/ɣ)VnV	cóoní	°coonee		coona	†coona f-	'soul'
*caac~cec	caac, cic	caaca	caac	caac, cec f-	caac, cic f-	'grandparent'
ᶜ*caafú	cëw, °cëwuu	cëëfú f-	caafu	cóofú °f-	°cëëf k-	'fly' (bug)
*caal		caal f-	caar		caal f-	'antelope'
*caangínV	céengëníi	cëgëní f-	caangin	°cegina f-	°cagín, †cégín f-	'large bird sp.'[14]
ᵇ*coot	†cot		coot 'go'	coot	†cot	'pass by, cross'
	˘cadam f-	†cadúm f-	candoom	°cëdúm	†caróm f-	'price'[15]
			curun	°cúrún f-		'fish'[16]
PC *k						
*kaɗ	kaɗ	kaɗ	kaɗ	(kaaɗ)[17]	†kar	'go'
*kaɗVɗ	kaɗeeɗ	(kaañiid)		kariɗ	°karad †k-	'tamarind tree'
*kal				kal	†kal	'take'
*kal-ís[18]	kéléebís			°këlís	kélís	'take off (of head)'
*kayoH	kayoh f-	kayoh f-	keeh	kaah	°kaah k-	'truth'
ᵇ*kaaɓaaɓ		kaaɓ	kaaɓaaɓ k-	°kabaap 'jaw'	†kakaab	'cheek'

---

12 While *oɣ becomes NdP /a'/, *ooɣ does not in *kooɣ 'God,' and as such it seems that the prefix had not fused with the root as *cooɣ in PC (note also the vowel length discrepancy arising from this vowel sequence). See outside cognates in Appendix 2.

13 Laalaa 'white-backed vulture.'

14 Laalaa 'falcon,' Noon 'vulture sp.,' others 'eagle.'

15 Perhaps borrowed from Wolof *dóom* 'ash,' cf. the polysemy in Sereer *ndaw* 'ash, debt.'

16 Borrowed from Saafi into Paloor, as no regular /r:r/ correspondence exists between them. This is regardless the only plausible PC word for fish (*ca-lún?).

17 In *bóy kaaɗ* 'Saafi,' which Thornell et al. give as meaning 'celui qui est parti.'

18 Pichl (1977) gives Ndut *kel* 'load onto head,' so *kel* may be the root here, with *kal* being unrelated. However the Khodaba Paloor form should have /í/ rather than /ë/ if the root is *kel*. The apparent Noon suffix is unaccounted for, and appears only in this word.

APPENDIX 1

(*cont.*)

	Noon	Laalaa	Saafi	Paloor	Ndut	
			PC *k			
b*kaal	kaal		kaal	kokaal		'hunt'
*kaalú	kóolúu	këëlú			†kúulú f-	'venomous snake'
b*kaaní	kéení	këëní			°kéení	'hot pepper'[19]
b*kaañ	kaañ	kaañ	kaañ	°kaañ	°kaañ	'be sharp/brave, dare'[20]
b*keɓ		keɓ	keɓ	keɓ	†keɓ	'fence' (v/n)
*fe-keɗ	fekiɗ f-	°fekeɗ			†feked	'millet chaff type'
*kel				°kel	†kel	'hear'
*kel-oH	keloh	kalah	kerah	keloh	keloh 'listen'	'hear'
*keen	keen	keen	keen	keen	keen	'fall'
c*keeñ	keeñ 'lung'	keeñ k-	keeñ °k-	°keeñ	°keeñ	'liver' (often also 'heart')
c*kilif	kelif f-/†k-			°kílíf m-		No. 'butter,' Pa. 'oil'
*kiih	†kii	kii	kii (nut)	°kiih (nut, oil)	°kii	'palm tree'
*kiil	kiil k-	kiil k-		kiil °k-	kiil k-	'braiding needle'
b*kílook	kílóok	cílóok	kilook	kílóok, °kúlok	†kílëk	'marry'
*kínd	kíd	kín	kind	kín~°d	†kín~d	'count'
*ki(i)sí		°kiisíi †f-		kísí °f-	†kísí f-	'ocean/sea'
b*kíiṛ (kV-híiṛ)	kíis k-	kíis k-	kiis k-	kíil	kíil †k-	'year'
*wu-(h)íiṛ	wiis	†wís	woyis			'this year'
*koɓ	koɓ	koɓ			°kob	'be sour'
c*koɗ	koɗ		°koɗ	koɗ	koɗ	'raise child'
*koɗ-ox	koɗuk	koɗok		°kodoh		'be polite/behave'
c*kof	kof 'shell'	kof		kof	†kof	'skin/flay'
*kol				°kol	kol	'raise'
*kol-ox	koluk	kolok	kuruk	koloh	koloh	'rise'
b*koleñ	koliñ f-, ‡koleñ			koloñ	†koleñ f-	'sand'
*kom	kom	°kom	kom	kom	°kom	'bring'

---

19 Borrowed from Manding (likely via Wolof), originally referring to the fruit of the *Xylopia aethiopica* tree, and later applied to new world hot peppers.

20 May not be borrowed with the sense 'be sharp,' but 'be brave, dare' seems to be borrowed, cf. Mandinka *háañi*, Joola Fonyi *-kaañen*, Bainunk Gubëeher *-xaañun*. However it is conspicuous that there are very few Mande borrowings in Proto-Cangin, and furthermore within Mande this word is only found in Mandinka, where h-initial words are themselves mostly borrowings. This is perhaps best seen as a Wanderwort among the coastal languages of Senegal.

PROTO-CANGIN LEXICAL RECONSTRUCTIONS

(cont.)

	Noon	Laalaa	Saafi	Paloor	Ndut	
			PC *k			
*kot	kot	kot	kot	kot	kot	'leg, foot'
*kooɗ	kooɗuk	kooɗ	kooɗuk	kooɗ 'bring'	(†kúd 'bring')	'carry on head'
*kooɣ[21]	kooh	koh f-	kooh	koope	koo (pe)	'god, sky'
*kuɗ	koɗ k-	koɗ k-	kuɗ	kud °k-	kud k-	'pestle' (der. *hoɗ 'pound')
*nju-kuɗ	joku' j-	jokoɗ j-				'small pestle'
ᶜ*kun	jokun j-	jokon j-	ndukun	kun	°kun	'finger'
*kuun	kuun c-	kuun c-			†kuun k- 'cake'	'ball(s) of millet'
*kúɓ(-ox)[22]	kúɓ	°kúu		°kúu	†kúuh	'carry (baby) on back'
*kúlmbVs	kúlmbís f-, °kúlmbús	kúlbísóh	kurmburus	°kúlbús f-	†kúlbús f-	'ant sp.'
*kúlndV[23]	kúldí	kúldí k-		kúlë	†kúllë k-	'couscous steamer'
ᶜ*kún	kún 'cover'	kún	kun 'cover'	kún	°kún	'close'
*kún-ís	kúnís 'uncover'	kúnís	kunis 'uncover'	kúnís	°kúnís	'open'
*kúC-iɗ-oɣ[24]	kúuɗoh			°kúyra'		'announce death'
ᶜ*kúum	kúum k-	kúum k-	kuum	kúum k-	°kúum k-	'honey'
*kúum		huum f-	kuum	kúum k-/°f-	kúum f-	'bee'
*kVm	kím	kím	kim	°kaam f-	†kaam m-	'morning/tomorrow'
	kéekíɗ			°keykiɗ		No. 'mock,' Pa. 'surprise'
			PC *ɓ			
*ɓaH		ɓah 'resemble'	ɓaah	ɓaah		'be related,' Pa. 'be part of'

---

21 NdP *pe* is unexplained; it is certainly not a determiner. There is no evidence that *k is a prefix in this word, and it likely cannot be connected with Sereer *Roog*.

22 The suffix could explain the NdP forms, but not Laalaa, in which the loss of the consonant is unexpected.

23 Perhaps originally *kul-hínde* if borrowed from Sereer (*g*)*o-hinde* < hypothetical earlier *gol-hinde*, itself borrowed from Wolof *hinde*.

24 Or with *u in the root, if the suffix is causative *-íɗ—but benefactive *-iɗ is more likely given the meaning. The consonant, if present, could be *h, *ɣ, *H, or *y. The root could conceivably be cognate with Bantu *kú 'die,' but it is unclear if these suffixes could yield the given meaning from a root 'die.'

242 APPENDIX 1

(*cont.*)

	Noon	Laalaa	Saafi	Paloor	Ndut	
			PC *ɓ			
*(ki-)ɓaHa²⁵		kea k-		ɓaha	ɓaha, †ɓaah	'old person'
ᵇ*ɓak	ɓak		ɓak 'beside'	°ɓëkíd 'move'		'set aside'
*ɓal, ɓan	ɓan	ɓal, ɓan		ɓal	†ɓal	'also'
*ɓang	°ɓag, †ɓang		ɓang	ɓaŋ	†ɓaŋ	'defeat, win'
*ɓap	ɓap	ɓap	ɓap	ɓap	°ɓap	'suckle'
*ɓap-id	ɓëpíd	ɓëpíd	ɓapid	ɓëpíd		'nurse'
ᵇ*ɓasíl			ɓasil	°ɓësíl	ɓësíil, †ɓësíl	'beget'
*ɓay/c	ɓay		ɓay, ɓac		ɓey	'bring'
*ɓaaɓ	ɓaaɓ	ɓaaɓ	ɓaaɓ	°ɓaaɓ	°ɓaab	'travel'
ᶜ*ɓaaɓ			ɓaaɓ	ɓaaɓ	ɓaaɓ	'morning'
ᵇ*ɓaat	ɓaat	ɓaat	ɓaat	ɓaat	ɓaat	'add, increase'
*ɓeɓ	ɓeɓ	°ɓeɓ			†ɓeɓ	'take'
*ɓeɓ-íd	ɓéɓíd	ɓiid			†ɓéyíd	'pick up'
ᵇ*ɓek	(ek)	(ek)	ɓek	ɓek	†ɓek	'put in'
*ɓek-ox	(ekuk), °bègək	(ekok)	ɓekuk	ɓekoh	°ɓekoh	'get dressed'
*ɓend	ɓed	°ɓen	ɓend-	ɓen	°ɓen~†d	'accompany'
*ɓes			ɓes	ɓes	†ɓes	'cut in half'
*ɓee?	ɓey	ɓee		ɓée		'call'
*ɓee-ít-oɣ?	ɓéyítoh	°ɓeetoh	ɓeedkoh	ɓéeta'		'call a meeting'
*ɓeen	ɓeed	ɓeen	ɓeen	°ɓeen	†ɓeen	'pick/harvest fruit'
*ɓeend-ox	ɓeeduk			ɓeedoh²⁶	†ɓeedoh	'be crippled'
*ɓeer-id	ɓestíd, °ɓéestíd	ɓéesíd	ɓeesdoh 'chat'	ɓíilíd	ɓílíd	'tell'
ᶜ*ɓííɓ	ɓííɓ	ɓííɓ	ɓííɓ	ɓííɓ	ɓííɓ	'breast'
ᶜ*pi-ɓil	piwil, ɓiwil	píil p-	piɓiir	°pihil		'lower abdomen'
*ɓis	⁻†ɓes	ɓes	ɓis	ɓis		'arrow'
ᶜ*ɓitif²⁷	ɓeti f- 'woman'?		ɓitif	ɓitif	°ɓitif	'old woman'

---

25 Likely derived from *ɓaH 'be related,' with the original sense of 'older relative, ancestor.' The long vowel in Saafi ɓaah is likely due to the regular development of word-final /ah/ in Saafi. The same explanation cannot hold in Paloor, but this may be a Saafi borrowing. Cf. Wolof *bokk* 'share, be related, be part of' and its derivative *mbokk* 'relative.'

26 Thornell et al. give ɓéedoh in Kajoor, and ɓeeroh in Baol. Since /ɗ/ has an allophone [d] between vowels, and intervocalic /d/ becomes /r/ in Baol, this word must in fact be ɓeedoh, though the ATR discrepancy is unexplained.

27 It is possible that the Ndut-Paloor word is borrowed from Saafi, in which case the PC form could be *ɓi-rif. In Northern and Padee Noon, ɓeti 'woman' (from *ɓe-reɓ) can optionally take f- agreement, which is unexpected for a human noun. This is explained if *ɓitif sur-

PROTO-CANGIN LEXICAL RECONSTRUCTIONS

(cont.)

	Noon	Laalaa	Saafi	Paloor	Ndut	
			PC *ɓ			
*ki-ɓí(s/r̥)	kíwíi k-, †kíwís	kiis k-, †kíwís	kiɓi k-	kíi °k-	°kíi k-	'fire'
*ɓít	ɓít	ɓít	ɓit	°ɓít	ɓít	'be heavy'
*ɓi-o'	ɓo' y-	ɓo' y-	ɓo' y-	ow~ɓó, °o'	ow (ɓëë)	'person'
*ku-ɓo[28]	kowu, koow, †kowo k-	kuu k-	kuɓu k-	kook 'baby'	këë, †kú k-	'child' (son/daughter)
*ku-ɓo i-noɣ	kowinoh k-, †koɓnoh[29]	kuunoh k-	kuɓno			'meat' (lit. 'child/fruit of cow')
*ɓof	ɓof	ɓof	ɓof	°ɓof	°ɓof	'cough'
c*ɓoɣ	ɓoh	ɓoh	ɓoh	ɓa'	ɓa'	'baobab'
*ɓop	ɓop	ɓop		ɓop		'carry baby in arms'
*ɓot	ɓot	ɓot	ɓot	ɓot	°ɓot	'vomit'
c*ɓoo(ɣ)[30]				ɓoo, °ɓo	†ɓoo	'wash (self)'
c*ɓoo(ɣ)-ox	ɓook	ɓook	ɓook	ɓooh	°ɓooh	'bathe'
b*ɓoof	ɓoof		ɓoof 'sit'		†ɓof	No. 'crouch w/ knees together,' Nd. 'lay down (said of camels)'
b*ɓool	ɓool		ɓoor	ɓool 'uproot'		'strip from a branch/stalk'
*ɓooñ-ox		ɓooñok		°ɓoñoh	°ɓooñoh	'wash self'
*ɓooy	†ɓooy		ɓooy	ɓooy		'pluck feathers'
c*ɓuh	(baay f-)[31]	ɓúu f-	ɓuu f-, ‡ɓu'	ɓuh f-	ɓuh f-	'dog'
c*ɓuk	ɓok	ɓok	ɓok	ɓuk °f-	°ɓuk f-	'mosquito'
*ɓuñ	ɓoñɓoñ	kuu-ɓooñ k-			°ɓuñ	'kidney'
*(n-)ku-ɓú	kúuɓ k-, ◇kuvu	kúu k-	nguɓu n-	ɓúk	ɓúk	'mouth'
*ɓi-Vɓ	ɓéeɓ	ɓeeɓ		ɓéeɓ	ɓéeɓ	'all'
b*ɓVVs	ɓaas		ɓuus		°ɓaas	'suck,' No. 'suck out venom'

---

vived in Noon, and the final consonant was reanalyzed as a class prefix before suffixed determiners on the independently-existing noun *ɓeti* (i.e. **ɓetif-∅-ii > ɓeti-f-ii*).

28 The diminutive of **ɓi-o* 'person,' and so more accurately **ku-ɓi-o'*, which accounts for the +ATR vowel in Ndut (via the intermediate form **ku-ɓó*).

29 Not found in the modern sources on Thiès Noon, but volunteered by Marie Christine Diop as the Thiès dialect form. Tastevin has *◇kop noh*.

30 Evidence for **ɣ* comes only from potential outside cognates (e.g. Sereer *ɓog-oox*). The loss of the resulting /h/ would be irregular in Saafi.

31 Noon form unrelated—note that the regular Noon outcome of **ɓuh* would be *ɓo'*, homophonous with 'person.'

APPENDIX 1

(cont.)

	Noon	Laalaa	Saafi	Paloor	Ndut	
			PC *ɗ			
*mi-ɗa	meɗaa m-, †maɗaa m-	meɗa m-	miɗa, meɗa m-	miraa, °mera m-	mira °m-	'salt'
c*ɗaɗ	ɗaɗ	ɗaɗoh, °ɗaɗ	ɗaɗ	°ɗaɗ	ɗaɗ	'tear/be torn, split'
*ɗaaɗ	ɗaaɗ	°ɗaaɗ	ɗaaɗ	ɗaaɗ	†ɗaad	'fermented/smoked fish'
*ɗaak	ɗaak	ɗaak	ɗaak	ɗaak		'hide/stash'
*ɗaas	ɗaah (<ɗaas-oh)	ɗaas		ɗaas	†ɗas	'dig out/hunt out'
*fi-ɗaas	feɗaaf f-, ⁻†faɗaaf	feɗaaf f-	fiɗaaf	firaas f-		'corpse'
*ɗeɓ	ɗeɓ	ɗeɓ	ɗeɓ	ɗeɓ	ɗeɓ	'be first'
b*ɗel?	ɗel			ɗeel		No. 'cut fruit,' Pa. 'cut skin'
c*pe-ɗe(e)m	peɗim p-	píɗïm p-	peɗeem, °peɗem	pereem	°pereem, †perem	'tongue'
b*ɗeem	†ɗeem		ɗeemb		°ɗeem	'bat (animal)'
*ɗeew	ɗeew	(ɗees)³²	ɗeew	ɗeew	°ɗeu	'lick'
b*ɗiñ	ɗiñ	°ɗeñ	ɗiñ	ɗiñ °f-	°ɗiñ f-	'louse'
b*ɗing	ɗig	ɗiŋ	ɗing	°ɗiŋ~g		'fence' (v/n)
c*ɗoɓ	ɗoɓ	ɗoɓ	ɗoɓ	ɗoɓ	°ɗob	'bite'
b*ɗof	ɗof	ɗof	ɗof	ɗof	†ɗof	'uproot'
*ɗooɓ	ɗooɓ	ɗooɓ	ɗooɓ	ɗooɓ	†ɗoob	'speak ill, slander'
*ɗook	ɗook	ɗook		ɗook	†ɗook	'thread' (v)
*ɗoon	ɗoon	ɗoon		ɗoon	†ɗoon f-	'calf' (cow)
*ɗúk	ɗúk	ɗúk			°ɗúkë'	'deceive'
*ɗúuk	ɗúuk	°ɗúuk	ɗuuk			'smoke' (v)
*ɗúuk-ú			ɗuuku r-	ɗúukú	ɗúukë	'smoke' (n)
	ɗíl			°ɗil		'crush'
			PC *y			
*yaH	yah	yak	yah		†yah	'go'
c*yaak	yaak 'scratch'	yaak	yaak	°yaak	†yaak 'break in two'	'cut w/ teeth,' Pa. 'break w/ hands'
*yaal	yaal	yaal	yaar	yaal	yaal	'man'
*yek	(yí'	yíi)	yek	yek	†yek	'kneel'

---

32 Likely *ɗeew with iterative *-iɽ or intensive *-is, but the deletion of *w would be irregular in Laalaa.

PROTO-CANGIN LEXICAL RECONSTRUCTIONS 245

(cont.)

	Noon	Laalaa	Saafi	Paloor	Ndut	
			PC *y			
ᶜ*yen	yen	yen	yen	yen	°yen	'laugh'
*pi-yen		peyen p-				'laugh' (n)
*yeek	yeek	yeek	yeek	yeek	yeek	'sing'
*yin	yín		yin	yin	°yin	'(be) small'
*yíh~díh[33]	yí'	díi	yii, †yi'	yíh	°díh	'knee'
*yíñ		yíñ, °yiñ, †yeñ	yiiñ	°yíñ f-	†yíñ f-	'guinea fowl'
ᶜ*yíp~yíp	yíp	yíp	yip	yíp, °yíp	yíp	'plant (e.g. a stake)'
*yoɓ	yoɓ	yoɓ	yoɓ	yoɓ	†yob	'cut (down)'
ᵇ*yof	yof				†yof	'cut dog's ear'
*yoH	†yooh	yoh		°yoh		'taste'
*yok		yok		°yog		'back of head'
*fi-yon[34]	fiyon f-			°fiyonoh	†fion	'cold,' NdP 'be cold'
*yuH	yoh	yoh	†yoh	yuh	°yuh	'bone'
*yu(u)y		yuuy		yuy	†yuc	'embers'
*yVm	yúm	yúm		°yím	†yím	'extinguish'
			PC *m			
ᶜ*maɓ	maɓ			maɓ		'close the mouth'
ᵇ*mal	mal	mal	mal	mal		'bring luck'
ᶜ*mand	mad	man	mand	man~d	man~d	'resemble'
*may	may	may		may	†may	'suck'
*maal			maar	maal 'fog'	°maal	'dew'
*maang	maag	maag	maang	°maaŋ		'stab,' Pa. 'stab w/ horn'
ᶜ*maañ	maañ	maañ	maañ	maañ	maañ	'last (long)'
*maas	maayoh, ˜maasoh			maas		'termite,' Pa. 'termite infestation'
ᵇ*maas	maas 'witness'	maas			maas	'be present'
ᵇ*meeɓ	˜meeɓ[35]		meeɓ	meeɓ	†meb	'lift'

---

33 The variants suggest palatalization of *d, but this change is seen in no other word. A hypercorrect depalatalization is also possible. Both forms likely co-existed in PC.

34 Both vowels are unexpected in Noon (*i should become /e/, unstressed *o should become /u/). However if the prefix fi- remained active in Noon until very recently (with stress on the root), this would explain both vowels. The consonant could instead be *y, which would not have deleted in Northern Noon after an active prefix.

35 Acts 27:27, describes what a storm does to a boat in the sea.

246   APPENDIX 1

(*cont.*)

	Noon	Laalaa	Saafi	Paloor	Ndut	
			PC *m			
b*meeɗ	meeɗ	†meɗ	meeɗ	°meed	°meed	'be used to'
c*meex-iṛ	meekis	miikis	meekis	meel	meel	'ask'
b*misaH		mesah		misah	†misah	'granary'
*misik	miik, °mesik	mesek	misik	misik	misik	'hurt' (intr.)
c*miis	miis m-	miis m-	miis m-	miis m-	miis m-	'milk'
*mílnd-oɣ			mirndoh	mílë'	míllë'	'be last'
c*mín	mín	mín	min	mín	mín	'be able'
*mond	mod 'roll cigarette'		mon, monduk	°mon~d	†mon	'twist/braid' (rope, Sa. hair)
c*mooɓ	móowíɗ			°moɓ		'smile'
*moond-íɗ	móodíɗ	móodíɗ		°moodíɗ	†mëdëh~ moddë	'whisper'
b*mooň	mooň			°mooň		'twist'
b*moos	moos	moos	moos	°moos	°moos	'wipe clean'
*mungul	†mungul 'cheek'		mungur	mugul		'eyebrow'
b*muus	muus	muus	muus °m-	múus	°múus m-, †f-	'cat'
c*mún	mún m-	mún m-	mun	mún m-	mún m-	'flour'
b*múň	múň	múň		°múň~j	†múň	'be patient'
*múuma			muuma n-	°múmë'	múumú f-	'(mythical) lion'
*múuy	múuy	°múuy	muuy	múuy		'disappear'
*múuy(-ox)		múu	muuy	muh, °múh		'sun go down'
*múuy-oɣ-aaɗ noɣ	múuyaah noh	múhaaɗ- noh	muyohaaɗ- noh			'west' ('where the sun sets')
			PC *n			
*na	na	na	na	na	na	'with', Nd. durative
*nah		†naa		°nah		'day after tomorrow'
*nand	nad	nad	nand	nan, nen °f-	°nen f-	'spider'
*nang-íɗ(-oɣ)	négíɗ, °nëgíɗoh, †nëngëɗoh	nígíɗóh		°nígírë'	†négér(é)	'gather'
*nax	nak	†nak 'inform'	nak 'ask'	naha', °nah	nah	'order, command'
*nay	nay		°ney	nay		'sift'
b*na(a)H[36]	nah, †naah	nah	naah	naah	°naah, †nah	'magic healer'

---

36   Likely with a short vowel as in Sereer *o-naq*. Earlier Saafi /ah/ becomes /aah/, and the Saafi word may have been borrowed into some Ndut-Paloor dialects. The Thiès Noon form has

PROTO-CANGIN LEXICAL RECONSTRUCTIONS

(cont.)

	Noon	Laalaa	Saafi	Paloor	Ndut	
PC *n						
*naaf		°naaf	naaf	°naaf	naaf 'take'	'take/snatch back'
*naal	naal	naal	naar	naal	°naal †f-	'bull/male animal'
*naand	naan		naand			'forget'
*naand-ís	níidís	níidís	naandis		°nédís	'remind/remember'
*-naaC?	yaanaaw	yaanaaw	yaanaw, yanaaw	naa'	°naa'	'white'
*neɓ	neɓ	neɓ	neɓ	neɓ	†neɓ	'be nice'
*neh	ne'	niiy (<*neh-idʼ)	ne'~ney	neh	neh	'draw water'
*nek	nek	nek	nek	nek	†nak	'porridge'
*nen[37]	nen	nen	nen	nen	†nen	'shave'
*ne(e)ɣ (ní-oɣ)	neeh	neh	neeh	ne'	nee'	'sleep' (cf. *paní)
*neeɓ		neeɓ			°neebb	'be angry'
*neex (nV-ox?)	néek, ˇniik	neek, °nëëkéy	neek		neeh	'fear' (v)
*niɣ-ís?	naas	naas	nihis	nís	nís	'remove'
ᶜ*nixiir̥	nikiis	niikiis	nikis	iniil	iniil	'four'
*níh	ní'	níi	nii, ‡ni'	níh	°níh	'rope'
*pi-níh		†píníi p-				'twine'
*níidʼ	níidʼ	níidʼ	niidʼ	níidʼ	†níid	'herd/keep live-stock'
*níidʼ-oH	níidoh	níidʼóh	niidʼoh	níidʼoh	†níidoh~ níirëh	'herdsman'
*níil	níil	níil	niir	níil	°níil	'root'
*(fi-)níin	níin		niin	finíin f-	finiin f-	'evening'
ᶜ*noɣ	noh	noh	noh	na'	na'	'sun'
ᶜ*i/fa-noɣ	enoh f-	enoh f-	inoh	fana' f-	fana f-	'cow'
*ki-noH[38]	kenoh k-	kenoh k-	kinoh	°kinoh	†kinoh k-	'waist'
*non(d)	non	nan	nond	non	°non	'be cooked, ripe'
*noodʼ			noodʼ	°noodʼ	noodʼ	'be deep'
*nook	nook	°nook	nook	nook		'pull'
ᶜ*nuf	nof	nof	nof	nuf	°nuf	'ear'
*nung	noŋ	nog	nung	°nuŋ	nuŋ	'hole (in ground)'

---

no available explanation.

37 Cf. Wolof *nel* 'shave head completely,' but the final consonant correspondence would not be regular for either a cognate or borrowing.

38 Not a nominalization of *ken* 'tie *pagne* at someone's waist.' *-oH* is an agentive suffix, and furthermore Saafi has *ken* for this verb, and *kinoh* for 'waist.'

248 APPENDIX 1

(*cont.*)

	Noon	Laalaa	Saafi	Paloor	Ndut	
			PC *n			
*nu(n)ɣund	nood	nogon	nuhun	nuun~d	nuŋun, †nugun	'point out'
*fa-núf	fónúf, ˚fënúf, †fënëf f-	fënúf f- 'eyelash'			˚fënúf	'body hair' No. also 'feather'
*núh	nú'	núuɓ[39]		˚nuh	†núh	'scoop grain/food w/ hand'
*núp	núp	núp	nup		†núp 'fear'	'flee'
			PC *ñ			
ᵇ*ñaɗ	ñaɗ	ñaaɗ 'be angry'	ñaɗ	ñaɗa'		'scold/argue'
ᶜ*ñam	ñam	ñam	ñam	ñam	ñam	'eat'
	ñaam	ñamah		˚ñahom	˚ñamaa	'right (hand)'
*ñangan	ñagan		ñangind	˚ñagan	†ñagan	'crawl'
*ñaaɓ			ñaaɓ	ñaaɓ	†ñab	'light fire'
*ñaam	ñaam	†ñaam	ñaam	ñaam	˚ñaam	'slave' (cf. Wolof *jaam*)
*ñaand	†ñaan		ñaand	ñaan	†ñan	'seat' (n)
*ñimin	yewin	yemen	ñimin	˚ñimin		'be many'[40]
*ñíf/ñif	ñíf	ñíf	ñíf m-	ñíf m-	ñíf m-	'blood'
*ñíf/ñif-iɽ	ñíwís	ñifis	ñifis	˚ñifil	†ñífíl	'bleed'
*ka-ñík	kéñí k-		kiñi	keñik	†kéñík k-	'bracelet'
*(kV-)ñíin			kiñin k-	ñíin	ñíin	'nose'
ᶜ*ñíind	ñíid	ñíid	ñiinɗuk	ñíin~d		'blow nose'
ᶜ*ñíiñ	ñíiñ	ñíiñ	ñiiñoh ˚f-	˚ñíin f-	˚ñíiñ f-	'ant'
*ñof	ñof	ñof		ñof	†ñof	'clog/block/stop up'
ᶜ*ñúus	ñúus (v)	ñúus (n)	ñuus (n)	ñúus (n, v)		'be dark/darkness'
*ñVVk-íɗ	ñéekíɗ			ñéekíɗ	†ñekit	'sew'
ᵇ*ñafaɗ~ñofaɗ	ñood, ˚ñafaɗ		ñafaɗ	ñafaɗ	ñofaɗ	'shoe'
			PC *ŋ			
ᶜ*ŋaɓ	ŋaɓ 'take big bite'	ŋaɓ	ŋaɓ	ŋaɓ	ŋaɓ	'hold between teeth'
*ŋaak		ŋaak n-			†ŋaak f-	'pied crow'

---

39 Dieye (2010: 349) gives only *ka-núuɓaa* [kënúuwaa] 'to go scoop up,' which does not provide evidence for /ɓ/. This may simply be *núu*, the expected outcome of **núh*.

40 Irregular denasalization in NL. Initial C must be *ñ, as *y is rare before a front vowel. Medial C must be *m, as *w would delete in Northern Noon.

PROTO-CANGIN LEXICAL RECONSTRUCTIONS 249

(*cont.*)

	Noon	Laalaa	Saafi	Paloor	Ndut	
			PC *ND			
ᵇ*mbaHane	baani	°baane	mbahne r-	baanu	°baane	'hat'
*mbaŋ		°baŋ	mban	°baŋ f-	†bang f-	'weaverbird sp.'
ᵇ*mbaal	baal, †mbaal		mbaal	(°mbal)		'sheep'
*mbaang	baag	°baaŋ		baaŋ	baaŋ	'stalk' (of millet)
*mbaangV	baagii	baagii		°baag⁴¹	baage	'palm oil'
ᵇ*mbec	†mbec		mbec	bec	°bec	'dance'
ᵇ*mbet			mbet	bet	°bet	'throw'
*mbílím	mbílím	°bílím			†bílím	'dance type'
*mbíing	bíig, †mbíiŋ			bíiŋ 'hip'	°bíiŋ	'back'
ᵇ*<u>ka</u>-mbot	kobut, °kobot °k-	kebot k-			†kabot	'debt'
*mboong-	boogaa, booginoh			bóogúl	†bëgúl, †bogú f-	'wasp,' No. 'bee'
*mboos	boos	boos			°boos	'well bucket'
ᵇ*mbúum	búum, †mbúumëd	búum		búum	búum	'be blind'
ᵇ*ndangal	dagal, †ndangal	dagal	ndangal	dagal °f-	°dagal f-	'scorpion'
*ndil			ndel	°dil	†díl	'sitting mat'
*<u>ka</u>-ndí(d)	kédí k-	këdí k-, jëdí j-	kandid	kedi	†kédí	'mortar' (NLS), 'pipe' (NNdP)
*ndíiŋ	díiŋ	ndíig	ndiŋ	díiŋ °f-	°díiŋ f-	'owl'
*ndook		°dook			†dook f-	'egret/heron sp.'
*nduul	duul	duul	nduur		°duul f-	'monitor lizard'
*ndúulú	dúulúu	dúulúu 'wasp'		°dúlú	†dúul	'insect'
*ndúut	dúut	°dúut		°duud f-	†dúut f-	'Abyssinian ground hornbill'
*ndVVd	dood, †ndod	dood	ndood	dúud	duud, †dood	'stick'
*njaɓul⁴²	jawul, †njawol	jawol		°jawul		'parakeet'
ᵇ*njakal	jakal	jakal	njakar	°jakal	†jakal f-	'lizard'
	jakakooɓ	jakooɓ j-, °jakkooɓ				'chameleon' (cf. Ser. a-koβ 'wild')
*njang		°jaaŋ	njang	jaŋ		'Palmyra palm'
*njol	jol		njol	°jol	†jol f-	'cricket'

---

41 Must be *baage* as in Ndut, with D'Alton mis-segmenting the /e/ as a definite suffix; if the root were truly consonant-final, D'Alton would have *baaŋ*.

42 *ɓ rather than *w, as *w would be deleted in Northern Noon (cf. *ɣawul > hool 'griot'). A glide sometimes emerges when *ɓ is lost in Laalaa and Paloor.

250 APPENDIX 1

(cont.)

	Noon	Laalaa	Saafi	Paloor	Ndut	
			PC *ND			
ᵇ*njotot			njotoot	°jotoɗ		'lip'
			njulañ	°juloñ	†júlíŋ	'ground squirrel'
ᵇ*ngakúɗ	gókúɗ	°gëkúɗ	ngakuɗ n-	°gëkút	†gokúɗ f-	'gecko'
*ngaal		gaal			°gaal	'calabash sp.'
*(n)helis	elis	geles		°gílís	†gelis	'burp'
ᵇ*ngiic	giic		ngiic	giic		'jujube tree'
ᶜ*ngol-ngol	golgol			°golgol	†golgol	'throat'
ᵇ*ngolVc	golic			°golac		'vomit milk'
*ngong	gog, goŋ	gog	ngoŋ 'viper'		°goŋ f-	'snake'
ᶜ*ngum			ngum 'heart'	gum	†gum	'gourd/calabash for liquid'
*ngumú	gómúu (f-), †ngómú f-, ˘gumuu f-	guumuu/ gúmú f-, °gumuu f-	ngumu °f-	gúmú °f-	°gúmú f-	'hyena' (borr. Ser. *(g)o-moon?*)
*ngúl	gúl (n, v)		ngul (n, v)	gúl (n, v)	°gúl (v)	'(make) hole'
ᵇ*ngúlfa(n)	gúwlan (n, v), °gúlfaa (v)	gúlfaad (n)		gulfoo, °gulfa'	†gúlfan f-	'mucus,' 'have a cold'
			PC *f			
*fas	fas	fas	faskoh 'reptile'	fas	†fas	'drag' (Sa. 'drag-REFL-AGENT')
*faaɗ	faaɗ	faaɗ	faaɗ	faaɗ		'winnow'
*faan[43]	faan f-	faan f-	faan	faan	faan	'body'
ᶜ*faan	faan	faan	faan	faan	†fan	'lay down'
ᶜ*faan-ox	faanuk	faanok	faanuk	faanoh	fanoh	'lie down'
ᶜ*fen[44]	fen f-	fen f-	fin f-, °fen f-	fen °f-	°fen f-	'hair'
*fe(e)y	°fey			fey, °feey f-	feey, †fey f-	'soil, dirt'
*fiil	fiil	fiil, ffil, °fiil	fiir	fiil	†fiil	'young man/ boyfriend'

---

43 If the initial consonant is indeed a prefix, the root *-aan resembles /ɓaal/ found in a number of other Atlantic groups (cf. Sereer *fo-ɓaal*), but the absence of /ɓ/ would be unexplained. The resemblance to *faan 'lay down' is likely coincidental, especially if the outside cognates for the verb are valid.

44 A prefix in this word would easily explain its class membership, and furthermore lines up well with the use of *fa- on a number of mass nouns. However the *f is more likely the root-initial consonant, lining up with w-initial roots for 'hair' in other Atlantic languages, e.g. Sereer *wil*, Manjak *ka-wɛl*.

PROTO-CANGIN LEXICAL RECONSTRUCTIONS

251

(cont.)

	Noon	Laalaa	Saafi	Paloor	Ndut	
			PC *f			
*fís		fís			°fis	'tree sp.'
ᵇ*fiis	fiis	fiis	fiis	fiis	°fiis	'draw, trace, write'
ᵇ*fool	fool 'run'	fool 'run'		fóol	fool, ᵗfël	'jump'
ᵇ*ku-fúc	kúuc k-	kúuc f-	kufic, kofooc k-, ᵗkufuc	°kúfúc k-	ᵗkúc k-	'needle'
ᶜ*fúɗ	fúɗ (v), fúɗaaɗ 'hearth-stone'		fuuɗ	°fuɗ	(ᵗfúl)	'kindle/light fire,' No. 'make charcoal'
*fúɗ-íɽ	fúɗĩs 'blow'	fúdĩs	fudis 'blow'		fúlíl	'breathe'
*fúdĩñ	fúdĩñ	fúdĩñ	‡fu'ñuk	°fúrëñë'	ᵗfúríñ	'whistle'
ᵇ*fulVl	folul			°fulil	ᵗfúlíl 'spindle'	'spin thread'
*fi-lond(o)?	fíldóo, ˇfíldoo		ᵗfilndo	filoon	filoon ᵗf-	'behind/under'
	funuuñ 'burrs'			°fúñúñoh 'itch'		
			PC *s			
ᵇ*sangalí⁴⁵	ségélíi	ᵗsagalí f-		sëgílí		'millet semolina'
ᶜ*saaf			saaf	saaf		'leaf'
ᵇ*saafu⁴⁶	saawu		saafu	°suufu		'soap'
*saak	saak	saak	saak de saakɗoh	saak		'tremble'
ᵇ*saak	saak		saak		ᵗsaak	'scratch about in ground'
*saand	saad	saad	saandoh 'flee'	saada' 'flee'		'escape'
*saangú	sóogúu f-, ᵗsóongú, ˇsëëgúu f-	°sëëgúu	saangu n-	sóogú °f-	°sëëgú f-	'shadow, shade'
ᵇ*saaw	saaw	saaw	saaw	saaw	ᵗsaaw	'firstborn'
*seH	sah	°sah	seh	°seeh		'Sereer (Siin)'
ᶜ*sel	sel	sel	sel	sel		'bird'

---

45 Borr. Wo. *sànqal*; in earlier sources this Wolof word is given with a final vowel: ⟨*sanglet*⟩ (De Chambonneau c. 1675), ⟨*sanglé*⟩ (Adanson c. 1750).

46 Proto-Fula-Sereer *b > Sereer /f/, explaining Sereer *saafu*, from Arabic *ṣābūn*, likely via Wolof *saabu*. The Noon word may be a more recent borrowing from Wolof as **saabu*, especially given the word-final short vowel. Probably not truly present in PC, as with all Arabic borrowings.

252 APPENDIX 1

(*cont.*)

	Noon	Laalaa	Saafi	Paloor	Ndut	
			PC *s			
*sex	sek	sek	sek	seh	°seh	'wait'
*seeɓ			seeɓ	°seeb		'fish w/ net'
ᵇ*seek	seek	seek	seek	°seek		'stop raining'
ᵇ*seek	seek	seek	seek	°sega	†seega	'dry season/harvest time'
*seengVñ		seegeeñ		°seegañ f-		'ant sp.'
*sifVɗ		sefaɗ (n, v)	sifaɗuk (v)	°sifiroh (v)	siipid f-	'thirst, be thirsty'
*sing(u)	seg	seŋ, †seg	suŋngu, °singu	sigu	°sugu	'left'
*sinja(a)n		sejan		sijaan		'back'
*sip		sep				'put sauce on food'
*mi-sip	miip, °mesip m-	mesep m-	misip m-	°misib m-	misip m-	'sauce'
ᵇ*siik	siik	siik		°síik 'rooster'	siik 'rooster'	'male animal'
ᵇ*siili	siilii	siilii		siili	siili	'Ndut-Paloor/ Sereer'
ᵇ*síɓ(-íɗ)	síɓ	síɓ 'knead,' °síwíɗ 'water' (v)		síiɗ		'pour hot water on couscous'
ᵇ*síɗ	síɗ	síɗ		síɗ		'strain, sift'
*síkíɗ-ox?	súkúɗúk	súkúɗúk 'hear'	sikiɗuk	sikiroh	síkírëh	'listen'
*(pi-)síl	tíil t-, †píil p-	písíl p-	sir	síl 'tendon'	°síl	'vein'
ᶜ*sís	sís	sís	sis	sís	sís	'tooth'
*sisíɓ			sisíɓ	°sisip	†sísíɓ	'smith'
ᵇ*síis[47]	síis	síis	siis	síis	°síis	'twin'
ᶜ*soɗ	soɗ	soɗ	soɗ	soɗ	°sodd	'fill (bag)'
*ti/pi-soH	peoh, †peeh p-, °tesoh t-	pesoh p-	tisoh	°tisoh	tisoh k-	'seeds'
*sox[48]	sok	sok	sok	soh	†soh	'sow'
ᵇ*so(o)mb	soob	soob		som~b	som~b	'pound (into flour)'
*soos	soos	soos	soos	°soos	°sos	'be cold'
*fi-soos	‡feyos					'cold'

---

47   Borrowed from Sereer *o-siid* after Cangin **t > *r̥, but before *t > *s; i.e. likely borrowed as *síit*, becoming *síis* by the Proto-Cangin stage.

48   This pair 'sow, seed' exhibits a unique *x~H alternation, which would have come from an earlier singleton/geminate alternation. Similar root-final alternations are found in Wolof and Sereer (cf. Sereer *sox* 'thresh millet,' *soq* 'millet threshing'), but are otherwise not found in Proto-Cangin. Alternately, both roots may be suffixed, and related to ʙᴋᴋ *-sʉgg, Balanta *sʊg* 'sow.'

PROTO-CANGIN LEXICAL RECONSTRUCTIONS

(cont.)

	Noon	Laalaa	Saafi	Paloor	Ndut	
			PC *s			
ᶜ*soox	sook	sook	sook	soo	°sooh	'urinate'
*mi-sook[49]	meek, °misook m-	mesook m-	misook m-	°sok 'urinal'	misook m-	'urine'
ᵇ*sooy	sooy		sooy	sooy	(†soyñ)	'be lost/disappear'
*su(u)ng[50]	suuŋ/suug	†sug	suung	°suŋ	°suŋ	'elbow'
*suul	suul	suul	suur	°suul f-	°suul f-	'vulture'
*(n-)ku-suun	guun	guusuud	kusun k-	kusiin	kusuun †k-	'navel'
*súh	sú'	†súu	suy	súh	†súh	'be dry'
ᵇ*súkút?	súgút f-		suket	°súkút f-	†síkét	'billy goat'
*(nju-)súun(d)	júud[51]		suun	súun		'top of palm tree,' Pa. 'palm leaf'
*súuṛ	súus	súusúus	suusus	°súul	°súul	'(be) black'
*sVf	soof	soof	soof 'displease'	sufis		'turn back'[52]
*sVkoñ[53]	sookooñ (f-)	saakoñ	sokoñ	sokoñ		'(fire)wood'
*sVVmi[54]	siimii		siim, siini	siimi, suumi	suum-	'bead'
			PC *ṛ			
*kV-ṛaaɣ	ki-saah[55]	kesah	°kisoh	kalaa	†kal	'last year'
*fV/a-ṛaal[56]	°fasaa f-		fisaa r-	alaal	°araal	'chest' (thorax)
*ma-ṛúɓ/ṛuɓ[57]	móoɓ, °músú m-	mësú m-	masuɓ m-	muluɓ °m-	muluɓ	'water'

---

49 The difference in final consonant between 'urinate' and 'urine' is unparalleled, and unexplained. The verb may contain the suffix *-ox.

50 Vowel length discrepancy would be regular for a prefixed form *su-ung.

51 Instead of containing the diminutive prefix, perhaps *n-súund, with *n-s resolving as *nj; however there is no independent evidence for this development.

52 The Saafi word may be borrowed from Wolof *soof* 'be uninteresting.' In Noon also 'be miscarried.'

53 Perhaps a compounded or prefixed form of *hoñ* 'burn'.

54 Perhaps with a prefix *su- as in *su-pi 'ring.' Cf. Ser. *o-feme*, Wo. *peme* 'carnelian (bead),' but deletion of *f would be regular only in Noon.

55 Found unprefixed in *saah-c-aa* 'past years'.

56 The absence of a final consonant in Noon is unexpected, as is the /r/ instead of /l/ in Ndut.

57 The ATR discrepancy may be related to the irregular loss of /ɓ/ in Laalaa and Padee Noon, if the sequence *uɓ developed > uw > ú. But it is not clear if Northern Noon /óo/ could regularly derive from the sequence /au/; note that it does not in *daso > *dau > doo 'we (inclusive).'

APPENDIX 1

(cont.)

	Noon	Laalaa	Saafi	Paloor	Ndut	
			PC *h			
ᶜ*haɓaang	awaag	aaŋ				'open the mouth'
*haɓaang-ís-ox	éwéegíik		aɓaangsuk	°hëbgísëh	°hëëgísë	'yawn'
*haɓaang-íɗ		ëëgíɗ				'be stupefied'
ᶜ*hac	ac	ac	ac	hac	hac	'dig'
*hal	al	al	al	hal	°hal	'forget'
*hamb	ab		amb	ham~b	ham~b	'hold'
*hamb-íɗ-oɣ	abɗoh		ambɗoh	(habda')[58]		'help'
*han	an	an	an	han	han	'drink'
ᵇ*han		an 'hearth'			ᵗhan	'hearthstone'
*hang	ag	ag	aŋ, °ang	haŋ~°g	°haŋ	'be wide'
*hap	ap	ap	ap	hap~w	hap~w	'kill,' Nd. 'beat (to death)'
ᶜ*has	as	as	as	has	has	'(be) new'
*hayl-ox[59]	ayluk		ayruk	hayloh		'be angry'
ᶜ*hay	ay	ay			hay	'lean'
ᶜ*ha(a)y	aay	ay	aay	haay, °hay	hay, ᵗhaay	'be spicy/bitter'
*haañí(nd)	ééñíin	ëëñín, ᵗëñíd	aañind	héeñí	°héeñí	'coal, charcoal'
*haaṛ	aas	aas	aas	haal	haal	'enter'
*te/pe-he'	tee' t-, °pee' p-	ᵗpeᵃ p-		°tehe'	ᵗteh k- 'straw'	'palm midrib,' Pa. 'palm fiber'
*heɓ	eeɓ		eɓ	°heb	ᵗheb	'pick'
ᶜ*hedVf	edíf, ˇedef	aɗaf	edef	heref, °heraf	°heref	'be lightweight'
*(h)en	en	en		en, hen 'do/go'	ᵗhen	'be' (incl. Pa. en)
*heng	eŋ	(iig)		heŋ~g 'throw'	ᵗhegë	'swing,' Nd. 'be stirred up'
*heng-íṛ-oɣ				héyla', °heela'	hégílë	'play'
*heend	eed		eend	heen~°d	ᵗhedd, her	'be quiet/calm'
ᵇ*heeñ	eeñ	ééñ 'smell'	eeñ 'smell'	heeñ	ᵗheñ	'smell good'
*heeñ-íɗ-ox	ééñduk	éénjúk				'smell (tr.)'
*heeñ-ís-ox				°heeñsoh	°héeñsëh, ᵗhínsë	'smell (tr.)'
ᵇ*(n-)hila	elaa	elaa	ngila r-	hila	ᵗhílë, °hílëër	'scuffle hoe' ('hilaire')
*híin		°íin		híin	°híin	'be hard'
ᶜ*híix	íik	íik	iik		ᵗhíh	'breathe'

---

58   Derived from *haɓ* 'hold' rather than *ham~b*.

59   Perhaps borrowed from a hypothetical Wolof form *haay-lu* 'be made wicked,' but the short vowel would be unexplained.

PROTO-CANGIN LEXICAL RECONSTRUCTIONS

(cont.)

	Noon	Laalaa	Saafi	Paloor	Ndut	
			PC *h			
*hoc	oc	oc	oc	hoc	†hoc	'scratch'
ᶜ*hoɗ	oɗ	oɗ	oɗ	hoɗ	†hoɗ	'pound (in mortar)'
*kuɗ (*ku-hoɗ)	koɗ k-	koɗ k-	kuɗ	kuɗ °k-	kuɗ k-	'pestle'
*nju-kuɗ	joku' j-	jokoɗ j-				'small pestle'
ᶜ*hon	on	on	on	hon	hon	'swallow'
*ki-hon-ay	koonaah k-	keonah k-				'throat'
ᶜ*hoñ	oñ	oñ	oñ	°hoñ		'burn'
*hot	ot	ot	ot	hot	°hot	'stink' (v)
ᶜ*huɓ	oɓ	°oɓ	oɓ	huɓ 'leaf'	huɓ 'leaf/bark'	'bark' (n)
*pV-huɓ	tóoɓ t-, °puuɓ	póo p-				'leaf'
*hund	on, †ond	od	und	°hun	°hun	'skin' (n)
ᵇ*hup			uup, °up	hup		'exceed'
ᵇ*húɗ	úɗ	úɗ	uɗ	°húd		'Guiera senegalensis'
*húfiṛ/hufiṛ	úwis	°úwís	ufis	hufil	°ufil, †hofel	'swell'
*húfiṛ-is	úwlis					'really swell'
*húñ	úñ			°hún	†húñ	'chew'
*hút	út 'bake'	út	ut	hút	°hút	'grill'
*hVṛ	ís	ísúk, °ís	is	hel	hel	'leave/let (go)'
			PC *x			
*ti/ka-xeyi[60]	(†)kakeey f-, ˇkakay f-	keke f-, °kekee f-	kekey~kehey	°tihi' k- 'sand'		'dirt' No. also 'sand'
*fi-xí	fíkíi f-	fíkíi f-	fiki	fii °f-	fii, †fíh	'face/before'
			PC *H			
*Hak	hak	hak	hak	hak	†hak	'acacia tree'
ᵇ*Hali	°hëlí, ‡hélí	hëlí	†hal	hël~hél, °hil	°hél	'bow' (weapon)
*Hambús	hóbús	hëbús		°huɓis	hëbús 'beside'	'side (of body)'
ᵇ*Haalís	héelís	hëëlís		heelís	°hélíis, †hílís	'money/silver'
*Hend			hend	hen	†hen	'fireplace'
*Heel	heel					'search for'

---

60 Cf. Mandinka *keñe*, Kobiana *gi-heeñí*, Kasanga *ti-keeñe*, Wolof *beeñ b-* (*bV-heñ?) 'sand,' possibly a Wanderwort. For *y in Noon, cf. *ku-ɓo > koow*.

256 APPENDIX 1

(*cont.*)

	Noon	Laalaa	Saafi	Paloor	Ndut	
			PC *H			
*Heel-iɽ-ox	heeleek	heelok		heltoh	heeltoh, °helsoh	'turn around/look back'
*Heey[61]	heey	heey	heey	°heej	heey	'dream' (v)
*pi-Heey		peheey p-				'dream' (n)
ᵇ*Híl	híl	híl		°hír[62]	ᵗhílí	'snore'
ᶜ*Hul	hol	ol	hor	hul	°hul	'star'
ᵇ*(H)umb-is	obis	hobes		hubis	ᵗhúbís	'rekindle'
*Húc(Vk)	húcúk	°húcúk	huc	°hucekoh		'rinse mouth'
*Húl	húlíiy 'resurrect'		hulit 'resurrect'	húl	°húl	'die'[63]
ᵇ*Húlúɓ	húlúɓ	°hëlúɓ	huluɓ	huluɓ	húlúɓ	'river/ravine'
*Húndís	húnís	húnís	hundis	hudis	húrís, ᵗhús	'friend/co-wife'
*Húy-íɗ, -ox	húyíɗ (n)	húuɓ (n)	‡huyi (n)	°huuh (v)	ᵗhúuh (v)	'cloud/be cloudy'
			PC *w			
*waɗ	waɗ	waɗ	waɗ 'gift'	waɗ (n), °waɗ	ᵗwod	'allocate,' Pa. also 'part' (n)
*waɗ-oy	waɗoh	waɗoh		waɗa'	°woda'	'share'
*waɣ	wah	wah	waah	wa'		'winnowing fan'
*walínd		wëlíd	wirind	yilin, °yíil	°yéníl	'pay'
*walínd-ox	oolduk	°wëldúk	wirnduk			'get revenge on'
*wañ(j)	wiñ			wañ~°j		'make holes for planting'
*wax	wak	wak	wak	wah	ᵗwah	'egg'
ᶜ*wax	wak	wak		°wah	ᵗwah	'be cured/healthy'
*waaɗ	waaɗ	waaɗ	waaɗ	waaɗ		'want, love'
*waak	waak 'visit'		waak	waak[64]		'search'

---

61 Perhaps related to Fula *hoyɗ-*.

62 Perhaps borrowed from a hypothetical Saafi form *hir*, but no word for 'snore' is recorded in existing Saafi sources.

63 The Saafi form is unlikely to descend from Proto-Cangin. The suffix seems to be borrowed from Sereer reversive *-it*, e.g. Sereer *xon-it* 'resurrect' from *xon* 'die,' and the fact that it contains /l/ rather than /r/ identifies it as a likely borrowing. The Noon form contains the reversive suffix *-is* followed by either causative *-íɗ* or benefactive *-id*; cf. Paloor *húlís* 'resurrect'.

64 Also 'like, love, want.' In Paloor there was apparently a conflation of native *waaɗ* 'want/love' and *waaɗ* 'search' borrowed from Sereer *waat* 'search.' The two senses of *waaɗ* were acquired by *waak*, originally only 'search.' Thornell et al. report that *waak* is used with both senses in Kajoor, and *waaɗ* in Baol.

PROTO-CANGIN LEXICAL RECONSTRUCTIONS

(cont.)

	Noon	Laalaa	Saafi	Paloor	Ndut	
			PC *w			
ᶜ*waaṛ	waas	waas	waas	waal	waal	'road'
*wet	wet	weet	wet	wet, yet	°yet	'ash'
ᵇ*wey			wey	°wec		'swim'
*wees	wees	°wees	wees	yees, †wes	°yees	'throw'
*wic⁶⁵	‡ɥit, (wiiy)	(°wii)	wic	wic, yic	wic	'horn'
ᵇ*ṯi/pi-wiñ	piiñ, pewiñ p-	píiñ p-	tiwiñ	tiwiñ °k-	tiiñ k-	'metal, iron'
*wík	ík	wík	wik	°yík		'give back'
*wíind	wíid	wíid	wiind	°yíin~d	°yíin~†d	'pour out/decant'
*wíiñ	wíiñ	wíiñ	wiiñ	yíiñ	°yíiñ	'hang dry'
ᶜ*wíiṛ	wíis	†wís	wiis	yiil, °yíl	°yíil	'dawn (v)'
*kooy wíiṛ	kuus, †°kuwis, ˇkooh-wíis	°koh-wíis	kooh wiis	koope yiil	†ko yíl	'tomorrow/sunrise'
*woh (an)	wo'	woo	woo, °wo'	won, wan	won	'say'⁶⁶
*woṛ	wos	wos	wos-, woos	wol	°wol	'send' (Sa. *wosuud* 'messenger')
*wot	wot	wot	wot	°wot		'borrow'
*woy	wuy	way, †woy		woy	†woy	'collect firewood'
ᵇ*woy	wuy	woy	woy 'heat'	°waj	†woy	'boil'
*wook	wook	wook	wook	°wok		'gather'
*wuṛ/úṛ	úwaay, °úsaay, (†)úyaay	wos	us	°wul	wul	'be far'
ᶜ*wa/wo-te	wati	wate	woti	wate, °watey f-	wote	'today'
			PC *l			
ᵇ*laɓ			laɓ	laɓ	laɓ	'beat, hit'
ᶜ*laɗ	laɗ		raɗis	°laɗ	†laɗ	'spread out (cloth)'
ᵇ*lam	lam	lam	lam	lam		'inherit'
*lap	lap	lap	rap	°lap~w	°lap	'mount, climb'
*las	las	las	las	°las	las	'winnow'
*la(a)x (*la-ox?)	laak	laak	raak	lah	lah	'have, happen'

---

65 Noon *wiiy* and Laalaa °*wii* appear to be from a variant form, but Noon *ɥit* (perhaps /wic/) given by Williams and Williams may represent original *wic*.

66 The verb root is *woh* 'say'; *an* is a complementizer 'that' which has fused with the verb root in Ndut-Paloor.

(cont.)

	Noon	Laalaa	Saafi	Paloor	Ndut	
			PC *l			
ᵇ*-laaɓ	†kolaɓ		koraaɓ	°palaab		'brush fire'
*laaH			laah	laah	laah	'marsh/river' (borr. Wo. *dex*?)
*laal	laal	laal	laar	laal 'be sated'	†laal 'be sated'	'be drunk'
*laan		laanuk, †laan	raan	°laan	†laan	'carry on head'
*laang	laag	laag		laaŋ		'palm leaf'
*leɓ	le'		reɓ	leɓ	†leɓ	'touch,' Pa. 'come close'
	lebidoh		leber	leber, °leɓer	†leɓer	'wrestle'⁶⁷
*leh~lah	le'	lee	ree, raa, †reh		†lah, †leh-	'arrive' (Nd. †*lehel* 'fail to arrive')
*leHet		laat	lahit	°lehed 'nape'	°lehet, †leet	'neck'
ᵇ*le(e)lu⁶⁸	leeloo	leloo	leero	lelu	†lelu	'middle/between'
*leef	leef	leef		leef	°leef	'coat w/ substance'
*-li(i)ɾ	wi-liis	w-iilis	wiriis	yilil		'other'
ᶜ*liil	liil	liil	liir	liil	°liil	'intestine'
*líh	li'			°líh	†líh 'cover up'	'flip over'
*lík	lík	lík	lik		†líkoh	'hang,' Nd. 'carry on shoulder'
ᵇ*líkít	líkët	líkët		°likit 'thread'	†lékít	'cotton'
*pi-líkít	pílkët p-	pílkët p-				'thread'
ᶜ*lím	lím	lím	rim	lím	†lím	'give birth'
*lín	lín	lín			lín	'cultivate'
*lis	lís	lís	ris	líis 'live'	†lis	'continue, (live)'
*liiɓ	liiɓ		riiɓ	†liiɓ		'be dirty'
ᵇ*liiɓ?⁶⁹			liiɓ	líɓ, liiɓ	(°níb)	'think'
*líif	líif	líif	riif	líif	líif	'be full'
ᵇ*líil	líil	líil		líil	líil	'piece of cloth'
ᶜ*líix	líik	líik	riik	°lí'	†líi	'fart'

---

67 Seemingly all borrowed from Ndut-Paloor *leɓer*, since /ɓ/ is [b] intervocalically in Ndut-Paloor; derived from **leɓ* 'touch/come close'; Pichl (1977) gives Ndut *leɓer* as both 'touch each other' and 'wrestle.' However compare Biafada *dəbwəl*, Pajade *səbbər* 'wrestle.'

68 From the Fula-Sereer root **reer*. Borrowing from an early Fula form **reer-ru > reed-u* would explain the final vowel, though Fula borrowings are rare.

69 The Ndut form could be a true cognate to Sereer *liiɓ*, rather than a borrowing, as it shows the regular sound correspondence /n/ for Sereer /l/.

PROTO-CANGIN LEXICAL RECONSTRUCTIONS

(cont.)

	Noon	Laalaa	Saafi	Paloor	Ndut	
			PC *l			
*lom	lom	lom	rom	lom	lom	'buy'
ᵇ*loŋ-loŋ	log-log	loŋ-loŋ	loŋ-loŋ	°loŋ-loŋ	°loŋ-loŋ	'earring'
*lox	lok	lok	rok	loh	°loh	'steal'
*loy	luy, †loy	loy	°loy	loy		'knot' (n/v)
ᵇ*loon	˜loon-haf 'skull'	lood	roon	loon	†loon	'calabash bowl'
*loox	look	look	rook	loo y-	loo	'belly'
*looy	looyuk 'mourn'	looy 'flow'	rooy	looy	looy	'cry'
ᶜ*luH(Vy)	looy, °lohoy	looy	rohoy	°luh	°lúh	'(be) short'
*luy	luy	loy	ruy	luy, †lóy	luuy, †lóy	'funeral'
*(n-)luuf	luf, *†luuf	lúuf	nduuf	luuf duuf	°luuf †dúf	'forest' 'thick bush'
*luun	luun	luun	ruun	°luun	°luun	'witch, sorcerer'
*luum	luumiin	°luumiin	ruumind	luum	°luum	'be red,' NL 'have light skin'
ᵇ*ku-lúɓ	˜kúlúɓ		kuluɓ k-	°kúlúb		'horn (instrument)'
*lúk	lúk			lúk	°lúk	'tail'
*ku-lúŋ	kúlúŋ k-	kúlúŋ k-⁷⁰		kuluŋ °k-	†kúlúŋ	'pot/jug'
*n-ku-lúŋ	gúlúŋ 'jug'			guluŋ	guluŋ	'gourd (spoon)'
*lúuk	lúuk			lúuk	°lúuk	'gang up on and attack'
*lúund	lúud	lúud		luun, °lún~d		'lend'
*ca/sa-lngis	celngis c-				†selgis f-	'steamed millet granules'
ᶜ*(n-)lVVn	leen	†len	reen		°diin, †déen, †len	'kapok tree'
			PC *r			
ᵇ*kV-ra⁷¹	ketaa k-	ketaa k-		°kula		'pot'
ᶜ*ɓe-reɓ	ɓeti (y-), †ɓedëɓ	ɓete f-	ɓitiɓ	ɓeleɓ	ɓeleɓ	'woman'
*reɓ	leɓ		riɓ			'female'

---

70 Given as *kúlúng* in Pichl (1981) with the meaning 'calabash wine bottle.' Dieye gives this word with the meaning 'extreme darkness,' but also as part of the compound *kúlúŋ-yoon* 'heart,' equivalent to a Noon compound *kuluŋ ñon* given by Williams and Williams.

71 A Wanderwort in the area, likely originally from Mande (e.g. Bambara *dàa*); cf. Wolof *ndaa* 'pot,' Tenda *er-ɗaa* 'beer pot'.

APPENDIX 1

(cont.)

	Noon	Laalaa	Saafi	Paloor	Ndut	
			PC *r			
c*ḵi-rik	kedik k-	kedek k-	kidik[72]	kilik k-	kilik †k-	'tree'
*fi-rik				filik f-		'grass'
c*(a-)roɣ	atoh (f-)	atoh	atoh °f-	la'	la', †ala[73]	'stone, rock'
			PC *y			
*yaɣ	yah	yah	yaah, °yah	ya'	ya'	'hand, arm'
b*yaH	yah	°yah	yah	yah		'destroy'
b*yamb	yab	yab	yamb	°yab	†yam~b	'accuse'
*yamb	yab			°yam~b	yam~†b	'alight' (for a bird)
*yaaɓ	yaaɓ		yaaɓ 'be tired'	yaaɓ	yaaɓ	'hunger' (n/v)
c*(y)eɗ	eɗ	eɗ	eɗ	yeɗ	yeɗ, †(y)ed	'give'
b*yeñ(j)	ye'	†yeñ	yenj	°yeej, °yeen	°yeñ	'push'
*(y)in	yen 'some-thing'	yin	in	yin	yin	'thing'
*(y)in-	enaama (y-)	°yinaama		inam		'thing'
c*yíp~yíp	yíp	yíp	yip	yíp, °yíp	yíp	'plant (e.g. a stake)'
*yíiɓ	yíiɓ	yíiɓ	yiiɓ		†yíɓ	'limp'
*ḵo-yo	†kuyu/kuuy, kui k-	koyo k-	kooy	koy k-	koy k-	'child' (NL 'girl')
*yon(d)	yon	yan		yon~°d	†yon	'thresh grain'
b*yooɓ	yooɓ	yooɓ	yooɓ	yooɓ	yooɓ	'be easy'
b*yool	yool	†yol		°yool		'hang down,' Pa. 'slide down'
*yoond	yood	yood	yoond 'move'	yoon~d	°yoon~d	'learn'
*yoond-íɗ	yóodíɗ	yóodíɗ	yoondiɗ 'shake'	yóodíɗ	°yoodíd	'teach'
*yul	yool, °yol	†yol	†yul		°yul	'digging stick'
*yul					yul	'arrive'
*yul-oH	°yoloh 'stand straight'	yoloh	yurah	°yuloh	yuloh	'go straight/for-ward'
*yup	yop	†yep		yup	†yúp	'herd' (n)
*fa-yúm	‡fëyum	fëyëm f-	fayum	fëyúm °m-	°fëyúm	'fat, grease'
*yú(u)k	yúuk	yúuk	yuuk	yuk	yúk	'shoulder'
*yúul	°yul	yúul			yúul	'sanctuary/altar'

---

72 Botne and Pouille give *kidig*, phonetically [kidik]. Better taken as *kidik* (as in Pouye), with voicing in definite forms (*kidg-i*, etc.).

73 Ndut *ala* 'a fetish stone on which libations are poured'.

PROTO-CANGIN LEXICAL RECONSTRUCTIONS

261

(cont.)

	Noon	Laalaa	Saafi	Paloor	Ndut	
			PC *y			
*yúun(d)	yúud	yúud	yun	yúun	yúun	'wake up'
*yVx[74]	yúk	yúukís	yuk	yoh	°yoh	'dry season'
(cf. Wo. yaay)	yiiy, yeey		yaay	°yeey	yaay f-	'mother'
			PC *ɣ			
*(n̲-)ɣaɓit	hawit c-	hayet f-, °haet	haɓit	geet	°geet	'dung'
*ɣac~ɣay	hay	hac	hay	ac~y	ac~y	'come'
ᶜ*ɣaf	haf	haf	haf	af	af	'head'
*(fi̲-)ɣal	hal 'door'	hal 'door'	har	(yal) 'door'	°fëël, †fël f-	'outdoors'[75]
ᶜ*ɣam	ham	ham			†am	'dance'
*ɣan	han	°han	han 'then'	an	an	'have just done'
ᶜ*ɣar̲/ɣír̲[76]	has	koas k-	has	°íl	íl	'eye'
*ɣawír̲	(nóoyís, °nёёwís)	(†noys)	haawis, °hawis	óyíl, °owil	°oyíl, †ëyíl	'reduce'
ᵇ*(ɓi̲-)ɣawúl[77]	hool, °huul	hёwúl	hawur	ɓóolú	†ɓёёlú, †ɓol k-	'griot'
*ɣaan	haan	haan	haan	aan	aan	'drum'
*ɣiñ	hiñ, °hej, °heñ	heñ		íñ		'war'
*ɣiñ-oɣ	hiñoh, °heñoh	heñoh	hiñoh	iña'	†íñ, (†íne)	'fight'
ᵇ*ɣíiñ	híiñ	híiñ		°íiñ	†íñ	'roll flour'
ᶜ*to̲-ɣo	tooh, °tohoo t-	too t-	toho r-	too k-	too k-	'millet'
*pV-ɣo	pooh p-	poo p-				'millet plant'
ᶜ*mu̲-ɣon	moon c-	moon m-	muhun	°moon m-	†mun m-	'tear (crying)'
ᶜ*ɣot	hot	hot	hot	ot~l	ot~l	'see'

---

74   This would be the only example of the sequence *úx or *íx, so it is possible that NdP regularly lowered +ATR vowels before *x.

75   Unprefixed 'door', spatial meaning with *fi-, seemingly eroded in Saafi. Unclear connection with Paloor yal and Saafi yarndeeh 'door'.

76   A high front vowel is common in Niger-Congo (cf. Sereer a-ngid, Bantu *-jícò), and so Cangin *i must be original. The NLS form with *a may be due to the preceding *ɣ, before which some vowels lower in NLS (see § 2.2.6). However this would be the only case of vowel lowering after *ɣ.

77   Noon suggests a variant *ɣawul.

262   APPENDIX 1

(*cont.*)

	Noon	Laalaa	Saafi	Paloor	Ndut	
			PC *ɣ			
*ɣooɓ	hooɓ	hooɓ	hooɓ	°owena'	†oowe/oe	'turn night'[78]
*ɣooɓ-icʼ	hóoɓicʼ	°hóyicʼ	hooɓicʼ 'turn night'			'be late at night'
*ɣooɓ-ox	hooɓuk	°hook	hooɓuk			'pass the day'
*ɣoocʼ	hoocʼ	°hoocʼ		oocʼ 'grow'		'be tall/deep'
*ɣooɽ	hoos	hoos	hoos	ool	†ool	'slit throat'
*ɣun		hon		un	un	'throat/voice'
*ɣut	(hoocʼiit)	hotiit	hut	ut	°ut	'be long'
*ɣúul	húul	húul		uul	°úul	'Palmyra palm'
			PC ∅/ʔ[79]			
ᶜ*(k-)anax	kanak	kanak	kanak	ana	anah	'two'
*nda-anax yaɣ	daaŋkeeh, °daaŋkah	dankeh, °daaŋkeah	ndaŋkiyaah			'ten' (*'at two hands')
*(ka-)aɣay(V)?	kaay, °kaahay	kaahaay	kahaay, †kaahai	eye	éeyë	'three'
*an-nd-?	†and		andiin 'tale'	andi 'tale'	anil, †and	'tell (story)'
ᵇ*eel	ˇyaayeel		eel	eel		'cloud'
*eend	eed	een			†een	'fig tree'
*ilaax?	elak, †alak	elak	iraak		°yalaah	'bean'
ᶜ*iñ	iñ y-	oñ y-[80]	iiñ 'snake'	iñ y- 'things'	iñ	'thing'
*-íno(h)	w-íinoo, winnoo, °wítnoo	w-íinó, °w-íinóo	yiino	yíno	yínëh	'one' (2nd and 3rd Noon forms used in counting)
ᵇ*íin	íin	íinúk	iin		†iin	'groan'
*omb	ob	ob	omb-	wom~b		'wean'
*on	on	on	on	on	on	'give/offer'

---

78   Ndut-Paloor 'good afternoon,' from *ɣooɓ with the imperative suffix -*e*, and in Paloor *na'* 'sun/day.' Paloor plural °*ëwënë'* with plural imperative -*í*.

79   See prefix consonant for: *ti-ix 'name,' *ca-oy 'elephant,' *tV-úH 'all,' *ɓi-o' 'person,' *ɓi-Vɓ 'all,' and all nouns with a C- prefix.

80   The unexpected /o/ may be related to the Laalaa *e > o change seen in Table 43, but all examples of this change involve a labial consonant, so there may be another explanation. Konyagi has a similar vowel discrepancy for 'thing,' which may be cognate to the Cangin form(s): *i-ỹín ~ i-ỹá* 'thing' alongside *ñóñǎ* 'nothing.' Bassari has *yèỹî* 'thing' and Bedik *jíñ* 'thing.' The root exhibits irregular developments in each language. A connection with BKK *k-onj 'thing' (cf. Kobiana *koñ*, Gujaher *xonj*) is also possible. If 'thing' is related between these three groups, the /o/ in the Laalaa form might be traced back much further, and be unrelated to the *e > o change.

PROTO-CANGIN LEXICAL RECONSTRUCTIONS 263

(cont.)

	Noon	Laalaa	Saafi	Paloor	Ndut	
			PC Ø/ʔ			
ᵇ*op		op	op	op	°opa	'sweat'
*ú(u)f	úf, ˟†úuf	úf	uuf	°uuf	†úf	'pagne'
	ee	eey	ee	ee, ii	†ii	'yes'
			Unclear			
*yún-oH?[81]	únoh, °ínoh	únóh	inah	yúh	yúh	'know'
*-(ɽ)ek?[82]	wek	wek	wek	elek	°elek	'night'
ᶜ*(H)íníŋ?	híníŋ, íníŋ	kíindíŋ (n)	iling, iliŋ (n/v)	híndíŋ~g	°híiníŋ, †(h)íníŋ	'thunder'
*nda/ɗa-(h)um	dóom, °duum	ɗom		doom	†dom	'not yet'
*(k̲-)aɓ?		kaɓ			†ab	'part'
ᶜ*kaɗ~ka'~kan?				kaa', kada', °kad	kaa', †ka'a, †kad	'refuse'
	kaa, ha-, °han-	kaa/caa, haɗ-/caɗ-	ka, kana, kin(a)	ka, ki na	ka, †kanka	prohibitive marker
	jutuut	jítúut	yisuut, yissut	jísúut	°yútúut	'small'
	melic	miiliic	meleñ	°ɓíríñ	°pilliŋ	'lightning'[83]
	wílal	wíil 'search'	wil	wil, °yiil	†yíd	'turn/spin around'[84]
	óodǐs	óodóos	puudis	purus, °puris		'wind'[85]

---

81 See Table 137 for *-oH. Initial *yú might explain /ú~í/ in NLS, but the developments would be irregular. If the NdP word is related, deletion of /n/ would be irregular.

82 Very irregular, if the two forms are related. Each is possibly prefixed, NLS with *w-, and NdP with *el-, perhaps an allomorph of some other prefix before a vowel (cf. Bantu class 5 *di-). Instead, it may be that the root was *-ɽek, allowing comparison with Bantu *bu-tíʼkù 'night' (also found in class 5 with the meaning '24-hour period'). The NLS form would then be an irregular development of *w-ɽek or *u-ɽek. Neither explanation has support from elsewhere in Cangin, and so both are very speculative.

83 The basic template LABIAL-LIQUID-VELAR/NASAL for 'lightning' is common nearby (cf. Bambara férɛn 'thunder,' Konyagi -viliñát) and throughout the world: Semitic *barak', Hungarian villám, Uto-Aztecan *piLok, Norwegian blink, Khmer phleek bantou, Kurmanji birûsk, etc. The Cangin forms are similarly sound-symbolic, and these forms could have in theory arisen even in isolation. The Proto-Cangin form likely had a similar form, but there is no evidence to prefer any particular reconstruction.

84 Cf. Sereer wiril, Wolof wër, but also similar to forms in many other languages, e.g. Proto-Nilotic *wir 'turn around,' Proto-Pama-Nyungan *wirni 'turn,' Proto-Indo-European *welH 'turn,' Proto-Austronesian *wili 'return,' Khmer wil 'turn around,' English whirl—seemingly iconic.

85 Not the class prefix *pi- in Saafi and Paloor. There is a cross-linguistic sound-symbolic association between 'wind/blow' and an initial labial consonant.

264 APPENDIX 1

(cont.)

	Noon	Laalaa	Saafi	Paloor	Ndut	
			Unclear			
	fabuy f-, †fumbuluy f-	fëbúy f-, †fúy f-	mbambaluug		°fuj f-	'brain'[86]
	‡kuluŋ ñon	kúlúŋ-yoon	‡ngum		°gumioon	'heart'[87]
	booy	ɓooy	ooy	wooy		'strangle'
		dúlfúlúf	burufruf	fúlfúlúf	†yúrúfúy	'lung'
	hiilii	hiiliil	hiilir			'(be) green'
			iiri	hílís	°hílís	'be wet'
	korkat 'thank you'		corkidʼ	°jolka', cole farah		'thank'
	ñodʼuwaa		ñolfit 'eye-brow'		†fúrfë	'eyelash'[88]
		jíp		°cíp	°cíp 'stake'	'pillar'[89]
	cuul~yuul				†col	'crouch'
	ɓëgúl 'chop wood'			°bígíl		'store firewood'
		bos		°posa'		'be rotten'[90]
			NLS only[91]			
*pambi	pabi, °pabu, †pambe f-	pabe f-	pambi f-	(paan)	(paan †f-)	'chicken'

86 For the longer forms in Thiès Noon and Saafi, cf. Sereer *mbunquluj/mbunguluuć/mbon-qoluj* 'yolk of egg, baobab fruit powder.'

87 The first word in the Noon-Laalaa compound is *kúlúŋ* 'gourd/jug.' The first word in the Ndut compound is †*gum* 'gourd (for palm wine),' and in Saafi the compound 'heart' has been truncated to only this first word, replacing the original meaning 'gourd.' The second word in the compound, *yoon*, is peculiar; it appears to be NLS **yoyon* 'field,' but the semantic connection between 'gourd of field' and 'heart' is unclear. The compound may have referred to a particular variety of gourd that resembles a heart.

88 The Noon and Ndut forms are plausibly related: Noon from **ñV-dúfa*, Ndut from **fa-dúfa*. The Noon and Saafi forms can be compared with Sereer *o-ñooroor*, which may have supplied the initial CV in these two languages through contamination, as **ñV-* is not otherwise identifiable as a prefix. The sequence /it/ in Saafi is a borrowing of the Wolof "individuative" suffix *-it* as found in *fell-it* 'fragment' from *fell* 'chip off,' etc.

89 Perhaps related to **yíp~yíp* 'plant (stake) in ground.'

90 Similar forms for 'rot/rotten' found throughout the world: Latvian *pūt*, Amharic *bäsäb-bäsä*, Proto-Malayo-Polynesian **busuk*, Proto-Bantu **-bòd*, etc. Seemingly iconic (perhaps of spitting out rotten food), and not derivable from a single PC form in Laalaa and Paloor.

91 Note that any instance of **ɣ* may in fact be **H. Most instances of short **o could instead be **u.

PROTO-CANGIN LEXICAL RECONSTRUCTIONS

(cont.)

	Noon	Laalaa	Saafi	Paloor	Ndut	
			NLS only			
*payVm	payum, ˇpayam	payamun	payuum	(°pacool)	(†pacoli)	'inlaw' (pfx. *pa-?)
*paangí	péegíi (f-)	paagii f-	paangi f-/n-			'grass'
*taal	téelís	taal	taal			'lower,' No. 'skim off cream'
*taamb	taab	taab	taamb			'follow'
*taañind[92]	téeñiin	†tañíd	taañind			'bedbug'
*toon	toon	toon	toon			'sell'
*tool	tool		toor			'move' (borr. Wo. toxal?)
*wu-tuɓa	wutuwaa	wotoa, °watoa	wotɓa	(aa')	(aa)	'yesterday'
*cambVnaɣ[93]	cobinaah	cobona f-	caɓnaah			'armpit'
*ca(n)kunaɣ[94]	coog(i)naah (f-)	cogona f-	cekna(a)~ cakna r-	(cigilaan)	(°cigilaan)	'fingernail/claw'
*cangíndo(ɣ)[95]	°cígídóo	cëgídóh f-	°ciɓndo'			'panther'
ᵇ*cíiɓ-is-ox	cíiwiik		ciiɓsuk			'tsk (Wo. cüpatu)'
*kaɣand	kaad f-	kaad f-	kahan, °kahand			'house'
*kañ	kañ (v)	kañuu (v)	kañeeh, kañis (n)			'(have) family name'
*kap	kap	kap	kap			'be full (sated)'
*kaak/x	kaak	kaak	kaak			'defecate'
*kaan	kaan	kaan	kaan			'die'
*ka-kaan	ˇkikaan k-	kakaan k-	kakaan			'death'
*ken	ken	ken	ken			'tie pagne'
*kíim	kíim	kíim	kiim			'ask, pray'
*kúl	kúl	kúl	kur 'land/ town'			'land/world'
*kúng	kúg		kung			'fold, bend'
*ɓas/r̥	ɓas	ɓas	ɓas			'insult'
*ɗafuk/x	ɗook	ɗook	ɗafuk			'above/over'
ᵇ*ɗaal	ɗaal	ɗaal	ɗaar			'stoop down,' Sa. 'be nonchalant'

---

92 Resembles *haañínd 'coal,' perhaps due to a folk-etymological contamination (cf. Wolof teeñ w- 'louse')—or else this is truly the same root with *tV-.

93 Contains the class prefix *ca(N)-, and perhaps *yaɣ 'arm' compounded with a root *wun/ won/pun/pon. Ndut has °poɓ, presumably unrelated.

94 Likely *ca(n)-kun-yaɣ, containing *kun 'finger' and *yaɣ 'hand.' Noon yognaah 'hoof' is presumably related. NdP *cangilaan has a different root.

95 In 'panther' as well as 'armpit,' there is no apparent explanation for /ɓ/ in Saafi.

APPENDIX 1

(cont.)

	Noon	Laalaa	Saafi	Paloor	Ndut	
			NLS only			
ᵇ*ɗaang	ɗaag		ɗaangiɗ			'be stuck up high,' Sa. causative
ᵇ*ɗaang-ís	ɗaagís	ɗëëgísúk 'fall'				'lower sth. stuck up high'
*ɗik/x	ɗek	ɗek	ɗik, ɗek	(°lik)	(°lik)	'be deaf'
*ɗisik	ɗiik ~ ɗesk-		ɗisik	(ɗíkë, °tíke)	(tígë)	'place' (n)
*ɗiif	ɗiif	ɗiif	ɗiif			'press down on'
*ɗood	dooɗuk		ɗood			'miss s.o.'
ᵇ*ɗúung	ɗúug 'squint'	ɗúug	ɗuung			'close eyes'
*fi̱-yaang	feyaaŋ f-, ˉfayaaŋ f-	feaŋ f-	fiyaang			'bed' (cf. Sereer *njong*)
*malak/x	malak	malak	marak			'watch'
*mey	miy, °ᵗmey	mey	mey			'leave/disappear'
*moɗ	moɗ	maɗ	moɗ			'be beautiful'
*naaw	naaw	naaw	naaw			'wash clothes'
*ka̱-no(ɣ)⁹⁶	kanu, ᵗkanoh k-	kano k-	kanoh			'calabash'
*nja̱-no(ɣ)	janu j-	jano j-	njenoh, °njanoh			'small calabash'
ᵇ*nop	nop	ᵗnop	nop	(°nëp)	(ᵗnob)	'rot'
*fi̱-nVɣo?	fenoo f-	fenoo	fino, finno, finho r-			'behind' ('rear')
ᵇ*ñakít-ox	ˉñëkítuk		ñaktuk, ñakit			'eat breakfast,' Sa. '(eat) lunch'
*ñaañ	ñaañ	ñaañ	ñaañ			'be smart'
*ñiin(d)	ñiid	ñiid	ñiin 'light'	(niiñ)		'moon,' (Pa. 'be clear')
*ñoɣok/x		ᵗñok	ñuhuk			'termite'
ᵇ*ndap	dap	dap	ndap			'granary'
*nga	ga	ga	nga			general preposition
ᶜ*ngúɗ	gúɗ	gúɗ	nguɗ			'cut'
ᵇ*saɓ-ís-oɣ	séwíyoh		saɓsoh			'separate,' No. 'break up fight'
*sang	sag	sag	sang			'hate, refuse'

---

96 Mbodj (1983: 125) analyzes the Saafi word as an instrument nominalization of the verb *an* 'drink,' which may be correct. If so, the original form might be *ku-han-oɣ with the applicative suffix, with the diminutive being *nji-han-oɣ, explaining the vowel change in Saafi.

PROTO-CANGIN LEXICAL RECONSTRUCTIONS

(cont.)

	Noon	Laalaa	Saafi	Paloor	Ndut	
NLS only						
*ko̱-se/ɽe	‡koye	kose f-, °kosee k-	kose k-			'tail'
ᵇ*sew	sewiñ		seew			'be thin/skinny'
ᶜ*sút	sút	sút 'fog'	sut			'fill w/ smoke'
ᶜ*(h)aɗ	aɗ	aɗ	aɗ k-			'famine'
ᶜ*(h)aɗ-ox	aɗuk	aɗok	aɗuk			'be hungry'
*(h)aam	aam		aam			'pour'
*(h)aañ	aañ 'win, shoo'	aañ 'send back'	aañ			'chase off'
*(h)aañ-íɗ-oy	éenjoh	ënjóh	añnjoh			'play'
*(h)et-oy	etoh		etoh			'need'
*(h)oy		oy	oy			'pierce'
*(ku̱-) (h)oomaay	oomaa(h)	oomah	komaak			'child'
*tu̱-(h)uy?	túuy, ᵗtúy	tuy, °tuuy	tuy, °tuuy			'hut, room'
*ɗa̱-(h)uy?	ɗóoy, °ɗuuy	ɗoy 'among'	ɗooy			'inside'
*(h)úl	úl	úl	ur			'squash' (n)
*(h)úm	úm		um			'bring bad luck'
ᵇ*(h)úul	úul	úul	ul			'cover'
ᶜ*(h)úumb	úub		uumb			'bury'
ᵇ*Hof/Huf		hof	hofiɗ 'frighten'			'be fearful'
ᵇ*Ho(o)m		hoom	hom			'tortoise'
ᵇ*waal	waal	waal	waar			'Wolof'
*weel	weel	weel	weer			'break'
ᵇ*ka̱-laɓ	kalaɓ	koloɓ f-	kalaɓ k-			'sword, machete'
*mV̱-leyi?	maleey m-	melaay~ melae m-	merey~ mereh m-			'sand'
*lamb	°lam	lab	ramb			'thigh'
*lang	lag	lag	rang			'close'
*lang-ís	légís	lëgís	rangis			'open'
ᶜ*ley	lah	lah	reh			'rainy season'
ᶜ*leey < lV-oy	leeh	leh	reeh			'be finished,' Sa. 'be used up'
*líis/ɽ		líis 'bean'	liis			'bean pod'
*ki̱-lo		keloo k-	kiro	(°koloj k-)		'pot'
*lúp	lúp	°lúp	rup			'thorn'
*lúund	lúud	lúud	ruund			'be ripe'
ᶜ*yak/x	yak, yaak	yaakaak	yak, yakak			'(be) big'
*yatús/ɽ	yótús	yítús	yatus			'five'
ᵇ*yeeɓ	yéeɓ 'rock baby'		yeeɓ			Sa. 'set down discretely'

268 APPENDIX 1

(cont.)

	Noon	Laalaa	Saafi	Paloor	Ndut	
			NLS only			
ᶜ*(y)íif	íif	†yíif	yiif	(°ef 'fill')		'pour'
*yoyon	yoon	yoon	yohon			'field'
*ki̱-yVVŋ?[97]	kuuŋ	kiyuuŋ k-, †kúuŋ k-	yooŋ			'shin'
	ya'ɓu		yaɓko			No. 'old woman,' Sa. 'old man'
*yaɓ	haɓ	haɓ				'be good'
*yaɓ-id	hóɓíd 'fix/build'	hëɓíd	haɓid 'do'			'make good'
ᵇ*yaaɓi	haawi (n-), †haaɓ(e)	haay †n-				'millet couscous'[98]
*yíy	híy	híy	hiy 'be drunk'	(°sëgíj)		'hiccup' (v)
*pi̱-yíy		píhíy p-				'hiccup' (n)
*yíil	híil	híil	hiir			'bow down'
ᵇ*yod	hod	hod	hood			'pigeon'
*yo(o)n-oy	hoonoh 'forbid'		honoh 'prevent'			
*yún		†hún	hun			'accompany'
*yVd	°had	had	hay, hed			'owner/master'
ᵇ*yVnd	híd	híd	hend			'be equal'

---

97 Based on Noon-Laalaa, the root-initial consonant appears to be *y, as it is regularly deleted in Noon but not Laalaa—if it is *y as in Saafi, this would be the only word in which *y is deleted in Noon. The irregular vowel correspondence further complicates the reconstruction.

98 This word is listed because of its interesting etymology. It is borrowed from the Proto-Fula-Sereer root *gaab 'millet' (Sereer ngaaf, Fula gaw-ri)—the presence of the final vowel may indicate borrowing from early Fula *gaab-ri. Its status as a borrowing is confirmed by the fact that the final vowel does not undergo regular lengthening in Noon—unprefixed Noon nouns with a final short vowel are almost all borrowings. Despite the seemingly recent borrowing of this term (post-dating the NL-exclusive final vowel lengthening change), it shows a labial stop as in PFS, rather than /w/ as in Fula, or /f/ as in Sereer. This suggests a rather late change from PFS *b to either Fula /w/ or Sereer /f/. Saafi has saay 'millet couscous,' from Sereer saac. Ndut-Paloor has kiid k- or kíid k-. It is likely that no term existed in Proto-Cangin.

APPENDIX 2

Outside Cognates

The Proto-Cangin reconstructions on the following pages have potential cognates in other Northern Atlantic languages. These can be compared with the borrowings identified in Table 69, mostly from Sereer and Wolof. These potential cognates differ from the borrowings in that most of them are found in Atlantic languages other than Sereer and Wolof, they show sound correspondences that would not be natural for a borrowing, and/or they tend to represent more basic vocabulary. Still, there is the possibility that some of these words are in fact borrowings, and some may be coincidental resemblances. A number of them appear to be sound-symbolic, or otherwise can be explained by cross-linguistically "universal" tendencies of form-meaning mapping (marked with a raised "u" before the gloss). Comparisons from nearby Mande languages are shown to suggest that some of these words may be Wanderwörter. Abbreviations used are: BKK = Proto-Bainunk-Kobiana-Kasanga, Bai. = Proto-Bainunk, KK = Proto-Kobiana-Kasanga, BP = Proto-Biafada-Pajade, JF = Joola Fonyi, JE = Joola Eegimaa, PB = Proto-Bantu, (P)BC = (Proto-)Benue-Congo ("pseudo-reconstructions" from De Wolf 1971). A plus sign below a reconstructed BKK or Bainunk vowel indicates +ATR; for Wolof and Joola, the acute accent is used instead, as in Cangin. Proto-Tenda *ə̣ is a higher central vowel than *ə. Accent marks for all other languages are tone markings. Forms from the Saalum dialect of Wolof which preserves /h/ and postvocalic /d/ are given in parentheses. Proto-Manjak reconstructions (taking into account all Manjak-cluster languages) are adapted from Doneux (1975b). Other reconstructions are my own—most can be found in Merrill (2018).

Table 149 presents my hypothesis for the regular consonant correspondences between Northern Atlantic groups (and Bantu). The table considers only singleton consonants, and not consonant clusters, geminates, or prenasalized sounds, including those that are the result of consonant mutation in various groups. In some groups (including Cangin), consonants develop differently in class prefixes, and these outcomes are not represented in the table. "#" represents a word boundary, and "$" a stem boundary. "$V_{rd}$" and "$V_{fr}$" indicate environments next to a round or front vowel. Some consonants have two regular reflexes in Joola, the reason for which is not currently clear. Proto-Bantu forms are from the BLR3 (Bastin et al. 2002), which reconstructs a consonant *j that likely represents multiple sounds, including ∅ in root-initial position. A number of the potential cognates in this appendix do not conform to the sound

© JOHN T.M. MERRILL, 2023 | DOI:10.1163/9789004546493_008

correspondences presented in Table 149, and these should be taken as much less likely cognate candidates, perhaps involving borrowing or simply coincidental resemblance. In a number of cases, a *CV root may have been "extended" with different frozen suffixes across groups.

TABLE 149 Regular development of singleton consonants in NW Atlantic groups and Bantu

Language								
*Bantu	p	t	c	k		"j"	b	d
Bijogo	$p, ∅	t	t, c	k, kp		∅	β	$r, d
Balanta	f, V_{rd} ∅	t	s	h			f, ∅#	θ
*Manjak	f, V_{rd}w	t>s	t, c	k	h		p, w#	ţ, [t(ʃ)]
*Joola	f, V_{rd}w	l/t	ɬ/t, s/c	∅/k			f/p, w#	t
Bedik	f	s	ʃ	h, ʃ	h		w	r
Bassari	f	s	ʃ	x, ʃ	x		w	r
Konyagi	f	r	s	x, s	x		w	l
*Tenda	f	r̥	ʃ	x, ʃV_{fr}	x		w	r
Pajade	f	s	s	∅wy, s	∅wy	w, ∅	p	r
Bialada	f	r	s	h, s	h	w, ∅	b	l
*Bialada-Pajade	f	r̥	s	h, sV_{fr}	h	#w, ∅	b	r
Kobiana, Kasanga	f	h, r	s	h, h	w/y		b	l
Bainunk	f	l	r, s	k, x	h		b	$p, r
*Bainunk-kk	f	r̥	s, ʃ	$k, x	h		b	d
Wolof	f	t	s	h, x[χ]	h		b	d
Sereer	f	t, d#	s	x[χ]	$h, x		f	r
Fula	f	t, t#	s	h			w	r
*Fula-Sereer	f	t, d#	s	x[χ]	h		b	r
*Cangin	$p, f	#t/$s, r̥	s	k	$H, x	h	$w, ∅	l
*Niger-Congo	p	t	t, c	k	x	h	b	d

TABLE 149   Regular development of singleton consonants in NW Atlantic groups and Bantu (*cont.*)

*Niger-Congo	*Cangin	*Fula-Sereer	Fula	Sereer	Wolof	*Bainunk-ᴋᴋ	Bainunk	Kobiana, Kasanga	*Biafada-Pajade	Biafada	Pajade	*Tenda	Konyagi	Bassari	Bedik	*Joola	*Manjak	Balanta	Bijogo	*Bantu
g	ɣ	g	ʔ/w/y	g k#	g	g	g	$g g,∅	g jVfr	g j	#k ∅ c	ɣ yVfr	$y/w ∅ y	$ɣ ∅ y	$ɣ ∅ y	k	k	g	g, (gb)	g/j
w	f	w	w	w	w	w	w	w	#w ∅	w ∅	w ∅	w	w	w	w	w	w	?	β	?
l	n	l	l	l	r	n	n	n	y	y	y	n	ḷ	n	l	l	l	l	∅	"j"
j~y	y/∅	y	y	y	y	y	y	y	y	y	y	y	y	y	y	y	y	y?	y/∅	j
ɓ	ɓ	ɓ	ɓ	ɓ	w/∅	∅	∅	∅	ɓ	b	b	ɓ	v	ɓ	ɓ	b	b	b	b	b
ɗ	ɗ	ɗ	ɗ	ɗ	l	r	n	r, d	ɗ	d	d	ɗ	ry	l	ɗ	d~r	d~r	d	ɖ	d
y	y	y	y	y	y?	y	y	y	y	j	j	y	y	y	y	j	j	j	j	j?
m	m	m	m	m	m	m	m	m	m	m	m	m	w̃	w̃	m	m	m	m	m	m
n	n	n	n	n	n	n	n	n	n	n	n	n	ḷ	n	l	n	n	l	n	n
ñ	ñ	ñ	ñ	ñ	ñ	ñ	ñ	ñ	ñ	ñ	ñ	ñ	ỹ	ỹ	ñ	ñ	ñ	ñ	ñ?	ɲ
ŋ	ŋ	ŋ	ŋ	ŋ	ŋ	ŋ	ŋ	ŋ	ŋ	ŋ	ŋ	ŋ	ỹ/w̃	ỹ	ŋ	ŋ?	ŋ	ŋ?	ŋ?	?

OUTSIDE COGNATES 273

Cangin	Fula-Seerer	Wolof	Other Atlantic	BC, Mande
*pe-ɗe(e)m	S. ɗelem F. ɗem-ngal	làmmiñ w-?	Kobiana jaaróm BP *bu-ɗeemä Tenda *-ɗim Joola *fu-rim 'voice' Manjak pə-rim 'speech' Manjak *pə-ndumənʈ Balanta gɪ-dèmét	PB *-dímì̧	ᵘ'tongue'
*huɓ[1]	*-xoɓ(ɓ) S. o-xoβ F. koɓ-al	xob w- 'leaf'	Gujaher gu-hubut Tenda *-xoɓɓ/xuɓɓ Pajade ka-ŋubɛ JF ka-kub Mankanya ka-huub Bijogo kɔ-kpa	PB *-kóbá 'baȑk/skin' Yamba kɔ̀b, etc.	'bark'
*ɣaɽ/ɣíɽ̥	*-gid S. a-ngid F. yit-ere	gët y- (archaic pl.)	BKK *ci-ggiɽ Tenda *-ɣəɽ BP *-gəɽä Joola *ji-kíl Manjak pə-kəs Balanta f-gít	PB *-jj̧cò PBC *i-lito[2]	'eye'
*tuHuɽ̥ (< Ser.?) NdP muluc < *mu-ɽuc?	*tuxud S. duxud F. tuut-	tëfli?	Bai. *-ɽoott Tenda *-ɽo BP *-ɽəmp Balanta tʊfaj Bijogo tu	PB *tú̧(-ij/id)	ᵘ'spit'
*soox (<sV- ox?)	S. sayid	saw, seben	BKK *-ʃa-et(t) Konyagi -sǽw̃ BP *sah Joola *-súr	PB *-cù(b)	'urinate'
*pe'	*ban-be S. fambe F. mbee-wa	béy w-	Bai. *fa-bȩ Tenda *ji-fe 'sheep' Manjak u-pɪ Bijogo e-βe	Idoma òpí Basa-Benue u-pi, etc.	ᵘ'goat'

---

1 Fula-Seerer, Wolof, and Bantu suggest **x, but Cangin, suggests **h. In other groups, the root-initial consonants could be traced to either sound. There are likely two roots represented here. The h-initial roots are perhaps cognate with Bantu *jùb~jòb 'peel/skin.'

2 E.g. Dzodinka -līt~mīt 'eye(s),' and many similar l~m alternations in Bantoid. The l~m are fused class 5~6 prefixes, so the form throughout Bantoid (including Bantu) must be traced to *-jito or similar. Gerhardt (1983: 226) reconstructs *-gis for a subgroup of the Plateau languages within Benue-Congo.

274 APPENDIX 2

(cont.)

Cangin	Fula-Sereer	Wolof	Other Atlantic	BC, Mande	
*koɗ	S. xoɗ 'make drink'?	(hudd), wudd 'raise livestock'? xol 'help to eat'?	Bai. *-kun (BKK *-kur?) Tenda *-xoɗ/xuɗ Pajade kud JF -kur	PB *kúd 'grow up' Bambara kólo	'raise child'
*i/fa-noɣ	*ge-nag S. naak F. nag-ge	nag w-	Konyagi ỹi-lì (<*ji-nVɣ) BP *-nagä	PBC *i-nak tiMap fə-ná, etc. Soninke ná	'cow'
*ɓiiɓ	*ɓir- 'milk (v)' S. ɓir F. ɓir-	ween w-	BKK *-ịn(d) Tenda *er-ɓər BP *ba-ɓɓər	PB *-béèdè~ béenè	'breast'[3]
*mooɓ[4]	S. muuy-oox F. moos-o-	muuñ	Kobiana -mozəzə(n) Pajade miñ Bijogo moj	PB *-mùè(ɲ)	'smile'
*ñam	*ñaam S. ñaam F. ñaam-	ñam w- 'food'	BKK *-ñaam Tenda *-ñamm 'gnaw' Manjak ñaam 'chew'	PB *-ɲàmà 'meat' Mundabli ɲām 'fufu'	ᵘ'eat'
*ɓuk	*gun-ɓog S. ɓook F. ɓow-ngu	yoo w- <*y-oh?	BKK *-ung~ux Joola *e-buk	PB *-bú Somyev tə-bogo	'mosquito'
*ɓuh	S. o-ɓox		Konyagi i-vé Pajade ci-baa Manjak u-bʊs? Bijogo e-booɟi?	PB *-búà	'dog'
*ki-rik	F. leg-gal 'tree,' lek-ki 'medicine' S. a-teex 'wood'		Tenda *gaŋ-ɽəx BP *ɓu-ɽe Bijogo ŋu-te	PB *tí Pinyin -tə́k Medumba -túx	'tree'
*nixiiɽ	S. naxik F. nai		Tenda *-nax Biafada nihi Balanta -tàllá?	PB *-nàị	'four'
Sa. cahuy < *ca-ɣuy	F. ngabb-u		BKK *ja-gʊ BP *wan-guwä Joola *e-kaw	PB *-gʊ̀bú	'hippopo-tamus'[5]

---

3 The second consonant was a voiced coronal in Proto-Niger-Congo. The Cangin word (if related) may be an altered nursery form.

4 Irregular final consonant. Sereer and Bijogo suggest **y, which perhaps labialized in Cangin under influence from the preceding vowel and consonant.

5 No word is recorded for other Cangin languages. There is evidence from other groups for both **b and **ɓ as the second consonant. In Cangin, **b would develop to ∅, and **ɓ would remain *ɓ. Either way Saafi /y/ is innovative if this root has outside cognates.

OUTSIDE COGNATES

(cont.)

Cangin	Fula-Sereer	Wolof	Other Atlantic	BC, Mande	
*fúɗ 'light fire,' *fúɗ-íṛ 'blow' *fúɗíñ 'whis- tle'	*wuuɗ S. wuuɗ 'blow, light' F. wuuɗ- 'whistle'		BP *fuur Joola *-fúuten Manjak fuʈ	PB *púd	ᵘ'blow (with mouth)'6
*paɓ	F. wibjo, wiifoongo		Tenda *gaŋ-waf Pajade mam-paafo	PB *-bàbá, *-pàpá	'wing'
*púl	F. ful-		BKK *-fuɗ Joola *-púr	PB *púduk 'escape, go out'	'leave'
*ɓoo(ɣ)-ox	S. ɓog-oox		Konyagi -vágwɔ́l̪ <*ɓoggən	Tikar ɓɔʔ <*ɓɔk	'bathe'
*kún	S. hul		Manjak kul	PB *kúnik	'cover,' also Ca. 'close'7
*mín		mën	BKK *-min BP *mən JF -manj 'know'	PB *màn(i)~màn ~mèɲ 'know'	'be able, know how'
*ca-oɣ			BP *wan-yoogä Bijogo ka-yoga	PB *-jògù	'elephant'
*(h)aɗ-ox, *(h)aɗ			Bijogo aɗ-ɔk (v), aaɗu (n)	PB *-jàdà (n)	'be hungry,' 'hunger'
*pang				PB *páng 'act, make'	'do'
*ɗaɗ				PB *ɗàd	'split'
*puuṛ				PB *pútá	'wound'
*kaɗ~ka'~kan				PB *káan	'refuse'
*nuf	*ru-nof S. nof F. nof-ru	nopp b-	BKK *ki-nuf Tenda *gaŋ-nəf BP *go-nəfa Joola *ka-nuu Balanta gɪ-lɔ́ Bijogo kɔ-nnɔ		'ear'
*fen	S. wil	kawar g-	Biafada ga-i Tenda *-waan Joola *ka-wal Manjak ka-wɛl Bijogo ɛɛ-βa		'hair'

---

6   Only the Fula-Sereer root can be cognate with Cangin based on the initial consonant.

7   Either the Bantu or Manjak root can be cognate to Cangin based on regular correspon- dences—the Sereer root with /h/ cannot be a regular cognate.

APPENDIX 2

(cont.)

Cangin	Fula-Sereer	Wolof	Other Atlantic	BC, Mande	
*sút	S. o-suun (n) F. cuur-ki (n)	suur	BKK *-sudd Tenda *-ʃən Biafada fu-cu (n) Bijogo ʈukp		'(fill with) smoke'
*(sa/ca-)pus	S. °foos (v)	focci (v)	KK *ta-mpooɽ Tenda *-fətter BP *-feeɽ (v), *gun-peeɽä Balanta gɪ-mfɛr	Mandinka fíri	ᵘ'flower/ bloom'
*toɓ	*toɓ F. toɓ- S. °doɓ	taw	Tenda *-ɽəɓ Joola *-lub Manjak sob Balanta tob		'rain (v)'
*ñíind	S. ñiit-oox F. ñitt-aa-	ñand	BKK *-ñiiɽ Tenda *-ñVtt Pajade ñinkət		ᵘ'blow nose'
*pi-ɓil	F. ɓer-nde 'heart'?	(biid), biir b- < *bV-id 'belly'	Bai. *bu-yẹd 'belly'	PB *-bàdì 'liver, heart'?	'lower abdomen'
*ŋaɓ	S. ŋaβ, F. ŋaaɓ-aa- 'gape'	ŋàpp 'gape'	Kobiana -ŋaappə(n) 'yawn' Joola *-ŋaf 'bite'		ᵘ'hold between teeth'
*to-yo	*ri-gaab S. kaaf (pl.) F. gaw-ri	dugub j-	Balanta b-ɔgɔ́		'millet'
*soɗ	*soɗ S. soɗ, F. soɗ-	sol (also 'wear')	Tenda *-ʃuɗɗ-a 'wear'? Manjak *tɔr		'fill (bag)'
*kun	*ru-xol S. nqol F. hon-ndu	baaraam b- <*ba-hVraam?	BKK *-kunum Manjak pə-konj	Bambara kɔni	'finger'
*has	S. xas, F. hes-	(hees), ees	Tenda *-xaʃ		'(be) new'
*wíiɽ	*beed S. feed, F. weet-	bët-set	BP *biiɽ		'dawn (v)'
*keeñ	*re-xeeñ S. xeeñ F. heeñ-ere		Bai. *bu-kiiñ Konyagi i-cə̀nj BP *bu-seeñ(i) Joola *fu-iñ, Pepel fñ Balanta f-húñɛ̀		'liver'
*noɣ	F. naa-nge		BKK *bi-nẹg Biafada nnagə Joola *-nak Manjak pə-nak 'noon' Balanta lĕy?		'sun'

OUTSIDE COGNATES

277

(cont.)

Cangin	Fula-Sereer	Wolof	Other Atlantic	BC, Mande	
*ɓoɣ	S. ɓaak F. ɓok-ki		Bai. Gubëeher si-ǫog Tenda *gaŋ-ɓakk, Konyagi -vu < *-ɓoɣ? JF bu-bak Manjak bə-bak		'baobab'
*yaak	S. yax F. yakk- 'chew, eat (meat/fruit)'		Bai. *-yaax 'eat' Tenda *-yaakk 'crunch w/ teeth' BP *-yah 'eat' Balanta gɪ-njáagám 'jaw'		'cut w/ teeth, etc.'
*ñíiñ	S. ñiiñax F. ñuuñ-u		BKK *-ñuuñ Tenda *-ñiññ/ñuññ Biafada gu-ññuñu Pajade ku-ñiñi Manjak *u-nɔɔn		'ant'
*Hul	*-xoor S. o-xoor F. hood-ere		BKK *gu-hųud Tenda *er-xor Pajade pu-oor Joola *e-ut		'star'
*caa-fú	*-wuC F. mbuubu S. buc̣		BKK *-wųrund Konyagi æ-nkú Joola *e-wú Manjak u-wu		'fly' (insect)
*mu-ɣon	S. o-gooniit F. gon-gol		Tenda *-ɣon(n) BP *man-gə(y) JF mu-kul Balanta f-ngólá		'tear' (cry- ing)[8]
*lím	*rim S. rim F. rim-		Bai. *-dį(i)m Tenda *-rəm BP *rəm		'give birth'
*ɣam	*gom/gam S. gom 'wrestling dance' F. 'am-/'om-		Kobiana -gom Tenda *-ɣam BP *gam		'dance'
*leɣ	S. ndiig (verb riig)		KK *boo-lug Tenda *-ruu BP *-rigV/rugV		'rainy sea- son'

---

8 Two roots are represented, one **n-final, and one **l-final; the Cangin root could come from
either, as these consonants merge as Cangin *n.

278 APPENDIX 2

(*cont.*)

Cangin	Fula-Sereer	Wolof	Other Atlantic	BC, Mande	
NdP gin < *ngin 'village,' perhaps *ca-ngin 'town'	S. gen		Bainunk *-gin Joola *-kin Manjak *-kin Bijogo ne-gen 'village'		'live (some-where)'
*k-úum	*-yuum S. yuum F. njum-ri		BKK *-yum Joola mu-kúm		'honey/ bee'
*waaṛ[9]	*gal-ɗat S. a-fat, F. ɗat-al		BKK *bi-(r)aaṛ BP *f-aaṛ(e)		'path, road'
*(y)iif	S. yip F. yupp-		Tenda *-yiif Joola *-yúw		'pour'
*faan-ox	S. wond-oox		Bai. *waan-ah Manjak wɛnʈa		'lie down'
*(y)eɗ	F. yeɗ-		Konyagi -yáɗ Bassari -yìl		'give'
*maañ	S. miñ		Bai. *-miñ		'last long'
*puh/poh	S. fox		Tenda *-foxa		'clap'[10]
*haɓaang-ís-ox	S. haɓaas		Manjak *habənʈ	Mandinka hábáasi	'yawn'
*hay	S. gec?		Tenda *-xaay		'lean'
*ɣaf		gopp y- (archaic pl.)	BKK *bu-gof Tenda *-ɣaf BP *bu-gafä Joola *fu-ków/kaw Balanta b-gɔ́ Bijogo bu		'head'
*mand		mel?	BKK *-mịnd Tenda *-mənd Biafada meel Pajade miir		'resemble'
*ngum		gamb b-	Tenda *gaŋ-ɣo(o)m Pajade pomm <*bu-gomm JF e-kómboon Manjak pə-kumbɛ		'calabash gourd (for liquid)'

---

9 It is unclear if these roots of the basic form /(ɗ)aat/ should be connected; if so the initial ɗ~∅ discrepancy is irregular, including in BKK (KK *bi-aaṛ, Bainunk *bi-naal). If these roots are related, Cangin *w would be a class prefix in this word.

10 Perhaps related to the widespread Niger-Congo root for 'ten,' e.g. Benue-Congo *pu, Wolof *fukk*.

OUTSIDE COGNATES 279

(cont.)

Cangin	Fula-Sereer	Wolof	Other Atlantic	BC, Mande	
Sa. seeh < *seeɣ		jasig j-	Bainunk *ja-reeg < *-seeg Biafada jaasugu Manjak *u-tuk Bijogo ɛ-ʈɛɛga		'crocodile'
*hon		(honn), wonn	Tenda *-xon BP *ŋun Joola *e-kondor 'neck'?		'swallow'
*hoɗ *kuɗ 'pestle'		(hol), wol	BKK *-hur Pajade wuud	Mandinka kudaa 'pestle'	'pound in mortar'[11]
*teɗ			BKK *-ṛiir Bedik -sęɗ < *-ṛiɗ Pajade seed < *-ṛeeɗ JF -liir, Manjak *ɬiir Balanta tud		'weave, braid'
*líix			BKK *-dịt(t) Tenda *-rɔcc Pajade ric JE ma-ttí, Manjak ʈịñ Balanta θɛ		'fart'
*(n-)leen~liin			BKK *-dẹen Tenda *gaŋ-riin Pajade bə-riin Joola Karon hi-téeni Manjak *pə-nʈụn		'kapok tree'
*meex-iṛ			Bai. *-miix Bassari -w̃ɔ̀ká Biafada meek Pajade məkəndaan		'ask'
*ɓitif 'old woman' (or *ɓi-rif?)			BKK *-def Tenda *-raf BP *-raf Manjak ʈaf		'be old'
*kof			BKK *keef-uṛ/kuuf-uṛ Tenda *-xuf Pajade woof		'flay/peel'
*luH(Vy)			BKK *-dox Konyagi -lɔ́kw		'be short'

---

11 A number of other Atlantic groups have a root for 'pestle' of the basic shape /hund/, but this would seem to be unrelated.

280 APPENDIX 2

(cont.)

Cangin	Fula-Sereer	Wolof	Other Atlantic	BC, Mande	
*saaf			BKK *-ɾuf? Pajade ka-taaf		'leaf'
*(y)in ~ iñ (La. oñ)			BKK *k-onj Tenda *yin~yiñ~yoñ?		'thing' (see note 8o in appx. 1)
*a-roɣ			Manjak *pə-laak Balanta f-làagí		'stone'
*hang			Tenda *-yang Pajade wank		'be wide'
*mún m- 'flour'	*'un S. 'un, F. 'un-	*gënn g- 'mortar'			'pound in mortar'
*híix 'breathe'	S. °xiiq F. hiik-	xiix			ᵘ'rasp, breathe with diffi- culty'
*laɗ	F. daɗɗ-	lal			'spread out (cloth)'
N. (h)íníŋ, etc.	S. o-xiiñ 'lightning'	xiin w- 'storm cloud'			'thunder'
*leeɣ < lV-oɣ	F. re'-	dee 'die'?			'be fin- ished'
*liil	*reer F. reed-u 'belly' S. a-ndeer 'inside'				'intestines'
*ɓaaɓ	F. ɓaɓɓ-ol				'morning'
*ki-lif		diw g-			'oil'
*-anax			Bai. *-nakk, KK *-naŋ		'two'
Sa. cookam			BKK *ja-kaam (also 'river')		'ocean'
*miis			Joola *míił		'milk'
*yak			Manjak yʌk		'be big'
*ha(a)y			Manjak *hay		'be spicy/ bitter'
		Unlikely cognates			
N. jutuut, etc.	S. ducuuc	tuuti	Bai. *-tiit Biafada -tiiti JF -tiiti		ᵘ'small/tiny'
*hac	*gas : S. gas, F. 'as-	gas	Tenda *-wəcc		'dig'
*ɣot	*gi'/ga'	gis	Bassari -yàt		'see'

OUTSIDE COGNATES

281

(*cont.*)

Cangin	Fula-Sereer	Wolof	Other Atlantic	BC, Mande	
			Unlikely cognates		
*yíp~yíp	S. cip		BKK *-sif-un Tenda *-ʃif Pajade -cif JF -cup		'plant (a stake)'
*sel	F. sondu (pl. colli)		Tenda *-ʃəɗ Pajade ku-cid		'bird'
*(h)úumb	S. 'uup, F. 'ubb-		BKK *-hųbb		'bury'
*ngol-ngol	F. holo-nde		Bassari e-gə̀là̧ Bedik e-gə́lá		ᵘ'throat'
*wax	(S. faax borr. Wo.)	baax 'be good'	Tenda *-fakk 'heal'?		'be cured'
*ngúɗ	(S. god borr. Wo.)	(god), gor 'chop down'	Tenda *-ɣuuɗ		'cut'
*ñúus 'be dark'		ñuul	KK *-ñuru		'(be) black'
*tar̰		taat w-	Tenda *ma-tta (pl.)		'buttock'
*heɗVf	S. yelef	(hoyof~hoyaf)			'be light-weight'
*ɓe-reɓ[12]	*ɓe-rew (pl.) S. rew, F. rew-ɓe				'woman'
*maɓ	S. muɓ, F. muɓɓ-				ᵘ'close mouth'
*yen	S. yeel 'laugh out loud'				'laugh'
*hoñ		xóoñ b- 'burnt rice'			'burn'
*wa/wo-te[13]		tey			'today'
*ɗoɓ			Joola *-rum Manjak *rɔm Balanta dɔm Bijogo num	PB *dúm	'bite'

---

12   If cognate, the Cangin root-final *ɓ might be a resegmented class prefix of the sort seen in Table 100. Recall that *w seems to have been lost root-finally in Cangin, so perhaps **ɓi-rew ɓ-i > *ɓe-re ɓ-i > *ɓe-reɓ-i 'the woman/women.' The case for cognacy is not particularly strong, given that PFS *w should correspond to Cangin *f, and Cangin *r has unclear outside correspondences. Borrowing is also possible, though unlikely for such a basic word.

13   Root-initial *t would be surprising for a native noun, so borrowing may be more likely.

APPENDIX 2

(cont.)

Cangin	Fula-Sereer	Wolof	Other Atlantic	BC, Mande
			Unlikely cognates	
*sís			BKK *-sir̥ 'tooth, mouth'	'tooth'[14]

---

14   Unlikely as cognates, since Cangin word-final *s cannot regularly derive from **t (the source of BKK *r̥). It is conceivable that there was an irregular palatalization of the final consonant in Cangin, or that it somehow escaped the lenition of root-final **t to *r̥, becoming *s by the later *t > *s lenition.

References

Babou, Cheikh Anta & Loporcaro, Michele. 2016. Noun classes and grammatical gender in Wolof. *Journal of African Languages and Linguistics* 37(1): 1–57.

Bastin, Yvonne, André Coupez, Evariste Mumba, and Thilo C. Schadeberg (eds). 2002. *Bantu lexical reconstructions.* http://linguistics.africamuseum.be/BLR3.html.

Becker, Charles. 1985. La représentation des Sereer du nord-ouest dans les sources européennes (xve–xixe siècle). *Journal des africanistes* 55:1–2: 165–185.

Blust, Robert. 2005. "Must sound change be linguistically motivated?" *Diachronica* 22:2: 219–269.

Botne, Robert & Adrien Pouille. 2016. *A Saafi-Saafi (Sébikotane Variety) and English // French Dictionary.* Köln: Rüdiger Köppe Verlag.

Casali, Roderic. 2008. ATR harmony in African languages. *Language and Linguistics Compass* 2: 496–549.

Crétois, Léonce. 1972–1977. *Dictionnaire sereer-français.* Dakar: Centre de Linguistique Appliquée de Dakar [CLAD].

D'Alton, Paula A. 1983. *Esquisse phonologique et grammaticale du Paloor, langue cangin (Sénégal).* Université de la Sorbonne Nouvelle (Paris 3), PhD Dissertation.

De Wolf, Paul P. 1971. *The Noun Class System of Proto-Benue-Congo.* The Hague: Mouton.

Diagne, Anna Marie. 2015. Le palor et le ndut : deux langues atlantiques sans classes nominales. *Les classes nominales dans les langues atlantiques*, ed. by Denis Creissels & Konstantin Pozdniakov. Köln: Rüdiger Köppe Verlag.

Dieye, El Hadji. 2010. *Description d'une langue Cangin du Sénégal: Le Laalaa.* Dakar: Université Cheikh Anta Diop, PhD dissertation.

Dieye, El Hadji. 2015. Les classes nominales en laalaa (léhar). *Les classes nominales dans les langues atlantiques*, ed. by Denis Creissels & Konstantin Pozdniakov. Köln: Rüdiger Köppe Verlag.

Diouf, Jean-Léopold. 2003. *Dictionnaire wolof-français et français-wolof.* Paris: Editions Karthala.

Doneux, Jean Léonce 1975a. Hypothèses pour la comparative des langues atlantiques. *Africana Linguistica* VI: 41–129. Tervuren.

Doneux, Jean Léonce. 1975b. *Lexique manjaku.* Dakar: Centre de Linguistique Appliquée de Dakar.

Doneux, Jean Léonce. Year unknown. *Ndut wordlist.* Available in Segerer G. & Flavier S. 2011–2021. *RefLex: Reference Lexicon of Africa*, Version 1.1. Paris, Lyon. http://reflex .cnrs.fr/

Dramé, Mamour. 2012. *Phonologie et morphosyntaxe comparées de trois dialectes Wolof.* Dakar: Université Cheikh Anta Diop, PhD dissertation.

Drolc, Ursula. 2003. Gibt es Ansätze von Anlautpermutation in den Cangin-Sprachen? *Afrika und Übersee* 86: 43–62.

Drolc, Ursula. 2004. A diachronic analysis of Ndut vowel harmony. *Studies in African linguistics* 33-1: 35–63.

Drolc, Ursula. 2005. *Die Cangin-Sprachen: Vergleichende Grammatik und Rekonstruktion*. Universität Köln, PhD dissertation.

Drolc, Ursula. 2006. L'évolution du système consonantique des langues cangin. *Afrikanistik online* Vol. 2006: 26.

Faidherbe, Louis. 1865. Étude sur la langue Kéguem ou Sérère-Sine. *Annuaire du Sénégal et Dépendances pour l'année 1865*. Saint-Louis: Imprimerie du Gouvernement.

Faye, Souleymane & Hillebrand Dijkstra. 2005. Glottalisées du sereer-siin, du saafi-saafi et du noon du Sénégal. *SudLangues* 4: 121–138.

Gerhardt, Ludwig. 1983. *Beiträge zur Kenntnis der Sprachen des Nigerianischen Plateaus* (Afrikanistische Forschungen IX). Glückstadt: J.J. Augustin.

Gottschligg, Peter. 2000. La morphologie nominale peule dans le cadre dialectal et nord-(ouest)-atlantique. *Areal and genetic factors in language classification and description: Africa south of the Sahara*, ed. by P. Zima, 61–89. München: Lincom Europa.

Güldemann, Tom. 2018. Historical linguistics and genealogical language classification in Africa. *African Languages and Linguistics*, ed. by Tom Güldemann, 58–444. Berlin: DeGruyter Mouton.

Hyman, Larry. 2014. Reconstructing the Niger-Congo Verb Extension Paradigm. *Paradigm Change: In the Transeurasian languages and beyond*, ed. by Martine Robbeets and Walter Bisang, 103–126. John Benjamins.

Kobès, Mgr. Aloyse & O. Abiven. 1923 [c. 1869]. *Dictionnaire Volof-Français*. Dakar: Mission Catholique.

Lopis-Sylla, Jeanne. 2010. *La langue noon*. Dakar: IFAN/UCAD.

Lüpke, Friederike & Anne Storch. 2013. *Repertoires and Choices in African Languages*. Berlin: Mouton de Gruyter.

Mbodj, Chérif. 1983. *Recherche sur la phonologie et la morphologie de la langue saafi (le parler de Boukhou)*. Université de Nice, PhD dissertation.

Merrill, John. 2018. *The Historical Origin of Consonant Mutation in the Atlantic Languages*. University of California, Berkeley, PhD dissertation.

Merrill, John. 2021. The Evolution of Consonant Mutation and Noun Class Marking in Wolof. *Diachronica* 38:1: 64–110.

Meyer, Gérard. 2001. *Éléments de grammaire du Badiaranke: Parler de la région de Koundara, Guinée*. Dakar.

Miehe, Gudrun, Brigitte Reineke, & Kerstin Winkelmann (eds). 2012. *Noun Class Systems in Gur Languages*. Vol. 2: *North Central Gur Languages*. Köln: Rüdiger Köppe Verlag.

Morgan, Daniel R. 1996. *Overview of Grammatical Structures of Ndut: A Cangin Language of Senegal*. University of Texas at Arlington, MA Thesis.

Ndiaye, Ousmane. 2013. *Contrastive study of Saalum-Saalum Wolof and Lebu: phonology and morphology*. Dakar: Université Cheikh Anta Diop, MA Thesis.

Pichl, Walter J. 1966. *The Cangin group: a language group in northern Senegal*. Pittsburgh: Duquesne University Press.

Pichl, Walter J. 1980 [1973]. Safen. *West African language data sheets 2*, ed. by M.E. Kropp Dakubu. Legon & Leiden: West African Linguistic Society (WALS); African Studies Centre (ASC).

Pichl, Walter J. 1977. *Vocabulaire Ndut*. Ms.

Pichl, Walter J. 1979. *Abrégé de grammaire ndout*. Ms.

Pichl, Walter J. 1981. *Abrégé de grammaire laala*. Ms.

Pinet-Laprade, Émile. 1865. Notice sur les Sérères. *Annuaire du Sénégal et Dépendances pour l'année 1865*, 129–171. Saint-Louis: Imprimerie du Gouvernement.

Pouye, Abdoulaye. 2015. *Pour une sauvegarde des langues en danger au Sénégal: Description synchronique du saafi-saafi*. Saint-Denis: Édilivre.

Pozdniakov, Konstantin & Guillaume Segerer. 2004. Reconstruction des pronoms personnels du proto-Cangin. *Systèmes de marques personnelles en Afrique* (Afrique et Langage 8), ed. by D. Ibriszimow & G. Segerer, 163–183. Louvain, Paris: Peeters.

Pozdniakov, Konstantin & Guillaume Segerer. 2017. A Genealogical classification of Atlantic languages. (Draft). To appear in *The Oxford guide to the Atlantic languages of West Africa*, ed. Friederike Lüpke. Oxford University Press.

Renaudier, Marie. 2012. *Dérivation et valence en sereer*. Université Lumière Lyon 2, PhD Dissertation.

Sambiéni, Coffi. 2005. *Le Proto-Oti-Volta-Oriental: Essai d'application de la méthode historique comparative* (Gur Monographs 6). Köln: Rüdiger Köppe Verlag.

Sapir, J. David. 1971. West Atlantic: An inventory of the languages, their noun class systems and consonant alternations. *Current trends in linguistics* 7, 45–112.

Segerer, Guillaume. 2000. L'origine des Bijogo: hypothèses de linguiste. *Migrations anciennes et peuplement actuel des Côtes guinéennes*, ed. by Gérald Gaillard, 183–191. Paris: L'Harmattan.

Soukka, Maria. 2000. *A Descriptive Grammar of Noon*. Lincom Europa.

Soukka, Maria & Heikki Soukka. 2011. *Esquisses phonologiques du laalaa et Paloor*. Göteborg Africana Informal Series, no. 8.

Stanton, Juliet. 2011. *A Grammatical Sketch of Saafi*. Ms., Indiana University.

Storch, Anne. 1995. *Die Anlautpermutation in den westatlantischen Sprachen*. Frankfurt-am-Main: Frankfurter Afrikanistische Blätter.

Taine-Cheikh, Catherine. 2008. *Dictionnaire zénaga-français: le berbère de Mauritanie présenté par racines dans une perspective comparative*. (Berber studies, 20). Köln: Rüdiger Köppe Verlag.

Tastevin, Rév. Constant F. 1936. Vocabulaires inédits de 7 dialectes sénégalais dont 6 de Casamance. *Journal de la Société des Africanistes* 6–1, 1–33.

Thornell, Christina, Marie Diouf, Mamadou Diouf, Ibrahima Ciss, Abdoulaye Diouf, & Fatou Diouf. 2016. *Grammaire de base sur la langue paloor au Sénégal.* Dakar: ASPAD/SIL.

Thornell, Christina, Marie Diouf, Mamadou Diouf, Ibrahima Ciss, Abdoulaye Diouf, & Fatou Diouf. 2016b. *Lexique langue cangin paloor—français.* Dakar: ASPAD/SIL.

Thornell, Christina, Ndiol Malick Tine, Roger Samba Faye, & Gilbert Guilang Thiaw. 2016 [Thornell et al. 2016c]. *Lexique: langue cangin laalaa-français.* Senegal: Sé Wínóo/SIL.

Thornell, Christina, Marie Diouf, Mamadou Diouf, Ibrahima Ciss, Abdoulaye Diouf, & Fatou Diouf. 2017. *Paloor au Sénégal, sa vitalité est-elle en déclin?* SIL International.

Voisin-Nouguier, Sylvie. 2002. *Relations entre fonctions syntaxiques et fonctions sémantiques en wolof.* Université Lumière Lyon 2, PhD Dissertation.

Wane, Mohamadou Hamine. 2017. *La grammaire du noon.* Leiden University, PhD Dissertation.

Williams, Gordon & Sara Williams. 1993. *Enquête sociolinguistique sur les langues Cangin de la région de Thiès au Sénégal.* Dakar: SIL.

Woodworth, N.L. 1991. Sound symbolism in proximal and distal forms. *Linguistics* 29, 273–299.

Wycliffe Bible Translators. Year unknown. *Hewhewii winéwíʼwii Kooh Kifiiliimunkii kiʼaskii* [God's good news of the new covenant]. (New Testament in Padee Noon).

Index

adjectives 93, 131, 136–139, 145, 146, 153–157, 159, 210
agentive 152, 222
allophony 18, 20–25, 26, 30, 42, 43, 53, 59, 134
animacy 94, 107, 108, 137, 141, 164, 168, 182
anticausative 160, 202, 203, 231
antipassive 230
applicative 127, 151, 158, 160, 200–202, 204, 210, 230
areal linguistics 79–88, 144, 172, 208–212, 213, 214, 222–224, 230
aspect 175–185
assimilation 46–49, 56, 61, 68, 69, 134, 221
associative marker 128, 145–147, 162, 170
Atlantic 1, 8, 41, 208, 232
ATR 58–62, 214, 221
auxiliaries 175, 177, 180–182, 186–192, 211

Bainunk-Kobiana-Kasanga 132, 221, 225, 227–229, 233
Bak 214, 226
Bantu 102, 146, 214, 220, 224, 226, 233
Berber 213
Biafada-Pajade 221, 225, 227
Bijogo 233
borrowing 22, 23, 27, 29, 33, 38, 39, 44, 53, 54, 79–88, 98, 101, 124, 150, 199

causative 157, 201, 202, 205
clitics 97, 137, 140, 165, 179, 196
coda nasalization 25
consonant clusters 72, 76, 220
consonant mutation 41, 221, 233

definite agreement 93, 137–139
deletion 23, 25, 42–46, 47, 66, 70–73, 195, 214, 229
denasalization 25, 215
determiners 44, 68, 69, 92, 96, 97, 127, 140–147, 166, 182, 209, 211, 224
devoicing 20, 40, 225–227
diminutives 94, 113, 120, 124

endangerment 8
epenthesis 19, 65, 96, 97, 124

extensions 198–207, 229–232

Fula 28, 41, 171, 221, 222
Fula-Sereer 40, 214, 225–227

geminates 47, 218–220
grammaticalization 96, 113, 142, 144, 153, 162, 179, 182, 187, 188, 192, 195–198, 211
Gur 224–226

hiatus 65–67, 70, 97, 101, 124, 179

implosives 20–25, 212
iterative 199, 202
itive 199, 206

lengthening 56, 63–66, 144, 165, 177, 183
lenition 18, 20–25, 39, 42–46, 101, 196, 213, 214–218, 221, 233
leveling 25, 59, 114, 149
lowering 51, 73–75

Mande 33, 35, 41, 269
mass nouns 102, 115, 118, 151, 225
mood 185–186
multilingualism 8, 212

negation 186–192, 206, 211
Niger-Congo 91, 110, 139, 172, 208, 214, 220, 222, 224, 228–232, 234
noun class 91–139, 222–229
  agreement 92, 128, 136–139, 148, 164, 182
  derivational 91, 135
  frozen prefixes 117, 125–127, 134, 137, 224
number marking
  nominal 101, 104, 114, 121
  verbal 192–195
numerals 93, 129, 145, 147–150

orthography 11–13, 26, 53

palatalization 171
passive 192–195
phonotactics 72, 76–78, 220
pluractional 204, 205
prenasalization 25–29, 87, 98, 212, 229

pretendative   205, 231
privative   187, 192, 199, 206
pronouns   162–172

raising   53, 56, 57
reduplication   110, 199, 205, 231
reflexive   203
relative clauses   183, 195–198
resegmentation   124, 127, 150
reversive   59, 203, 216, 231

Sereer   2, 8, 28, 32, 35, 38, 39, 76, 79, 86, 87, 143, 171, 199, 202, 205, 208–212, 212, 214, 221, 222–224, 230

shortening   144, 167, 218
subgrouping   3, 90, 232
syncope   70–73

Tenda   218, 221, 225, 227, 233
tense   175–185

voicing   18, 30, 42, 44, 97, 134, 221, 229

Wolof   28, 32, 35, 50, 59, 79, 86, 87, 104, 129, 133, 143, 171, 186, 194, 199, 202, 205, 208–212, 212, 214, 218, 221, 222–224, 225, 227, 228, 230

Printed in the United States
by Baker & Taylor Publisher Services